ARBITRATION AND CONTRACT LAW IN SAARC COUNTRIES

with Case Law on UNCITRAL Model Law

ARBITRATION AND CONTRACT LAW IN SAARC COUNTRIES

with Case Law on UNCITRAL Model Law

G. K. KWATRA, LL.M. (Harvard)
Executive Director, Indian Council of Arbitration
Asstt. Secretary General, FICCI

Foreword by
Hon'ble Justice Altamas Kabir
Judge Supreme Court of India

ICA
INDIAN COUNCIL OF ARBITRATION

Universal
Law Publishing Co. Pvt. Ltd.

2008 Edition

ISBN: 978-81-7534-648-2

Published by
INDIAN COUNCIL OF ARBITRATION
Federation House, Tansen Marg, New Delhi, India
Phones: 91-11-23719103, 23738760-70
Fax: 91-11-23320714, 23721504
E-mail: ica@nda.vsnl.net.in
ica@airtelbroadband.in
Web site: ficci.com/icanet

Distributed by
UNIVERSAL LAW PUBLISHING CO. PVT. LTD.
C-FF-1A, Dilkhush Industrial Estate,
(Opp. Hans Cinema, Azadpur) G.T. Karnal Road, Delhi-110 033
Tel : 011-27438103, 27215334, 42381334
Fax : 011-27458529
E-mail *(For sales inquiries)* : sales@unilawbooks.com
E-mail *(For editorial inquiries)* : edit@unilawbooks.com
Website : www.unilawbooks.com

Recommended citation: *Arbitration and Contract Law in SAARC Countries*, G.K. Kwatra (New Delhi: Universal Law Publishing Co. Pvt. Ltd., 2008)

Computer Typeset at Aesthetic & *Printed* at Sita Fine Arts Pvt. Ltd., New Delhi.

Altamas Kabir
Judge
Supreme Court of India

17, Safdarjung Road
New Delhi – 110011
Ph.: 23017059
23015962

September 27, 2007

FOREWORD

It gives me immense pleasure to write the foreword for this book, which has been authored by Mr. G.K. Kwatra, Executive Director, Indian Council of Arbitration, who, on account of his experience on the subject, is eminently suited for the purpose.

Arbitration as a mode of resolving disputes has been in existence in different forms from ancient times. Before the establishment of common law courts, arbitration was resorted to under customary practice and traditions and even under the personal law of the parties. With the increase in trade and commercial activities and the opening of borders between different countries, arbitration acquired a new importance, which ultimately came to be recognized by way of Statute Law which, however, had various limitations involving judicial intervention at different stages of the arbitral proceedings. What was intended to be a quick method for resolution of disputes, became instead a lengthy process thereby defeating the very object for which the laws were enacted.

The legislative history of arbitration in India begins in 1937 with the enactment of the Arbitration (Protocol and Convention) Act, 1937, which was followed by the Arbitration Act, 1940, which continued to be in operation till its repeal in 1996 with the enactment of the Arbitration and Conciliation Act. In between, the Foreign Awards (Recognition and Enforcement) Act was enacted in 1961 to make it possible to execute foreign awards in the Indian Courts following the adoption of the New York Convention adopted in 1958. Since the aforesaid enactments and similar enactments in other countries proved inadequate in the wake of global expansion of commercial activities involving different countries, which gave rise to disputes having an international character, the United Nations took the initiative through its Commission on International Trade Law to come out with a model law on the subject and the same, which came to be known as the UNCITRAL Model was formerly adopted by the United Nations General Assembly on 21st June, 1985. Most of the member countries of the United Nations, including India, adopted the UNCITRAL model and enacted new Laws in conformity therewith. In India, the acceptance of the said model resulted in the enactment of the Arbitration and Conciliation Act, 1996.

Apart from the majority of the member countries, India and the other members of the South Asian Association of Regional Co-operation (SAARC) with the exception of Pakistan, adopted the UNCITRAL model and enacted new laws accordingly. Pakistan continued to retain the Arbitration Act of 1940. Mr. Kwatra has, in his book, made a comparative study of the arbitration laws existing in the SAARC countries, which besides being informative will also prove to be of great assistance in understanding the recent trend in arbitration in the SAARC countries. By including chapters on the law of limitation and contract and institutional arbitration, and the relevant judicial decisions on the different provisions of the Arbitration and Conciliation Act, 1996, and the UNCITRAL Model Law, Mr. Kwatra has provided an insight into the arbitration laws as are being administered by different countries which have adopted the UNCITRAL Model which will prove to be of immense help to corporate and non-corporate bodies, and the legal fraternity. Mr. Kwatra has laid special emphasis on Institutional Arbitration, which, in fact, was earlier the accepted procedure which was adopted in most countries, including India. In view of the increase in global commerce, Mr. Kwatra has highlighted the benefits of institutional arbitration which provides for a more regulated procedure in arbitral proceedings and also for quick disposal of such proceedings, which is one of the main objectives of settlement of disputes by arbitration.

Mr. Kwatra has taken great pains to point out the positive aspects of Institutional Arbitration which, I am sure, will result in harmonizing the concept of Institutional Arbitration in the SAARC region thereby encouraging and facilitating global trade and commerce, both within the SAARC region and in the global context.

Justice Altamas Kabir

PREFACE

Regional co-operation has not only come to stay – as a matter of fact, it has intensified in most parts of the world.

In this perspective it is reassuring to observe that the regional economic co-operation has finally take off and milestone SAFTA Agreement has been signed and ratified by member counrties.

As trade expands between the countries of SAARC and the process of economic integration moves forward, it is imperative to address the practical problems of doing business whether it is tariff or non-tariff barriers, infrastructure, taxation or settlement of commercial disputes, etc.

With economic integration, the need has arisen to integrate the dispute resolving mechanisms (specially of commercial disputes) with special regard to ADR. The first step in this direction is this publication which examines the systems available in each of the SAARC countries for the resolution of commercial disputes and the need for evolving a common regional mechanism.

Indian Council of Arbitration (ICA) is delighted to bring out and present this publication on "Arbitration and Contract Law in SAARC Countries". The book has been updated with new cases on UNCITRAL Model Arbitration Law and also on the Arbitration and Conciliation Act, 1996 of India. A revised chapter has been added on the Arbitration Regime in Bangladesh, which had adopted the UNCITRAL Model Law.

I am confident that all segments of policy makers, businessmen and the legal communities shall find it a useful and comprehensive document. I compliment Mr. G.K. Kwatra, Asstt. Secretary General, FICCI and Executive Director, Indian Council of Arbitration for his efforts in bringing out this publication.

We would feel that our efforts have been successful if it can expedite the establishment of a SAARC arbitral institution which shall be of considerable benefit to the business community and which we have proposed for this region.

Habil Khorakiwala
President
Indian Council of Arbitration

COMMENT

It is a pleasure for me to introduce this concise but intensive analysis of the law of contract and the law of arbitration in the SAARC countries. With his usual indefatigable energy Mr. G.K. Kwatra has examined the laws in each of the SAARC countries and made this most useful publication which will be of great interest not merely to those who advise in legal matters but all those in business and industry as well. Regional trade can only increase if there is an interchange of accurate information which this volume provides.

Fali S. Nariman
Hony. Chairman,
International Council for
Commercial Arbitration (ICCA)

COMMENT

I would like to congratulate Mr. G.K. Kwatra for his work "Arbitration and Contract Law in SAARC countries". The book makes a comparative study of the arbitration laws of the SAARC countries. The coverage is comprehensive and the style is lucid. A special feature of the work is the section on the Law of Contract in the SAARC countries. This adds immensely to the practical utility of the work. There is also a special chapter devoted to Institutional Arbitration available in these countries.

The growth in interaction and co-operation amongst the countries in the region in the recent past has brought about new challenges and opportunities. Indeed the South Asian Free Trade Agreement, when it becomes functional, will have a significant impact in commercial and economic activity in the region, when the need for a work of this nature will be even more pronounced. This book meets a long felt need and, therefore, the contributors deserve special appreciation.

I am sure that with this book, India will lead the way in bringing about harmonisation of the law in this region. I am sure the book will prove to be of immense use and value not only for lawyers but also for entrepreneurs and business houses in the region who have to frequently resort to arbitration for dispute resolution.

(K.K. VENUGOPAL)
Former President, SAARC LAW,

CONTENTS

TABLE OF CASES

A

B

Gay Constructions PTY Ltd. and Spaceframe Buildings (North Asia) Ltd. *v.* Caledonian Techmore (Building) Limited and Hanison Construction Co. Ltd. 319

Gibson *v.* Manchester City Council, (1979) 1 All ER 192 109, 129

Global Company *v.* M/s. National Fertilizer, 1999 AIHC 3644 (Del) 58

Globe Union Industrial Corp. *v.* G.A.P. Marketing Corp., [1995] 2 Western Weekly Reports, 696 340, 365

Godrej Properties & Investments Ltd. *v.* Tripura Constructions, Mumbai, 2003 (2) Arb LR 195 (Bom): (2003) 8 CLA-BL Supp (Snr) (Bom) 3 55, 58, 62, 63

Government of Kerala *v.* Luiz Paul, (1998) 28 CLA (Snr) 4 (Bom) 35

Government of Kerala *v.* Som Dutt Builders Ltd., (2003) 7 CLA-BL Supp (Snr) 28 (Ker) 63, 66

Grand Cashew Corporation *v.* Gibbs Nathaniel (Canada) Limited, AIR 1984 Ker 33 26

Great Northern Rly. Co. Ltd. *v.* Witham, (1873) LR 9 CP 16 110, 129

Grid Corpn. of Orissa Ltd. *v.* AES Corpn., (2002) 7 SCC 736 47, 53

Guangdong Agriculture Company Limited *v.* Conagra International (Far East) Limited, (1993) 1, Hong Kong Law Reports; 1992, Hong Kong Law Digest, H11 329, 343

Gulf Canada Resources Ltd. *v.* Arochem International Ltd., 66 British Columbia Law Reports (2d), 113 325, 341, 345, 346

H

H. Small Limited *v.* Goldroyce Garment Limited, (1992) ADRLJ 235, (1992) ADRLJ 240, (1993) ADRLJ 240, (1993) ADRLJ 100 and (1994) ADRLJ 49 317

H.P. State Council for Child Welfare *v.* Unique Mixers and Furnaces Pvt. Ltd., 2001 Arb WLJ 109 (HP): AIR 2001 HP 22 73

H.V.S. Technologies, Inc. *v.* Aeronautical Development Agency, 2002 Al HC 755 (Kar) 41

Hadley *v.* Baxendale 126

Hari Shankar Singhania *v.* Gaur Hari Singhania, AIR 2006 SC 2488 56

Harinarayan G. Bajaj *v.* Sharedeal Financial Consultations (P.) Ltd., (2003) 7 CLA-BL Supp 48 (Snr) 63

Harvey *v.* Facey, 1893 AC 552 102, 108, 128

Haryana State Agricultural Marketing Board, Karnal *v.* Jagdish Chand Contractor, 2003 (1) Arb LR 476 (P&H) 58

Haryana Telecom Ltd. *v.* Sterlite Industries (India) Ltd., 1999 Arb WLJ 591 (SC): 1999 (2) Arb LR 685 (SC): (1999) 5 SCC 688: AIR 1999 SC 2354 39

Hawkes *v.* Saunders (1782) 1 Cowp 289 139

Hindusthan Petroleum Corporation Ltd. *v.* Pink city Midway Petroleums, (2003) 6 SCC 503 55

Hissan Trading Co Ltd. *v.* Orkin Shipping Corporation, [1992] ADRLJ 235, [1992] ADRLJ 240, (1993) ADRLJ 240, (1993) ADRLJ 100 and (1994) ADRLJ 49: 1992, Hong Kong Law Digest, H8 315, 317, 330

Hotel Marina *v.* Sushil Kumar Raut, [2003] 8 CLA-BL Supp (Snr) 16 (Del) 52

L

M

N

O

T

ARBITRATION LAW IN SELECTED SAARC COUNTRIES*

A COMPARATIVE PERSPECTIVE

The SAARC countries present a variety of models, as regards their enactments relating to arbitration; and the subject is an interesting one for a comparative study. Some of the relevant aspects are dealt with here. The countries covered are – Bangladesh, India, Pakistan, Nepal and Sri Lanka.

The Acts in Force

(a) In Bangladesh, Arbitration Act, 2001 came into effect on 10th April, 2001, it was repeated from the previous Arbitration Act, 1940. The Act follows closely the UNCITRAL Model Law and provides a united formula for both international commercial arbitration and domestic arbitration by consolidating the entire law of arbitration in one single Act.

(b) India has revised its enactment on the subject and the law relating to arbitration is now contained in the Arbitration and Conciliation Act, 1996. This is largely modelled on the UNCITRAL Model Law on International Commercial Arbitration.

(c) In Pakistan, the pre-1947 enactment (in force in the Indian sub-continent), *i.e.*, the Arbitration Act, 1940, is still in force.

(d) Nepalese legislation on the subject is the Nepal Arbitration Act, 1999 (April 1999). This Act incorporates some features of the UNCITRAL Model law, but also contains some provisions not found in the Model law or elsewhere.

* SAARC Countries being – Bangladesh, India, Pakistan, Nepal and Sri Lanka.

(e) The Arbitration Act No. 11 of 1995, which came into force on August 1, 1995 makes comprehensive legal provision for the conduct of arbitration proceedings, enforcement of awards and recognition and enforcement of foreign awards in Sri Lanka.

Variety of Models

Thus, from the point of view of chronological order, we have very recent Acts (Bangladesh and Nepal), fairly recent Acts (Sri Lanka and India), and a not so very recent Act (Pakistan), on the subject.

In point of content and style, again, there is a good deal of difference, amongst the various countries. India, Sri Lanka and Bangladesh by substantially adopting the UNCITRAL Model, have tried to promote three main principles, namely:—

(a) party autonomy;

(b) freedom for the arbitrators; and

(c) finality of the arbitral award.

The Pakistan Act is not so liberal. Nepal seems to stand mid-way between a liberal approach and a conservative approach.

Classes of Arbitration

The Indian Act of 1996 recognises only one class of arbitration, namely, arbitration initiated without court intervention.

In Pakistan three classes of arbitration are still recognised, namely:—

(a) arbitration without court intervention;

(b) arbitration, where no suit is pending, but through court; and

(c) arbitration in suits (through court).

Of course, in all the three cases mentioned above, the basis of arbitration is an agreement between the parties.

The Nepal Act (like the Indian Act) primarily concentrates on arbitration without court intervention.

The Sri Lankan and Bangladesh (like the Indian and Nepal Acts) are concerned with arbitrations without court intervention. Although the earlier Arbitration Ordinance and certain provisions of the Civil Procedure Code were repealed by the Act, provisions in the Code which deal with Court administered arbitration on application of parties in pending actions are still operative.

Arbitration Agreement

Under all the Acts, a written agreement is required in order to constitute an arbitration agreement. But there are several differences in point of detail.

(a) The Indian Act requires that the dispute must relate to a "defined legal relationship" (whether contractual or not). This sophistication does not appear in the Act applicable in Pakistan. The Nepal Act provides that the dispute must concern "a specific legal issue (whether contractual or not)". The Nepalese version is simpler and yet more expressive.

As regards the form of the agreement, the Indian Act, while insisting on the requirement of writing, elaborates that requirement in detail, by drawing upon the UNCITRAL Model.

(b) The legislation in Pakistan, simply requires writing.

(c) The Nepal Act amplifies the concept of "writing" by specifically covering messages "where records can be maintained in a written form". Here again, the Nepalese version is simpler, and yet, more expressive.

(d) The Sri Lankan Act and Bangladesh Act (like the Indian Act) defines an arbitration agreement as an agreement by the parties to submit to arbitration all or certain disputes which have arisen or which may arise between them in respect of a defined legal relationship, whether contractual or not. An arbitration agreement must be in writing and contained in a document signed by the parties or in an exchange of letters, telexes, telegrams or other means of telecommunication which provide a record of the agreement.

Arbitrators

The number of arbitrators can be determined by agreement. But the Indian Act prohibits an even number. The Pakistan Act contains no such restriction. The Nepal Act permits an even number, but, in that case, the arbitrators must choose an additional arbitrator.

Failing a provision in the arbitration agreement (as to the number of arbitrators), the number shall be:—

(a) one, under the Indian and Pakistan Acts, and

(b) "ordinarily three", under the Nepal Act.

(c) three, under the Sri Lankan Act and Bangladesh Act.

The Sri Lankan Act and the Bangladesh Act require the arbitral tribunal to act in an impartial, practical and expeditious manner in dealing with any dispute submitted to it for arbitration.

The Nepal Act prescribes a written oath of impartiality and honesty to be taken by the arbitrator. In addition, it also gives a list of disqualifications of the arbitrator. For example, a person who has been convicted of an offence involving moral turpitude cannot become an arbitrator in Nepal.

Section 11 of the Act gives full liberty to the parties to determine the number of arbitrators. The arbitral tribunal consist of three arbitrators in line with the UNCITRAL Model Law provisions.

Removal of Arbitrator

Generally, arbitration laws provide for the removal of an arbitrator, who is guilty of undue delay, etc. and the Acts in force in India and Pakistan possess this feature. The Sri Lankan and Bangladesh Acts also provide for challenging an arbitrator if circumstances give rise to justifiable doubts as to his impartiality and independence.

The Nepal Act goes further. For example, an arbitrator can be removed in Nepal, if "he frequently commits mistakes or irregularities in the performance of his functions".

Pleadings

Pleadings constitute the basis of any formal adjudication, including arbitration. But arbitration laws may adopt varying approaches in this regard.

(a) In the Indian Act, there is a brief provision dealing with the obligation of parties to file pleadings, the contents of the pleadings and the time within which the pleadings should be filed.

(b) The Pakistan, Bangladesh and Sri Lankan Acts do not contain any details about pleadings. In fact, expressions like "statement of claim" and "statement of defence", do not occur in these Acts.

(c) The Nepal Act contains elaborate provisions on the subject. It even takes care to deal specifically with counter-claim, as well as rejoinder to the counter-claim. It also gives the arbitrator a power to extend the various time limits for pleadings, upto seven days. It further deals, in detail, with the material (documents) that should accompany the pleadings. In this respect, the Nepal Act has the merit of specificity, without sacrificing simplicity.

Challenge to Jurisdiction

Regarding challenge to the arbitrator's jurisdiction, the position is as under:

(a) Under the Indian Act, it is for the arbitrator to determine such questions, if the question is raised by a party. There is no right given to the party, aggrieved by his ruling, to approach the court immediately. However, after the award is pronounced, he can move the court, for setting aside the award on this ground. In the meantime, the arbitration proceedings can go on.

(b) In the scheme of the Act in force in Pakistan, such a challenge can be made before the competent court, and pending decision by the court, the arbitration will ordinarily be stayed. The arbitrator himself is given no power to determine the issue of jurisdiction in the Act in force in Pakistan.

(c) In the Nepal Act, there are elaborate provisions as to the procedure to be followed. When an objection is raised as to the jurisdiction of the arbitrator or as to the legality of the agreement, an "appeal" can be filed to the Appellate Court within 30 days against the arbitrator's decision on these points. But the proceedings before the arbitrator will, in the meantime, continue. The Nepal Act, thus, seems to strike a compromise between a theoretical approach and practical considerations.

(d) The Sri Lankan Act and Bangladesh Act confers on the arbitral tribunal the power to rule on its jurisdiction. Any party to the arbitral proceeding could apply directly to court for a determination on the jurisdiction of the arbitral tribunal. The arbitral tribunal is not precluded from proceeding, pending the determination of such a question by court.

Procedure

(a) The Indian Act (following the UNCITRAL Model) contains a few procedural provisions. While excluding the application of the Code of Civil Procedure, 1908, it takes care to confer, on the arbitral tribunal, power to regulate the conduct of the arbitration in such manner as it thinks fit. It also recognises the right of the parties to regulate the procedure by agreement, on several matters.

(b) The Act in force in Pakistan and Bangladesh is silent on most matters, concerning procedure, pleadings, evidence and so on.

(c) The Nepal Act more or less follows the same approach as the Indian Act, *i.e.*, it leaves the matter to the agreement of the parties or (failing that) to the arbitrator. But it contains certain additional provisions also, which are worth noting:

(i) Under the Nepal Act, the arbitrator must start the proceedings immediately after receiving the pleadings;

(ii) The arbitrator must keep records of the proceedings in the case file;

(iii) Where there are three or more arbitrators and one of them is absent at a particular hearing, the remaining arbitrators may carry on the proceedings. Of course, in the final decision, all arbitrators must participate;

(iv) The arbitration proceedings shall be held in-*camera*, unless the parties otherwise decide. (This is the practice in most of the countries, but a statutory provision is helpful).

(d) Under the Sri Lankan Act and the Bangladesh Act, the parties are given the freedom to agree on the procedure to be followed by the arbitral tribunal in conducting the proceedings.

Award

(a) The Indian Act requires a written award, which must give reasons (unless the parties agree otherwise). There is no formal time limit, as such, for pronouncing the award. The award, when pronounced, has the status of a court decree (though it can be set aside by the competent court on certain grounds).

(b) The Bangladesh Act does not require reason to be given by the arbitral tribunal if the parties have agreed that no reasons are to be given.

(c) The Act in force in Pakistan are not specific as to the arbitrator's duty to give reasons for the award. There is no time limit, as such, laid down for pronouncing the award.

(d) The Nepal Act, in contrast, is fairly elaborate on these matters. The award must give reasons. It must state briefly, particulars of the matter referred to arbitration and the decision and reasons for the decision. The amount awarded as principal and interest should be mentioned in the award and the decision has to be read out by the arbitrator.

(e) The Sri Lankan and the Bangladesh Act require the award to be in writing, signed by the arbitrators or a majority of them, stating the date, place of arbitration and the reasons upon which it is based, unless the parties have agreed that no reasons be given or the award is one made on agreed terms at the request of parties.

The tribunal can correct, modify, make an additional award and where parties have so agreed, give an interpretation of a specific point or part of the award.

Status of the Award

(a) The Indian Act and the Bangladesh Act confer, on the award, the status of a decree (subject to the possibility of the award being challenged on certain grounds before the competent court).

(b) Under the Act in force in Pakistan, the winning party has to approach the court to obtain a decree in terms of the award. Also, the award can be set aside on certain grounds.

(c) Under the Nepal Act, the award (if not challenged on the specified grounds) must be implemented by the district court.

(d) Subject to the provisions relating to applications for setting aside and recognition of awards, an award made under the Sri Lankan Act is final and binding on the parties to the arbitration proceedings. If the need arises, a party can make an application to court within one year after the expiry of fourteen days of the making of the award for its enforcement. If there is no challenge pending before the court and the court sees no reason to refuse recognition and enforcement, it will proceed to file the award and give judgment according to the award. A decree will thereafter be entered on the judgment. Such a decree can be executed as a normal decree entered in terms of the provisions of the Civil Procedure Code.

Challenge to the Award

All the Acts relevant to the present discussion contain provisions under which the award of an arbitrator can be challenged before the competent court. However, the grounds of challenge vary from country to country. It is not possible at this place to present an exhaustive enumeration of the grounds of challenge. However, some salient points (of the Indian Act) can be mentioned, as under:

(I) In India, the grounds for interference with an award can be summarised as—(i) want of jurisdiction, (ii) invalidity of the agreement, (iii) award going beyond the agreement, (iv) arbitrator not qualified, (v) breach of the Act or arbitration agreement, (vi) breach of natural justice, (vii) conflict with the public policy of India, and (viii) the matter not being arbitrable. Interference on the merits of the case is not permissible under the present Indian Act.

(II) The legislation in force in Pakistan is, on its face, worded in narrow terms. But judicial decisions have expanded the scope of judicial intervention with arbitral awards. The arbitrator's "misconduct", and the fact that "the award has been improperly procured", or is otherwise invalid, are the main grounds for setting aside the award. But the judicial trend has been to cover, *inter alia*, errors of law apparent on the face of the record, and this latter concept itself has had the effect of widening the jurisdiction of the court to a very large extent.

(III) Under the Nepal Act, the award may be challenged on a petition filed within 35 days of receipt of a copy by the petitioner.

(IV) Fraud, corruption or conflict with public policy of Bangladesh, violation of principles of natural justice, etc. are the grounds available for setting aside the award, under the Bangladesh Act.

(V) The following are the principal grounds of challenge in Nepal:—

(i) Incompetence of a party or invalidity of the agreement;

(ii) Notice of the proceedings not given to the petitioner;

(iii) Decision was rendered:—

(a) on a matter related to the dispute not referred to the arbitrator, or

(b) in a manner contrary to the prescribed conditions, or

(c) by acting beyond the arbitrator's jurisdiction.

(iv) Procedure or designation of the arbitrators or their functions, etc., does not conform to the agreement or the Act.

(v) The matter is not arbitrable under the law of Nepal.

(vi) The award as is likely to prove detrimental to "public interests or policies".

(VI) An award made under the Sri Lanka Act can be challenged on substantially the same grounds provided for in the Nepal Act. An application for setting aside the award has to be made to court within sixty days of the receipt of the award.

ARBITRATION LAW IN BANGLADESH

The new Bangladesh Arbitration Act, 2001 ("the Act") which came into effect on 10 April, 2001 repealed the previous Arbitration Act, 1940. The Statement of Objects and Reasons described the salient features of new Act as follows: (a) establishing a modern and independent procedure for resolution of dispute based on an arbitration agreement between parties; (b) resolution of dispute within a short frame of time; (c) procedure for dispute resolution without interference by the court; (d) granting of comprehensive power to the arbitrators to resolve dispute; (e) increasing party autonomy; (f) role of District Judge and Chief Justice in resolving disputes arising from appointing arbitrators; (g) granting the award of arbitration the status of a decree of Court; (h) limitations of Court and parties in setting aside an arbitral award; (i) power to set aside arbitral award that are against public policy; (j) reduction in expenditure of Government etc.

The Act follows closely the UNCITRAL Model Arbitration Law and provides a united formula for both international commercial arbitration and domestic arbitration by consolidating the entire law of arbitration in one single Act.

The Act consists of 59 sections in 14 chapters. Chapter III of the Act provides definition of an arbitration agreement. An arbitration agreement that would be recognized by the court includes written documents signed by the parties, exchange of letters, telex, telegrams, fax, e-mails or other means of telecommunication providing a record of the agreement or an exchange of statement of claim and defence in which existence of the agreement is alleged by one and not denied by the other. Some of the salient features of the Act are discussed below.

Composition of Arbitral Tribunal

Chapter IV of the Act deals with the composition of arbitral tribunal. Under section 11 of the Act, full liberty is given to the parties to determine the number of arbitrators. Failing such determination, the arbitral tribunal shall consist of three arbitrators in line with the UNCITRAL provisions. A person of any nationality may be chosen as an arbitrator or Chairman if that is accepted by the parties involved in the dispute.

Where the parties appoint an even number of arbitrators, the latter would jointly appeal for an additional arbitrator who would be the Chairman of the tribunal. The grounds for challenging the appointment of an arbitrator is provided in section 13 of the Act which states that such challenge can be set aside if circumstances exist that give rise to justifiable doubts as to his independence or impartiality, or he does not possess the qualification agreed to by the parties. Section 14 sets out the challenge procedure. A party is duty bound to put its objections on record. Parties are free to agree on a challenge procedure. In absence of an agreement, the arbitral tribunal can itself decide on the challenge to its independence and impartiality. Any party aggrieved by the decision of the arbitral tribunal can appeal to the High Court Division. If a challenge to the arbitral proceeding fails, the tribunal shall continue the proceedings and render an award and the court cannot interfere with the proceedings of the tribunal at that stage.

Section 154 sets out the circumstances, e.g., death of arbitrator, which results in the termination of its mandate and section 16 provides the procedure for substitution of an arbitrator whose mandate has been terminated.

Settlement other than Arbitration

Section 22 of the Act speaks of the arbitrator's power and also the duty to encourage settlement of disputes through mediation, conciliation or other procedure with the agreement of parties. Agreements reached in the above procedures are accorded the same status as an arbitration award and are referred to as arbitral awards on agreed terms.

Reduction of Court Intervention

The involvement of the judicial system has been kept to a minimum level essential for the effective operation of the tribunal's work. No judicial authority is normally to hear any legal proceedings filed by one party to the arbitration agreement against the other till the arbitration process is exhausted and that hearing has to be done in a manner prescribed by this Act. The Court's power to intervene is restricted to the following:

1. Power to refer parties to arbitration where there is an arbitration agreement (sec. 10).
2. Power to appoint arbitrators on parties' failure to approve arbitrators as per the agreement or on failure of the two appointed arbitrators to appoint the third arbitrator (sec. 12).
3. Appeal against the decision of the arbitral tribunal challenging the arbitrator [sec. 14(4)].
4. Power to decide on the termination of the mandate of the arbitrator in the event of his inability to perform his functions or failing to act without undue delay [sec. 15(2)].
5. Power of the High Court Division in deciding jurisdiction (sec. 20).
6. Power to enforce interim measures taken by the arbitral tribunal [sec. 21(4)].
7. Power to issue summons upon the application of the arbitral tribunal (sec. 33).
8. Power to set aside awards (sec. 45).
9. Power to enforce foreign arbitral award (sec. 45).
10. Power of the Appellate Division to hear appeals (sec. 48).
11. Power to resolve dispute as to arbitrator's remuneration of costs (sec. 50).
12. Power to direct determination of any question in connection with insolvency proceeding by arbitration under certain circumstances (sec. 52).
13. Power of the Supreme Court to make rules in certain cases (sec. 58).

Award Enforceable as a Decree

The arbitral award and also an arbitral award on agreed terms are treated as decrees of the Court and are therefore enforceable in the same manner as a decree. Section 39 states that an award shall be final and binding on the parties and persons claiming under them respectively. The High Court Division for arbitral award made in respect of an international commercial dispute and a District Court in respect of domestic commercial disputes can set aside an arbitral award if an application is made by an involved party within sixty days from the receipt of the award. Section 44 further states that where the time for making an application to set aside the award under section 42 has expired, or such an application having been made has been rejected, the award shall be enforceable in the same manner as if it were a decree of the Court.

Enforcement of Foreign Awards

Bangladesh is a party to the New York Convention on the Recognition and Enforcement of Foreign Arbitral Awards. Chapter X of the Act sets out provisions dealing with recognition and enforcement of foreign arbitral awards. Section 45 of the Act states that foreign arbitral award shall on the application being made to it by any party, be enforced by execution by the Court under the Code of Civil Procedure, in the same manner as if it were a decree of the Court. Application for the execution has to be accompanied by the original arbitral award or an authenticated copy of the award, original or authenticated agreement for arbitration and evidence proving that the award is a foreign award.

Grounds for refusing recognition or execution of foreign arbitral awards are set out in section 46 of the Act and includes, amongst others, incapacity of any party, invalidity of the arbitration agreement, inadequate notice of arbitration to the party against whom award is invoked, subject matter of the dispute not capable of being settled by arbitration and award being in conflict with the public policy of Bangladesh.

Party Autonomy

The Act recognises maximum possible party autonomy in matters relating to arbitration. Autonomy starts from the formation of the arbitral tribunal and appointment of arbitrators. Parties are free to determine the number of arbitration as per section 11(1). Some other instances of party autonomy are: Parties challenging an arbitrator [sec. 14(1)], procedure for appointing a substitute of an arbitrator whose mandate has been terminated [sec. 16(1)] or determining the nationality of the arbitrator(s) [sec. 12(2)]. There is autonomy in deciding upon the jurisdiction of the arbitral tribunal (sec. 17), procedures for conducting the proceedings of the arbitral tribunal [sec. 25(1)], time and place of holding the proceedings [sec. 25(3)(a)], place of arbitration [sec. 26(1)] and language of the proceedings [sec. 25(3)(b)]. Power of the arbitrator to make order pertaining to interim measures under section 21, appointment of the expert under section 32, making an award by majority under section 37, costs of arbitration under section 38(7)(a) are several other aspects which can be determined by party autonomy.

Grounds of Challenge of Award

Section 43 of the Act provides the grounds for setting aside arbitral awards. Fraud, corruption or conflict with public policy of Bangladesh, violation of principles of natural justice, acting beyond the terms of the submission and deciding on matters which are legally not arbitrable are the grounds available for setting aside the awards.

Interim Award

Arbitral tribunals have been endowed with the power to pass an interim award which is enforceable like a final award by the Court. Under section 21 of the Act, the arbitral tribunal may, at the request of a party, order a party to take any interim measure of protection as the arbitral tribunal considers necessary in respect of the dispute and such an award is not appealable.

Reasoned Award

The Act does not require reasons to be given by the arbitral tribunal if the parties have agreed that no reasons are to be given or the award is an arbitral award on agreed term [s. 38(3)].

Code of Civil Procedure and Evidence Act

Section 24 of the Act states that the arbitral tribunal shall not be bound either by the Code of Civil Procedure of Bangladesh or the Evidence Act. Parties are free to agree on the procedure to be followed by the arbitral tribunal in the conduct of the proceedings under section 25 of the Act. However, the Limitation Act, 1908 is made applicable.

Power of Arbitral Tribunal

An arbitral tribunal has the following powers, amongst others:

1. By section 17 and 10 respectively, the Act confers competence on the arbitral tribunal to rule on its own jurisdiction and to consider objections with respect to the existence or validity of the arbitration agreement.
2. Apart from the power to correct any clerical, typographical or other similar error, the Act by section 40 further empowers the arbitrators if so agreed by the parties, to give an interpretation on a specific point or part of the award.
3. The arbitral tribunal may, if deemed fit, make interim awards under section 21.
4. The arbitral tribunal is empowered to continue the proceedings in the absence of any one party and make an award on the basis of evidence before it.
5. The arbitral tribunal has the power to follow either the legal system of Bangladesh or any other foreign legal system or system of international bodies, if so desired by the parties.

Proceedings which Commenced Before the Act Came into Force

The Arbitration (Protocol and Convention) Act, 1937 and the Arbitration Act, 1940 have been repealed by section 59(1). The saving clause provides that the repealed enactment shall be applied in relation to the proceedings which commenced before the Act came into force.

ARBITRATION LAW IN INDIA

India has undertaken major reforms in its arbitration law in recent years as part of the economic reforms initiated in 1991. Simultaneously, many steps have been taken to bring judicial reforms in the country, the thrust being on the minimization of court's intervention in the arbitration process by adoption of the United Nations Commission on International Trade Law (UNCITRAL) Model Law on international commercial arbitration. The focus of the government has been as much on the simplification of the law as on its rationalization in order to meet the requirements of a competitive economy. These reforms have resulted in increased Foreign Direct Investments (FDI).

Since 1990, Foreign Direct Investment (FDI) flows have become the largest and fastest growing single component of external finance for the developing world. As the noted economist Dr. Raja Chelliah has pointed out, "simplicity, transparency and perceived functions are essential for attracting the much needed foreign investment". These have been the guiding principles of the Government policy over the last seven years.

The Government has been encouraging private investment in infrastructure facilities, particularly in the power, highways and telecom sectors. The government's emphasis is now on the upgradation of technology and the promotion of foreign exchange earnings.

India has entered into bilateral investment protection agreements with the United Kingdom, Germany, the Russian Federation, the Netherlands, Malaysia and Denmark. Each agreement makes provisions for settlement of disputes between an investor of one contracting party and an investor of the other contracting party through the following Alternative Dispute Resolution (ADR) procedures—negotiation, conciliation and arbitration.

India is also a party to the Convention establishing the Multilateral Investment Guarantee Agency which provides for settlement of disputes between State parties to the Convention and Multilateral Investment Guarantee Agency through negotiation, conciliation and arbitration. There are number of agreements in other sectors to which India is a party, which similarly contain provisions for resolution of disputes through ADR procedures. However, India has not acceded to the Washington Convention *i.e.,* International Centre for Settlement of Investment Disputes (ICSID) Convention.

Presently there is a wide divergence and disparity in the laws relating to various aspects of business contracts in different countries. Such disparities create practical difficulties and legal problems in the smooth and swift flow of international business. With a view to promote uniformity atleast on fundamental principles in the various business laws, UNCITRAL has either made model laws/conventions or has prepared guidelines on various subjects. The conventions are intended to provide useful means of reconciling the existing conflicts and diversities between civil law, common law and several other legal systems prevailing in different parts of the world. The Government of India has already taken up the task of harmonization and globalisation of the legal framework relating to international trade and arbitration laws. The present arbitration law in India is based on the UNCITRAL Model Law on international commercial arbitration. In addition, India has acceeded to the UN Convention on Multimodal Transport of Goods (1980). The business community as well as the Indian Council of Arbitration are making all out efforts to induce the Government to adopt the other conventions/model laws as also to formulate appropriate legislation with reference to such conventions etc.

OVERVIEW OF LAW OF ARBITRATION IN INDIA

In the past, statutory provisions on arbitration were contained in three different enactments, namely, the Arbitration Act, 1940, (hereinafter referred as 1940 Act), the Arbitration (Protocol and Convention) Act, 1937 and the Foreign Awards (Recognition and Enforcement) Act, 1961. The 1940 Act laid down the framework within which domestic arbitration was conducted in India, while the other two Acts dealt with foreign awards. The Arbitration and Conciliation Act, 1996 (hereinafter referred as 1996 Act) has repealed the 1940 Act and also 1937 and 1961 Acts. The 1996 Act has brought out many changes relating to domestic arbitration, international commercial arbitration and enforcement of foreign arbitral awards and also defined the law relating to conciliation. It has consolidated the entire law relating to arbitration into a single enactment.

However, there are provisions regarding arbitration in some other central and State enactments also, *e.g.*, labour legislations.

The 1996 Act has several advantages over the 1940 Act The most important departure made by the 1996 Act from the previous law is in regard to judicial intervention with the process and product of arbitration. There are many distinctive features in this Act. First, where there is an arbitration agreement, the court is required to direct the parties to resort to arbitration as per the agreement (section 8). However, in such situations, parties seeking arbitration are expected to make an application to the court either before or at the time of filing a written statement on merits before the court. Second, the grounds on which award of an arbitrator could be challenged before the court under the 1940 Act have been severely cut down. Such a challenge, now, is permitted only on the basis of invalidity of the agreement, want of jurisdiction on the part of the arbitrator, or want of proper notice to a party of the appointment of the arbitrator or of arbitral proceedings, or a party being unable to present its case (section 13). At the same time, an award can now be set aside if it is in conflict with "the public policy of India"—a ground which covers *inter alia* fraud and corruption. Third, the powers of the arbitrator himself have been amplified by inserting specific provisions on several matters, such as the law to be applied by him, power to determine the venue of arbitration failing agreement, power to appoint experts, power to act on the report of a party, power to apply to the court for assistance in taking evidence, power to award interest, and so on. Fourth, obstructive tactics sometimes adopted by parties in arbitration proceedings are sought to be thwarted by an express provision whereunder a party who knowingly keeps silent and then suddenly raises a procedural objection will not be allowed to do so. Fifth, the role of arbitral institutions in promoting and organizing arbitration has been recognized for the first time in law. Sixth, the Act provides considerable improvement in the nature of the appointment of arbitrators, with the formulation of the Chief Justice scheme (section 11) which takes the task of selecting an arbitrator by courts outside the litigation process and makes it an administrative act. It is the prerogative of the parties to nominate their own arbitrator. It is only when there is a difference between the parties on the appointment, that the court intervention becomes necessary. The Act also empowers the court to nominate arbitrator (failing agreement between the parties) or designate an institution or a person to make such appointment. Accordingly, some of the institutions in India are under the consideration of the Chief Justice of High Courts for such designation. Seventh, under the 1940 Act there was a time limit of four months within which the arbitrators had to make the award. However, this time limit used to be extended by the arbitration tribunal with the agreement of the parties and failing such agreement, by the court. This resulted in delay. The time limit for making awards has now been deleted. Eighth, the importance of trans-national commercial arbitration has been recognized and it has been specifically provided that even where the arbitration is held in India, the parties to the contract would be free to designate the law applicable to the substance of the dispute. Ninth, the requirement of a formal arbitral agreement under the 1940 Act has now been relaxed to include even an informal agreement (section 7). Tenth, the 1996 Act has clothed the arbitrator with the power to grant interim orders in respect of the preservation of property and for ordering security. This is in addition to the interim orders that can be passed by a court (sections 9 and 17). Eleventh, the arbitrator can now decide on his own jurisdiction. This will help considerably to reduce interference by courts. Prior to the 1996 Act, the Supreme Court in *Renusagar Power Co.* v. *General Electric Co.*, (1984) 4 SCC 679, had restricted the power of the arbitrator to decide on the question of jurisdiction and, consequently, if a dispute was raised in respect of jurisdiction almost invariably the parties had to approach courts for adjudication which caused enormous delay. The 1996 Act, having defined the jurisdiction of the arbitrator, will surely prevent interim intervention by courts and consequent delay (section 16). Twelfth, the 1996 Act also provides for various other time saving measures such as requiring an arbitrator to disclose any possible bias at the threshold itself (section 12). Thirteenth, when an arbitrator is replaced, the proceedings conducted by him are protected. This will save time as it would otherwise require *de novo* proceedings before the new arbitrator (section 15). Finally, unless the agreement provides otherwise, the arbitrators are required to give reasons for the award. The award itself has now been vested with the status of a decree, in as much as (subject to the power of the court to set aside the award) the award itself is made executable as a decree and it is no longer necessary to apply to the court for a decree in terms of the award.

International arbitration can take place either within India or outside India in cases where there are ingredients of foreign origin relating to the parties or the subject matter of the dispute. The law applicable to the conduct of arbitration and the merits of the dispute may be Indian law or foreign law, depending on the contract in this regard, and the rules of conflict of laws.

The most significant contribution of the 1996 Act is the categorical definition of International Commercial Arbitration. Clause (f) of sub-section (1) of section 2 of the 1996 Act defines "international commercial arbitration" as an arbitration relating to disputes arising out of legal relationships, whether contractual or not, considered as commercial under the law in force in India and where at least one of the parties is:—

(i) an individual who is a national of, or habitually resident in any country other than India; or

(ii) a corporate body which is incorporated in any country other than India; or

(iii) a company or an association or a body of individuals whose central management and control is exercised in any country other than India; or

(iv) the government of foreign country.

It is clear from the above definition that international arbitration can take place in India in accordance with the same procedure as domestic arbitration.

CONCILIATION

Conciliation is a technique of Alternative Dispute Resolution (ADR) which has now acquired statutory recognition in the 1996 Act. Contrary to arbitration, conciliation can be used to settle or to resolve any conflict or dispute which has arisen between parties in respect of a defined legal relationship, whether contractual or not, and is not controlled or based on any prior agreement between the parties—the idea being that two willing parties can, at any stage, resolve a dispute in the presence of a conciliator. This technique can be used even after parties resort to litigation, and in fact would be most useful to persons whose cases are pending in courts for several years without any foreseeable outcome.

The chief elements in the conciliation process are the identification of the causes of the disputes and the creation of options to resolve the conflict. In this technique, the parties are encouraged to visualize options which provide solutions keeping in view the interests and priorities of the parties in question.

The 1996 Act provides a certain structure to the technique of conciliation, whilst at the same time retaining its flexibility and informality. It further provides that if the parties enter into conciliation and reach an agreement on a settlement of the dispute, then the said agreement will have the same status and effect as if it was an arbitral award (sections 73 and 74). This will have the effect of preventing parties from resiling from a settlement, thus giving this technique of alternate dispute resolution greater sanctity. The Act also provides for confidentiality in respect of all matters in the conciliation proceedings and in the settlement agreement except where disclosure is necessary for the purposes of implementation and enforcement. This makes it a useful tool for conflict resolution even in complex commercial disputes (section 75).

The Indian Council of Arbitration (ICA), a specialised arbitral body at the national level consisting of about 5,000 members, has been conducting workshops on the techniques of mediation and conciliation, in order to develop the new profession of mediators and conciliators. In addition to the efforts made by arbitral institutions like the ICA, Government has also felt the urgent need for the judiciary to develop court-annexed ADR schemes and make ADR a part of the judicial repertoire of dispute management. Accordingly, legislative changes have been made in the Code of Civil Procedure, 1908 which aims at giving impetus to arbitration, conciliation, mediation, judicial settlement within specified time limits. In other words, the new provision seeks to bring court-annexed ADR methods in India. The ICA has appealed to the Government and the public sector undertakings to resort to ADR methods by incorporating mandatory ADR provisions in their contractual undertakings.

ENFORCEMENT OF FOREIGN AWARDS UNDER THE CONVENTIONS

A foreign award can be enforced in India under the multilateral international conventions to which India is a party, namely, the Geneva Convention of 1927 or the New York Convention of 1958, if the said Convention applies to the relevant arbitration. The foreign award must have been made in a country which has ratified the Geneva Convention of 1927 or the New York Convention of 1958.

India had enacted legislation earlier to implement the two Conventions. The Arbitration (Protocol and Convention) Act, 1937 which came into force on 4th March, 1937 provided for the enforcement of foreign arbitral awards to which the Geneva Convention of 1927 applied. Similarly, the Foreign Awards (Recognition and Enforcement) Act, 1961 which came into force on 30th November, 1961 had been enacted pursuant to the New York Convention of 1958 and it prescribed the law and procedure for the enforcement of foreign awards in India, to which the said Convention applied. The Geneva Convention does not apply to those awards to which the New York Convention applies.

India had made two reservations while ratifying the Convention namely:

(i) It would apply the Conventions to the recognition and enforcement of an award only if it was made in the territory of another contracting State. In pursuance of the said reservation, the two implementing Acts of 1937 and 1961 provide that the Government of India will notify the names of countries to which the Convention would apply and which countries had made reciprocal provisions for the enforcement of Indian awards in those countries.

(ii) It would apply the Convention only to differences arising out of legal relationship which are considered 'commercial' under Indian Law. Courts have interpreted the term 'commercial dispute' under the two Acts in certain decisions where the question was at issue. The concept of commercial relationship in section 2 of 1961 Act, therefore, takes within its ambit all relationship which arise out of or are ancillary and incidental to business dealings between citizens of two States. The concept takes within its fold all legal relationships pertaining to international trade in all its forms between the citizens of different States.

The 1996 Act has repealed both the Arbitration (Protocol and Convention) Act, 1937 and the Foreign Awards (Recognition and Enforcement) Act, 1961. Part II of the 1996 Act, however, re-enacts the operative portions of both these repealed enactments. The three Schedules to the 1996 Act also reproduce the provisions of the New York Convention (in Schedule I), Geneva Protocol (in Schedule II) and Geneva Convention (in Schedule III). In other words, India continues to be a party to three important international instruments on the recognition and enforcement of foreign arbitral awards. There is no change in the legal position relating to enforcement of foreign arbitral awards in India. But a material change has been made in the 1996 Act, in as much as sub-section (b) of section 9 in the 1937 as well as 1961 Act, which provided that those Acts shall not apply to any award made on arbitration agreement governed by the law of India, has been omitted in Part II. So, any award given outside India, whether or not made on an arbitration agreement governed by the law of India, will henceforth be treated as a foreign award. To such foreign award, if the same be a convention award, the provisions of Part II and not the provisions of Part I of the 1996 Act will apply.

Although India has enacted the 1996 Act based on the UNCITRAL Model Law of international commercial arbitration, the international legal community has since been asking as to how Indian courts have responded towards interpretation and application of the various international conventions and the new law. The Indian courts have dealt with a number of complex issues in respect of enforcement of foreign awards. The law as settled by the courts on certain issues in the following cases continues to be valid under the 1996 Act.

Clause (f) of sub-section (1) of section 2 of the 1996 Act speaks about disputes arising out of legal relationship, whether contractual or not, considered as commercial under the law in force in India. The question of "commercial relationship" has been considered by various courts in number of cases. In *R.M. Investment Trading Co. Pvt. Ltd.* v. *Boeing Co.*, AIR 1994 SC 1136: (1995) CLA Supp 95, the Supreme Court of India has concluded this issue with the following observations:

> "While construing the expression 'commercial' in section 2 of the Act, it has to be borne in mind that the Act is calculated and designed to subserve the cause of facilitating international trade and promotion thereof by providing speedy settlement of disputes arising in such trade through arbitration and any expression or phrase occurring therein should receive, consistent with its literal and grammatical sense, a liberal construction".

Emphasizing the ambit of an activity which takes the character of the commercial relationship in the context of Article 301 of the Constitution of India, the Supreme Court further noted:

> "Trade and commerce do not mean merely traffic in goods, *i.e.*, exchange of commodities for money or other commodities. In the complexities of modern conditions, in their sweep are included carriage of persons and goods by road, rail, air, and waterways, contracts, banking, insurance, transactions in the stock exchanges and forward markets, communication of information, supply of energy, postal and telegraphic services and many more activities — too numerous to be exhaustively enumerated which may be called commercial intercourse."

On the above logic, the Supreme Court ruled that a consultancy service for the promotion of sale is a commercial transaction and any dispute arising thereunder is a commercial dispute. Therefore, as far as the meaning of "commercial" is concerned, the absence of a formal definition has not hindered an expansive interpretation.

REFERENCE TO ARBITRATION BY JUDICIAL AUTHORITY

The recognition and enforcement of an arbitration agreement precedes the issue of recognition and enforcement of arbitral awards. In a situation where one of the parties to the arbitration agreement institutes a suit in a court of law of the contracting State inspite of the fact that there was an arbitration agreement, section 45 of the 1996 Act empowers the judicial authority to refer the parties back to arbitration, if the following conditions are satisfied:

(i) There is an agreement to which the New York or Geneva Convention applies.

(ii) The authority is seized of an action by one of the parties against another.

(iii) The action relates to a matter agreed to be referred to arbitration.

(iv) One of the parties or a person claiming through or under him makes a request to the authority.

(v) The authority is satisfied that the agreement is not null or void nor inoperative or incapable of being performed.

(vi) The existence of a dispute/difference arising out of the legal relationship whether contractual or not.

(vii) That such differences are considered as commercial under the law in force in India.

The procedure for the enforcement of awards under the Geneva Convention of 1937, the New York Convention of 1958, and section 49 of the 1996 Act is much the same. Any person interested in enforcing a foreign award may apply in writing to any court having jurisdiction over the subject matter of the award. The "court" for the purpose of the proceedings would be the principal city civil court of original jurisdiction in a District and the High Court exercising the ordinary original civil jurisdiction over the subject matter if it were a civil suit. In addition to filing of the award and the agreement on which it is based as required by the Convention, the 1996 Act requires that evidence as to the award being a foreign award has to be filed.

The competent court in which the award is to be filed is the court which will have jurisdiction over the subject matter of the award. The application will be numbered and registered in the court. An award shall become a decree on the court being satisfied that the foreign award is enforceable. There is no provision for the issue of a notice to the affected party before the court enters satisfaction.

In India, a foreign award can be sought to be enforcement, although a foreign judgment was given in terms of the award. Merger of the award into the judgment in the country of origin does not have extra-territorial effect and therefore the award remains the cause of action for enforcement in other countries on the basis of the convention [*Northern Sales Company Ltd.* v. *Reliable Extraction Industries Pvt. Ltd.*, AIR 1985 Bom 332]. In *M/s Kochi Navigation. Inc.* v. *M/s Hindustan Petroleum Corporation Ltd.*, AIR 1989 SC 2198, the Supreme Court has pointed out that the meaning of the foreign award should be interpreted in the light of the New York Convention and its implementing legislation in India. The award must be executed as it is. The only ground which may compel the court to modify the award is its ambiguity.

Article V of the New York Convention elaborates the general grounds for non-enforcement by the courts of a foreign state. Section 48 of the 1996 Act lists various grounds upon which the court may refuse to enforce an otherwise enforceable foreign arbitral award. Briefly stated, they are—(a) invalidity of the arbitral agreement; (b) a violation of due process; (c) the arbitrator exceeding his authority; (d) irregularity in the composition of the arbitral tribunal or the arbitral procedure; (e) failure of the award to become binding, or its being set aside or suspended in the country in which, or under the law of which, that award was made; (f) non-arbitrability of the dispute; and (g) violation of public policy. A court may, on its own motion, on either of the last two grounds decline to enforce a foreign arbitral award.

Therefore, in proceedings for enforcement of a foreign arbitral award under Chapter I of the 1996 Act, the scope of enquiry is limited to grounds mentioned in section 48 of the 1996 Act.

PUBLIC POLICY OF INDIA

One of the circumstances in which enforcement of the award may be refused is that it is contrary to the public policy of India. The Explanation to section 48 of the 1996 Act also provides that an award would be deemed to be in conflict with the 'public policy of India' if the making of the award was induced or affected by fraud or corruption. Indian courts have been called upon to interpret directly the extent and content of public policy in India. The content of "public policy" as used in the 1996 Act as a legal standard has been set by the Supreme Court of India in *Renusagar Power Co.* v. *General Electric Co.*, AIR 1994 SC 860: 1994 CLA Suppl 1 (SC). According to the verdict of the Supreme Court of India in *Renusagar's* case, there are three patterns of the operation of the doctrine of "public policy" in the field of recognition and enforcement of foreign arbitral awards. First, an Indian court will refuse, on grounds of public policy, to recognize and enforce a foreign arbitral award if such enforcement is contrary to "fundamental policy of Indian law", that is to say, if the foreign award involves a violation of the Indian laws or non compliance with a court's orders. However, the bar of limitation will not operate as a bar of public policy.

There is a second pattern of public policy invocation. A court will refuse, on grounds of public policy, to recognize and enforce a foreign arbitral award if such enforcement is detrimental to the "interest of India". The words "interest of India" are of general import and the court has not clearly spelt them out. It is evident, however, that whatever is detrimental to the national interest or may lower the image of the country cannot be required to be enforced by a court.

In *C.O.S.I.D. Inc.* v. *Steel Authority of India*, AIR 1986 Del 8, the Delhi High Court refused to enforce an award on the ground that the Government of India had to ban the export shipments of coils with immediate effect because of the acute shortage of HR coils existing in the country at the relevant time.

The third pattern of operation of public policy is that in which the enforcement of foreign award would be contrary to justice or morality.

FOREIGN AWARD IS FINAL ON MERITS

Section 46 of the 1996 Act provides that any foreign award which would be enforceable under the Chapter shall be treated as binding for all purpose on the persons as between whom it is made. A foreign award cannot be challenged on merits, being final, conclusive and binding for all purposes, except the circumstances set out in section 48 in which the enforcement of the award will be refused. Domestic courts cannot set aside or annul a foreign award. The scope of the court's jurisdiction is restricted to a decision on whether the award is enforceable *(Ludwing Wunscha & Co.* v. *Raunaq International*, AIR 1983 Del 247).

LIMITATION

Hitherto, the enforcement of a foreign award was governed by the provisions of the Acts of 1937 and 1961, which did not make the Limitation Act, 1963 applicable to proceedings thereunder. The Delhi High Court has held in *Ludwing Wunscha & Co.* v. *Raunaq International*, AIR 1983 Del 247, that Article 119 of the Schedule to the Limitation Act, 1963 refers to Arbitration Act, 1940, and would not therefore apply to foreign awards. The court, however, held that, Article 137 of the Schedule to the Limitation Act, 1963 or the directions that may be given by the Court seized of the matter would apply. The court applied the provisions of section 47 of the Arbitration Act, 1940, which provides that the provisions of the said Act would apply to all arbitrations, save in so far as is otherwise provided by any law for the time being in force.

In view of the Bombay High Court decision, however, in the absence of a specific provision in the 1937 and 1961 Acts, the Limitation Act, 1963 would not apply and a foreign award can be enforced at any time without limitation (*Francesco Corsi* v. *Gorakram Gokalchand*, AIR 1960 Bom 91).

Section 43 of the 1996 Act has set this controversy at rest by making the Limitation Act, 1963 applicable to domestic arbitrations as it applies to proceedings in court. Section 43 will not cover Part II of the Act which deals with foreign awards and Part III which provides for conciliation.

APPLICABILITY OF THE CODE OF CIVIL PROCEDURE, 1908

In *Oriental Middle East Lines Ltd.* v. *Brace Transport Corporation of Munrovia*, AIR 1986 Guj 62, the Gujarat High Court has held that the 1961 Act is not a self-contained code excluding recourse to the Code of Civil Procedure or any other statute while considering the procedure to be adopted in enforcing a foreign award thereunder. The Court further held that section 41 of the 1940 Act read with or without the aid of Article III of the New York Convention means that the procedure for enforcing a foreign award has to be the same as for enforcing a domestic award, subject, however, to the implied condition that the Act of 1961 shall prevail if there is any inconsistency between the provisions of the said Act and any other Act, which might apply to domestic awards.

The Kerala High Court also took the view that the Code of Civil Procedure, 1908, would apply in respect of proceedings under the Act of 1961 (*Grand Cashew Corporation* v. *Gibbs Nathaniel (Canada) Limited*, AIR 1984 Ker 33). It was a case where a decree was obtained against the firm and the question arose whether that could be enforced against the partners.

NOTICE AND APPEAL

While section 49 of the 1996 Act provides that a foreign award shall become a decree of the court where the court is satisfied that the foreign award is enforceable, there is no provision for the issue of a notice to the affected party before the court enters such satisfaction.

Section 50 of the 1996 Act provides for an appeal from an order refusing to—

(a) refer the parties to arbitration under section 45;

(b) enforce a foreign award under section 48.

Such appeal would lie to the court authorized to hear appeals from such order. There shall be no second appeal, subject, however, to the right of appeal to the Supreme Court. There is no right of appeal against the recording of satisfaction by the court under section 49.

ENFORCEMENT OF AWARDS TO WHICH THE CONVENTIONS DO NOT APPLY

Foreign awards which are made in countries which are not parties to either the Geneva Convention or the New York Convention cannot be enforced with the same facility as in the case of foreign awards to which the Conventions apply.

Such foreign awards are, however, enforceable in India on the same grounds and in the same circumstances in which they are enforceable under the general law on grounds of justice, equity and good conscience. They can be enforced by an action brought before a court of law. The principles and conditions of enforcement of foreign awards as stated in some of the judgments of Indian courts are as follows:

(i) that there was a contract between the parties, whereunder, disputes between them were referred to arbitration to a arbitral tribunal in a foreign country,

(ii) that the award is in accordance with the terms of the agreement,

(iii) that the award is not invalid according to the law governing arbitration proceedings, obtaining in the country where the award was made,

(iv) that it was a subsisting award on the date of suit.

A foreign award will not be enforced by the courts in India, if its enforcement would be contrary to the public policy or the laws of India.

There is not much case law on the circumstances in which a foreign award can be challenged, assuming that it is made in accordance with a valid agreement to arbitrate and that it is valid and final according to the law governing the arbitration proceedings. There are also few cases in which a foreign award has been denied recognition or enforcement on grounds of public policy or on the ground that it is against the laws of India. A foreign award will be deemed to be against the laws of India if it violates, for instance, provisions relating to exchange control, import-export control or similar mandatory provisions.

CASE LAW ON INDIAN ARBITRATION AND CONCILIATION ACT, 1996*

Interpretation of Provisions

- *Sundaram Finance Ltd.* **v.** *NEPC India Ltd.,* **(1999) 2 SCC 479: AIR 1999 SC 565**

Held, that the provisions of the Act have to be interpreted and construed independently and, in fact, reference to Act of 1940 may actually lead to misconstruction. In order to get help construing these provisions, it is more relevant to refer to the UNCITRAL Model Law rather than the 1940 Act.

Also see: ***Anil Constructions* v. *Vidharbha Irrigation Developments Corpn.,* 2000 Arb WLJ 270 (Bom): 2000(2) All MR 119.**

- *Konkan Railway Corp. Ltd.* **v.** *Rani Construction (P) Ltd.,* **(2002) 2 SCC 388: AIR 2002 SC 778**

The Arbitration and Conciliation Act, 1996 has been drafted according to the UNCITRAL Model Law. The Act and the Model Law are however not identical and, therefore, the judgements and the literature thereon cannot be taken as a guide to the interpretation of the Act of 1996.

- *Ashok Traders* **v.** *Gurumukh Das Saluja,* **(2004) 3 SCC 155**

Held, that cases decided under the preceding Act of 1940 have to be applied with caution for determining the issues arising for decision under the new Act.

---

* Assisted by Abhay, Jyoti and M. Sailaja, Students, Amity Law School and Chhavi Kapoor, Student, School of Law & Legal Studies, G.G.S.I.P.U.

- ***Shin Etsu Chemical Co. Ltd.* v. *Aksh Optifibre Ltd.*, (2005) 7 SCC 234**

Held, that decisions rendered under the previous Acts should be considered with caution, since the 1996 Act purports to bring a new approach to arbitration. Further, the US position is very different from the Indian position and therefore, it is not very helpful in considering the 1996 Act.

Preamble, Statement of Objects and Reasons

- ***Decor India P. Ltd.* v. *National Building Const. Corpn. Ltd.*, EFA (OS) No. 18/2006 (decided on 3-7-2007)**

Held, we may refer to the Introduction, Statement of Objects and Reasons and Preamble to the Arbitration & Conciliation Act, 1996. The sum and substance of these sub-headings in the Arbitration & Conciliation Act, 1996 is that the outdated Arbitration Act, 1940 was replaced by the Arbitration & Conciliation Act, 1996 to make it more responsive to contemporary requirement; to make provisions for an Arbitral procedure which is fair, efficient and capable of meeting the needs of specific arbitration; to minimize the supervisory role of the courts in the arbitral process and to provide that every final Arbitral Award is enforced in the same manner as if it were a decree of the Court.

- ***Bhatia International* v. *Bulk Trading S.A.*, (2002) 4 SCC 105: AIR 2002 SC 1432**

Held, that the Act is a consolidated and integrated Act, having the general provisions such as those given under sections 9 and 17 applicable to all types of arbitration and not repeated in all chapters.

Such provisions are to apply to all arbitrations unless expressly barred or where other provisions have been made in a particular chapter or part.

It has also been held that Part I of the Act applies compulsorily to all arbitrations held in India and all proceedings relating thereto. The parties can only derogate from the provisions to the extent permissible.

- ***Food Corporation of India* v. *Indian Council of Arbitration*, (2003) 6 SCC 564**

The legislative intent underlying the 1996 Act is to minimize the supervisory role of the courts in the arbitral process and quick nomination/appointment of arbitrator, leaving all contentious issues to be decided by him.

- ***Dharma Prathishthanam* v. *Madhok Construction (P) Ltd.*, (2005) 9 SCC 686**

The essence of arbitration is to honour the intention of the parties to resolve the dispute through a tribunal of their own choosing without intervention of the Court. The jurisdiction of the arbitrators to hear and decide the dispute is derived from the arbitration agreement and the consent of the parties.

Section 1

- ***Fuerst Day Lawson Ltd.* v. *Jindal Exports Ltd.*, AIR 2001 SC 2239: 2001 Lab IC 2073**

Held, that from the plain and literal interpretation of section 1(3) of the Act and the Gazette Notification, it is clear that the Act came into force on 22-8-1996 but the purposive reading would show that the Act came into force in continuation of the first Ordinance which was brought into force on 25-1-1996. Thus, for all practical and legal purposes it shall be deemed to have been effective from 25-1-1996, particularly when the provisions of the Act are similar and there is nothing in the Act to the contrary so as to make the ordinance ineffective, as to either its coming into force on 25-1-1996 or its continuation up to 22-8-1996.

Section 2

- ***P. Anand Gajapati Raju* v. *P.V.G.Raju*, (2000) 4 SCC 539: AIR 2000 SC 1886**

Held, that the court before which the award shall be challenged is the court as defined in section 2(1)(e) and not the court to which application under section 8 is made.

- ***Nirma Ltd.* v. *Lurgi Energie und Entsorgung Gmbh*, (2003) 8 CLA-BL. Supp (Snr) 17 (Gujarat)**

It was held that where in the case of commercial arbitration the parties have agreed that the agreement, including the arbitration thereunder, shall be governed according to the laws of India and an award is made in pursuance to such an agreement, it shall be considered as 'domestic award' and, thus, held that the Indian court would be the competent court to entertain application for setting aside of award, subject to other provisions of part I [section 2(1)(e) read with section 34].

- ***Jagdish Raj & Brothers* v. *Jagdish Raj*, (2003) 7 CLA-BL Supp (Snr) 11 (P&H)**

An award could be challenged before the court as defined in section 2(1)(e) and not the judicial authority or the court before which an application under section 8 for reference of dispute to arbitration is filed.

- ***Union of India and another* v. *East Coast Boat Builders & Engineers Ltd.*, 1999 Arb WLJ 345 (Del): 1998 (2) Arb LR 702: 1999 (2) RAJ 221 (Del)**

The decision of the arbitral tribunal on the issue of nature of dispute *i.e.*, whether it is arbitrable or not is the one which amounts to a decision as to jurisdiction of the tribunal. It is not an award and hence not liable to be set aside under section 34.

- ***Manohar Lal* v. *Vinesh Anand*, 2001 Arb WLJ 387 (All) (*sic*: SC)**

An Arbitral Tribunal is not a Court within the meaning of section 195 of Cr. P.C. If it was the intention of the legislature it could have added a provision as existing in the Debt Recovery Act, Income Tax Act etc., granting such status.

- ***Stock Exchange, Mumbai* v. *Vinay Bubna*, 1999 Arb WLJ 633 (Bom): AIR 1999 Bom 266: 1999 (2) RAJ 290 (DB)**

Bye-laws of a society providing for the appointment of even number of arbitrators will prevail over the inconsistent provisions of section 10 of the Act because such bye-laws have the statutory back up and are saved by section 2(4).

- ***Shreejee Traco (I) (P) Ltd.* v. *Piperline International Inc.*, (2003) 9 SCC 79**

The Supreme Court laid down that the Act is applicable only when the place of arbitration is in India.

Section 4

- ***Krishna Bhagya Jala Nigam Ltd.* v. *G. Harischandra Reddy*, AIR 2007 SC 817**

Held, in case where both the parties accepted that there was an arbitration agreement between them and proceeded on that basis and submitted the arbitration proceedings before the Arbitrator, later on they cannot be allowed to contend that the Contract did not constitute an arbitration agreement.

- ***Narayan Prasad Lohia* v. *Nikunj Kumar Lohia*, (2002) 3 SCC 572: AIR 2002 SC 1139**

It was held that if a party to arbitration does not object to the composition of the arbitral tribunal (before the tribunal itself) within the time prescribed under section 16(2), it would be deemed that the party has waived his right to object.

- ***Union of India* v. *Maa Agency,* (2003) 8 CLA-BL Supp (Snr) 10 (Bombay)**

Held, that the petitioner can challenge either the jurisdiction of the arbitral tribunal to adjudicate upon an additional claim without a formal reference by the competent authority to the arbitrator, or raise the plea that the tribunal is exceeding the scope of its authority. Not doing so, and on the contrary proceeding with the defence to additional claim on merits attracts the principle of waiver embodied under section 4. The petitioner thereby clearly waives his right to object to the arbitral award on the ground that any requirement of the arbitration agreement has not been complied with (section 4 read with section 34).

- ***State of Goa* v. *M/s Heera Construction,* 2002 Arb WL 48 (Bom): 2000 (1) All MR 206: AIR 2001 Bom 45**

Held, that when a party knows that in accordance with the terms of the agreement, the new Act shall be the governing law and does not raise objection to the proceedings being held under the old Act and allows the proceedings to conclude and also does not take such a plea while answering the objections of the other party under section 30 or 33 to the award so passed, it is deemed that the party has waived his right to applicability of the provisions of the new Act to such proceedings.

Also see: ***Sardar Sarover Narmada Nigam Ltd.* v. *Aarti Steel Industries,* 2001 Arb WLJ 526 (Guj): 2001 (2) GCD 1332 (Guj).**

Section 5

- ***Union of India* v. *Popular Construction Co.,* (2001) 8 SCC 470**

Keeping in view the scheme of the Act which is "to minimise the supervisory role of courts in the arbitral process" and the same objective being reflected in section 5 (which prescribes the extent of judicial intervention in no uncertain terms) the court concluded that that the time limit prescribed under section 34 to challenge the award is absolute and unextendable by court under section 5 of the Limitation Act.

- ***SBP & Co.* v. *Patel Engineering Co.,* (2005) 8 SCC 618**

An arbitral tribunal is a creature of a contract of the parties, and this feature does not change even if the Chief Justice constitutes it. Therefore, the orders passed by the Arbitral tribunal can be corrected only as per the provisions of the Act and are incapable of being considered by the High Court under Article 226 or 227.

- ***United India Insurance Co. Ltd* v. *M/s Kumar Texturisers,* 1999 Arb WLJ 621 (Bom): AIR 1999 Bom 118**

In this case, a petition was made to the court seeking a declaration that since the claim was fully satisfied, there existed no arbitrable dispute between the parties to be referred to arbitration and also prayed for injunction to restrain the arbitrator from proceeding. It was held, that the court can intervene only in cases provided for by sections 14(2), 34 and 37. Thus the court cannot interfere in such a case/situation and held that the petition was not maintainable.

- ***Mankanner Jain Social Welfare Society* v. *Anil Kumar Doshi*, 2002 Arb WLJ 25 (Mad.): 2001 (2) Arb LR 242 (Mad)**

In this case the Madras High Court held that the new Act has widened the powers of the arbitral tribunal to decide upon the questions relating to appointment of the arbitrator, jurisdiction of the arbitral tribunal etc. Hence, for such preliminary issues, a party cannot approach the civil court as such intervention has been prohibited *vide* section 5 of the Act. The civil court can intervene only where it has been expressly provided for by the Act. If the challenge fails and the tribunal passes the award, the party can challenge the award under section 34 as provided for in section 16(6). This is the only remedy available.

Similarly the Allahabad High Court in ***Anil Constructions* v. *Vidarbha Irrigation Development Corp.*, 2000 Arb WLJ 270: 2000 (2) All MR 119** and the Bombay High Court in ***United India Insurance Co. Ltd.* v. *M/s. Kumar Texturises*, 1999 Arb WLJ 621 (Bom): AIR 1999 Bom 118: 1999 (2) RAJ 225** have spelt the scope of this section holding that the judicial intervention is not possible, except where expressly provided for.

- ***CDC Financial Services (Mauritius) Ltd.* v. *BPL Communications Ltd.*, (2003) 12 SCC 140**

Held, that under section 5, courts are restrained from interfering with arbitration except in the manner provided for under the Act. Thus, whatever may be the merits of a writ application, the writ court should have due regard to section 5 of the Act.

Section 7

- ***The Iron and Steel Company Limited* v. *Tiwari Road Lines*, AIR 2007 SC 2064**

Held, for settlement of dispute by arbitration, the agreement executed between the parties is to be given importance and an agreed procedure for appointment of Arbitrator is to be placed on high pedestal.

- ***P.B. Jagtyani and Co.* v. *Gaurav Agencies*, OMP No. 100/2000 (decided on 1-6-2006)**

Held, an arbitration agreement should be in writing i.e. its terms should be reduced to writing. But if the agreement is not signed and is established by another written contemporaneous document, it will be binding between the parties. The Hon'ble Supreme Court in **Jugal Kishore Remeshwardas v. Goolbai Hormusji, AIR 1955 SC 812** held that in order to constitute an arbitration agreement in writing, it is not necessary that it should be signed by the parties, and it is sufficient if the terms are reduced to writing and the agreement of the parties thereto is established.

It is not necessary that there should be a formal agreement or that the terms should also be contained in one document. No particular form is obligatory. All that is necessary is that the parties should agree in writing to submit present or future differences to arbitration. Such an agreement may be found in correspondence consisting of a number of letters. Under Section 7 of the Arbitration and Conciliation Act, 1996 an arbitration agreement should be in writing - it could be in the form of a document signed by the parties or by exchange of letters, telex, telegrams or other means of telecommunications.

- ***Wellington Associates Ltd.* v. *Kirit Mehta,* (2000) 4 SCC 272: AIR 2000 SC 1379**

The court held that section 7 does not cover situation where parties agree that they "may" file a suit in case of dispute or "may" enter into arbitration proceedings. "Arbitration agreement" under section 7 means "an agreement by the parties to submit to arbitration". It postulates an agreement, which necessitates or mandates the parties to appoint an arbitrator and then submit their disputes to arbitration.

- ***S N Palanitkar* v. *State of Bihar,* AIR 2001 SC 2960**

The case dealt with both section 7 and section 8. It was held that the presence of an arbitration clause in an agreement (in relation to commercial transaction) would not be a bar to criminal prosecution against a party in breach whose act constitutes a criminal offence (even if a case is made out *prima facie*).

- ***P. Anand Gajapati Raju* v. *P.V.G. Raju,* 2000 Arb WLJ 377 (SC): (2000) 4 SCC 539: 2000 AIR SCW 1489**

An application made to the Court and signed by all the parties stating that they have agreed to refer their disputes to arbitration can be considered equivalent to the arbitration agreement.

- ***Owners and Parties interested in the Vessel M.V. "Baltic Confidence"* v. *State Trading Corporation of India Ltd.,* 2001 Arb WLJ 625 (SC): 2001 AIR SCW 3220**

The arbitration agreement of one contract may be incorporated into that of the other contract, which does not contain any such clause. But such incorporation should not lead to inconsistency, insensibility and absurdity.

Also see: ***Pyrites, Phosphates and Chemicals Limited* v. *Sebilan Compania,* 2002 Arb WLJ 619 (SC): AIR 2002 SC 2341** and ***Prem Laxmi and Company* v. *Trafalgar House Construction India Limited, Bombay,* 1998 Arb WLJ 606 (Bom): 1998 (4) Bom CR 830: 1998 (3) Mah LJ 695. *Government of Kerala* v. *Luiz Paul,* (1998) 28 CLA (Snr) 4 (Bom)** also deals with the same aspect. It was held in this case that if a contract specifically excludes arbitration, recourse to it cannot be made on the ground that this contract by incorporation makes the rules of other contract applicable, which contains an arbitration clause.

- ***Build India Construction System* v. *Union of India,* 2002 Arb WLJ 621 (SC): AIR 2002 SC 2437**

The unilateral modification of arbitration clause is not allowed. If it is done and accepted, it will not apply retrospectively, unless otherwise agreed.

- ***Nirman Sindia* v. *Indal Electronics Ltd., Coimbatore,* 2000 Arb WLJ 342 (Ker): 2001 (1) Arb LR 144 (Kerala)**

If the arbitration agreement provides for some pre-requisites to be complied with by the party before taking the steps to initiate the arbitration proceedings those must be fulfilled. Otherwise the request for reference will be considered as pre-mature and will not be allowed.

- ***UP Sugar Factories Federation Ltd* v. *P.S. Mishra,* (2003) 8 CLA-BL Supp (Snr) 7 (All)**

Held, that where the arbitration agreement contains a jurisdiction clause which merely provides that a particular court would have jurisdiction to deal with any court proceedings arising out of the dealings between the parties, and it does not either by intention or by specific words or by inference exclude the jurisdiction of other courts which might deal with that matter because the cause of action or part thereof has accrued within the territorial jurisdiction of such courts, such jurisdictional clause cannot be construed to mean that it ousts the jurisdiction of such courts.

- ***M.M. Aqua Technologies Limited* v. *Wig Brothers Builders and Engineers Ltd.,* 2002 Arb LR 301 (Del): 2002 Arb WLJ 492 (Del)**

Held, that a person not a party to arbitration agreement cannot invoke it merely on the ground that a part of the job under the main contract containing the agreement had been assigned to him.

- *Firm Ashok Traders* **v.** *Gurumukh Das Saluja,* **(2004) 3 SCC 155**

Held, that an arbitral clause is separable from other clauses of the partnership deed under the scheme of the 1996 Act as such an arbitration clause constitutes an agreement by itself.

Section 8

- *P. Anand Gajapati Raju* **v.** *P.V.G.Raju,* **(2000) 4 SCC 539: AIR 2000 SC 1886**

Held, that there was no bar to refer the parties to arbitration if the application is moved after the submission of the first statement, if the other party who instituted the suit does not object to the reference.

Also held that the language of the section is preemptory and the court is under an obligation to refer the parties to arbitration once the conditions stated in section 8(1) and (2) are satisfied.

Further, it was held that the phrase "which is subject to arbitration agreement" covers an arbitration agreement brought into existence while the action was pending. It does not require that the arbitration agreement must already be in existence before the action is brought in the court. Even the court of appeal can refer the parties to arbitration if an arbitration agreement is brought into existence while the appeal is pending.

Also held that once the reference is made, the proceedings in civil action stands disposed of and the rights and obligations of the parties would be now governed by the new act including the right to challenge the award.

- *Kalpana Kothari* **v.** *Sudha Yadav,* **(2002) 1 SCC 203: AIR 2002 SC 404: (2002) 1 Andh LT 30 (SC)**

It was held that the dismissal of an earlier application under section 34 of the old Act cannot constitute any legal impediment for having recourse to and avail avenues open to parties under the 1996 Act (section 8).

Differentiating section 34 of the old Act and section 8 of the new Act, the court held that there was no need for obtaining a specific stay of judicial proceedings under the new Act as under the old Act.

- *Wankanner Jain Social Welfare Society, rep. by President, Chennai* **v.** *Jugal Kishore Sapani,* **2002 Arb WLJ 628 (Mad): 2001 (3) Arb LR 423 (Mad)**

Held, that the words "first statement on the substance of the dispute" do not necessarily mean a written statement. It may even be a counter-filed in an injunction application based on merits of the suit (as in the present case). And an application for reference to arbitration after the filing of any such statement or first statement may be dismissed.

- ***Palinder Singh Bedi* v. *The National Rifle Association of India*, 2001 AI HC 1738 (Del)**

The Delhi High Court, observing that section 8 of the new Act substantially corresponds to section 34 of the old Act and thereby referring to a judgment under the old Act (wherein it was held that the mere existence of an arbitration agreement does not by itself operate as a bar to a suit in the court and also that it does not impose any obligation on the court to stay the suit), held as follows:

> That the defendant in the present case was actively participating in the suit by seeking adjournments time and again for filing the written statement. He also failed to file an application for reference to an arbitration. The court held that the defendant's behaviour had resulted in the waiver of his right to file an application to get the matter adjudicated through arbitration.

- ***Parampal Singh* v. *Punjab State Ware House Corpn., Chandigarh*, 2000 (1) Arb LR 467 (P&H): 2000 Arb WLJ 360 (P&H): AIR 2000 P&H 53**

Section 8 requires that an application for reference to arbitration has to be accompanied by the original agreement or a duly certified copy thereof. In the present case, a copy of the original agreement was filed along with the plaint by the plaintiff. Subsequently, the defendant before filing the written statement made an application for referring to arbitration. The court held that such an application may be entertained as copy of the arbitration agreement had been filed earlier, albeit by the opposite party.

- ***Pamvi Consultancy Services Ltd.* v. *Global Syntex (Bhilwara) Ltd.*, 2003 (1) Arb LR 204 (Bom)**

Held, that there was no question of the court *suo motu* directing the parties to arbitration and the court shall do so only when the conditions in section 8 (that of application by the parties and a copy of the original agreement being submitted) are satisfied by the parties.

- ***Navin Kumar* v. *Standard Restaurant*, (2003) 8 CLA-BL Supp (Snr) 2 (Del)**

When there is an arbitration agreement, and application is made for reference to arbitration, a party cannot raise an objection or contend that there are serious allegations of fraud and falsifications and hence the matter should be decided in open court and not by an arbitrator in terms of the agreement between the parties. Arbitration clauses cannot be given a go-by simply on the basis of what type of the allegations are chosen to be made by the parties, except when there are serious disputes regarding fraud in relation to the execution of the arbitration agreement itself. The parties have to be sent to arbitration and the arbitrator is the competent person to decide all the disputes under the agreement between the parties.

- ***Asokan, Managing Partner Karthiyani Oil Mills* v. *Jayan,* 1998 Arb WLJ 490 (Ker): 1998 (2) Arb LR 123 (Ker): AIR 1998 Ker 256**

Whether a dispute falls within the purview of the arbitration clause is not the issue to be decided by the judicial authority. If the demand comes and the agreement contains the arbitration clause, court must refer it for arbitration under section 8.

The Bombay High Court in ***Garden Finance Limited* v. *Parkash Industries Limited,* 2002 Arb WLJ 579 (Bom): 2002 (1) Arb LR 122: AIR 2002 Bom 8,** however held that the dispute, if requested to be referred to arbitration, should relate to the same subject matter in respect of which the arbitration agreement exists. The judicial authority otherwise is not bound to refer the dispute to arbitration agreement.

- ***Varun Seacon Limited* v. *Bharat Bijlee Ltd.,* 1998 Arb WLJ 399 (Guj): AIR 1998 Guj 99: 1997 (3) Guj LR 2553: 1997 (3) Arb LR 559**

A party is disentitled to make a request for referring the matter to arbitration if such request was not made while filing the written statement. Such statement should be on the substance or merits of the dispute. Merely filing an application asking for more time to submit the written statement cannot be regarded as a statement on the substance of dispute and hence does not debar the party from making an application for referring the dispute to arbitration. Also, it was held that it is immaterial whether an application to refer is made independently or in the suit.

Also see: ***L.D. Industries* v. *Hindustan Wires Ltd.,* Arb WLJ 497 (P&H): 1998 (1) Arb LR 576 (P&H)** and ***Wankanner Jain Social Welfare Society, rep. by President, Chennai* v. *Jugal Kishore Sapani,* 2002 Arb WLJ 628 (Mad): 2001 (3) Arb LR 423 (Mad).**

- ***Maruti Udyog Limited* v. *Mahalaxmi Motors Ltd.,* 2002 Arb WLJ 541 (Del): 2002 (1) Arb LR 271 (Del)**

When there is no dispute existing in a suit, demand for reference to arbitration is not valid.

Also see: ***Pandey Company* v. *Power Grid Corporation of India Ltd.,* 2000 Arb WLJ 599 (MP): 2001 (1) Arb LR 382 (MP).**

- ***Vinod Kumar Chopra* v. *Sunshine Travels India Ltd.*, 2002 Arb WLJ 265 (Del): 2002 (1) Arb LR 69**

The specific Relief Act confers discretionary powers upon the courts to grant the temporary or permanent injunction. But still such matters can be validly referred to arbitration.

Also see: ***Haryana Telecom Ltd.* v. *Sterlite Industries (India) Ltd.*, 1999 Arb WLJ 591 (SC): 1999 (2) Arb LR 685 (SC): (1999) 5 SCC 688: AIR 1999 SC 2354.**

Held: Question of winding up of a company is not a matter referable to arbitration.

***Mahendra Kumar Poddar* v. *M/s. Bansal Builders*, 2001 Arb WLJ 382 (Cal): AIR 2001 Cal 58.**

Held: Dispute as to dissolution of partnership firm can be decided by the arbitrator.

- ***Bombay Gas Company Limited* v. *Parmeshwar Mittal*, 1998 Arb WLJ 351 (Bom): AIR 1998 Bom 118: 1998 (3) RAJ 53 (Bom)**

Held:

(1) Allegation about fabrication of record is not a sufficient reason to refuse the reference of dispute to arbitration.

(2) Section 8 of new Act differs from section 34 of the old Act in two respects. Firstly, stay was discretionary under section 34 while it is mandatory under section 8. Secondly, the pre-requirement of reference under section 34 was that the party must be ready to do all things necessary for the proper conduct of arbitration but there is no such requirement under section 8.

- ***Tamil Nadu Electricity Board* v. *Sumathi*, 2000 Arb WLJ 369 (SC): AIR 2000 SC 1603: (2000) 4 SCC 543**

The new Act does not permit reference to arbitration through the intervention of Courts. Hence, the High Court erred in referring the dispute to arbitrator through the intervention of the Court and then in making it a rule of the Court.

- ***ITU Classic Finance Limited* v. *Grapco Mining and Company Limited*, (1998) 28 CLA 408 (Cal)**

The arbitration clause in an agreement should not be vague and uncertain. A vague and uncertain clause of arbitration will not bind the court to refer the dispute to arbitration.

Section 9

- ***Adhunik Steels Ltd.* v. *Orissa Manganese and Minerals Pvt. Ltd.*, 2007 (4) CTC 340**

Held, that the intention behind Section 9 of the Act is the issuance of an order for preservation of the subject matter of an arbitration agreement — Power under Section 9 of the Act is not totally independent of the well known principles governing the grant of an interim injunction that generally govern the Courts in this connection.

- ***Sundaram Finance Ltd.* v. *NEPC India Ltd.*, (1999) 2 SCC 479: AIR 1999 SC 565**

Held, that the word "before" in section 9 means before the arbitral proceedings commenced as under section 21 and, therefore, it would not be necessary to give notice of invoking the arbitration clause to the other party. Also held that if an application is so made, the court will first have to be satisfied that there exists a valid arbitration agreement and the applicant intends to take the dispute to arbitration. Only when the court satisfies itself of such an intention of the applicant, it shall have the jurisdiction to pass interim measures.

This case was referred by Delhi High Court in ***Buddha Films Private Limited* v. *Prasar Bharti*, 2001 Arb WLJ 449 (Del): AIR 2001 Del 241.**

- ***Deepak Mitra* v. *District Judge, Allahabad*, 2000 Al HC 864 (All)**

The Court held that the power of the court under section 9 is not unbridlled. It is subject to limitations and restrictions. The interim directions can be issued under section 9 only for the purpose of arbitration proceedings and with a view to protect interest of the parties which otherwise cannot be protected or safeguarded by the arbitral tribunal. The power to pass orders with respect to interim measures cannot be exercised by the court if it would prejudice the powers vested in the Arbitrator and renders him incapable to resolve the dispute between the parties. To allow the jurisdiction under section 9 to be invoked for interim direction, one has to be cautious and circumspect keeping in view the intendment of the new Act which is to minimise the scope for intervention of courts in arbitration matters.

- ***Smt. Ila Mitra* v. *Shri Justice Amitava Banerji (Retd. Chief Justice)*, 2001 Al HC 434 (All)**

The Court in this case, held that the remedy under section 9 (and section 34) is an appropriate alternative remedy to negate a challenge before the High Court in the nature of a writ petition.

- ***HVS Technologies, Inc.* v. *Aeronautical Development Agency,* 2002 Al HC 755 (Kar)**

The High Court of Karnataka held that petition before a civil court for injunction or an interim measure would not be maintainable if it does not concern the issues referred to the arbitrator or subjected to arbitration though related to the issue.

- ***Anil Constructions* v. *Vidarbha Irrigation Development Corporation, and another,* 2000 Arb WLJ 270 (Bom): 2000 (2) All MR 119**

The provisions of section 9 are in aid of arbitration proceedings and cannot be used for its derogation.

Hence the party cannot, by using these provisions, ask the Court to restrain other party from approaching the Arbitration Tribunal.

- ***Nepa Limited* v. *Manoj Kumar Agrawal,* 1999 Arb WLJ 281 (MP): AIR 1999 MP 57: 1999 (2) RAJ 246**

The jurisdiction to grant interim measures under section 9 vests in the Court as defined in section 2(e) of the Act. High Court is not the appropriate Court in this regard.

- ***Shiva Carriers* v. *Royal Projects Ltd.,* 2000 (1) Arb LR 20: 2000 Arb WLJ 411 (Cal): AIR 2000 Cal 138**

By the operation of section 42, the Court in which an application for interim relief is initiated gets the exclusive jurisdiction on all the subsequent matters related to that arbitration.

- ***Kifayatullah Haji Gulam Rasool* v. *Smt. Bilkish Ismail Mehsania,* 2001 Arb WLJ 36 (Bom): 2001 (1) Arb LR 10 (Bom): 2001 (1) RAJ 133 (Bom)**

The interim measures ordered under section 9 continue to be operative till the arbitration proceedings get over.

- ***Narain Sahai Aggarwal* v. *Smt. Santosh Rani,* 1998 Arb WLJ 332 (Del): AIR 1998 Del 144: 1997 (2) Arb LR 322**

An application for compelling the production of documents is not maintainable under section 9.

- ***Steel Authority of India Limited* v. *Feegrade & Co. Private Limited,* 2000 Arb WLJ 616 (Del): 2000 (1) Arb LR 308 (Del)**

The application under section 9 praying the Court to defer the arbitration proceedings because of a pending Special Leave Petition in the Supreme Court in respect to the law involved in arbitration, is not maintainable.

- ***Kamala Solvent* v. *Manipal Finance Corporation Limited, Manipal*, 2002 Arb WLJ 210 (Mad): AIR 2001 Mad 440**

Though section 9(ii)(e) is widely worded to give discretion to the court to pass any interim measures appearing just and convenient, it cannot be used in allowing the application of the party seeking the injunction to restrain the arbitrator from proceeding with the arbitration, especially where the named arbitrator and venue was agreed upon by the parties.

- ***Baba Arya* v. *Delhi Vidyut Board*, 2002 Arb WLJ 508 (Del): 2001 (3) Arb LR 547 (Del)**

Relief under section 9 cannot be granted where the dispute does not arise from the breach of terms of agreement or from their non-compliance.

Section 10

- ***Narayan Prasad Lohia* v. *Nikunj Kumar Lohia*, (2002) 3 SCC 572: AIR 2002 SC 1139**

Answering the question whether section 10 is a derogable provision or not in the affirmative, the court held that an arbitration agreement will not be held invalid merely because it provides for the appointment of two or even number of arbitrators. Giving reasons, the court said the parties may choose to challenge the composition of the arbitral tribunal [before the tribunal itself within the time (section 16)] or they may even choose not to. Thus, a conjoint reading of sections 10 and 16 shows that this matter is derogable.

The court also said that in case the agreement provides for two arbitrators, two arbitrators should then appoint (preferably in the beginning) a third arbitrator under section 11(3) who then shall act as the presiding arbitrator. They can also do so at a later stage *i.e.*, if and when there is a difference of opinion between the two, so that the arbitration proceedings are not frustrated. The two arbitrators may even agree and give a common award and there would be no frustration of the proceedings.

- ***National Aluminium Company Limited* v. *Metalimpex Ltd.*, 2001 Arb WLJ 248 (SC): 2000 (3) Arb LR 422 (SC): (2001) 6 SCC 372**

Arbitration agreement providing for even number of arbitrators is not invalid.

Also see: ***M.M.T.C. Limited* v. *Sterlite Industries (India) Ltd.*, 1997 ATLR 119 (SC): (1996) 6 SCC 716.**

Held: There is nothing in section 7 to indicate the requirement of the number of arbitrators as part of the agreement. Section 10 is a part of machinery provision for the working of the arbitration agreement and cannot render the agreement invalid. The Bombay High Court relied on this judgement in the case of ***Smt. Satya Kailashchandra Sahu and Others* v. *Vidarbha Distillers, Nagpur,* 1998 Arb WLJ 376 (Bom): AIR 1998 Bom 210: 1998 (2) RAJ 447.**

- ***Sri Venkateswara Construction Company* v. *Union of India,* 2001 Arb WLJ 399 (AP): AIR 2001 AP 284**

If the agreement provides for even number of arbitrators, the arbitral tribunal will consist of the sole arbitrator. Section 10(2) clearly provides that the arbitration tribunal will consist of sole arbitrator if the parties fail to provide for the odd number of arbitrators.

Section 11

- ***Ion Exchange (India) Ltd.* v. *Paramount Limited,* 2006 (4) Bom Cr 545**

Held, on failure of a party to appoint its nominee on the arbitral tribunal it was the Chief Justice who would have jurisdiction to make appointment and in no case could the arbitrator appointed by one party assume jurisdiction as sole arbitrator— Act of arbitrator of assuming jurisdiction as sole arbitrator was patently illegal, it was not only contrary to the arbitration clause but was also contrary to the provisions of **Section 11** of the Act — Therefore, he had no jurisdiction to make the award.

- ***Shri Ashwani Kohli Sole Proprietor, Jyoti Enterprises* v. *Municipal Corporation of Delhi,* Arb P No. 312 of 2005 (Decided on 24-5-2006)**

Held, the court went in favour of the view taken in ***Union of India* v. *R.R. Industries,* 120 (2005) DLT 572**, where it was held that once a party does not supply the vacancy or fails to supply the vacancy before filing of a petition under Section 11(6) of the Arbitration and Conciliation Act, 1996 he forfeits the right to supply the vacancy in terms of the arbitration clause. What remains is only the arbitration clause, i.e. the dispute has to be resolved under the mechanism of Alternative Dispute Redressal scheme but no right survives to the party to supply the named Arbitrator in the arbitration clause.

Section 11(6)

- ***Punj Lloyd Ltd.* v. *Petronet MHB Ltd.,* (2006) 2 SCC 638**

Held, the court considered the applicability of Section 11(6) and held that once notice period of 30 days had lapsed, and the party had moved the Chief Justice under Section 11(6), the other party having right to appoint arbitrator under arbitral agreement loses the right to do so.

- ***Union of India (UOI)* v. *Bharat Battery Manufacturing Co. (P) Ltd.*, CA No. 3692 of 2007 (Decided on 13-8-2007)**

Held, in cases arising under Section 11(6), if the opposite party has not made an appointment within 30 days of demand, the right to make appointment is not forfeited but continues, but an appointment has to be made before the former files application under Section 11 seeking appointment of an arbitrator. Only then the right of the opposite party ceases.

- ***SBP & Co.* v. *Patel Engineering Co.*, (2005) 8 SCC 618**

The case of ***Konkan Railways Corp. Ltd.* v. *Rani Constructions (P) Ltd.*, (2002) 2 SCC 388** stands over-ruled by seven Judge Constitutional Bench decision of the Supreme Court. It holds that the power exercised by the CJ or his designate under section 11 of the Act is not an administrative power but a judicial power. The CJ is bound to give consideration as to the existence of—territorial jurisdiction; valid arbitration agreement in terms of section 7; the fact that applicant is a party to the said agreement; and the arbitrability of the dispute. This power can be delegated to the other judges of the respective High Courts or the Supreme Court and no non-judicial body, authority or institution can be designated for entertaining an application under section 11(6). Although under section 11(8) it is open to seek the opinion of an institution in the matter of nominating an arbitrator, the decision will be that of the CJ or his designate alone.

In the case of an order being passed by the CJ of the High Court a writ petition under Article 226 is not maintainable but it is open to the aggrieved party to move the Supreme Court under Article 136. However, where the order has been passed by the CJI, then no such appeal or writ lies. This judgment has prospective operation and it does not affect past appointments or concluded proceedings.

- ***Datar Switchgears Ltd.* v. *Tata Finance Ltd.*, (2000) 8 SCC 151**

Held, that under section 11(6), if one party demands the other party to appoint an arbitrator and the opposite party fails to meet the demand within 30 days, the right to appoint an arbitrator is not automatically forfeited after the expiry of 30 days. The opposite can still make an appointment but before the other party has moved the court.

It was also held that the power of nomination given in arbitration clause amounts to power of appointment and it does not require concurrence of other party unless so specified.

- ***Konkan Rly. Corpn. Ltd* v. *Mehul Construction Co.,* (2000) 7 SCC 201: AIR 2000 SC 2821**

The Apex court, in this landmark judgment, held that an order of appointment by the Chief justice or his designate is an order of administrative nature and, therefore, would not be subject to judicial review under Article 136 or Article 32. The nature of the function performed by the Chief Justice being essentially to aid the constitution of the arbitral tribunal immediately and the legislature having consciously chosen to confer the power on the Chief Justice and not a court, it is apparent that the order passed is an administrative order. Even an order refusing to appoint an arbitrator would not be amenable to challenge, but an order of refusal which has decided contentious issues would be an act of non-performance of duty and the authority concerned could be directed by mandamus to perform its duty. [*Note*: This case is no longer good law. See ***SBP & Co.* v. *Patel Engineering Co.,* (2005) 8 SCC 618.**]

- ***Wellington Associates Ltd.* v. *Kirit Mehta,* (2000) 4 SCC 272: AIR 2000 SC 1379**

Held, that even if the Chief Justice or his designate under section 11(12) is to be treated as an administrative authority, the position is that when the said authority is approached seeking appointment of an arbitrator under section 11 and a question is raised that there is no arbitration clause at all between the parties, the Chief Justice has to decide the said question. [*Note*: This logic has been followed even where this power is held to be judicial by the case of ***SBP & Co.* v. *Patel Engineering Co.,* (2005) 8 SCC 618.**]

- ***Nimet Resources Inc.* v. *Essar Steels Ltd.,* AIR 2000 SC 3107: (2000) 1 SCC 497: 2000 (3) Arb LR 342 (SC)**

Held, that though it is permissible under section 11 to decide the question of existence or otherwise of the arbitration agreement, but when such matter is not clear from the correspondence or exchange of documents between the parties, the appropriate course is to let the arbitrator decide such question under section 16, reason being that the power exercised under section 11 is administrative in nature. [*Note*: This case is no longer good law. See ***SBP & Co.* v. *Patel Engineering Co.,* (2005) 8 SCC 618** where this power was held to be judicial and it was held that such a question has to be decided by the CJ or his designate and this is binding on the arbitral tribunal.]

- ***Malaysian Airlines Systems-II* v. *Stic Travels (P) Ltd.,* (2001) 1 SCC 509: (2001) 104 Comp Cas 29: (2001) 2 An LT 8 (SC)**

The apex court held that the word "may" used in section 11(9) is not intended to be read as "must" or "shall". It is not mandatory that the nationality of the arbitrator should necessarily be different from the nationalities of the parties. In other words, the nationality of the arbitrator is a matter to be kept in view, but it does not follow that the arbitrator of the same nationality as of either party is necessarily disqualified.

- ***Konkan Railways Corp. Ltd.* v. *Rani Constructions (P) Ltd.*,(2002) 2 SCC 388: AIR 2002 SC 778**

The UNCITRAL model law was only taken into account while drafting the Arbitration and Conciliation Act 1996. The model law and the new Act are not identical. The model law and judgements cannot therefore be taken as a guide in interpreting the provisions of the Arbitration and Conciliation Act, 1996 and especially section 11 of the Act.

The court also decided that the appointment of an arbitrator by the Chief Justice or his designate is not a judicial function and, therefore, does not result in an adjudicatory order. The order of appointment is, thus, not open to challenge under Article 136 of the constitution of India. The only purpose of appointment is to see that due care is taken in the appointment of the arbitrator, and that the appointment is made by a person occupying a high judicial office. This in turn will lead to the appointment of a competent and impartial arbitrator. They affirmed the earlier decision in ***Konkan Railway Corp. Ltd.* v. *Mehul Construction Co.*, (2000) 7 SCC 201**. The court also decided as to the procedure for challenge of the arbitrator appointed by the Chief Justice or his designate. A party having justifiable doubts as to the independence and impartiality of the arbitrator may challenge the appointment of the arbitrator. The schemes formulated by the Chief Justice under section 11(10) cannot go beyond the ambit of section 11.The scheme is vitiated if it is contrary to section 11of the Act. [*Note:* This case is no longer good law for the point where it holds the power of appointment of the Chief Justice under section 11 as an administrative power. See ***SBP & Co.* v. *Patel Engineering Co.*, (2005) 8 SCC 618.**]

- ***Narayan Prasad Lohia* v. *Nikunj Kumar Lohia* , (2002) 3 SCC 572: AIR 2002 SC 1139**

The parties may by agreement provide for the appointment of 5 or 7 arbitrators. In cases where the parties fail in the appointment of arbitrators, section 11 does not expressly provide for the contingency but rather the provisions made under the section apply *mutatis mutandis*, providing for the appointment of 5 or 7 arbitrators.

- ***Grid Corpn. of Orissa Ltd.* v. *AES Corpn.*, (2002) 7 SCC 736**

The court in this case decided upon the appointment process of the presiding arbitrator by the two appointed arbitrators. The appointment should be made on the basis of prior consultation between the two original arbitrators. The parties should be informed as to the appointment. The appointment may, however, not be in writing. The arbitrators also need not meet physically nor are they obliged to include the parties in the consultation process. The appointment of an arbitrator not belonging to nationality of either party is not a mandatory provision and the appointing arbitrators may, after consultation, decide upon a person of a third nationality as the presiding arbitrator. The court relied on the decision in ***Malaysian Airlines Systems BHD (II)* v. *Stic Travels (P) Ltd.*, (2001) 1 SCC 509.**

- ***UB Global Corporation Ltd* v. *Kaveri Impex*, 2001 Al HC 2730 (Kar)**

The court refused to agree with the petitioner's contention that having regard to the decision of the Supreme Court in ***Konkan Railway*, AIR 2000 SC 2821,** the power exercised by the Chief Justice or his nominee is administrative, and therefore the Chief Justice or his nominee have no power to examine the matter under any circumstances and should mechanically appoint an arbitrator and held that such contention was against all principles of law. The court, held, that the Chief Justice or his nominee can refuse to appoint an arbitrator if they believe or if it is clear in their minds that there is no arbitration agreement existing which is *prima facie* evident from the material produced. It would be a travesty of justice if they appoint an arbitrator and leave the matter to the arbitrator to decide about existence of arbitration agreement. Also held that the issue of arbitrability of the disputes be left to the arbitrator. [*Note:* This case is no longer good law. See ***SBP & Co.* v. *Patel Engineering Co.* (2005) 8 SCC 618.**]

- ***K. Srinivasulu Reddy* v. *D.K. Audikesavulu*, 2001 Al HC 4097 (Kar)**

It was held that a writ of *Mandamus* cannot be issued against the order of appointment of arbitrator by the Chief Justice or his nominee as such orders are passed in performance of duty imposed or obligations imposed under section 11 of the Act of 1996 and a writ of *Mandamus* can be issued to quash the orders which are judicial in nature or quasi-judicial in nature, but not with respect to administrative order. [*Note:* The same conclusion has been reached in ***SBP & Co.* v. *Patel Engineering Co.*, (2005) 8 SCC 618,** however on a totally opposite reasoning.]

- ***The Indian Oil Corporation Ltd.* v. *M/s D.K.Gupta and Co.,* 2002 AI HC 4537 (Ori)**

An order of appointment was passed in exercise of powers under section 11 without sufficient notice to the opposite parties. The court held that the order was liable to be recalled as it was violative of the principles of natural justice even though such order may not affect any substantive right of the party and will still leave the party to agitate his contention before the arbitrator.

- ***Indian Engineering Works (Bombay) Pvt. Ltd.* v. *Chairman, Coal India Ltd.,* 2003 (1) Arb LR 443 (Jhar)**

Held, that the court has to be approached for the appointment of the arbitrator only after the procedure prescribed under the arbitration agreement is exhausted or it becomes difficult. If an application is made without setting in motion the procedure set up in the agreement, it shall not be maintainable as being premature.

- ***MWC Market Services Pvt Ltd.* v. *State of Manipur,* 2003 (1) Arb LR 454 (Gau)**

Held, that when a matter comes before the Chief Justice or his nominee under section 11, it is imperative on their part to bear in mind the legislative intent that the arbitral process should be set in motion without any delay whatsoever and all the contentious issues be left to be raised before the arbitral tribunal itself.

- ***Madhava Hytech Engineers Pvt. Limited, Secunderabad* v. *Union of India, South Central Railway, Secunderabad,* 2003 (1) Arb LR 611 (AP)**

An objection of limitation was raised to an application for the reference of the dispute to an arbitrator and the appointment thereby. The court held that the scope and jurisdiction of the court is very limited and cannot go into the merits of the matter. Keeping in view the object of the Act which is to expedite and move the arbitral proceedings without any loss of time, the Chief Justice or his designate is not obligated to go into the contentious issues.

- ***Muddu Krishna Rangaiah* v. *Union of India rep. by General Manager, S.C. Rly,* 2003 (1) Arb LR 642 (AP)**

Held that while appointing arbitrator either civil court or this court cannot ignore binding covenant or clause between the parties. If the parties specifically agree that a particular matter is not arbitrable, it would not lie in the mouth of the party to urge before this court that notwithstanding the given factual matrix still arbitrator can be appointed.

- ***National Building Construction Co.Ltd* v. *M.V. V. Sathyanarayana*, (2003) 8 CLA-BL Supp (Snr) 3 (AP)**

Under section 11(6), if the appointment of the arbitrator by the Chief Justice is contrary to the terms of the agreement and is in clear disregard to the qualifications required of the arbitrator, then the order is liable to be set aside, being misconceived and suffering from an error apparent on the face of the record.

- ***Karnataka Power Corporation Ltd.* v. *G J Fernandez*, (2003) 8 CLA-BL Supp (Snr) 9 (Kar)**

The power of the designated judge to appoint arbitrator flows from arbitration clause in the agreement between the parties. If there is no arbitration clause in the agreement, power under section 11(6) cannot be exercised.

- ***Sudhir Goel* v. *S.P. Sabarwal*, (2003) 7 CLA-BL Supp (Snr) 20 (Del)**

When the court has appointed the arbitrator with the consent of the parties, the appointment cannot be challenged through a writ petition on the ground that no notice under section 21 was served as such notice is not mandatory. Also, in view of section 16, all contentions relating to jurisdiction of arbitrator must be raised only before him. (Section 11 read with sections 21 and 16)

- ***A. Mohammad Yunus (dead) by L.Rs.* v. *Food Corporation of India*, 2000 Arb WLJ 399 (SC): 2000 (2) Arb LR 2 (SC)**

When an arbitrator is appointed contrary to the agreed stipulation in the arbitration agreement and the appointment is not covered under section 8(1)(a) or (b), the award given by such an arbitrator is *quorumnon-judis*.

- ***Sunrise Enterprises* v. *Union of India*, 2002 Arb WLJ 498 (Del): 2001 (3) Arb LR 654 (Del)**

The court in this case decided that when contentious issues are raised at the time of consideration of application under section 11, the right course of action would be to allow the application, leaving the contentious issues to be raised before the arbitral tribunal under section 16.

- ***Sri Venkateswara Construction Co.* v. *Union of India*, 2001 Arb WLJ 399 (AP): AIR 2001 AP 284**

The Chief Justice or his designate, while exercising the power under section 11, cannot decide contentious issues. The duty of the Chief Justice or his designate officer is only as to the appointment.

- ***Smt. Satya Kailashchandra Sahu* v. *Vidarbha Distillers, Nagpur,* 1998 Arb WLJ 376 (Bom): AIR 1998 Bom 210: 1998 (2) RAJ 447**

When named arbitrators are provided for in the agreement but the same refuses to act, then the procedure for appointing the arbitrator is exhausted and the appointment can be made only by the Chief Justice or his designate.

- ***Marshall Corporation Ltd.,Vishakapatnam* v. *Union of India rep. by the Engineer-in-Chief, Army Headquarters, New Delhi,* 1998 Arb WLJ 540 (AP): 1998 (2) Arb LR 175 (AP)**

The court cannot at the time of appointment of the arbitrator, embark upon an inquiry into matters which are excepted matters and are excluded from arbitration. Such matters should be left for the consideration of the arbitrator.

- ***Rail India Technical and Economic Services Ltd.* v. *M/S. Vidyawati Construction Company,* 2002 Arb WLJ 107 (All): AIR 2001 All 259**

The question as to whether the Chief Justice or his designate has jurisdiction to entertain an application under section 11 has to be decided with reference to section 11(12) read with section 2(1)(e), by considering the question as to which principal civil court of original civil jurisdiction has the jurisdiction to decide the question forming the subject matter of arbitration if the same has been the subject matter of the suit.

- ***State of Maharastra and others* v. *M/s. Khanzode Engineers (Pvt.) Ltd.,* 2002 Arb WLJ 145 (Bom): 2001 (3) All MR 555**

The agreed procedure for appointment of arbitrators may be deviated from by the agreement of the parties.

- ***M.M.T.C. Limited* v. *Sterlite Industries (India) Ltd.,* 1997 ATLR 119 (SC): (1996) 6 SCC 716**

When proceedings are commenced after the coming into force of the new Act, the provisions of the new Act will apply to the proceedings. When the agreement made before the coming into force of the new Act provided for appointment of Umpire by the other two arbitrators, then on failure of the two arbitrators the appointment will be made according to section 11(4)(b) by the Chief Justice of the High Court or his designate.

- ***Kamala Solvent* v. *Manipal Finance Corporation Ltd., Manipal,* 2002 Arb WLJ 210 (Mad): AIR 2001 Mad 440**

When an arbitrator is named in the arbitration agreement then it is implied that the procedure for appointment has been agreed to by the parties and an appointment made by the Chief Justice or his designate in such cases is without jurisdiction.

- ***Naginbai C. Patel* v. *Union of India,* 1999 Arb WLJ 572 (Bom): 1999(2) Arb LR 343 (Bom): 1999 (1) Mah LJ 745**

The appointment of an arbitrator by the appointing authority has to be made within 30 days. On failure of the appointing authority to appoint an arbitrator, the procedure may be undertaken by the Chief Justice or his designate. The appointment made by the appointing authority during the pendency of the application under section 11(6) is not an appointment in the eye of law.

- ***Avtar Singh Chadha* v. *Municipal Corporation of Delhi,* 1998 Arb WLJ 254 (Del): 1998 (2) RAJ 111: 1998 (1) Arb LR 397 (Del)**

The right of the appointing authority to appoint an arbitrator is not forfeited if the authority does not make the appointment within the stipulated period of time.

Section 12

- ***Konkan Railways Corp. Ltd.* v. *Rani Construction (P) Ltd.,* (2002) 2 SCC 388: AIR 2002 SC 778**

The right to challenge the appointment of the arbitrator is a right that is vested in the aggrieved party.

The party that has justifiable doubts as to the independence and impartiality of the arbitrator may challenge the appointment of the arbitrator.

- ***Saurabh Kalani* v. *Tata Finance Ltd.,* (2003) 7 CLA-BL Supp (Snr) 6 (Bom)**

Allegations raising doubts as to arbitrator's impartiality and independence cannot be made in a casual and frivolous manner without substantiating the allegation on facts. No doubts would arise merely because the arbitrator was employed in distant past with another public company of the same group (a party) (section 12 read with section 34).

- ***Kitiku Imports Trade Private Ltd.* v. *Savitri Metal Limited,* 1999 Arb WLJ 577 (Bom): 1999 (2) Arb LR 405 (Bom): 1999 (1) RAJ 56 (Bom)**

A petition for removal of arbitrator on the ground that he is biased can be before the Arbitral Tribunal itself. Such a petition, if filed directly before the Court is not maintainable.

Section 13

- ***Konkan Railways Corp. Ltd.* v. *Rani Construction (P) Ltd.*, (2002) 2 SCC 388: AIR 2002 SC 778**

The appointment of the arbitrator can only be challenged by the party that has justifiable doubts as to the independence and impartiality of the arbitrator and has reasons to believe that the arbitrator is not acting impartially or independently.

- ***Satish chander Gupta & Sons* v. *Union of India*, 2003 (1) Arb LR 589 (P&H)**

Dealing with the question whether sections 13(5) and 34 are *ultra vires* and contrary to each other, held, that two sections are harmoniously construable and there is absolutely no anamoly or any conflict or contradiction. Section 34 does not provide a ground of misconduct and malafide on the part of Arbitrator or challenge to the appointment of the arbitrator itself which is provided for in section 13.

Section 14

- ***Ashalata S. Lahoti* v. *Hiralal Lilladhar*, 2000 Arb WLJ 47 (Bom): 1999 (3) Arb LR 462 (Bom): 1999 (2) RAJ 384 (Bom)**

An Arbitral Tribunal consisting of even number of arbitrators is not in accordance with section 10 of the Act. Hence the Court can under section 14 (2) decide about the termination of the mandate of such a tribunal.

Section 14 and section 15

- ***Hotel Marina* v. *Sushil Kumar Raut*, [2000] 0 CLA-BL Supp (Snr) 16 (Del)**

There is no power of the appointing authority to recall a duly appointed arbitrator. His mandate is terminated or withdrawn only by way of events mentioned in sections 14 and 15, when he fails to act or it becomes impossible for him to act as arbitrator. When no such withdrawal of mandate has taken place, the order of any substitute arbitrator in which he purports to act as sole arbitrator is *non est* and without any jurisdiction and is liable to be struck down.

- ***Kifayatullaha Haji Gulam Rasool* v. *Smt. Bilkish Ismail Mehsania*, 2001 Arb WLJ 36 (Bom): 2000 (4) All MR 431: 2001 (1) RAJ 133 (Bom): 2001 (1) Arb LR 10 (Bom)**

Parties can agree as to the termination of mandate of the arbitrator. But such a termination does not amount to the termination of arbitration proceedings which is governed by section 32 of the Act.

Section 16

- ***Modern Food Industries (India) Ltd.* v. *International Engineers and Project Consultants Limited (IEPCL) (Intercorp. Division)*, OMP No. 53/2006 (decided on 26-7-2007)**

Held, that the award made by an Arbitrator can be set aside if the Arbitrator acts beyond jurisdiction, and, to find out whether the Arbitrator has traveled beyond jurisdiction, it would be necessary to consider the agreement between the parties containing arbitration clause. In order to determine whether the arbitrator has acted in excess of his jurisdiction what has to be seen is whether claimant can raise a particular claim before the arbitrator. If there is a specific term in the contract or the law which does not permit the parties to raise a point before the arbitrator and if there is a specific bar in the contract, the raising of the point then the award passed by the arbitrator in respect thereof would be in excess of jurisdiction.

- ***SBP & Co.* v. *Patel Engineering Co.*, (2005) 8 SCC 618**

The arbitral tribunal does not have exclusive jurisdiction under section 16 to decide on the existence and the validity of the arbitration agreement. The same can also be decided by the concerned fora under sections 8, 9 and 11. Where the jurisdictional issues are decided under section 11 or section 8, it is not open to the arbitral tribunal to ignore the said decisions given by the judicial authority or the Chief Justice and the tribunal is bound by it.

- ***Wellington Associates Ltd.* v. *Mr. Kriti Mehta*, 2000 Arb WLJ 188 (SC): 2000 AIR SCW 1165: 2000 (1) Arb LR 690 (SC)**

Section 16 of the new Act is an enabling provision. It empowers the arbitration tribunal to decide upon the questions relating to the existence of arbitration agreement and hence removes the disability, which once existed. The section uses the word "may" which indicates that it does not give an exclusive power to the arbitration tribunal to decide upon such questions. The Chief Justice can also decide upon such questions if it is raised by the respondent in reply to the petition filed for the appointment of an Arbitrator under section 11. [*Note:* This case has been clarified and continues to hold as good law subsequent to the decision in ***SBP & Co.* v. *Patel Engineering Co.*, (2005) 8 SCC 618.**]

- ***Grid Corpn. of Orissa Ltd.* v. *AES Corpn.* (2002) 7 SCC 736**

An appointment made by the Chief Justice or his designate may be challenged before the arbitral tribunal. The objection may be with regard to the improper constitution of the arbitral tribunal. Such an objection may be raised before the arbitral tribunal itself. [*Note:* This case is no longer good law. See ***SBP & Co.* v. *Patel Engineering Co.*, (2005) 8 SCC 618.**]

- ***Konkan Railways Corp. Ltd.* v. *Rani Construction (P) Ltd.*, (2002) 2 SCC 388: AIR 2002 SC 778**

If the arbitrator appointed by the Chief Justice has been appointed before the expiry of 30 days then such an appointment is improper. The aggrieved party may, in such cases, require the tribunal to rule on its own jurisdiction.

- ***MWC Market Services Pvt Ltd.* v. *State of Manipur*, 2003 (1) Arb LR 454 (Gau)**

Section 16 gives the power to the arbitral tribunal to rule on its own jurisdiction including ruling on any objections with respect to the existence or validity of the arbitration agreement, and for this purpose, an arbitration clause which forms part of a contract shall be treated as an agreement independent of the other terms of the contract *i.e.*, even when the contract containing the arbitration clause is terminated, the clause does not go with the contract.

- ***Nirma Ltd.* v. *Lurgi Energie und Entsorgung Gmbh*, (2003) 8 CLA-BL Supp (Snr) 17 (Guj)**

A ruling by the arbitral tribunal on its jurisdiction is an order/decision and not an award. The legislature has clearly made a distinction between order/decision and an award and provided that such a ruling would be an order/decision against which an appeal shall lie under section 37(2) and not under section 34 (section 16 read with sections 34 and 37).

- ***Sarkar Enterprises* v. *M/s. Garden Reach Shipbuilders and Engineers Ltd.*, 2002 Arb WLJ 475 (Cal): AIR 2002 Cal 65**

A question as to the jurisdiction of arbitrator cannot be raised for the first time before the Court in an application to set aside the arbitration award if it was not raised under section 16, provided that such question was based on the factual matrix. This is because the principle of acquiescence/waiver applies in such a case. However if the question is one which relates to the inherent lack of jurisdiction by the arbitrator, it can be raised at any stage.

In the case of ***Olympus Superstructures Private Limited* v. *Meena Vijay Khaitan*, AIR 1999 SC 2102: 1999 (5) SCC 651,** the Supreme Court left this question open.

- ***Scan Organics Ltd.* v. *Mukesh Babu Financial Services Ltd.*, 1998 Arb WLJ 519 (Bom): 1998 (1) Arb LR 685 (Bom): 1998 (1) Arb LR 685 (Bom)**

The arbitrator is not bound to decide upon the question of jurisdiction as the preliminary issue. He can decide it along with other issues.

- ***M. Mohan Reddy* v. *Union of India*, 1999 Arb WLJ 564 (AP): 2000 (1) Arb LR 39 (DB) (AP)**

Sections 13(4) and 16(5) are Constitutionally valid and do not violate Article 14 as there is an intelligible differentia for the different treatment of the party invoking the arbitration and the party subjected to the arbitration. Also there is a nexus for the object to be achieved which is the speedy disposal of arbitration proceedings.

***Rail India Technical and Economic Services Ltd.* v. *M/s. Vidyawati Construction Company*, 2002 Arb WLJ 107 (All): AIR 2001 All 259**

The order of the Chief Justice appointing an arbitrator under section 11 can be challenged before the arbirtral tribunal so constituted but, writ petition against such an order will not lie.

Also see: ***M/s. Gautam Packaging Industries* v. *M/s. Gold Crest Finance (India) Ltd.*, 2002 Arb WLJ 189 (Kar): AIR 2001 Kant 510.** It was held in this case that the order under section 11 appointing the arbitrator is not amenable to the writ jurisdiction but the order under this section refusing to appoint can be challenged under Article 226. [*Note:* This case does not operate as good law any more. The position in this matter has been clarified by the Supreme Court in ***SBP & Co.* v. *Patel Engineering Co.*, (2005) 8 SCC 618.**]

- ***Hindusthan Petroleum Corporation Ltd.* v. *Pink city Midway Petroleums*, (2003) 6 SCC 503**

It was held that section 16 of the Act makes it clear that if there is any objection as to the applicability of the arbitration clause to the facts of a case, the same will have to be raised before the arbitral tribunal concerned. The contention that this question will have to be decided by the civil court first, as the applicability of the arbitration clause to the facts of a case goes to the very root of the jurisdiction of the reference to arbitration, cannot be accepted.

Section 18

- ***Godrej Properties & Investments Ltd.* v. *Tripura Construction*, (2003) 8 CLA-BL Supp (Snr) (Bom) 3**

Held, that the section 18 by itself is not a ground to challenge an award. An award can only be challenged under sub-section (2) of section

34 and not under section 18. Section 18 merely provides that the parties shall be treated equally and at the highest, section 18 can be invoked only to point out that the petitioner were denied an opportunity of presenting the case.

Section 20

- ***Hari Shankar Singhania* v. *Gaur Hari Singhania*, AIR 2006 SC 2488.**

Held, that where the negotiations were taking place between the parties by way of various letters written by both the parties, the right to apply for arbitration can be said to accrue when it becomes necessary *i.e.* when a dispute in fact arose. The Supreme Court also observed that right to apply under Section 20 accrued to the petitioners on the last day of communication between the parties.

- ***Sanshin Chemicals Industry* v. *Oriental Carbons & Chemicals Ltd.*, (2001) 3 SCC 341: AIR 2001 SC 1219**

Held that the decision of the arbitral tribunal on the question of venue under section 20 would not come within making of an arbitral award under sections 28 to 33. The said decision on the question of venue will not be either an award or an interim award so as to be appealable under section 34 of the Act. But once the award is finally given, it can be challenged under section 34(2) on the ground that incorrect decision as to venue of arbitration had a bearing on procedure ultimately followed in arbitral proceedings.

Section 21

- ***Shetty's Constructions Company Private Limited* v. *Konkan Railway Construction*, 1998 Arb WLJ 625 (SC): AIR 1998 SC 1535: (1998) 5 SCC 599**

Section 21 of the new Act provides a test for determining the date of commencement of the proceedings. It is the date on which the request for referring the dispute to arbitration was received by the respondents. This date, in turn, is helpful to determine the law applicable to the arbitration proceedings, which is the one in force that day, unless the parties otherwise agree.

Also see: ***Reddy and Company Contractors* v. *A.P.S.R.TC.*, 1999 Arb WLJ 772 (AP): 2000 (1) RAJ 470 (AP); *Sardar Sarover Narmada Nigam Ltd.* v. *Aarti Steel Industries*, 2001 Arb WLJ 526 (Guj): 2001 (2) GCD 1332 (Guj); *Integrated Informatics (P) Ltd.* v. *Indian Telephonic Industries*, 1998 Arb WLJ 598 (All): 1999 (3) Arb LR 618 (All) and *Bombay Gas Co. Ltd.* v. *Parmeshwar Mittal*, 1998 Arb WLJ 351(Bom): AIR 1998 Bom 118: 1998 (3) RAJ 53 (Bom).**

- ***Milkfood Ltd.* v. *GMC Ice Cream (P) Ltd.*, (2004) 7 SCC 288**

Held, that change in constitution of arbitral tribunal is irrelevant for determining when arbitration proceedings commenced within the meaning of section 21.

Section 23

- ***G. Tech Stone Ltd.* v. *BFIL Finance Ltd.*, 2002 Al HC 4798 (Bom)**

It was decided that the order allowing the amendment of claim is not proper when the arbitrators failed to consider relevant law and facts and by recording contradictory findings and also there were no reasons given by the claimants for the delay. [Section 23(3)].

Section 28

- ***Shree Vinayak Cement Clearing Agency* v. *Cement Corporation of India*, FAO (OS) 129/2006 (Decided on 25-7-2007)**

Held, the Arbitral Tribunal as well as the Court cannot ignore the provisions of Section 28(3) of the Act which enjoins the Arbitral Tribunal to decide disputes before it in accordance with the terms of the contract, and while doing so to take into account the usages of the trade applicable to the transaction.

- ***Oil & Natural Gas Corporation Limited* v. *Saw Pipes Ltd.*, (2003) 8 CLA-BL Supp (Snr) 14 SC**

It is the duty of the arbitrator under section 28(3) to enforce the terms of the contract to uphold its sanctity. Hence, where the contract specifically provided for that the interest will not be payable on disputed claim, arbitrator cannot award the interest.

- ***G. Tech Stone Ltd.* v. *BFIL Finance Ltd.*, 2002 AIHC 4798 (Bom)**

An award, which violates the principle of natural justice and is contrary to section 28, is liable to be set aside because it will amount to the directions given by the arbitrator beyond the scope of the agreement. It is a duty of the arbitrator to decide the disputes within the terms of the contract and not beyond that.

Section 31

(1) Signing the award

- ***G. Tech Stone Ltd.* v. *BFIL Finance Ltd.*, 2002 AIHC 4798 (Bom)**

Section 31 makes it mandatory for the arbitrator to sign the award and in case of more than one arbitrator, all or majority can sign it, provided the reason for omission to sign by others is given. If some arbitrators give different award and do not agree with the majority, it is a valid reason of not signing the award. Such an award will be an arbitral award, though it was not signed by all.

(2) Awarding Interest

- ***Bhagwati Oxygen Ltd.* v. *Hindustan Copper Ltd.*, (2005) 6 SCC 462**

Provided the agreement does not prescribe the rate of interest, the arbitral tribunal has the power and the jurisdiction to grant a reasonable rate of interest for all the three stages of the proceedings, *viz.* pre-reference period, *pendente lite* and post-award period.

- ***Vastu Finvest & Holdings Private Ltd.* v. *Gujarat Lease Financial Ltd.*, 2001 Arb LJ 371 (Bom)**

The matters relating to interest are clearly in the discretion of the arbitral tribunal and it can award the interest on payment even when the agreement does not provide for.

- ***Haryana State Agricultural Marketing Board, Karnal* v. *Jagdish Chand Contractor*, 2003 (1) Arb LR 476 (P&H)**

If the arbitration agreement does not prohibit the Arbitrator to award interest for the pre-reference period, he can do so by invoking section 31(7)(a) of the Act. Also the Interest Act, 1978 confers express power on the Arbitrator to award interest for the pre-reference period.

- ***Godrej Properties & Investments Ltd.* v. *Tripura Constructions, Mumbai*, 2003(2) Arb LR 195 (Bom)**

Section 31(7) empowers the Arbitral Tribunal to award the interest at the contractual rate. But if the contract does not provide for the rate of interest, it will not exceed the statutory rate of 18%.

(3) Delivery of arbitral award

- ***Union of India* v. *Tecco Tricy Engineers & Contractors*, (2005) 4 SCC 239**

The delivery of an arbitral award under section 31(5) is not a mere formality. It is only after the conditions under section 31 are satisfied that the procedure under section 32 arises. The delivery of the arbitral award has to be "received" by the party which sets in motion the several periods of limitation. Therefore, this is matter of substance and it is an important stage in the arbitral proceedings.

Section 33

- ***Global Company* v. *M/s. National Fertilizer*, 1999 AIHC 3644 (Del)**

The new arbitration Act incorporates a specific provision (section 33) empowering Arbitral Tribunal to give interpretation of the award on a specific point or to correct any typographical, clerical or similar other errors. Keeping in view the above provisions, the High Court cannot proceed to give interpretation or remove clerical mistakes of the award, if the applicant did not take any steps to move the tribunal under section 33.

Section 34

- ***P. Kandasamy* v.: *Neyveli Lignite Corporation Ltd. rep. by its Deputy General Manager/Fertilizer Factory and Shri S. Sankaran,* C.R.P.N PD No. 1425 of 2005 (decided on 8-6-2007)**

Held, by examining the matter from any angle, it is thus apparent that the Court in which application under Section 34 of the Arbitration and Conciliation Act can be filed is the principal Civil Court of original jurisdiction in a district. Moreover, as per the definition clause contained in the Arbitration and Conciliation Act, any Civil Court of a grade inferior to the principal Civil Court is specifically excluded. In view of the specific provision contained in Section 2(1)(e) of the Act read with Section 2(4) of the Code of Civil Procedure, it must be taken that the expression "Court" as contained in Sections 34 and 36 of the Act is the principal Civil Court of original jurisdiction in a district, that is to say, the District Court or the District Judge.

- ***Ark Shipping Co. Ltd.* v. *GRT Shipmanagement Pvt. Ltd.,* Arb P No. 25 of 2007 (Decided on 26-7-2007)**

Held, grounds as raised in the present petition were based on **Section 48** similar to the grounds of **Section 34 of the Arbitration Act**, in the facts and circumstances of the present case, where the grounds specially in reference to the existence of Arbitration agreement and their clauses have already been decided by the Tribunal and against which no appeal is preferred by the respondents allowing the respondents to re-agitate the same issue and to challenge the said foreign award as contemplated under Section 34 of the Arbitration Act, as contended by the learned Counsel appearing for the petitioners is impermissible. In the present case the place of Arbitration is at Singapore. The English Law has been made applicable. The remedy of challenging the Arbitral award under Section 34 of the Arbitration Act is not available to the respondents. In the present case, there is admittedly, no such challenge made to the awards under Section 34 of the Arbitration Act.

(1) Setting aside the award

- ***M.M.T.C. Limited* v. *Sterlite Industries (India) Ltd.,* (1996) 6 SCC 716**

It was held that an arbitral award cannot be challenged on the ground that the agreement is invalid because it provided for even number of arbitrators. The validity of arbitration agreement depends upon section 7. Section 10 which provides for the number of arbitrators is a part of machinery provision for the working of the arbitration agreement and hence will not effect the validity of the agreement.

This case was relied upon by the Bombay High Court in the case of ***Satya Kailashchandra Sahu* v. *Vidarbha Distilleries, Nagpur*, AIR 1998 Bom 210.**

- ***Rajinder Krishan Khanna* v. *Union of India*, 1998 Arb WLJ 599 (SC): AIR 1999 SC 463: 1998 (2) Arb LR 619 (SC): 1998 (7) SCC 129: 1998 (7) JT 128 (SC)**

Where the issues referred to arbitration were those related to the compensation for destruction of houses, crops, garden and reclamation of lands and the arbitrator awarded compensation for loss of potential of lands, it was held that the arbitrator exceeded the scope of reference and the award was liable to be set aside under section 34(2)(iv).

- ***Olympus Superstructures (P) Ltd.* v. *Meena Vijay Khetan*, (1999) 5 SCC 651: AIR 1999 SC 2102**

  It was held that:

  (1) Use of the word "terms of the submission to arbitration" in section 34(2)(a)(iv) refers to the terms of arbitration clause. It is clear after the perusal of section 28 (which uses the words "dispute submitted to arbitration") and section 43(3) (which uses the words "submit future disputes to arbitration") that such is the meaning of the word "submission".

  (2) Section 34(2)(b)(i) does not prohibit the reference to arbitration of a dispute relating to specific performance. The right to specific performance arising out of a contract of sale is a contractual right and as such can be referred to the arbitration if the parties agree so to do.

- ***Narayan Prasad Lohia* v. *Nikunj Kumar Lohia*, (2002) 3 SCC 572: AIR 2002 SC 1139**

Section 34(2)(a)(v) provides for setting aside of the arbitral award if the composition of the arbitral tribunal or the arbitral procedure was not in accordance with the agreement of the parties. If such composition or procedure was in accordance with the agreement of the parties though in conflict with the provisions of Part I of the Act, the award cannot be challenged. Same is true for vice-versa *i.e.*, a composition or procedure not in accordance with the agreement but in accordance with the Act, will attach validity to the award and such an award cannot be challenged under section 34.

- ***Sanshin Chemicals Industry* v. *Oriental Carbons and Chemicals Ltd.*, (2001) 3 SCC 341: AIR 2001 SC 1219**

The decision of arbitration tribunal as to the venue of arbitration is not an award with in the meaning of section 2(6). This is because such conclusion is not an independent judicial determination but the one based upon the guidelines given in the arbitration agreement. Hence, it cannot be challenged under section 34 of the Act.

But it does not mean that such a decision cannot be assailed in the ultimate arbitration award. If the decision as to venue has effected the procedure followed in the arbitration proceedings, then it can be challenged under section 34(2), but only as a part of ultimate arbitration award.

- ***Indian Commercial Company Ltd.* v. *Amrish Kilachand*, 2003 (1) Arb LR 10 (Bom)**

In this case the Bombay High Court held:

(1) That the inadequacy of evidence brought before the Arbitrator or the suppression of certain matters by the witness of the opposite party cannot be a ground of fraud.

(2) That the legal misconduct of an arbitrator cannot be decided by the Court in execution, since it is not a question relating to execution, discharge or satisfaction of decree, but involves the determination of the manner in which the Arbitrator conducted the proceedings. Also legal misconduct is not one of the grounds provided under section 34 for setting aside the award.

- ***Sarkar Enterprises* v. *M/s. Garden Reach Shipbuilders and Engineers Ltd.*, 2002 Arb WLJ 475 (Cal): AIR 2002 Cal 65**

Insufficiency of evidence cannot be a ground to challenge the award under section 34.

- ***R.K. Textiles, Mumbai* v. *Sulabh Textiles Pvt. Ltd., Mumbai*, 2003 (1) Arb LR 303 (Bom)**

The question of jurisdiction of the arbitrator cannot be raised in the execution proceedings. The award can be challenged only in accordance with section 34 of the Act otherwise it becomes final and binding.

- ***M.C.D.* v. *Jasbir Singh, Prop., Jaseb Enterprises*, 2003 (1) Arb LR 336 (Del)**

The reason that the arbitration award suffered from legal infirmity because it was time barred cannot be a ground to set aside the arbitration award under section 34. With the introduction of section 34 of the new Act *"a sea change has occurred in the matter of challenging the award"*. The new Act has shrunken the grounds and has limited the scope for challenging the award to the cases expressly provided for under section 34.

- ***Godrej Properties & Investments Ltd.* v. *Tripura Constructions, Mumbai,* 2003 (2) Arb LR 195 (Bom)**

The reason that the parties were not treated equally by the arbitrator (which is his duty under section 18 of the Act) cannot be a ground for setting aside the award as it is not made so by section 34.

- ***Deepak Mitra* v. *District Judge, Allahabad,* 2000 AIHC 864 (All)**

It was held that:

(1) An order of arbitral tribunal recording the "mere findings of fact" is not an "interim award" and hence cannot be challenged under section 34.

(2) The proper court to entertain application under section 34 is the principal civil court of original jurisdiction *i.e.,* the District Judge and not the High Court.

(3) The intention of the new Act is to minimise the scope for intervention of Courts in arbitration matters. The jurisdiction of the court under section 34 is limited as expressly indicated in it.

Hence it has no jurisdiction to examine the correctness of the award on merits. While exercising jurisdiction under section 34, a court cannot sit in appeal over the views of the arbitrator by re-examining and re-assessing the materials.

- ***Shri Vishnu Cements Ltd.* v. *M/s. S.R.K. Transport Service,* 2002 AIHC 4161 (AP)**

A document recording the minutes of a meeting conducted to resolve some ambiguities of the original contract, is a part of the original contract and the arbitrator can rely upon it to reach the final conclusion. An award relying on such a document is not improper and hence cannot be set aside under section 34

- ***BFIL Finance Ltd.* v. *G. Tech Stone Ltd.,* [2003] 7 CLA-BL Supp (Snr) 6 (Bom)**

An award cannot be set aside on ground of public policy and non-application of mind, merely because another view of the matter is possible. Judicial review in arbitration does not permit to look into the merits, legality or validity except what is provided in section 34.

Also a challenge under section 34 merely to the reasoned award signed by the majority cannot, under the garb of liberal interpretation, be construed as a challenge to the final award signed by all. Only the final operative award is executable and it should be challenged specifically.

- ***Oil and Natural Gas Company Ltd.* v. *Saw Pipes Ltd.,* (2003) 7 CLA-BL Supp (Snr) 5 (Bom)**

An award cannot be set aside under section 34 on the ground of rejection of a demand for the joinder of a party with whom there was no dispute.

- ***Continental Construction Ltd.* v. *Food Corporation of India,* (2003) 7 CLA-BL Supp (Snr) 12 (Del)**

Where the arbitrator has recorded some findings based upon certain facts, court will not interfere with it just because a different view was also possible.

- ***Harinarayan G. Bajaj* v. *Sharedeal Financial Consultations (P.) Ltd.,* (2003) 7 CLA-BL Supp 48 (Snr)**

Every order or decision of the arbitral tribunal is not an award. Hence, it cannot be challenged separately but with the award in which such order will be taken to be merged, if such challenge was available under section 34(2).

- ***Government of Kerala* v. *Som Dutt Builders Ltd.,* (2003) 7 CLA-BL Supp (Snr) 28 (Ker)**

Even though the award falls with in the terms of reference to the arbitration but it is not contemplated by the contract, it will be open to challenge under section 34(2)(a)(iv).

- ***Godrej Properties and Investments Ltd.* v. *Tripura Constructions,* (2003) 8 CLA-BL Supp (Snr) 3 (Bom)**

The interest awarded can be challenged as unreasonable under section 34(2)(b)(i) of the Act, if it was contrary to the terms of the contract or exceeded the statutory rate of interest *i.e.,* 18% per annum.

- ***Suresh Kabra* v. *Trusted Share and Investments Ltd.,* (2003) 8 CLA-BL Supp (Snr) 5 (Bom)**

Having regard to the limited parameters of section 34, the Court cannot interfere with the award upon a reappraisal of evidence or by substituting its own opinion for the reasons given by arbitral tribunal.

- ***Em and Em Associates* v. *D.D.A.,* (2003) 8 CLA-BL Supp (Snr) 4 (Del)**

Where on perusal of relevant clauses of the contract, many views are possible, the Court cannot, under section 34, impose its own interpretation on that of the Arbitrator, when view of the Arbitrator is also a possible one.

(2) Limitation Period

- ***Union of India* v. *Popular Construction Co.,* (2001) 8 SCC 470**

Section 34(3) provides for a period within which an application for setting aside the arbitration award can be filed. The use of words *"in accordance with"* in section 34(1) and the words *"but not thereafter"* in section 34(3) suggest that there is express exclusion of the Limitation Act. The Arbitration Act is a special Law and provides for a limitation period different from the Limitation Act.

Hence the limitation period provided for under the Arbitration Act will apply. Award will not be allowed to be challenged after that period. This is because now under section 36, award directly becomes a decree of the Court and achieves finality as soon as the limitation period under Arbitration Act gets over. Hence the parties cannot be allowed to rely upon section 5 of the Limitation Act.

- ***Vastu Finvest & Holdings Private Ltd.* v. *Gujarat Lease Financial Ltd.,* 2001 Arb LJ 371 (Bom)**

Section 34(3) is absolute and excludes the application of the Limitation Act. This section applies even when the party applies for the amendment to raise a new ground of challenge *i.e.,* a party cannot apply for such amendment after the limitation period of 3 months and the grace period of 30 days gets over.

- ***Turnkey Constructions Private Ltd., Bangalore* v. *Mrs. V.R. Dijur,* 2001 AIHC 4210 (Kar)**

Section 34(3) of the new Act prescribes the period of limitation within which an application to set aside the award can be filed. The proviso to the section prescribes the condonable period of delay.

Contents of this section expressly exclude the application of the Limitation Act. Hence application for condonation of delay beyond the said period was not maintainable.

Also, in ***MIC Electronics Ltd., Hyderabad* v. *Union of India,* 2002 AIHC 1074 (AP HC)** it was held that use of the words "but not thereafter" in section 34(3) is crucial and amounts to an express exclusion with in the meaning of section 29(2) of the Limitation Act. Application of Limitation Act to condone the delay beyond the expressed period mentioned in section 34(3) of the new Arbitration Act would render the clause "but not thereafter" wholly otiose.

Also see: ***National Hydroelectric Power Corp. Ltd.* v. *Asian Techs. Rani Constructions Joint Venture,* (2003) 7 CLA-BL Supp (Snr) 11 (UTR)** and ***Rajeev Sharda* v. *Executive Engineer, HP PWD, Theog,* 2000 Arb WLJ 550 (HP).**

(3) Stay of Proceedings

- ***Midex Overseas Ltd.* v. *M/s. Dewas Saya Ltd.,* 2001 Arb WLJ 523 (MP): 2001 (2) MPLJ 391: 2001 (3) MPHT 140**

The grounds on which the court can stay the proceedings under section 34(4) should be such which will give an opportunity to the arbitration tribunal to correct the mistakes, which made the award liable to be set aside. Section 34(4) does not provide for any specific grounds. But, as the aim is to give an opportunity to the arbitration tribunal to set aside the award, the grounds for the stay should be in conformity with that objective.

(4) If ultravires *to other provisions of the Act*

- ***Satish Chander Gupta & Sons* v. *Union of India,* 2003 (10) Arb LR 589 (P&H) (DB)**

Section 13(5) and section 34 of the new Act are not *ultravires* and contrary to each other. The Parliament has enacted this Act on the lines of the Model Law on International Commercial Arbitration as approved by the General Assembly of the United Nations. Under the Model Law, a party has been given a right to challenge the appointment of the Arbitrator before the Arbitrator himself. If the Arbitrator decides against him, he can go to the Court before waiting for the award. However, Indian Parliament has made certain changes in that respect, with a view to prevent dilatory tactics. The unsuccessful party is not allowed to challenge the arbitrator till he makes the award. The two said sections are in conformity with the said object and can be harmoniously construed.

(5) Public Policy: Meaning

- ***Oil & Natural Gas Corporation Limited.* v. *Saw Pipes Ltd.,* (2003) 8 CLA-BL Supp (Snr) 14 SC**

Section 34(2)(b)(ii) *inter-alia* provides that an award can be set aside if it is against public policy of India. However, this phrase is not defined in the Act. It was held that this term should be interpreted in the context of the jurisdiction of the court where the award is challenged. A revisional or an appellate court can set aside an award which is patently illegal (*i.e.,* in violation of any statutory provisions) because it will amount to breach of public interest. An illegality of trivial nature can be avoided but not of a patent nature. The illegality must go to the root of the matter.

- ***Nirfabrics Ltd.* v. *Nirlon Ltd.,* 1999 AIHC 1061 (Bom)**

A proposition of law (not mere conclusion) based upon the interpretation of statute, on which the Arbitral Tribunal proceeded to pass the award, can be interfered by the Court by virtue of section 34 of the Act under the clause of "against the Public Policy".

- ***Union of India* v. *Modi Enterprises,* (2003) 7 CLA-BL Supp (Snr) 28 (Bom)**

Mere error of law does not amount to the breach of public policy. It should be clearly established that there was such breach.

- ***Government of Kerala* v. *Som Dutt Builders Ltd.,* (2003) 7 CLA-BL Supp (Snr) 28 (Ker)**

Explanation to section 34(2)(b)(ii) is not exhaustive. It merely provides for the illustrations, which can be taken as amounting to the breach of public policy. These are without prejudicing the generality of the meaning of the word "public policy".

(6) Section 34: If a good alternate remedy to the writ petition

- ***Smt. Veena Ojha* v. *U.P. Stock Exchange Association Ltd.,* 1999 AIHC 3854 (All HC)**

Applicant cannot approach the High Court under Article 226 to set aside the arbitral award passed *ex parte* because:

(1) Such an award can be challenged under section 34 of the new Act which is a good alternate remedy.

(2) It might involve some disputed facts like, whether proper notice was given or not and High Court while exercising writ jurisdiction cannot take evidence (except in exceptional circumstances) to decide upon such disputed questions.

Also see: ***Smt. Ila Mitra* v. *Shri Justice Amitava Banerji,* 2001 AIHC 434 (All).**

(7) Section 34 and section 36: Enforcement of award

- ***National Buildings Construction Corporation Ltd.* v. *Lloyds Insulation India Ltd.,* (2005) 2 SCC 367**

There is no power in a Court to direct execution of an award when a challenge to the award under section 34 is pending. For the purposes of section 36, the Court cannot go behind the award and a challenge to the award or the process of arriving at the award would render the award as a whole unenforceable.

- ***M. Anasuya Devi* v. *M. Manik Reddy,* (2003) 8 SCC 565**

Held, that an award cannot be set aside under section 34 for want of stamping and registration.

(8) Section 34(3), proviso: "Sufficient cause"

- ***National Aluminium Co. Ltd.* v. *Pressteel & Fabrications (P) Ltd.,* (2004) 1 SCC 540**

Held, that delay caused due to *bona fide* prosecution of application in wrong forum to be condoned.

Section 36

- ***S. Kumar* v. *D.D.A.,* (2003) 8 CLA-BL Supp (Snr) 4 (Del)**

Under the 1996 Act, an award is enforceable under section 36 as a decree of the Court. There is no provision under the 1996 Act for making the award a rule of the Court as was under the 1940 Act.

Once the application under section 34 is refused, the award becomes a decree and the date of this decree remains same that is the date of award.

- ***Ramaswamy* v. *Principal Subordinate Judge,* (1998) 28 CLA 23 (Ker)**

Because of section 36 of the new Act, award will now be considered as a decree of the Court and the executing Court cannot insist for a decree to accept the execution application.

- ***Khaleel Ahmed Dakhani* v. *Hatti Gold Mines Co. Ltd.,* (2000) 3 SCC 755: AIR 2000 SC 1926**

The executing court cannot entertain the execution application till the application under section 34 to set aside the arbitral award has been disposed of. This is because the award does not attain finality pending such application.

- ***I.C.D.S. Ltd.* v. *Mangala Builders Private Ltd.,* 2001 Arb WLJ 685 (Kant): 2001 (3) Arb LR 334**

The proper court for execution of arbitral award is the one to which the application under section 34 can be filed. This is because before execution, the Court has to satisfy itself as to the finality of the award in terms of challenge under section 34. Also, in the new Act the award is given a status of the decree of the Court. This means that the Court entitled to enforce such decree would be the one which had the jurisdiction to decide upon the subject matter of the dispute, and hence the challenge.

Section 37

- ***ITI Ltd.* v. *Siemens Public Communications Network Ltd.,* (2002) 5 SCC 510: AIR 2002 SC 2308**

The prohibition on filing of the second appeal does not bar the remedy to file for revision in the High Court. The application of CPC has not been expressly excluded. Hence its provisions will apply.

- ***Nirma Ltd.* v. *Lurgi Lentjets Energietechnik Gmbh,* (2002) 5 SCC 520**

A Special Leave Petition before the Supreme Court against the appellate order of the civil court will not lie because an efficacious alternate remedy in the form of revision petition to the High Court, already lies.

- ***Sanshin Chemicals Industry* v. *Oriental Carbons and Chemicals Ltd.,* (2001) 3 SCC 341: AIR 2001 SC 1219**

Decision as to the place of arbitration cannot be appealed under section 37 as it is not the one among appealable orders.

- ***Cref Finance Limited* v. *Puri Construction Ltd.,* AIR 2001 Del 414**

Section 37(3) uses the expression *"order passed in appeals"*. It is provided that no appeal lies from such orders. This means that no second appeal lies including the Letters Patent Appeal.

- ***Nirma Ltd.* v. *Lurgi Energie und Entsorgung Gmbh,* (2003) 8 CLA-BL Supp (Snr) 17 (Guj)**

An order or decision of arbitral tribunal is not an award and hence cannot be challenged under section 34. Such an order or decision can be appealed for under section 37, if it falls among the appealable orders.

Section 42

- ***Siroj Export Co. Ltd.* v. *Indian Oil Corporation Ltd.,* (1997) 27 CLA (Snr) 22 (Raj)**

In view of section 42 now only that High Court and other subordinate courts under it will have the jurisdiction on all the subsequent matters relating to the arbitration to which the first petition was filed and not any other High Court or its subordinate courts.

- ***ITI Ltd., Allahabad* v. *District Judge, Allahabad,* 1998 Arb WLJ 614 (All): 1998 (2) Arb LR 670 (All): AIR 1998 All 313**

Application for setting aside the arbitral award cannot be transferred by the District Judge to the Additional District Judge. This is because section 42 uses the expression *"with respect to an arbitration agreement"* and the application for setting aside the arbitration award is an application with respect to the arbitration agreement.

- ***Shiva Carriers* v. *Royal Projects Limited,* 2000 Arb WLJ 411 (Cal): AIR 2000 Cal 138**

It was held that in view of section 42, the Court in which an application for interim relief under section 9 was initiated gets the jurisdiction to decide all the subsequent applications relating to that arbitration matter.

- ***Sarkar Enterprises* v. *M/s. Garden Reach Shipbuilders and Engineers Ltd.,* 2002 Arb WLJ 475 (Cal)**

If the party files the first application under section 9 before the High Court it would amount to giving that High Court the jurisdiction with respect to all other subsequent applications.

- ***Garden Finance Limited* v. *Prakash Industries Ltd.,* 2002 Arb WLJ 579 (Bom): AIR 2002 Bom 8**

Section 42 is attracted only when the application with regard to arbitration agreement is made to the Court. An order under section 11 made by the Chief Justice is the order of administrative nature and not a judicial order. Hence an application before the Chief Justice for the appointment of arbitrator is not an application before the court and section 42 will not apply.

Section 45

- ***Shin Etsu Chemical Co. Ltd.* v. *Aksh Optifibre Ltd.,* (2005) 7 SCC 234**

The Court is required to take only a *prima facie* view for making a reference under section 45. The test to be adopted is whether it is "plainly arguable" that the arbitration agreement was in existence. An order refusing to refer the parties to arbitration under section 45 is appealable. However, there is no provision for filing an appeal if the authority refers the party to arbitration.

- ***Owners and Parties Interested in the Vessel M.V. "Balitic Confidence"* v. *STC,* (2001) 7 SCC 473**

Court should refer a dispute to arbitration even if the arbitration agreement is incorporated by reference into the earlier contract between the parties. Such an agreement should not be rendered nugatory by adopting the literal and technical interpretation. Intentions of the parties should be given effect.

- ***Society Commercial De Coreales & Financiers SA* v. *State Trading Corporation,* (1998) 30 CLA (Snr) 2 (Guj)**

The proceedings are to be stayed if there is no pleading, much less any material on record, to show that the arbitration agreement is null and void, inoperative or incapable of being performed.

- ***International Investor KLSC (Kuwait)* v. *Sanghi Polyesters Ltd.*, [2003] 8 CLA-BL Supp (Snr) 18 (AP)**

It was held that:

(1) It is for the party against whom foreign award is to be enforced to prove that the award is unenforceable for one or some of the grounds indicated in section 48.

(2) If a party wishes to rely on a foreign law, it must plead that in the same way as any other fact. This is the principle embodied in section 48.

(3) The expression 'agreement' referred to in section 48(1)(a) should be understood to cover an arbitration clause in the agreement between the parties.

Sections 46 to 49

- ***Fuerst Day Lawson Ltd.* v. *Jindal Exports Ltd.*, (2001) 6 SCC 356: AIR 2001 SC 2293: 2001 Lab IC 2073**

The application for enforceability and execution of the foreign award can be filed in the same proceedings. There is no need to file two different applications.

It was held: "*Since the object of new Act is to provide speedy and alternative solution to the dispute,* the same procedure of 1940 Act to award a decree of the Court cannot be insisted upon as it is advisedly eliminated, ... it would only contribute to protracting the litigation and adding to the sufferings of a litigant in terms of money, time and energy."

Section 73

- ***Mysore Cements Ltd.* v. *Svedala Barmac Ltd.*, (2003) 8 CLA-BL Supp (Snr) 1 (SC)**

The courts in this case took the view that the conciliator can formulate a settlement agreement as per section 73 considering its acceptability to both parties. The conciliator may reformulate his draft after receiving the observations of the parties. The agreement shall be final and binding on the parties when they sign it. The arbitrator shall furnish a copy of the agreement to both parties. The agreement so reached shall be binding on the parties and persons claiming under them.

Section 74

- ***Mysore Cements Ltd.* v. *Svedala Barmac Ltd.*, (2003) 8 CLA-BL Supp (Snr) 1 (SC)**

The procedure prescribed under section 73 is a pre-requisite under section 74. Any agreement that has been made without following the procedure prescribed under section 73 does not have the effect or status of an arbitral award under section 30.

Section 76

- ***Mysore cements Ltd.* v. *Svedala Barmac Ltd.,* [2003] 8 CLA-BL Supp (Snr) 1 (SC)**

A memorandum of conciliation proceedings that have not been legitimately assigned the status of a 'settlement agreement' under section 73 cannot be considered as an interim award and cannot be enforced directly until the conciliation proceedings are terminated as per section 76(a) and (d).

Section 82

- ***Sundaram Finance Ltd.* v. *NEPC India Ltd.,* (1999) 2 SCC 479: AIR 1999 SC 565**

The Supreme Court held that the High Courts should make use of the powers vested in them by section 82 which provides them with the power to make rules to carry out the provisions of the Act.

The High Courts should make rules regarding the procedure to be followed by the court under section 9 of the Act. The rules should relate to the manner in which the application is to be filed, the documents that should be made available to the court, and the manner in which such documents are to be dealt with by the courts. Supreme Court, therefore, requested the High Courts to frame the rules as soon as possible so as to facilitate quick and efficient disposal of arbitration cases.

Section 85

- ***Fuerst Day Lawson Ltd.* v. *Jindal Exports Ltd.,* (2001) 6 SCC 356: AIR 2001 SC 2293: 2001 Lab IC 2073**

In this case the Supreme Court held that a foreign award rendered after the commencement of the Arbitration and Conciliation Act, 1996 would be governed by the new Act even if the proceedings were initiated and had commenced prior to the commencement of the Act. The court affirmed its earlier decision in ***Thyssen Stahlunion Gmbh* v. *Steel Authority of India Ltd.,* (1999) 9 SCC 334.**

- ***National Aluminium Co. Ltd.* v. *Metalimpex Ltd.,* (2001) 6 SCC 372**

The Supreme Court held that arbitral proceedings relating to an agreement entered into under the old Arbitration Act of 1940 which was to commence subsequent to the enforcement of the new Arbitration Act, 1996 would be governed by the Arbitration and Conciliation Act, 1996.

- ***Sukhwant Rai*** **v.** ***Justice D.V. Sehgal,*** **(1999) 9 SCC 5**

The Supreme Court held that when a new arbitrator is to be appointed and the resignation of the earlier one was during the coming into force of the new Act, then the appointment of the new arbitrator is to be made as per the provisions of the new Act.

- ***Thyssen Stahlunion Gmbh*** **v.** ***Steel Authority of India Ltd.,*** **(1999) 9 SCC 334**

The section 85(2)(a) is a saving clause and saves the act from complete obliteration as far as pending cases are concerned under the old Act. Due to this provision the accrued right under the old Act is preserved. The parties may however agree to exclude the application of the new Act in relation to any arbitral proceedings that commenced before the new Act came into force and, therefore, it can be said that the provisions of the old Act apply to all proceedings which commenced before the coming into force of the new Act unless agreed to by the parties. They cannot agree to be governed by the old Act if even after the commencement of the new Act the proceedings have not yet commenced. The parties can also agree to be governed by the new Arbitration Act, 1996 even before the coming into force of the Act.

The Court held that the term proceeding used in the section includes proceedings for the enforcement of award rendered in the arbitration pending at the commencement of the new Act.

- ***Shetty's Constructions Co. Pvt. Ltd.*** **v.** ***Konkan Railway Construction,*** **1998 Arb WLJ 625 (SC): AIR 1998 SC 1535: 1998 (2) ARB LR 314 (SC): 1998 (5) SCC 599: 1998 (6) JT 643 (SC)**

The applicability of the new Act does not depend on the date of execution of the contract, neither does it depend on the date of completion of the work, rather it depends on the date of commencement of arbitral proceedings. Section 21 of the new arbitration Act states as to when the abitral proceedings commence.

- ***National Hydroelectric Power Corporation Ltd.*** **v.** ***Asian Techs Rani Constructions Joint Venture,*** **(2003) 7 CLA-BL Supp (Snr) 11 (UTR)**

If the arbitration proceedings are commenced when the Arbitration Act, 1940 was in force but the award is made and signed after the enforcement of the Arbitration and Conciliation Act, 1996, the proceedings shall be governed by the new Act of 1996. Where, however, the parties agree in terms of the contract for the enlargement of time for making the award after coming into force of the new Act without any intentional relinquishment of their rights, then their act will not be considered as a waiver of the applicability of the 1996 Act.

- ***Marshall Corporation Ltd. Vishakhapatnam* v. *Union of India, Rep. By the Engineer–in–Chief, Army Headquarters, New Delhi,* 1998 Arb WLJ 540 (AP): 1998 (2) Arb LR 175 (AP)**

The case is in a series of cases which lay down the test for commencement of arbitral proceedings. To decide whether the arbitral proceedings had commenced or not during the time the old Act was in force, the provision in section 21 of the new act cannot be considered. The test under the old Act is that the proceedings commence when the arbitrator shows his willingness to act as an arbitrator.

- ***H.P. State Council for Child Welfare* v. *Unique Mixers and Furnaces Pvt. Ltd.,* 2001 Arb WLJ 109 (HP): AIR 2001 HP 22**

When the arbitral proceedings commence much before the new Act came into force and the arbitration agreement also provided for the application of the old Act, then the proceedings will be governed by the old Act.

- ***Rakesh Kumar* v. *Superintending Engineer,Circle I, Irrigation Works,Meerut,* 2002 Arb WLJ 260 (All): 2001 (3) Arb LR 54 (All)**

When arbitral proceedings are commenced before 26-1-1996 or a request has been made before that date for the commencement of arbitral proceedings, the proceedings shall be governed by the old Arbitration Act. The appointment of the arbitrator at a later date *i.e.,* after 26-1-1996 will not be compelling for the application of the provisions of the new Arbitration Act, 1996. The passing of an award at a later date will also have no effect on the applicability of the old Act.

- ***Rani Constructions Pvt. Ltd.* v. *H.P. Electricity Board,* 1998 Arb WLJ 644 (HP): 1998 (2) Arb LR 322 (HP): 1999 (1) RAJ 332 (DB) (HP)**

Section 85(2)(a) provides that the old Act would apply to arbitration proceedings that had commenced before the new Act came into force. The parties can however agree to be governed by the new Act.

Such an agreement should be made only after the coming into operation of the new Arbitration Act.

- ***Reshma Constructions Goa* v. *State of Goa,* 1999 Arb WLJ 192 (Bom): 2000 (1) RAJ 552 (Bom)**

Section 85(2)(a) uses the term 'unless otherwise agreed' by the parties in the sense of arbitration agreement that has already been entered into by the parties prior to the enforcement of the new Act as also the agreement entered into after the enforcement of the new Act. The term otherwise agreed to by the parties refers not to the time factor but to the intention of the parties regarding the application of the new or the old Act.

- ***State of Goa* v. *Heera Constructions,* 2001 Arb WLJ 48 (Bom): 2001 (1) Arb LR 240 (Bom)**

The term 'unless otherwise agreed to' used in the section includes an agreement entered into between the parties even prior to the enforcement of the new Act. The parties can agree to the applicability of the new Act even before the new Act came into force. Section 85(2)(a) does not expressly bar the parties from agreeing to do so.

- ***Varun Seacon Ltd.* v. *Bharat Bijlee Ltd.,* 1998 Arb WLJ 399 (Guj): 1997 (3) Arb LR 559 (Guj)**

When an application for stay is pending on the date of the commencement of the new Act, then application will be governed by section 8 of the new Act and not by section 34 of the old Act.

ARBITRATION LAW IN NEPAL

In April, 1999, Nepal enacted the Arbitration Act, 1999, which came into force at once. The principal object of the Act was to update the current legal provisions relating to arbitration (as stated in the Preamble). The Act borrows some propositions incorporated in the UNCITRAL Model Law on the subject. But it does not blindly copy them. Besides this, it tries to put, in simple language, the governing principles, without a slavish imitation of the conservative style of drafting. A look at some of its important provisions would be useful.

Arbitration Agreement

Arbitration agreement is the foundation of arbitration under the Nepal Act. It must be an agreement for the settlement (through arbitration) of any dispute concerning any specific legal issue, arising under a contract or otherwise. The Act avoids the vague words "defined legal relationship" occurring in the UNCITRAL Model Law (and in the Indian Act of 1996). It is clarified that letters, telex, telegrams or telefax messages, or any other similar messages "whose records can be maintained in a written form" can form an arbitration agreement. Not raising an objection to the other party's claim for reference to arbitration also amounts to an arbitration agreement [section 2(a)].

Counter-claim is expressly recognised, and so is a "Rejoinder" to a counter-claim [section 2(f) and (g)]. Once there is an arbitration agreement in respect of a dispute, then resort to arbitration is mandatory [section 3(1)]. Arbitration in a pending suit is permitted by agreement [sections 3(2) and 4].

Arbitrators and Chief Arbitrator

The number of arbitrators can be determined by agreement, failing which, it should ordinarily be three [section 5(1)].

If an even number is provided for, then the arbitrators must choose an additional arbitrator [section 5(2)]. Subject to agreement, the process of appointing arbitrators must be started within 30 days from the date when the "reason for the settlement of a dispute through arbitration arises" [section 6(1)].

The method of appointment is left to the agreement. Failing agreement, each party shall appoint one arbitrator and the arbitrators so appointed shall appoint a third arbitrator, who shall work as "chief arbitrator" [section 6(2) to (4)].

The concept of "chief arbitrator" is not to be found in the Indian Act of 1996. The "presiding arbitrator" mentioned in the Indian Act does not have that status.

Under the Nepal Act, where the agreement is silent about the appointment of arbitrators or where no arbitrator can be appointed according to the agreement, then a party may apply to the Appellate Court for appointing three arbitrators (section 7).

Appropriate provision is made for filling up of vacancies in the post of arbitrators [section 8(1)]. Here also, the "Appellate Court" has a role to play, if the parties fail to act [section 8(2)].

Oath to be Taken by Arbitrators

The Nepal Act contains an interesting provision (not usually found in Arbitration Acts) requiring the arbitrator to take a written oath of impartiality and honesty, for which a Form is provided in the Schedule. A copy is to be sent to the Appellate Court. Any matters raising a reasonable doubt about impartiality or independence of an arbitrator must be cleared by the arbitrator before signing the oath (section 9).

Qualifications

A very interesting provision, found in the Nepal Act, relates to the qualifications of arbitrators. The following persons shall not be qualified for appointment as arbitrators:

(a) Those who are disqualified for entering into contracts under "current law" – a phrase which expresses the concept of "any law for the time being in force".

(b) Those who have been punished by a court on criminal charges involving a moral turpitude. This is a very interesting provision, not found in most Arbitration Acts.

(c) Those who have become insolvent or who have been declared bankrupt.

(d) Those who have any personal interest in the dispute that is to be settled through arbitration.

(e) Those who do not possess the specific qualifications laid down in the arbitration agreement (section 10).

Removal of Arbitrators

The Nepal Arbitration Act contains a rather drastic provision for the removal of arbitrators. The matter can, of course, be dealt with by agreement. But, failing that, the Act provides that a party may "apply" to the arbitrator, requesting for permission to remove the arbitrator. The wording is a quaint but polite form of language. The gist seems to be that the arbitrator can be called upon to resign.

This procedure can be resorted to, in the following circumstances:—

(a) Where the arbitrator clearly shows bias instead of working in an impartial manner.

(b) Where the arbitrator engages in improper actions or commits fraud in the course of arbitration.

(c) "In case any arbitrator frequently commits mistakes or irregularities in the arbitration proceedings". (This is rather an extreme provision, as "mistake" is a very wide word).

(d) If the arbitrator does not attend meetings for more than three months, without furnishing satisfactory reasons, in order to delay the proceedings in an improper manner.

(e) If the arbitrator takes any action opposed to the principle or rules of natural justice.

(f) If the arbitrator lacks the requisite qualifications or ceases to be qualified.

The arbitrator must take a decision (on the application to remove him) within 30 days. Against his decision, an appeal may be filed with the Appellate Court, whose decision shall be final (section 11).

Venue

The "office" of the arbitrator under the Nepal Act is to be located at the place chosen by the parties. If the parties fail to agree, then the office shall be at the place, specified by the arbitrator in the light of all the circumstances. However, (unless the parties have made other arrangement) the arbitrator may record the statements of witnesses, obtain opinion of experts and inspect any document, object or place at any time (section 12).

Language

Language of the arbitration proceedings shall be that chosen by the parties. Failing such choice, it will be the language used in the agreement, (section 13).

Claim, "Objection", Counter-claim and Rejoinder

A noteworthy feature of the Nepal Arbitration Act is the detailed provisions, which it makes, regarding the claim, and subsequent pleadings of the parties, and annexures thereto. The rather long provision in the Act (section 14) can be summarised for the present purpose as under:

(a) The claim must be made in writing, explicitly mentioning the details of the subject matter of the dispute and the remedy sought, along with the evidence. Copy is to be given to the other party.

(b) To the claim so filed, the other party shall submit its "objection" (defence).

(c) The other party can, along with the "objection", submit a counter-claim.

(d) To the counter-claim, the claimant can file a "rejoinder" (with copy to the opposite party).

Time Limits for Various Pleadings and Claims

The Nepal Act also lays down time limits for filing the various categories of claims mentioned above. Subject to an agreement between the parties laying down a different time limit, these time limits are as under:

- to be filed within three months from the date when the dispute arose or when the arbitrator is appointed (whichever is later);
- to be filed within thirty days from the date of receipt of the claim;
- same time limit as is mentioned above;
- to counter-claim, a rejoinder is to be filed within 15 days from date on which counter claim is filed;

The arbitrator is empowered to extend the time limit for not more than seven days (section 14).

Material to Accompany the Pleadings

The Nepal Act has a provision of considerable practical use, regarding the material that should accompany the pleadings (*i.e.*, claim, objection, counter-claim or rejoinder). The following must be submitted along with the pleadings:—

(a) documents intended to be relied upon,

(b) evidence substantiating the documents,

(c) list of witnesses proposed to be produced, [section 1(5)].

Failure to Submit Claims

If there is failure to submit the claim within the prescribed time limit, the arbitration proceedings "shall terminate" – unless the agreement provides to the contrary. If there is failure to submit the "objection" (*i.e.,* the defence) within the specified time limits, then the arbitrator must still proceed to determine the claim on the merits (section 15).

Challenge to Jurisdiction

The Nepal Act contains a fairly elaborate provision as to the procedure to be followed, where a party raises an objection:

(i) that the arbitrator has no jurisdiction over the dispute referred to him, or

(ii) that the contract "because of which the dispute has emerged" is itself illegal or null and void.

Such objection must be raised before expiry of the time limit laid down for filing the defence to the main case.

Any party not satisfied with the arbitrator's decision on such an objection may appeal to the Appellate Court within thirty days. The decision of the Appellate Court is final. But the filing of the appeal shall not be deemed to have prejudiced the power of the arbitrator to continue his proceedings and to pronounce his decision before the petition is finally disposed of by the court (section 16).

One may be permitted to add here, that generally, the question of the procedure to be followed in respect of objections to jurisdiction is a vexing one. The Indian Act of 1996 does not permit an interim appeal against the decision of the arbitrator, rejecting the objection to jurisdiction. The proceedings must go on, but the aggrieved party can raise the point again, when he challenges the award before the competent court [section 34, Arbitration and Conciliation Act, 1996 (India)].

The position under the Nepal Act is somewhat different. An interim appeal can be taken to the Appellate Court, as stated above. But the Nepal Act also takes care to expressly provide that the proceedings must go on, in the meantime. This is a good compromise; and whoever thought of it, deserves the grateful compliments of the business community. Of course, lovers of legalism are likely to argue that if the objection to jurisdiction is ultimately allowed by the Appellate Court, then the arbitration proceedings (which are allowed to be held in the meantime) would become infructuous. This is theoretically true. But, in practice, it is found that more often than not, the objections to jurisdiction or to arbitrability are ill-founded (if not totally frivolous).

Working Procedure

The Nepal Act deals with the procedure to be followed by the arbitrator, as under:

(a) The parties may, in the arbitration agreement, lay down the procedure. Failing agreement, the procedure laid down in the Act shall be followed.

(b) If, on a particular matter, the Act is silent, the arbitrator can seek the consent of the parties on that matter.

If the parties fail to reach an agreement on any procedural matter, the procedure (in that respect) "shall be as prescribed by the arbitrator himself" [section 17(1)].

The arbitrator must start the arbitration proceedings "immediately" after receiving the pleadings [section 17(2)].

He has to keep records of the proceedings in the case file, [section 17(3)].

Absence of One Arbitrator

A very useful provision in the Nepal Act deals with the absence of one of the arbitrators at a particular hearing. It is provided that where the dispute is referred to three or more arbitrators, the arbitrators who are present may conduct all arbitration proceedings, other than taking the final decision or issuing the final order [section 17(4)].

Ex Parte Proceedings

It is further provided in the Nepal Act that if any party does not present itself at the arbitration proceedings after due notice, the arbitrator may nevertheless continue the arbitration proceedings and pronounce his decision on the basis of the available material [section 17(5)].

Conclusion of the Proceedings

On completion of the hearing, the arbitrator has to issue an order that the hearing has concluded. The Act lays down that "evidence may not be examined or the parties heard thereafter" [section 17(6)].

Award

Unless the agreement provides otherwise, the arbitrator must read out his written decision, within 30 days of the order closing the hearing [section 17(7)]. This provision in the Nepal Act (as to reading out the award) does not occur in the Indian Act of 1996. (*See* also "Award: time limit", *infra*).

Hearing In-*camera*

The Nepal Act expressly provides that the arbitration proceedings shall be held in-*camera*, unless the parties otherwise decide (section 19).

Applicable Law

The Nepal Act provides that the Nepal law shall be the substantive law applicable, unless the agreement provides otherwise. But the arbitrator must settle the dispute according to the "conditions stipulated in the concerned contract". He has also to take into account the applicable commercial usages (section 18).

Bank Guarantee from Foreigners

An interesting provision found in the Nepal Act relates to foreigners. If any of the parties is a foreigner, so that the decision pronounced by the arbitrator is not likely to be implemented, then the arbitrator has power to obtain a bank guarantee or other appropriate guarantee, as prescribed by the arbitrator [section 21(1)(d)].

Interim Orders

The Nepal Act also confers on the arbitrator power to issue (on the request of a party) preliminary orders or interim or provisional orders, in respect of any matter connected with the dispute or to take a "conditional decision" [section 21(1)(g)]. The Act does not, however, elaborate this provision. Case law on the subject has to be awaited.

Certified Copies

The Nepal Act also confers on the arbitrator the power to issue certified copies [section 21(1)(h)]. This is a very useful provision, as many documents tend to be locked up before the arbitrator.

Appeal

Against the various, interim orders issued by the arbitrator under section 21(1) of the Nepal Act, an appeal lies to the Appellate Court [section 21(2)].

Equal Opportunity

The Nepal Act provides that each party shall be provided with an equal and adequate opportunity to present its case, "subject to this Act", [section 22(1)]. With this, one may compare section 18 of the Indian Act of 1996, which reads as under:

"*Section 18*. The parties shall be treated with equality and each party shall be given a full opportunity to present his case."

Two points of difference may be noted:

(a) The Indian Act contemplates "full opportunity", while the Nepal Act provides for "equal and adequate" opportunity. The Nepal wording is preferable.

(b) The Nepal Act makes the provision subject to the Act, which also is more precise than the Indian provision.

Appearance by the Parties

Under the Nepal Act, any party may attend the arbitration proceedings:—

(a) either personally, or

(b) by proxy, or

(c) through legal practitioner, [section 22(2)].

Court Assistance

Court assistance may be requested by the arbitrator, to examine any evidence concerning the dispute, (section 23).

Award: Time Limit

The Nepal Act does contain provisions regarding the time limit for pronouncing the award, as under:

(a) Subject to agreement between the parties, the award must be pronounced within 120 days from the date on which the process of submission of pleadings is complete (section 24).

(b) However, this is subject to the provision (already noted above) in section 17(7), under which the award must be pronounced within 30 days of the date on which the hearing is "closed" by a formal order, [section 24, read with section 17(7)]. (See "Award", *supra*).

Majority and Minority Decision

The Nepal Act provides that where there are three or more arbitrators, the decision of the majority prevails. But what about cases where there is no majority view on a particular matter? This situation, not dealt with specifically in the Indian Act of 1996, is specifically dealt with in the Nepal Act. It provides that in such cases, the decision of the chief arbitrator prevails.

It may be recalled that the Nepal Act specifically contemplates the designation of an arbitrator as, "chief arbitrator" under section 6(4). (See "Arbitrators and chief arbitrator", *supra*).

Finally, the Nepal Act requires every arbitrator to sign the award. If there is any special reason for his not signing, the other arbitrators, while signing shall explicitly mention that fact. Dissent is, of course, allowed.

Contents of the Award

Subject to a contrary provision in the agreement, the award under the Nepal Act must give brief particulars of the matter referred to arbitration, the grounds for deciding that the arbitrator had jurisdiction (where such a point had been raised) and reasons for the decision (section 27).

The amount awarded and interest, etc. should be mentioned, (section 27). The decision of the arbitrator has to be read out (section 28).

Corrections in the Award

Correction of arithmetical or clerical mistakes in the award is permitted under the Nepal Act.

If a point made in the claim has not been decided by the arbitrator he can be requested to do so, within the prescribed period (section 29).

Challenge to the Award

An award may be challenged on a petition filed before the Appellate Court within 35 days from receipt of a copy by the petitioner. The grounds of challenge are as under:

(a) Incompetence of a party to sign the agreement or invalidity of the agreement.

(b) Notice of arbitration proceedings not given to the petitioner.

(c) Decision has been rendered:

  (i) on a matter not referred to the arbitrator; or

  (ii) in a manner contrary to the prescribed conditions; or

  (iii) by acting beyond the arbitrator's jurisdiction.

(d) Procedure of designation of arbitrators or their functions and actions do not conform to the agreement or the Act.

(e) The matter is not arbitrable under the law of Nepal.

(f) The award is likely to prove detrimental to the "public interests or policies", (section 30).

Interest

In a monetary award (subject to agreement to the contrary), award of interest is compulsory under the Nepal Act. The interest is to be paid at the rate prescribed by the arbitrator in the light of the nature of the business connected with the dispute, ensuring that it is not higher than the rate of interest currently charged by commercial banks in respect of similar transactions (section 33).

Implementation of the Award

The award is to be implemented by the District Court on a petition filed within 30 days from the date of expiry of the time limit prescribed for implementing it. The time limit is 45 days (sections 31 and 32).

Interest not Awarded

The Nepal Act is silent as to the situation where the award itself is silent about interest. The situation does not fall within the power of "correction" conferred by section 29. In fact, section 29(1) expressly prohibits review in points of substance.

It would have been better if the Act had contained a provision that if the award is silent on this point, then it shall be deemed to have awarded interest at the rate of, say, 12 per cent per annum.

The date from which interest is to run, is also not mentioned in the Nepal Act.

Conclusion

Notwithstanding some minor omissions, the Nepal Arbitration Act of 1999 is likely to prove an eminently workable measure. It has struck a compromise between a doctrinnaire approach and a practical one. The grounds for setting aside the award should, however, be made more narrow, by providing that substantial injustice should be proved, before setting aside an award. There should also be a provision that if the award is silent as to interest, the interest shall run at 12 per cent per annum from the date on which the cause of action arose.

ARBITRATION LAW IN PAKISTAN

The Statute

The law of arbitration in Pakistan is contained in the Arbitration Act, 1940 (a pre-partition enactment, which still continues in force). Its main features are summarised as under.

The Act provides for three classes of arbitration:—

(a) arbitration without court intervention (Chapter II, sections 3-19);

(b) arbitration where no suit is pending (but through court) (Chapter III, section 20), and

(c) arbitration in suits (through court) (Chapter IV, sections 21-25).

The Act also contains further provisions, common to all the three types of arbitration (Chapter V, sections 26-38).

Arbitration Agreement

Whatever be the class of arbitrations, there must be an arbitration agreement. As defined in the Arbitration Act, 1940, it means a written agreement to submit present or future differences to arbitration, whether an arbitrator is named therein or not [section 2(2)].

Arbitrators

The number of arbitrators can be one, two, three or even more. In the case of an even number of arbitrators, an umpire is to be appointed according to the procedure given in the Act (First Schedule). Where the arbitration agreement does not specify the number, the arbitration shall be by a sole arbitrator (First Schedule).

An arbitrator may be named in the arbitration agreement or may be left to be appointed by a designated authority (First Schedule).

Where the arbitration agreement is silent about the mode of appointment of arbitrators and the parties cannot agree about the choice of the arbitrator, the Act gives power to the court to make the appointment, after following the prescribed procedure (sections 8-10).

An arbitrator who does not diligently conduct the proceedings, or who is guilty of misconduct, can be removed by the court after due inquiry (section 11).

Death of a party does not terminate the arbitration proceedings, if the cause of action survives (section 6).

The arbitrator has got certain statutory powers, including the power to administer oaths to witnesses, power to "state a case" for the opinion of the court etc.

Court Intervention

If a party to an arbitration agreement refuses to go to arbitration, the other party can seek intervention of the court to compel a reference to arbitration (section 20).

Procedure

The Arbitration Act, 1940, is totally inadequate in regard to matters of procedure. Of course, the arbitrator must observe the essentials of natural justice, failing which the arbitrator's award can be set aside for misconduct (section 30). But various stages of the process are not dealt with, in the Act.

In practice, arbitration is conducted on the basis of (i) the pleadings (statement of claim and statement of defence), whereupon (ii) issues may be framed (if necessary), followed by (iii) affidavits, (iv) oral evidence, and (v) arguments.

The Award

The award must be prounounced within the time limits laid down in the arbitration agreement or (failing such agreement), within 4 months of the commencement of hearing. However, the time limit can be extended by the court in certain circumstances (section 28, and First Schedule).

The award has to be in writing and signed by the arbitrator. If there are more than one arbitrator, the majority view prevails. The Act itself does not provide that the arbitrator shall give reasons for the award. When the award is a non-speaking award, the scope for interference by the court with the award becomes somewhat limited.

Court Control Over the Award

An award cannot be enforced, by itself. Judgment of the court has to be obtained in terms of the award (section 17).

In the scheme of the Arbitration Act, 1940, the court may:—

(a) pass judgment in terms of the award (section 17), or

(b) modify or correct the award (section 15), or

(c) remit the award (on any matter referred to arbitration), for reconsideration by the arbitrator or umpire (section 16), or

(d) set aside the award (section 30).

In short, the court may—(i) totally accept the award, or (ii) totally reject it, or (iii) adopt the intermediate course of modifying it or remitting it.

Modifying the Award

The Court may, by order, modify or correct an award:—

(a) where it appears to the court that a part of the award is upon a matter not referred to arbitration and can be separated from the other and does not affect the decision on the matter referred, or

(b) where the award is imperfect in form, or contains an obvious error which can be amended without affecting such decision, or

(c) where an award contains a clerical mistake or an error arising from an accidential slip or omission (section 15).

Remitting the Award

The court may remit the award (or any matter referred to arbitration):—

(a) where the award has left undertermined certain matters or where it determines matters which are not referred to arbitration, and which cannot be separated from the rest, or

(b) where the award is so indefinite, as to be incapable of execution, or

(c) where an objection to the legality of the award is apparent on the face of it (section 16).

Setting Aside the Award

The court can set aside the award, only on one or more of the following grounds, namely:—

(a) that the arbitrator or umpire has misconducted himself or the proceedings, or

(b) that the award has been made after issue, by the court, of an order superceeding the arbitration, or

(c) that an award has been improperly procured or is otherwise invalid (section 30).

Misconduct of the Arbitrator (Setting Aside the Award)

One of the principal grounds for setting aside the award under the Act of 1940 is the ground of misconduct. Section 30 of the Act expresses it in rather cryptic terms by phrasing it in this manner "the arbitrator has misconducted himself or the proceedings". No exhaustive definition of "misconduct" in this context can be given because misconduct is as large as life itself.

Because of the endless variety of situations in life, treatment of the subject in an exhaustive manner is likely to degenerate into a mere catalogue of instances. It will be more useful if selected instances of misconduct are collected and are classified under a few convenient groups. In arranging the cases under such group, one should bear in mind the fact that misconduct may arise from the arbitrator's conduct of the case, the arbitrator's relations with the parties, the arbitrator's mode of arriving at the decision (in regard to the materials relied on by the arbitrator or the tests applied), and the arbitrator's mode of formulating his award.

Specific Heads of Misconduct

Here are some specific heads of misconduct which recur frequently in practice:—

- proceeding *ex parte*, without justification (and analogous acts)
- private inquiries by the arbitrator
- absence of the arbitrator
- delegation by the arbitrator, or the arbitrator associating strangers with the arbitration
- use of wrong criteria by the arbitrator
- use of wrong material by the arbitrator
- irregularities in the award

Proceeding *Ex Parte* and Analogous Acts

It is misconduct for an arbitrator:—

- to hear only one party in the absence of the other; or
- to fail to give notice of hearing; or
- to amend the issues behind the back of the parties, thereby causing prejudice.

But it is not misconduct on his part to amend the issue at the time of writing an award, if no prejudice is caused to the parties.

Competent Court

The court competent to exercise various powers under the Arbitration Act, 1940, is the civil court, which would be competent to entertain a civil suit, if a suit were to be filed on the cause of action which forms the basis of the arbitration.

Private Inquiries

An arbitrator must decide on the evidence on record, and not on material obtained otherwise. It is misconduct on his part:—

- to import his personal knowledge into the decision
- to hold a private conference with a party
- to hold a private meeting behind the back of the party
- to make a private inquiry behind the back of the party
- to listen to confidential information, adverse to a party, even if the arbitration agreement gives him full latitude, (though the position may be different, if the parties had the opportunity of checking and contradicting the information so proposed to be utilised)
- to communicate with one party, behind the back of the other party

Absence of Arbitrators

Where there are more than one arbitrator, they must all act together. The award is bad, if one arbitrator is absent. The position may be different if what was done during the absence of one arbitrator is done all over again by all the arbitrators, or if the act performed in the absence of one arbitrator is only ministerial, such as looking into an account book.

Joint Deliberations

All arbitrators must deliberate jointly. However, the parties may waive the irregularity.

Delegation by Arbitrator, or Associating Strangers with the Arbitration

An arbitrator cannot delegate his functions to another person. It follows, that if the award is given by a person to whom the arbitrator delegates his functions, the award is a nullity. There is, however, an exception to this rule, where the delegation is:—

(i) with the consent of all the parties, or

(ii) a purely ministerial act.

An arbitrator cannot associate a third person with the decision-making process. Here again, there is no misconduct, if there was consent of all the parties, to such a course being adopted.

Use of Wrong Criterion by Arbitrator

Sometimes, an arbitrator, while not guilty of procedural lapses (as in the above categories of misconduct), employs a wrong criterion for coming to a conclusion. The award may then be set aside on that ground. Examples are:

(i) assessment of damages for breach of contract, on the basis of rates prevailing in the black market (instead of the controlled rates);

(ii) ignoring very material documents, at a stage when the evidence has not yet been closed.

Errors of Law

Questions of difficulty arise, when the arbitrator's decision is challenged, for an erroneous conclusion reached by the arbitrator on matters of law. The position appears to be a bit complex and cannot be stated with absolute certainty. However, broadly speaking, one can state the law on the subject in the form of the following propositions:—

(a) where a question of law has been specifically referred to the arbitrator for his decision, then his ruling on that question, if bona fide and if not suffering from any other defect, is not open to challenge, merely because it is erroneous;

(b) if a question of law has not been specifically referred to the arbitrator, his ruling on the point of law (if material to the result) may render the award void.

First as to situation (a) above. Where an arbitrator is called upon to decide the effect of the agreement, he has to really to decide a question of law, (*i.e.*, in interpreting the agreement), and hence his decision on the point is not open to challenge.

In situation (b) above, the award of the arbitrator can be set aside on the ground of an error of law on the face of the award. However, for this purpose, the court cannot look into a document not referred to, in the award.

Generally, the question of error of law can arise only if reasons are given in the award. However, if the very relief granted by the award is illegal, the position is different. Thus, an arbitrator cannot grant specific performance of a contract of service. Nor can a contract for the sale of movable property be enforced specifically, save in exceptional cases.

Decision to be According to Legal Rights

An arbitrator must decide according to legal rights, and not according to his own notions of fairness. There may, of course, be special situations where a different intention of the parties may be inferred and upheld judicially.

Basis of Interference by Court

The logical basis on which the jurisdiction of the court to interfere for apparent error can be justified, needs first to be explained. The general principle is that an arbitrator is a final judge, both of fact and of law. So far as questions of fact are concerned, this jurisdiction has been limited to decisions pronounced after serious procedural lapses, which reveal breach of natural justice or other technical misconduct. So far as errors of law are concerned, the jurisdiction of the court, (though not conferred in so many words by section 30), seems to have been based on the assumption that if the parties have not specifically referred a question for the decision of the arbitrator, then it is implied that the general power of the court to determine legal questions between the parties remains unimpaired. In theory, the jurisdiction can also be supported on the ground that the ultimate arbiters of questions of law should be the courts, so that uniformity is maintained.

Reasoned and Unreasoned Awards

Where the award is an unreasoned one, the court cannot interfere on the ground of an error therein. If the arbitrator chooses to give reasons, then the award can be set aside on the ground of error of law, although, in general, the reasonableness of the reasons themselves cannot be challenged.

Interpretation of Contracts

The same principle is also followed, regarding questions of interpretation of contract as determined in the award. Court can interfere only if the award is a speaking award. It is only if the line of interpretation is set out in the award that the court can interfere.

Breach of Natural Justice

Of course, the arbitrator would be guilty of misconduct, if there is a breach of natural justice.

Thus, it is well established that the arbitrator cannot depend on personal knowledge or arrive at a conclusion behind the back of the parties.

But where the arbitrator decides a question of fact on the basis of the evidence and on the basis of answers given by the parties in response to queries from the arbitrator, the award cannot be said to be based on personal knowledge and cannot be set aside on that ground.

Arbitrator's award may be set aside, if it awards charges for extra work, escalation charges and damages claimed by the construction contractor without any supporting material.

ARBITRATION LAW IN SRI LANKA

The formulation of a Model Arbitration Law by UNCITRAL has proved to be an event of great importance for the legal and commercial world. Countries all over the world have re-modelled their arbitration laws in the light of the U.N. Model. Sri Lanka is one of them. In 1995, it enacted a fresh Arbitration Act (No. 11 of 1995). As stated in the Preamble, one of its objects is to make "comprehensive legal provision" for the conduct of arbitration proceedings and the enforcement of arbitral awards. The second object is to make legal provision to "give effect" to the principles of the Convention on the Recognition and Enforcement of Foreign Awards of 1958 (the New York Convention).

General Approach

The Sri Lankan Act very largely follows the UNCITRAL Model law. At the same time, certain departures from, or additions to, the rules given in the Model Law have been considered necessary. Important departures and additions will be referred to, in this chapter, at the appropriate place.

Arbitration Agreement and Court Proceedings

The Sri Lankan Act provides that an arbitration agreement shall be in writing. It can be contained in a signed document or in an exchange of letters, telexes, telegrams or other means of telecommunications which provide a record of the agreement (section 4).

The Sri Lankan Act provides that by an agreement "any dispute" can be determined by arbitration "unless the matter in respect of which the arbitration agreement is entered into, is contrary to public policy or is not capable of determination by arbitration" (section 4).

(The Act does not elaborate the two exceptions mentioned above).

If legal proceedings are instituted in court by a party to an arbitration agreement, in respect of a matter covered by the arbitration agreement, the court shall have no jurisdiction to hear and determine the same, if the other party objects (section 5).

Arbitrators and Chairman

Parties are free to determine the number of arbitrators. But if it is an even number, then the arbitrators so appointed shall jointly appoint an "additional arbitrator" who shall act as the Chairman. Where the parties do not determine the number, it shall be three (section 6).

The parties are free to agree on the procedure for appointment. Failing such agreement, the High Court can make the appointment. If the agreed procedure fails, then also, the High Court has power to make the appointment (section 7).

Termination of Mandate

The mandate of an arbitrator terminates, if the arbitrator becomes unable to perform his functions or, for any other reason fails to act without undue delay or dies, or withdraws from office or if the parties agree on the termination. It may be noted that the provision for terminating the mandate by agreement is not found in many Arbitration Acts.

In case of undue delay by an arbitrator, the aggrieved party may move the High Court to remove him and to appoint another person in his place.

It is further provided that where the mandate of an arbitrator is terminated, the proceedings shall not be held *de novo*, unless the parties otherwise agree (sections 8-9).

Challenge to Arbitrator

An arbitrator has to disclose circumstances raising justifiable doubts as to his impartiality or independence. If circumstances exist which give rise to such doubt, a party may challenge an arbitrator. If the arbitrator does not resign, the matter can be taken to the High Court (section 10).

Challenge to Jurisdiction

If an arbitrator's appointment is challenged (this includes a challenge about the existence or validity of the arbitration agreement), then the arbitrator determines the matter in the first instance. But the aggrieved party may "apply" to the High Court for a determination of such question.

In the meantime, the arbitral tribunal may continue the proceedings (section 11).

Interim Measures

The Sri Lankan Act provides for interim measures of protection to be ordered by the arbitrator to protect or secure the claim (section 13).

Settlement

It is provided that it shall not be incompatible with arbitration proceedings, for an arbitrator to encourage settlement. Further, with the agreement of the parties, the arbitrator may use at any time during the arbitral proceedings:

(a) mediation;

(b) conciliation; or

(c) any other procedure

to encourage settlements [section 14(1)].

It the parties settle the dispute, the settlement is recorded as an award on agreed terms [sections 14(2) to (4) and 25].

Procedure: Arbitrator's Duties

The arbitrator must deal with the dispute in an "impartial, practical and expeditious manner" [section 15(1)].

He must afford all the parties "an opportunity of presenting their respective cases and of examining all documents and other materials furnished by the other party or by any other person" [section 15(2)].

Proceedings

An arbitral tribunal is authorised by the Sri Lankan Act to continue the arbitral proceedings and to determine the dispute on the available material, notwithstanding the failure of a party without reasonable cause:—

(a) to appear before it, or

(b) to comply with any order made by it [section 13(3)].

Amendment as to Relief

An interesting and useful provision to be found in the Sri Lanka Arbitration Act relates to amendment of pleadings in relation to relief. Parties are allowed to introduce new prayers for relief, provided:—

(a) such prayers fall within the scope of the arbitration agreement, and

(b) it is not inappropriate to accept them, having regard to the point of time at which the new prayers are submitted and other circumstances.

Parties are also allowed to amend or supplement the prayers for relief already introduced and to rely on new circumstances, in support of their respective cases [section 15(4)].

This is also a useful provision. However, it is somewhat strange that the main provision as to pleadings – section 15(2) – is not very elaborate and does not set out the contents of pleadings, time limits for the same and points of detailed nomenclature, such as "statement of claim", "defence", "rejoinder" etc. (In this respect, the Nepal Arbitration Act, 1999 is much more specific).

Venue

Parties may determine the venue of arbitration, by agreement. Failing agreement, the arbitrator decides it, having regard to the "circumstances of the case, including the convenience of the parties" [section 16(1)].

But (subject to a contrary agreement between the parties), the arbitral tribunal may meet at any place considered appropriate for consultation among the members, hearing the witnesses, inspection, etc. [section 16(2)].

Procedure Generally Including Evidence

Subject to the provisions of the Act, the parties can agree on the procedure of the arbitral tribunal in conducting the proceedings. The Act (section 17) further provides as under:

> "The power conferred upon the arbitral tribunal shall include the power to determine the admissibility, relevance and weight of any evidence".

Decision

Subject to an agreement to the contrary, the following provisions apply under the Sri Lankan Act in regard to any decision made in the course of arbitral proceedings:—

(a) the decision shall be by a majority of the arbitrators;

(b) failing a majority, the decision of the arbitrator appointed by the other arbitrators shall be binding [section 6(3)];

(c) where, in terms of the agreement or the Act, there is a Chairman, then the decision of the Chairman shall be binding [section 19(1)].

Where there is a Chairman, he has the power "to administer the conduct of the arbitral proceedings" [section 19(2)].

Summon and Oath

A party may, with the written consent of the arbitral tribunal, apply to the High Court for summons to witnesses [section 20(1)].

A person is not to be compelled to answer any question or to produce any document, which he could not have been compelled to answer or produce, at the trial in an action before the court [section 20(1)].

Penalty is provided for failure to attend or refusal to take oath etc. (section 21).

It may be mentioned that the arbitrator is expressly empowered to administer oath, unless otherwise agreed upon by the parties [section 22(2)]. [The power to administer oath is not provided in the Indian Act of 1996 though it was provided in the Act of 1940].

Evidence

The Sri Lankan Act contains two important provisions regarding evidence before the arbitral tribunal, as under:

(a) Unless otherwise agreed upon by the parties, evidence before the arbitral tribunal may be given orally or in writing or by an affidavit. This provision seems to confer a wide discretion on all concerned [section 22(1)].

(b) Unless otherwise agreed upon by the parties, an arbitral tribunal "shall not be bound by the provisions of the Evidence Ordinance" [section 22(3)].

It may be recalled that it is for the arbitral tribunal to determine the "admissibility, relevance and weight of any evidence" [section 17].

However, the Sri Lanka Act is silent about the "materiality" of the evidence—a concept expressly mentioned in section 19(4) of the Indian Act of 1996.

Representation of the Parties

Subject to a written agreement to the contrary, a party to an arbitration agreement may appear before the tribunal:—

(a) personally, or

(b) where the party is a body corporate or not corporate, then by an officer, employee or agent of that body, or

(c) through an attorney at law, if the party so desires (section 23).

Applicable Law

Most Arbitration Acts (including those following the UNCITRAL Model law) usually allow the parties to choose the substantive law to be applied, if it is a *transnational contract*. The Sri Lanka Act goes a little further. The material part of section 24(1) provides as under:

"(1) An arbitral tribunal shall decide the dispute in accordance with such rules of law as are chosen by the parties as applicable to the substance of the dispute."

Here, there is no limitation that the (main) contract should have a *foreign element*. Thus, even two Sri Lankan residents or companies can (it seems), choose a foreign law by an agreement between them. Of course, this provision applies "only to the extent agreed to by the parties" – as is emphasised in section 24(3), section 24(1) and 24(3).

Section 24(2) provides that failing any such designation (of the applicable law) by the parties, the arbitral tribunal shall apply the law determined by the conflict of laws rules, which it considers applicable. However – and this is somewhat unusual – section 24(3) provides that this provision shall apply "only to the extent agreed to by the parties". The question naturally arises, as to what is to happen, if the parties have neither chosen a particular system of substantive law nor opted for the conflict of laws rules. It is submitted that even in such a case, the arbitrator (like a civil court) will apply the rules of conflict of laws. This would be a reasonable course to adopt in the circumstances [section 24(2) and section 24(3)].

Considerations of "general justice and fairness" can be applied, only if the parties have expressly authorised the arbitral tribunal to do so. This provision in section 24(4) of the Sri Lankan Act is understandable (though the language is different from that adopted in the UNCITRAL Model Law). What is not understandable, is the provision given in section 24(4), as under:

"The arbitral tribunal shall decide according to .... trade usages only if the parties have expressly authorised it to do so."

This would mean that trade usages will be relevant, only if the agreement adopts them. This approach is contrary to the UNCITRAL Model Law. The Sri Lankan draftsmen had to adopt this course, presumably in view of some peculiarities of the commercial and legal scene in that country.

The Award

The award is to be made in writing and signed by the arbitrators. The majority may sign, giving reasons for the omitted signature [section 25(1)].

Reasons must be stated (unless the parties agree otherwise or unless it is an agreed award [section 25(2)]. Subject to the provisions of the Act, the award is final and binding on the parties (section 26).

Correction and Interpretation

The Act provides for correction and interpretation of the award as well as for its modification, in case of an omitted matter. Certain time limits are provided for in this regard (section 27).

Interest

The Sri Lanka Act makes a fairly comprehensive provision as to interest to be awarded by the arbitrator. Its salient features are as follows (under section 28):

(a) In an award for the payment of money, interest can be awarded, whether it is a claim for liquidated or unliquidated amount (section 28).

(b) The rate is that agreed between the parties or (in the absence of agreement), it will be the "legal interest" (section 28).

(c) The expression "legal interest" is defined in section 50, as meaning interest at the rate specified in an order made under section 192 of the code of Civil Procedure and for the time being in force. Interest is awarded on the principal sum awarded from the date of commencement of arbitration proceedings to the date of the award (section 28).

(d) As regards subsequent period, the Act provides that the arbitral tribunal may award further interest at the aforesaid rate on the aggregate sum so awarded, from the date of the award to the date of payment or such earlier date as the arbitral tribunal thinks fit (section 28).

Compensation of Arbitrators

The Sri Lanka Act contains a specific provision as to compensation of the arbitrators, to the effect that the parties shall be jointly and severally liable for the payment of reasonable compensation to the arbitrators constituting the arbitral tribunal, for their work and disbursements [section 29(1)]. [There is no saving regarding any provision in the agreement to the contrary.] There are detailed provisions as to deposit etc. [sections 29(1) to (6) and 30].

Enforcement of the Award

The award can be enforced by the High Court, on an application made to the High Court within one year after the expiry of fourteen days of the making of the award [section 31(1)].

Subject to provisions regarding setting aside the award, the High Court shall, on a day notified to the parties "proceed to file the award and give judgment according to the award". Upon the judgment so given, a decree shall be entered [section 31(6)].

Thus, the intention seems to be that the decree so entered shall be executed like any other decree of a civil court.

Setting Aside the Award

The award can be set aside by the High Court (on an application made within sixty days) on grounds which are substantially similar to those laid down in the UNCITRAL Model Law (section 32).

LAW OF CONTRACT IN SELECTED SAARC COUNTRIES

LAW OF CONTRACT IN BANGLADESH

Essentials of a Contract

The general law of contracts in Bangladesh is contained in the Contract Act, 1872. The Act defines "contract" as an agreement enforceable by law. The essentials of a (valid) contract are:

(a) intention to create a contract;

(b) offer and acceptance;

(c) consideration;

(d) capacity to enter into a contract;

(e) free consent of the parties;

(f) lawful object of the agreement.

Writing is not essential for the validity of a contract, except where a specific statutory provision requires writing. An arbitration clause must be in writing.

Offer and Acceptance

There must be an offer and its acceptance. If there is no offer, there is no contract, because there is no meeting of minds. Again, if there is an offer by one party, but it is not accepted by the other party or if the ostensible acceptance of the offer is defective, then also, there is no agreement and therefore no "contract".

Concept of Offer

An offer (or a "proposal") is not defined by statute. It is generally understood as denoting the expression, by words or conduct, of a willingness to enter into a legally binding contract. By its terms, it expressly or impliedly indicates that it is to become binding on the offerer, as soon as it has been accepted, usually, by a return promise or an act on the part of the person (the offeree), to whom it is so addressed.

An acceptance, in relation to an offer, is a final and unqualified expression of assent to the terms of the offer.

Offer followed by acceptance, is an "agreement".

If an agreement is enforceable by law, it is a "contract".

Offer By and To Whom

An offer must be made by a person legally competent to contract to on his behalf, by someone authorised by him to make the offer. It is usually made to a person (or to a number of persons), but it can be made to the entire world.

Statements which are not Offers

Every statement of intention is not an offer. A statement must be made with the intention that it will be accepted and will constitute a binding contract. Following are not offers:

(a) Statement made during negotiation, without indicating that the maker intends to be bound without further negotiation.

(b) A statement which invites the other party to make an offer (*e.g.*, a notice inviting tenders).

(c) Statement of lowest price [*Harvey* v. *Facey*, 1893 AC 552; *Macpherson* v. *Appanna*, AIR 1951 SC 184. (It is regarded as an invitation to make offers.)].

(d) A quotation [*Mylappa Chettiar* v. *Aga Mirza*, (1919) 37 MLJ 912].

Display of goods in a shop with price tags is not an offer, but is merely an invitation to make an offer, so that the trader may not accept the offer if the price is incorrectly marked.

Intention to be Bound

A definite intention to be bound by the agreement must exist.

Termination of Offer

Until an offer is accepted, it creates no legal rights and it may be terminated at any time in a variety of ways. Principal modes of termination of offer are:

(a) By the offerer revoking (or withdrawing) the offer before acceptance.

(b) By the offeree rejecting the offer outright or by making a counter-offer.

(c) By lapse of time (if the offer is stated to be open only for a fixed time).

Quality of Acceptance

Acceptance of an offer must be absolute and must correspond with the terms of the offer.

The court must look at the entire correspondence to decide whether an apparently unqualified acceptance did, in fact, conclude the agreement.

Consideration

(a) As a rule, an agreement without "consideration" is void. The Act defines "consideration" as follows:

> "When, at the desire of the promisor, the promisee or any other person has done or abstained from doing, or does or abstains from doing, or promises to do or abstains from doing, something, such act, abstinence, or promise is called a consideration for the promise."

(b) A mere promise to give a donation, either orally or in writing, is not enforceable. Settlement of *bona fide,* but doubtful claims involves a bargain between the contracting parties and is, therefore, based on consideration. Money is not the only form of consideration. A consideration may consist sometimes in the doing of a requested act, and sometimes in the making of a promise by the offeree. Forbearance to sue at the promisor's desire constitutes good consideration.

(c) Consideration is not required for a promise to compensate, wholly or in part, a person who has already voluntarily done something for the promisor or something which the promisor was legally compellable to do. It is also not required for a written and signed promise by the debtor (or his duly authorised agent) to pay a time-barred debt to the creditor.

Capacity of the Parties

(a) A person is competent to contract if, at the time of making it, he is of sound mind, major and not disqualified from contracting under law. Where he has not attained the age of 18 years (or being under the care of Guardian, has not attained the age of 21 years), he cannot contract.

(b) Agreements made by minors are void. Minors cannot, on attaining majority, ratify agreements entered into during their minority. But if a minor makes a fraudulent misrepresentation about his age and obtains a loan, he can be required (at the discretion of the court) to refund it or to make compensation for it. An unadjudged lunatic can enter into a valid contract during lucid intervals. A corporation can contract subject to certain limits.

Consent

When consent to a transaction is procured by coercion, undue influence, fraud or misrepresentation, the agreement is voidable at the option of the party whose consent was so procured.

Cases of undue influence arise where the transaction is *ex facie* unconscionable and one party was in a position to dominate the will of the other. Where parties are bound by a fiduciary relationship (as in the case of father and son, doctor and patient, master and servant, advocate and client), the law protects the weaker party, throwing on the other party the burden of proving that no undue influence was exercised. Mutual mistake in respect of material facts in the formation of a contract renders the agreement void. A unilateral mistake, however, does not render an agreement void. Nor does a mistake of law affects its validity.

Unlawful Agreements

An agreement whose consideration or object is unlawful, is void. The consideration or object of an agreement is unlawful, if it is forbidden by law or if it would defeat the provisions of any law, is fraudulent, or involves or implies injury to the person or property of another or the court regards it as immoral or opposed to public policy.

A party to an illegal agreement who has advanced money under it to the other party is entitled to recover it, if the illegal purpose has not been partly or wholly carried out.

Agreements in restraint of marriage, trade and legal proceedings are void. The seller of the good-will of a business may, however, validly agree with the buyer to restrain from carrying on a similar business within specified local limits, provided the limits are reasonable.

Persons Bound by Contract

Promises bind the promisors and (in case of death of promisors before performance) their legal representatives, unless there is contract to the contrary, or the nature of the contract is such that it depends upon the personal qualifications of any party.

Performance and Frustration

There are special provisions dealing with the case where time is the essence of contract. In commercial contracts, it is better to provide specifically that time is of the essence. A contract is validly discharged by faithful performance, by release or remission by the promisee, by "frustration" (under law) or by "novation" (by agreement).

Frustration occurs when unexpected developments subsequent to the making of the contracts render performance impossible. Novation occurs when the old agreement is replaced by a new agreement.

Subsequent Events and Frustration

If, subsequent to the making of the contract, some event happens, which the parties could not control so that the agreement cannot be performed, the contract is said to be "frustrated" because the contract then becomes impossible of performance. Frustration may occur by a change in the law, destruction of the subject-matter, supervening incapacity of the contracting party to perform the contract or fundamental change in circumstances after the contract is made. Mere strike, lock-out in the factory, rise in price of the contracted goods or other commercial difficulties do not, as such, render the contract "impossible" of performance.

Frustration leads to automatic termination of the contract, and exempts the parties from performance or further performance of the contract without rendering any of them liable for damages. Where, however, any party has received any benefit under the agreement, he must restore it or make compensation for it to the other party.

Remedies for Breach of Contract

The principal remedies for breach of contract are:

(a) damages;

(b) specific performance of the contract; and

(c) injunction.

When a contract has been broken, the party who suffers by such breach is entitled to receive, from the party who has broken the contract, compensation for any loss or damage caused to him thereby, being loss or damages which naturally arose in the usual course of things from such breach or which the parties knew, when they made the contract, to be likely to result from the breach of it.

Such compensation is not to be given for any remote and indirect loss of damage sustained by reason of the breach.

The same principle applies for determining damages for breach of an obligation arising from quasi-contract.

In estimating the loss or damage arising from a breach of contract, the means which existed of remedying the inconvenience caused by the non-performance of the contract must be taken into account.

Penal Stipulations

If a sum is named in the contract as the amount to be paid in case of breach of contract, or if the contract contains any other stipulation by way of penalty, the party complaining of the breach is entitled, whether or not actual damage or loss is proved to have been caused thereby, to receive from the party who has broken the contract, reasonable compensation not exceeding the amount so named or the penalty stipulated for.

A stipulation for increased interest from the date of default may be regarded as a stipulation by "way of penalty". The court is empowered to reduce it to an amount reasonable in the circumstances.

Specific Performance

In certain special cases dealt with in the Specific Relief Act, 1877, the court may direct against the party in default "specific performance" of the contract, that is to say, the party may be directed to perform the very obligation which he has undertaken by the contract.

LAW OF CONTRACT IN INDIA

The Statutory Framework

The Law of Contracts in India is principally dealt with, in the Indian Contract Act, 1872. It deals with the general principles of the law of contracts, and also with certain special contracts such as guarantee, indemnity, bailment, pledge and agency.

The law relating to sale of goods, partnerships and negotiable instruments are dealt with in separate Acts. Parliament enacted in 1972 the Hire-Purchase Act, but it has not yet been brought into force.

Essentials

The Contract Act defines "contract" as an agreement enforceable by law. The essentials of a (valid) contract are:

(a) intention to create legal relations;

(b) offer and acceptance;

(c) consideration;

(d) capacity to enter into a contract;

(e) free consent of the parties;

(f) lawful object of the agreement.

Writing is not essential for the validity of a contract, except where a specific statutory provision requires writing. An arbitration clause must be in writing.

Intention to Create Legal Relations

The parties must have had an intention to create legal relations. Thus, an offer made by way of a joke, or a mere social obligation cannot create a contract [*Balfour* v. *Balfour*, (1919) 2 KB 571].

Offer and Acceptance

In order to constitute a contract, there must be an offer and its acceptance. If there is no offer, there is no contract, because there is no meeting of minds. Again, if there is an offer by one party, but it is not accepted by the other party or if the ostensible acceptance of the offer is defective, then also, there is no agreement and therefore no "contract".

A large bulk of commercial litigation, however, requires the court to deal with the basic questions, which are:

(i) Whether there has been an offer at all in the particular case, or whether there is something less than an offer?

(ii) Whether there has been an acceptance of the offer?

(iii) If there is an acceptance; is it in the proper form?

(iv) Whether the acceptance has been communicated to the offerer.

Requirements of a Valid Offer

An offer (or proposal) is generally understood as denoting the expression, by words or conduct, of a willingness to enter into a legally binding contract. By its terms, it expressly or impliedly indicates that it is to become binding on the offerer as soon as it has been accepted, usually, by a return promise or an act on the part of the person (the offeree), to whom it is so addressed.

An acceptance, in relation to an offer, is a final and unqualified expression of assent to the terms of the offer.

Offer followed by acceptance, is an "agreement". If an agreement is enforceable by law, it is a "contract".

Statements which are not Offers

Every statement of intention is not an offer. A statement must be made with the intention that it will be accepted and will constitute a binding contract. Following are not offers:—

(a) Statement made during negotiation, without indicating that the maker intends to be bound without further negotiation.

(b) A statement which invites the other party to make an offer (*e.g.*, a notice inviting tenders).

(c) Statement of lowest price [*Harvey* v. *Facey*, 1893 AC 552, *Macpherson* v. *Appanna*, AIR 1951 SC 184]. It is regarded as an invitation to make offers. [Re *Webster*, (1975) 132 CLR 270].

(d) A quotation [*Mylappa Chettiar* v. *Aga Mirza*, 1919 MLJ 912].

Display of goods in a shop with price tags is not an offer, but is merely an invitation to make an offer, so that the trader may not accept the offer if the price is incorrectly marked [*Fisher* v. *Bell*, (1960) 3 All ER 731].

Offer By, and To whom

An offer must be made by a person legally competent to contract or on his behalf, by someone authorised by him to make the offer. It is usually made to a person (or to a number of persons), but it can be made to the entire world, as happened in *Carlill* v. *Carbolic Smoke Ball Co.*, (1893) 1 QB 256: (1891-94) All ER R 127. In that case, the defendants (manufacturers of medicinal smoke balls) promised to pay £100 to anyone who, after having bought and used their smoke balls, caught influenza. Plaintiff did so and caught influenza. Plaintiff was held entitled to recover. It was no defence that there was no particular individual to whom the announcement was addressed. Such contracts are sometimes called "unilateral contracts" – not a very happy term, because a contract can never be "unilateral". There must be two parties. It is really a case of innumerable offers, made to all potential readers of the announcement.

Intention to be Bound

A definite intention to be bound is required. This is highlighted in *Gibson* v. *Manchester City Council*, (1979) 1 All ER 192. In 1970, *M* adopted a policy of selling council houses to tenants. In February 1971, the City Treasurer wrote to *G*, stating that council "may be prepared to sell the house to you at £2,180 (freehold)". The letter asked *G* to make a formal application. This he did, and the council took the house off the list of council-maintained properties. Before the completion of the normal process of preparation and exchange of contracts when property is sold, control of the council changed hands and the policy of selling council houses was reversed. The new council decided only to complete those transactions where exchange of contracts had already taken place. In the Court of Appeal, it was held (by a majority) that a contract had been made between *G* and *M*. Lord Denning suggested that "there is no need to look for strict offer and acceptance" in every case. In this particular instance, a price had been agreed and the parties intended to carry through the sale. However, the House of Lords held that the February letter was (at the most) an "invitation" of treat. *G's* application was an offer and not an acceptance. (Informal agreements for the sale of houses are not likely to be held as binding contracts, because, otherwise, buyers may find themselves committed before securing mortgage finance.)

Termination of Offer

Some parties clearly indicate that their statements or documents do not constitute offers, *e.g.*, estate agents. The caution is expressed usually in specific terms.

Until an offer is accepted, it creates no legal rights and it may be terminated at any time in a variety of ways. Principal modes of termination of an offer are:

(a) By the offerer revoking (or withdrawing) the offer before acceptance. (However, in such a case communication is necessary.)

In *Great Northern Rly. Co. Ltd.* v. *Witham*, 1873 LR 9 CP 16, Great Northern Railway advertised for tenders for the supply of such stores as they might require for one year. *W* submitted a tender to supply the stores in such quantities as Great Northern Railway might order from time to time and his tender was accepted. Orders were given for some time, but eventually *W* was given an order which he refused to carry out. It was held that *W* was in breach. A tender of this kind was a standing offer which was converted into a series of contracts as Great Northern Railway made their orders. *W* might revoke his offer for the remainder of the period covered, but must supply the goods already ordered. Revocation of an offer is effective, only when communicated to the offeree.

(b) By the offeree rejecting the offer outright or by making a counter-offer.

(c) By lapse of time (if the offer is stated to be open only for a fixed time).

Acceptance to be Absolute and Unconditional

(a) When parties carry on lengthy negotiation, it may be hard to say exactly when an offer has been made and accepted [*Butler Machine Tool Co. Ltd.* v. *The Ex. Cello Corp. (Eng.) Ltd.*, (1979) 1 WLR 401 (CA)].

(b) A conditional offer, if accepted, must be accepted along with the conditions [*Shyam Sunder* v. *Mun. Chairman*, AIR 1984 Orissa III 113].

(c) The court must look at the entire correspondence to decide whether an apparently unqualified acceptance did, in fact, conclude the agreement.

(d) However, in regard to international agreements governed by the UN Convention on Sale of Goods, there is a slight qualification. (*See* article 19 of the Convention).

Communication

Acceptance must be communicated [*Bhagwandas* v. *Girdharilal*, AIR 1966 SC 543].

Consideration

As a rule, an agreement without "consideration" is void. The Act defines "consideration" as follows:

> "When, at the desire of the promisor, the promisee or any other person has done or abstained from doing, or does or abstains from doing, or promises to do or abstains from doing, something, such act, abstinence, or promise is called a consideration for the promise."

A mere promise to give a donation, either orally or in writing, is not enforceable. Settlement of *bona fide* but doubtful claims involve a bargain between the contracting parties and is, therefore, based on consideration.

Money is not the only form of consideration. A consideration may consist sometimes in the doing of a requested act, and sometimes in the making of a promise by the offeree. Forbearance to sue at the promisor's desire constitutes good consideration.

Consideration is not required for a promise to compensate, wholly or in part, a person who has already voluntarily done something for the promisor or something which the promisor was legally compellable to do. It is also required for a written and signed promise by the debtor (or his duly authorised agent) to pay a time-barred debt to the creditor.

Capacity of Parties

Parties must be competent to contract. A person is competent to contract if, at the time of making it, he is of sound mind, major and not disqualified from contracting under law. Where he has not attained the age of 18 years (or being under a court of wards, has not attained the age of 21 years), he cannot contract. Agreements made by minors are void. Minors cannot, on attaining majority, ratify agreements entered into during their minority.

But if a minor makes a fraudulent misrepresentation about his age and obtains a loan, he can be required (at the discretion of the court) to refund it or to make compensation for it. An unadjudged lunatic can enter into a valid contract during lucid intervals. A corporation can contract subject to certain limits.

Consent

When consent of a party to a transaction is procured by coercion, undue influence, fraud or misrepresentation, the agreement is voidable at the option of the party whose consent was so procured. Cases of undue influence arise where the transaction is *ex facie* unconscionable and one party was in a position to dominate the will of the other. Where parties are bound by a fiduciary relationship (as in the case of father and son, doctor and patient, master and servant, advocate and client), the law protects the weaker party, throwing on the other party the burden of proving that no undue influence was exercised.

Mutual mistake in respect of material facts in the formation of a contract renders the agreement void. A unilateral mistake, however, does not render an agreement void. Nor does a mistake of law affect its validity [*Kalyanpur Lime Works Ltd.* v. *State of Bihar*, AIR 1954 SC 163].

Unlawful Agreements

An agreement, whose consideration object is unlawful, is void. The consideration or object of an agreement is unlawful, if it is forbidden by law or if it would defeat the provisions of any law or is fraudulent, or involves or implies injury to the person or property of another or the court regards it as immoral or opposed to public policy.

A party to an illegal agreement who has advanced money under it to the other party is entitled to recover it, if the illegal purpose has not been partly or wholly carried out.

The Monopolies and Restrictive Trade Practices Act, 1969 now deals with the law relating to trade combinations.

Agreements in restraint of marriage, trade and legal proceedings are void. The seller of the good-will of a business may, however, validly agree with the buyer to restrain from carrying on a similar business within specified local limits, provided the limits are reasonable.

Persons Bound by the Contract

Promises bind the promisors and in case of death of promisor (before performance) their legal representatives, unless there is contract to the contrary, or the nature of the contract is such that it depends upon the personal qualifications of any party.

Performance

There are special provisions in the law dealing with the case where time is the essence of contract. In commercial contracts, it is better to provide specifically that time is of the essence. A contract is validly discharged by faithful performance, by release or remission by the promisee or by "frustration" (under law) or by "novation" (by agreement).

Subsequent Events and Frustration

If, subsequent to the making of the contract, some event happens, which the parties could not control so that the agreement cannot be performed, the contract is said to be "frustrated" because the contract then becomes impossible of performance. Frustration may occur by a change in the law, destruction of the subject-matter, supervening incapacity of the contracting party to perform the contract or fundamental change in circumstances after the contract is made. Mere strike, lock-out in the factory, rise in price of the contracted goods or other commercial difficulties do not, as such, render the contract "impossible" of performance.

Frustration leads to automatic termination of the contract, and exempts the parties from performance or further performance of the contract without rendering any of them liable for damages. Where, however, any party has received any benefit under the agreement, he must restore it or make compensation for it to the other party.

Introduction of the permit system by statute does not absolve the promisor from supplying the goods. He must make reasonable efforts to procure the permit to fulfill his agreement. Change in market conditions also does not justify a supplier in demanding a price higher than that stipulated, unless there is an "escalation" clause.

Remedies for Breach of Contract

The legal remedies for breach of contract are:

(a) damages;

(b) specific performance of the contract; and

(c) injunction.

In practice damages constitute the main remedy.

When a contract has been broken, the party who suffers by such breach is entitled to receive, from the party who has broken the contract, compensation for any loss or damage caused to him thereby, being loss or damages which naturally arose in the usual course of things from such breach or which the parties knew, when they made the contract, to be likely to result from the breach of it.

Such compensation is not to be given for any remote and indirect loss of damage sustained by reason of the breach.

The same principle applies for determining the quantum of damages for breach of an obligation arising from quasi-contract.

In estimating the loss or damage arising from a breach of contract, the means which existed of remedying the inconvenience caused by the non-performance of the contract must be taken into account.

Liquidated Damages and Penal Stipulations

If a sum is named in the contract as the amount to be paid in case of breach of contract, or if the contract contains any other stipulation by way of penalty, the party complaining of the breach is entitled, whether or not actual damage of loss is proved to have been caused thereby, to receive, from the party who has broken the contract, reasonable compensation, not exceeding the amount so named or the penalty stipulated for.

A stipulation for increased interest from the date of default may be regarded as a stipulation by "way of penalty". The court is empowered to reduce it to an amount which is reasonable in the circumstances.

Specific Performance

In certain special cases (dealt with in the Specific Relief Act, 1877), the court may direct against the party in default "specific performance" of the contract, that is to say, the party may be directed to perform the very obligation which he has undertaken, by the contract. This remedy is discretionary and granted in exceptional cases.

LAW OF CONTRACT IN MALDIVES

Contract Law

In Maldives, the law of contracts is contained in the "Contract Law" (No. 4 of 91).

"Contract" is referred to a formal agreement entered into between one or more parties and as such, it should be legally valid or acceptable by law (section 2).

Acceptance

"Executors" of a contract (*i.e.,* acceptors) should show their willingness to the contents, without being forced. Executors should also be acceptable by law, *i.e.,* they should be persons over 16 years of age and of sound state of mind (section 3).

Format and Formation

Format of a contract need not be of a particular pattern, unless otherwise specified by law (section 4).

"Submission" (offer) should be followed by acceptance. Then it becomes a contract in law (section 5).

Offer

The submission (offer) should not be confusing or uncertain and should form into a concrete idea so as to bind legally. An invitation to offer should not be treated as an offer.

An offer can be made to a particular person (or persons) or generally to all (section 6).

Acceptance and Revocation of Offer

When the offer is understood by whom it is to be accepted, then it is completed. Before acceptance, the offer can be cancelled. But it will be treated as cancelled, only when the party to whom it was made is made aware of the cancellation [section 7(a), (b), (c)].

Irrevocability

Where validity of an offer is specified, then, until such time the validity is expired, it cannot be withdrawn [section 7(d)].

It should be noted that this is a departure from the common law rule and seems to have been suggested by the U.N. Convention on Sale of Goods.

Acceptance

Acceptance of an offer can be conveyed specifically, or by conduct [section 8(a)].

For acceptance of an offer, no condition should be imposed [section 8(b)].

If the offer is to be accepted in a specified manner, acceptance should be conveyed in that particular manner; otherwise, acceptance should be conveyed in the generally practised manner [section 8(c)].

Completion of Acceptance

"On confirmation of acceptance of the submission, acceptance thereof is completed" (section 9).

Probably, "confirmation" here means communication.

Offer Beyond Acceptance

An offer is beyond acceptance in the following cases:—

- where a specific time limit is given to convey acceptance and lapse occurs prior to acceptance
- where a condition is imposed for acceptance, and the same is fulfilled before acceptance of the offer or occurrences of similar nature
- withdrawal of the offer on legal grounds
- non-acceptance of the offer (section 10).

Change of Circumstances

An interesting provision in the Maldives Act deals with change of circumstances, as under:

(a) the contract will become void, when the circumstances on which the contract is based change, whether within or without the reach of the contractors;

(b) change of circumstances, mentioned in (a) above, refers to "changing of an important portion of the contract" [section 11(a) and (b)].

The word "portion" here seems to refer to, an aspect or component of a contract.

This provision seems to go beyond the common law. At common law an event within the control of a contracting party does not terminate the contract.

It may also be mentioned that there is some overlap between section 11 and section 22.

Ignorance of Law

Ignorance of the laws in force is not a reason to nullify a contract [section 11(c)].

This is an interesting provision, codifying a rule which already exists at common law.

Consent Vitiated

A contract made "forcibly on false grounds" or through threat or by using undue influence is not a valid contract (section 12).

Threats and Force

If a contract is "forcibly" entered into, it becomes an invalid contract.

"Threat" here refers to acts which show intention of torturing or using influence of any kind (sections 13 and 14).

Undue Influence

Undue influence refers to using influence or position (section 15).

False Grounds

Something which is obviously unreal but deceitfully shown real, means false grounds (section 16).

Illegality

In the following circumstances, a contract becomes unlawful (section 17):—

- contracts prohibited by law
- contract to achieve illegal objectives
- a contract specifying illegal acts to be acted upon (*i.e.*, a contract whose object is unlawful).

Restraint of Trade

Where a clause of a contract prohibits refrain from carrying out of a person's occupation or urging a person to indulge in prohibited activities, that particular clause will be treated invalid, unless otherwise specified activity is proved to be reasonable [section 18(a)].

The section has been quoted above as contained in the (unofficial) transaction of the Maldives Act.

Legal Proceedings

Where a clause prohibits legal action, that particular clause is invalid.

If arbitration is allowed by any clause, that particular clause is valid [section 18(b)(c)].

Implementing International Law

In case of any dispute arising out of any clause in the contract, if implementation of international law is allowed, that particular clause is valid [section 18(d)].

Completion of a Contract

Under the following circumstances a contract may be treated as completed:—

(i) contractors fulfilling their obligations, as per contract;

(ii) contractors agreeing that the particular contract is acted upon;

(iii) due to legal or unforeseen constraints, it becomes absolutely obligatory on the part of the contractors to wind up the contract (section 19).

This section seems to provide for release, novation, accord, etc.

Adherence to the Contract: Performance

Unless otherwise deviated, a contract should be adhered to strictly as laid down in the contract [section 20(a)].

A contract can be carried out by the contracted parties or their nominees or Attorneys. However, if the contract strictly requires the contractor to fulfill his/her obligations, it is absolutely necessary on the part of her/him to do so personally.

Unless otherwise specified, the contract should be acted upon within a reasonable period.

Where a condition is imposed to act upon, then, unless the condition is fulfilled, it is not obligatory to act upon the contract (section 20).

This section seems to refer to contingent contracts.

Mutual Agreement

Obligations under a contract can be fulfilled as per mutual agreement of all contractors.

Such agreements should be within the legal framework (section 21).

Impossibility or Illegality

It will be treated as the contract has been acted upon (discharged) if adherence thereto becomes impossible due to legal constraints or otherwise.

If it becomes "difficult" or expensive to adhere to the contract it will be treated as difficulty to adhere to the contract.

But a difficult situation arising out of negligence of the contractors will not be treated as difficulty to adhere the contract.

Claims under a contract may be lodged before contracted party becomes aware of difficulty in continuation of the contract. After the situation arises, the contractor will not be bound to pay back such claims (section 22).

It should be pointed out that section 22 overlaps with section 11.

Compensation for Breach etc.

(a) The contractor who "does a detrimental act" will have to pay reasonable compensation.

(b) Detrimental acts, as per (a) above, for which compensation is payable, are:

  (i) Direct losses by violating the contract.

  (ii) Losses "that the contractor may be aware of, by violating the contract". [The idea seems to be to cover contemplated losses].

(c) For losses that may be arising out of inadequate security measures, no compensation is payable (sections 23-24).

Specific Performance

A contractor suffering losses due to detrimental acts can request the court to order the other party to act upon in a particular manner, in case compensation paid is considered to be insufficient to cover the losses.

Courts can issue such orders that the defendant should act upon in a "particular manner", in case the court feels the compensation given is insufficient.

"Particular manner" herein refers to such acts that may be laid down in the agreement that can be enforced by the court (section 25).

This simple provision is intended to deal with the whole law of specific performance.

Joint and Several Responsibility of the Contractors

Unless specified in the contract, liabilities arising out of the contract by more than one person, can be a responsibility of all contractors or individual contractors (section 26).

Enforcement and Practising Regulations

President of Maldives has the authority to make regulations for enforcement and practising of this law (section 27).

Definitions

(a) Unless specified in law, "The President" refers to the President of Maldives.

(b) Except in the case of section 3(b), (age and mental incapacity) this law is common and includes companies and associations.

(c) Any word used in singular form here, includes plural of the same. Likewise, any word in plural form also includes its singular (section 28).

LAW OF CONTRACT IN NEPAL

Nepal enacted, in 1966, a fairly detailed enactment on the law relating to contracts, which came into force on 16th December, 1966 (corresponding to Poush 1, 2023 according to the Nepalese calender).

Scheme of the Act

The Nepal Act contains 19 sections in all. Sections 1 and 2 contain preliminary provisions, including definitions. Section 3 deals with contracting parties. Sections 4, 5 and 6 contain detailed provisions as to offer, acceptance and their revocation. Sections 7 and 8 deal with—

(i) contracts, which may be avoided by a party; and

(ii) contracts which are invalid.

Section 9 deals with "indirect contracts" – these are really quasi-contracts.

Sections 10 and 11 are the key provisions, dealing with contractual liabilities. Alternations in the contract and delegation of work under contract are taken care of by section 12. Matters concerning time, manner, and place of performance are dealt with in sections 13 and 14.

Section 15 is devoted to the important topic of compensation for breach of contract, while section 16 deals with restitution to be made, when a contract is terminated (with mutual consent) or otherwise cancelled.

The relationship of the 1966 Act with other current Nepal laws is governed by sections 17 and 18. Section 19 repeals certain laws, but the Government Contracts (Arrangements) Act, 1963, is saved by an express proviso.

The Nepal Act, thus, seems to present in a simplified form, some of the basic principles of contract, in a manner suitable to the needs of the country.

Definitions

The Nepal Act contains, in section 2, only three definitions, as under:

(a) "contract" is defined as an agreement concluded between two or more parties for performing or not performing any work. This has to be read with section 4(1), which provides that if any person "advances" any proposal to any other person and the latter gives his acceptance thereto, they shall be deemed to have concluded a contract.

The definition of "contract" in section 2(a) is noteworthy, for two reasons:

(i) It expressly covers a multi-party transaction (note the words – "two or more parties");

(ii) Further, it covers negative agreements also – *vide* the words "agreement .... for .... not performing any work".

These words seem to take in (for example), restrictive covenants, *e.g.*, covenants in restraint of trade.

(b) "proposal" is defined as a proposal put forward by one person to another, with the expectation of obtaining his "consent for performing or not performing any work".

The definition expressly brings out one element, which (in many other models) is left to implication, namely, that the proposer desires to elicit a response from the person to whom the proposal is made.

(c) "consent" is defined as meaning consent given by a person "in the same sense in which the proposer has taken the substance of the proposal presented by him to the former".

Obviously, the object of this elaborate definition is to incorporate the juristic concept of "consensus *ad idem*".

In this manner, the intellectual aspect of consent is adequately dealt with in the Nepal Act. The psychological and moral aspects (which are also relevant, when there is fraud, undue influence or coercion), are not dealt with in the definition. However, section 7 takes care of all such factors which corrupt consent. (*See* "Free consent", *infra*).

Competence to Contract

The effect of section 3 of the Nepal Act is that a minor (*i.e.*, a person below 16 years) or a person of unsound mind, cannot enter into a contract. But his guardian can do so, "in his interest" and on his behalf.

Proposal and Acceptance

Sections 4, 5 and 6 of the Nepal Act contain very elaborate provisions as to—(i) proposal, (ii) acceptance, (iii) cancellation of proposal or acceptance, (iv) offer to the general public, etc.

The rest of the Act is couched in simple and short provisions, but these sections are found to be much more elaborate. Perhaps, some actual problems must have arisen in the country, necessitating a statutory clarification.

Section 4(1) of the Nepal Act lays down the basic proposition, that if a person "advances" a proposal to a person who "gives his acceptance" thereto, they shall be deemed to have concluded a contract. Section 4(2) contains a specific provision, by laying down that if a person making a proposal states that he should be given notice of the acceptance of the proposal within a specified period, but does not receive such notice within such period, then no contract shall be deemed to have been concluded. Under section 4(3), if no time limit is specified in the proposal, then it must be accepted within reasonable time. Section 4(4) provides that an offerer cannot bind the offeree by a stipulation that if the offerer is not given notice of rejection within a specific time limit, then he shall be deemed to have accepted the offer.

Section 5 contains detailed rules as to cancellation of an offer, while section 6 deals with offer made to the general public and is obviously reminiscent of the English case of *Carlill* v. *Carbolic Smoke Ball Co.*

Free Consent

Section 7 of the Nepal Act provides that in certain circumstances, contracts "may be made void by the party aggrieved thereby". In this context, the following factors are mentioned:

(a) coercion;

(b) undue influence;

(c) fraud;

(d) deceit (which is distinct from fraud and may cover even innocent misrepresentation). [*See* "Fraud and deceit", *infra*].

In regard to undue influence, one finds certain special features in the Nepal Act. "Undue influence" means influence exercised by a person upon another person "who is under his influence or is amenable to his wishes", with the intention of deriving some advantage for personal benefit or to fulfill some such interests. Explanations give specific instances, one of which deals with persons of physical or mental weakness, while another speaks of persons who can be subjected to economic pressures.

Incidentally, the draftsmen in Nepal seem to have found the Indian legislative practice of inserting an "Explanation" to be very useful.

Fraud and Deceit

Section 7(c) of the Nepalese Contract Act which defines "fraud", covers wilful deception, whether it be in the nature of *suggestio falsi* or *suppressio veri*.

Section 7(d) deals separately with deceit and seems to cover even a misrepresentation made innocently, because the Explanation states that a person commits deceit, if, without the intention of committing fraud, he does the acts enumerated in clauses (a), (b) and (c). Of these, clause (c) runs as under:

> "(c) causes any mistake or error to be committed in respect to the particulars of the contract, out of ignorance."

These words definitely cover innocent misrepresentation. Incidentally, the draftsman, by using the two words "mistake or error", seems to show his awareness of the fine distinction, between the two. "Mistake" leads to positive action, while "error" covers even inaction (resulting from misrepresentation).

Illegality, Immorality and Public Policy

Certain agreements are declared invalid by section 8 of the Nepal Act. Section 8, clauses (a) to (f) mostly cover agreements tainted by illegality or immorality or violating the public interest, agreements in restraint of trade or marriage, etc. But two clauses of the section are worth notice, as quoted below:

> "(a) Contracts preventing any person from enjoying the privileges or facilities already being enjoyed by the general public;
>
> (b) Contracts seeking to prevent the legal rights of any person from being made applicable by any government officer or court."

Uncertainty

In section 8 of the Nepal Contract Act, uncertainty seems to have been taken care of, by the following clauses:

> "(g) contract which cannot be carried out, because the parties thereto do not exactly know about the matter in relation to which it has been concluded;
>
> ***
>
> (i) contract which is not explicit, because there is lack of a reasonable interpretation thereof."

Impossibility

A simple provision in the Nepalese Contract Act [section 8(h)] declares, as invalid, a contract, "work in respect to which is considered impossible at the time it is conducted or after it has been conducted".

Indirect Contracts

Under the heading of "indirect contracts", the Nepalese Act, in section 9, deals with five situations of unjust enrichment.

Liability of the Parties

Section 10 of the Nepalese Contract Act spells out the obligation of each party to a contract, "to meet his liabilities". In the case of a joint contract, the liability is joint and several. A joint promisor can be compelled to perform a contract and can (on such performance) demand contribution from the other co-promisors.

A party must (under section 11) extend, to the other party, such facilities as are required, so that the other party may render performance of the contract.

A contract can be abandoned, or the time for performance extended, by mutual consent, under section 11 of the Nepalese Contract Act.

Time, Manner and Place of Performance

Sections 13 and 14 of the Nepal Act deal with the time, manner and place of performance of contracts. These are governed by agreement or (in the absence thereof) by the test of "reasonableness". The Act is silent as to the circumstances in which time shall be deemed to be of the essence. The matter must therefore be left to be decided on the facts of each case.

Damages for Breach of Contract

The thorny topic of damages for breach of contract is dealt with, in a fairly simple provision, in the Nepal Act.

Section 15 reads as under:

"(1) In case any party fails to carry out the contract, the opposite party may realise compensation thereof.

(2) In case the contract specifically provides for compensation for specific matters, compensation shall be paid accordingly, and where no compensation is specified in the contract, the party claiming compensation may receive compensation to the extent to which he has actually suffered losses or damages.

Compensation shall not be realised for indirect or imaginary losses or damages".

This provision is of considerable interest, for more reasons than one. In the first place, where the damages are liquidated by the contract, then the section steers clear of the various controversies as to whether the damages are "penal", or whether proof should be given of actual loss and so on. Secondly, if the damages are not liquidated, then, (under the section) compensation can be claimed for loss actually suffered. Obviously, the plaintiff will have to prove it. Thirdly, by prohibiting recovery for indirect or imaginary losses, the section incorporates the doctrine of "ordinary and natural consequences of breach" and thus, in a sense, brings the Nepalese law very near to section 73 of the Indian Contract Act, 1872, and the common law rule in *Hadley* v. *Baxendale*.

LAW OF CONTRACT IN PAKISTAN

Essentials of a Contract

The general law of contract in Pakistan is contained in the Contract Act, 1872. English decisions (where relevant) are also cited in the courts. The Act defines "contract" as an agreement enforceable by law. The essentials of a valid contract are:

(a) intention to create a contract;

(b) offer and acceptance;

(c) consideration;

(d) capacity to enter into a contract;

(e) free consent of the parties;

(f) lawful object of the agreement.

Writing is not essential for the validity of a contract, except where a specific statutory provision requires writing. An arbitration clause must be in writing.

Offer and Acceptance

It is an essential ingredient of a contract, that there must be an offer and its acceptance. If there is no offer, there is no contact, because there is no meeting of minds. Again, if there is an offer by one party, but it is not accepted by the other party or if the ostensible acceptance of the offer is defective, then also, there is no agreement and therefore no "contract".

These propositions may appear to be elementary. A large bulk of commercial litigation, however, requires the parties to deal with the basic questions, which are:

(a) Whether there has been an offer at all in the particular case, or whether there is something less than an offer;

(b) If there is an acceptance; whether it is in the proper form;

(c) Whether there has been an acceptance of the offer;

(d) Whether the acceptance has been communicated to the offerer.

Concept of Offer

An offer (or a "proposal") is not defined by statute. It is generally understood as denoting the expression, by words or conduct, of a willingness to enter into a legally binding contract as soon as it has been accepted, usually, by a return promise or an act on the part of the person (the offeree), to whom it is so addressed.

An acceptance, in relation to an offer, is a final and unqualified expression of assent to the terms of the offer.

Offer, followed by acceptance, is an "agreement", if an agreement is enforceable by law, it is a "contract".

Offer By, and To Whom

An offer must be made by a person legally competent to contract or on his behalf, by someone authorised by him to make the offer. It is usually made to a person (or to a number of persons), but it can be made to the entire world, as happened in *Carlill* v. *Carbolic Smoke Ball Co.*, (1893) 1 QB 256: (1881-94) All ER 127. In that case, the defendants (manufacturers of medicinal smoke balls) promised to pay £100 to anyone who, after having bought and used their smoke balls, caught influenza. Plaintiff did so and caught influenza. Plaintiff was held entitled to recover. It was no defence that there was no particular individual to whom the announcement was addressed. Such contracts are sometimes called "unilateral contracts"—not a very happy term, because a contract can never be "unilateral". There must be two parties. It is really a case of innumerable offers, made to all potential readers of the announcement.

Statements which are not Offers

Every statement of intention is not an offer. A statement must be made with the intention that it will be accepted and will constitute a binding contract. Following are not offers:—

(a) Statement made during negotiation, without indicating that the maker intends to be bound without further negotiation.

(b) A statement which invites the other party to make an offer (*e.g.*, a notice inviting tenders).

(c) Statement of lowest price [*Harvey* v. *Facey*, 1893 AC 552]. It is regarded as an invitation to make offers [Re *Webster*, (1975) 132 CLR 270 (Australia)].

(d) Display of goods in a shop with price tags (It is merely an invitation to make an offer, so that the trader may not accept the offer, if the price is incorrectly marked [*Fisher* v. *Bell*, (1960) 3 All ER 731].

Intention to be Bound

A definite intention to be bound is highlighted in *Gibson* v. *Manchester City Council*, (1979) 1 All ER 192. In 1970, *M* adopted a policy of selling council houses to tenants. In February, 1971, the City Treasurer wrote to *G*, stating that council "may be prepared to sell the house to you at £2,180 (freehold)". The letter asked *G* to make a formal application. This he did, and the council took the house off the list of council-maintained properties. Before the completion of the normal process of preparation and exchange of contracts when property is sold, control of the council changed hands and the policy of selling council houses was reversed. The new council decided only to complete those transactions where exchange of contracts had already taken place. In the UK Court of Appeal, it was held (by a majority) that a contract had been made between *G* and *M*. Lord Denning suggested that "there is no need to look for strict offer and acceptance" in every case; a price had been agreed and the parties intended to carry through the sale. However, the house of Lords held that the February letter was (at the most) an "invitation" of treat. *G's* application was an offer and not an acceptance. (Informal agreements for the sale of houses are not likely to be held as binding contracts, because, otherwise, buyers may find themselves committed before securing mortgage finance.)

Termination of Offer

Some parties clearly indicate that their statements or documents do not constitute offers, *e.g.*, estate agents. These particulars do not form, nor constitute any part of an offer, or a contract, for sale.

Until an offer is accepted, it creates no legal rights and it may be terminated at any time in a variety of ways. Principal modes of termination of an offer are:

- by the offerer revoking (or withdrawing) it before acceptance
- by the offeree rejecting the offer outright or by making a counter-offer
- by lapse of time, if the offer is stated to be open only for a fixed time

In *Great Northern Rly. Co. Ltd.* v. *Witham*, (1873) LR 9 CP 16, Great Northern Railway advertised for tenders for the supply of such stores as they might require for one year. *W* submitted a tender to supply the stores in such quantities as Great Northern Railway might order from time to time and his tender was accepted. Orders were given for some time, but eventually *W* was given an order which he refused to carry out. It was held that *W* was in breach. A tender of this kind was a standing offer which was converted into a series of contracts as Great Northern Railway made their orders. *W* might revoke his offer for the remainder of the period covered, but must supply the goods already ordered. Revocation of an offer is effective, only when communicated to the offeree.

Quality of Acceptance

Acceptance of an offer must be absolute and must correspond with the terms of the offer. This rule is a key constituent of the basic premise and does not always accord with the realities of complex business contract negotiations today. Such negotiations may indeed proceed through a series of proposals, counter-proposals, withdrawals, variations and qualifications, before agreement (or otherwise) is reached. When parties carry on lengthy negotiations, it may be hard to say exactly when an offer has been made and accepted. [*Butler Machine Tool Co. Ltd.* v. *The Ex Cello Corp. (Eng) Ltd.*, (1979) 1 WLR 401]. The court must look at the entire correspondence to decide whether an apparently unqualified acceptance did, in fact, conclude the agreement.

A conditional offer, if accepted, must be accepted along with all the conditions.

However, in regard to international agreements governed by the U.N. Convention on contracts for international sale of goods, there is a slight clarification, in as much as, article 19 of the Vienna Convention provides that non material variations between offer and acceptance do not make a difference.

Consideration

As a rule, an agreement without "consideration" is void. The Contract Act defines "consideration" as follows:

> "When, at the desire of the promisor, the promisee or any other person has done or abstained from doing, or does or abstains from doing, or promises to do or abstains from doing, something, such act, abstinence, or promise is called a consideration for the promise."

A mere promise to give a donation, either orally or in writing, is not enforceable. Settlement of *bona fide* but doubtful claims involve a bargain between the contracting parties and is, therefore, based on consideration. Money is not the only form of consideration. A consideration may consist sometimes in the doing of a requested act, and sometimes in the making of a promise by the offeree. Forbearance to sue at the promisor's desire constitutes good consideration.

Consideration is not required for a promise to compensate, wholly or in part, a person who has already voluntarily done something for the promisor or something which the promisor was legally compellable to do. It is also not required for a written and signed promise by the debtor (or his duly authorised agent) to pay a time-barred debt to the creditor.

Capacity of the Parties

A person is competent to contract if, at the time of making it, he is of sound mind, major and not disqualified from contracting under law.

Where he has not attained the age of 18 years (or being under a court of wards, has not attained the age of 21 years), he cannot contract. Agreements made by minors are void. Minors cannot, on attaining majority, ratify agreements entered into during their minority. But if a minor makes a fraudulent misrepresentation about his age and obtains a loan, he can be required (at the discretion of the court) to refund it or to make compensation for it.

An unadjudged lunatic can enter into a valid contract during lucid intervals.

A corporation can contract subject to limits imposed by its documents of incorporation.

Consent

When consent of a party to a transaction is procured by coercion, undue influence, fraud or misrepresentation, the agreement is voidable at the option of the party whose consent was so procured. Cases of undue influence arise where the transaction is *ex facie* unconscionable and one party was in a position to dominate the will of the other. Where parties are bound by a fiduciary relationship, (as in the case of father and son, doctor and patient, master and servant, advocate and client), the law protects the weaker party, throwing on the other party the burden of proving that no undue influence was exercised.

Mutual mistake in respect of material facts in the formation of a contract renders the agreement void. A unilateral mistake, however, does not render an agreement void. Nor does a mistake of law affect its validity.

Unlawful Agreements

An agreement whose consideration or object is unlawful, is void. The consideration or object of an agreement is unlawful, if it is forbidden by law or it would defeat the provisions of any law or is fraudulent, or involves or implies injury to the person or property of another or the court regards it as immoral or opposed to public policy.

A party to an illegal agreement who has advanced money under it to the other party is entitled to recover it, if the illegal purpose has not been partly or wholly carried out.

Agreements in restraint of marriage, trade and legal proceedings are void. The seller of the good-will of a business may, however, validly agree with the buyer to restrain from carrying on a similar business within specified local limits, provided the limits are reasonable.

Persons Bound by the Contract

Promises bind the promisors and in case of death of promisor (before performance) their legal representatives, unless there is contract to the contrary, or the nature of the contract is such that it depends upon the personal qualifications of any party.

Performance and Frustration

There are special provisions dealing with the case where time is the essence of contract. In commercial contracts, it is better to provide specifically that time is of the essence. A contract is validly discharged by faithful performance, by release or remission by the promisee, by "frustration" (under law) or by "novation" (by agreement).

Frustration occurs when unexpected developments subsequent to the making of the contracts render performance impossible. Novation occurs when the old agreement is replaced by a new agreement.

Subsequent Events and Frustration

If, subsequent to the making of the contract, some event happens, which the parties could not control so that the agreement cannot be performed, the contract is said to be "frustrated" because the contract then becomes impossible of performance. Frustration may occur by a change in the law, destruction of the subject-matter, supervening incapacity of the contracting party to perform the contract or fundamental change in circumstances after the contract is made. Mere strike, lock-out in the factory, rise in price of the contracted goods or other commercial difficulties do not, as such, render the contract "impossible" of performance.

Introduction of the permit system by statute does not absolve the promisor from supplying the goods. He must make reasonable efforts to procure the permit to fulfill his agreement. Change in market conditions also does not justify a supplier in demanding a price higher than that stipulated, unless there is an "escalation" clause.

Frustration leads to automatic termination of the contract, and exempts the parties from performance or further performance of the contract without rendering any of them liable for damages. Where, however, any party has received any benefit under the agreement, he must restore it or make compensation for it to the other party.

Remedies for Breach of Contract

The principal remedies for breach of contract are:

(a) damages;

(b) specific performance of the contract; and

(c) injunction.

When a contract has been broken, the party who suffers by such breach is entitled to receive, from the party who has broken the contract, compensation for any loss or damage caused to him thereby, being loss or damages which naturally arose in the usual course of things from such breach or which the parties knew, when they made the contract, to be likely to result from the breach of it.

Such compensation is not to be given for any remote and indirect loss of damage sustained by reason of the breach.

The same principle applies for determining damages for breach of an obligation arising from quasi-contract.

In estimating the loss or damage arising from a breach of contract, the means which existed of remedying the inconvenience caused by the non-performance of the contract must be taken into account. This is referred to, as the duty to mitigate.

Illustration: A stipulation for increased interest from the date of default may be regarded as a stipulation by "way of penalty", if the amount is excessive. The court is empowered to reduce it to an amount reasonable in the circumstances.

Specific Performance and Injunctions

In certain special cases dealt with in the Specific Relief Act, the court may direct against the party in default "specific performance" of the contract, that is to say, the party may be directed to perform the very obligation which he has undertaken, by the contract. This relief is awarded only in exceptional cases.

The same Act also deals with permanent injunctions. Temporary injunctions are governed by the provisions of order of the Code of Civil Procedure, 1908.

LAW OF CONTRACT IN SRI LANKA*

Sources of the Law

The law of contracts in Sri Lanka (like the law on other subjects) is derived from a variety of sources, as under:

(a) The Roman Dutch law;

(b) The English law;

(c) The personal law;

(d) Sri Lanka's statute law;

(e) Indigenous customs.

This is mainly due to two factors. The political history of the country is the first factor, as the country was in the last five centuries, ruled successively, by the Portuguese, the Dutch and the British, until it became independent. The second factor is the heterogeneous character of its population.

Personal Law

As to personal law (mentioned above), it consists of:

(i) the Kandyan law;

(ii) the Thesawalamai; and

(iii) the Muslim law.

The Thesawalamai is a system of personal law, applicable to "Malabar inhabitants of the Province of Jaffna" and was codified by the Dutch in 1707.

---

* This Chapter deals with the law of contracts as in force in Sri Lanka. In preparing this Chapter, considerable assistance has been derived from C.G. Weeramantry *Law of Contracts*. (The book is hereafter referred to as "*Weeramantry*".)

Roman Dutch Law

The Roman Dutch law is not applicable in its entirety in Sri Lanka but only so much thereof as may be shown to have been introduced into Sri Lanka. The jurists most commonly referred to (in the context of Roman Dutch law) are the following:

(a) Voet (who is the most respected);

(b) Grotius;

(c) Simon Van Leeuwen;

(d) Van der Keessel;

(e) Van der Linden;

(*Weeramantry*, p. 38).

Roman Dutch law is regarded as the "common law" of Sri Lanka, but statute law may provide a different rule.

English Law

English law has worked its way into Sri Lanka, partly through statutes which themselves enacted rules of English law, partly by tacit adoption of judicial decisions and partly by tacit use of English legal concepts (*Weeramantry*, p. 44).

Among the statutes directly introducing English law into Sri Lanka is the Civil Law Ordinance No. 5 of 1852 (Cap. 79), which, by sections 2 and 3, introduced the law of English and in maritime and commercial matters (unless there is a contrary provision in a statute of Sri Lanka).

Sri Lanka Statutes

Again specific statutes of the country have replaced Roman Dutch Law on particular matters. Thus, the age of majority in Roman Dutch law which was 25 years, was replaced by the Age of Majority Ordinance (Cap. 66) which introduced the age of majority as obtaining in English Law.

Similarly the Roman Dutch institution of "Community of spouses" was abrogated in Sri Lanka by the Matrimonial Rights and Ordinance (15 of 1876).

Essentials of a Contract

The essentials of a contract according to the legal system of Sri Lanka are as under:

(a) agreement between the parties;

(b) actual or presumed intention of the parties to create a legal obligation;

(c) due observance of prescribed forms or modes of agreement;

(d) legality and possibility of the object of the agreement;

(e) capacity of the parties to contract.

[*Weeramantry*, p. 81].

[The Common law doctrine of "consideration" does not apply to civil law systems, such as the Roman Dutch law.]

Offer and Acceptance

It is an elementary rule, that every contract requires an offer and an acceptance. Hence an offer or promise which is not accepted, is not actionable [*per* Mr. Justice Weerasooriya in *Muthukuda* v. *Sumanatwathie*, (1962) 65 NLR 205 (208, 209)]. It has been stated that it is a very elementary proposition of law, that a contract is concluded, when in the mind of each contracting party there is a consensus ad idem. [*Noorbhai* v. *Karuppan Chetty*, (1925) 27 NLR 325 (PC) (*per Lord Wrenbury*)]

An offer is a promise, which is in its terms, conditional upon an act, forbearance or return promise being given in exchange for the promise or its performance [Pollock *Contract*, (13th Edn.), p. 4].

An offer must be definite. An invitation to treat, and preliminary negotiations, do not amount to an offer. An advertisement of willingness to sell or let out a house, is not an offer [*Lallyet* v. *Negris & Co.*, (1911) 14 NLR 247].

A "tender" notice is not an offer. It is the tenderer's positive reply to such notice, that becomes an "offer" [*Attorney General* v. *Vithilengam*, (1941) 43 NLR 117 (118)].

Withdrawal of Offer

In English and in Indian Law an offer can be withdrawn before it is accepted [*Dickinson* v. *Dodd*, (1876) 2 Ch D 463].

However, in Roman Dutch law, if an offer is made with a stipulation that it shall be kept open, then it cannot be revoked during the stipulated period or if no period is stipulated, it cannot be revoked for a reasonable period (*Weeramantry*, pp. 140-141, 142, para under the head "options"). This difference seems to arise primarily because of the fact that Roman Dutch law (unlike the common law), does not recognise the need for "consideration" in a contract.

There has emerged the concept of "option" (in Roman Dutch law) which is an offer to keep open, for a definite or indefinite period, an offer that has already been made. In such a case, the offer cannot be withdrawn for the specified period. If the "option" is accepted, then legal consequences may ensue, even if the (substantive) offer is not yet accepted. Thus, a "contract" to keep an offer open is valid (in Roman Dutch law), though there is no consideration for such an undertaking.

Intention to Create Legal Relations

Legal writers generally emphasise that in order that a contract in the eye of the law can come into existence, there should be an intention (on the part of the parties), to enter into a legal relation. [Law Revision Committee (UK), 6th Interim Report, page 15]. In Roman Dutch law also, the proposition is recognised, that either such an intention must exist, or there must be circumstances from which it can be presumed. [Lee *Roman Dutch Law,* (5th Edn.) p. 220, 221, cited by *Weeramantry,* p. 155. f.n. 1].

Normally, the doctrine does not receive separate treatment in common law because, at common law "consideration" (which is an essential component of contract in law) ensures that the parties were serious about the transaction entered into. Nevertheless, there are cases where this aspect may become relevant, even in common law [Cf. *Balfour* v. *Balfour,* (1919) 2 KB 571].

Besides this, there do arise situations where, though there is a vague desire to enter into a contract at a future date, there may be no firm resolve present to enter into a legally binding agreement [Cf. *Rose and Frank* v. *Crompton,* (1923) 2 KB 261; on appeal (1925) AC 445 (HL)].

So far as Roman Dutch law (which is, by and large followed in Sri Lanka on matters and expressly subjected to English law) is concerned, it does seem to recognise that "the evidence should establish clearly that the intention of the parties was to create a legal obligation" [Lee *Roman Dutch Law,* 5th Edn., p. 221; *Weeramantry,* p.156 and f.n. 7 and 8].

"Honour Clauses"

It follows, from the above discussion, that an agreement which expressly provides that it is not to be justiciable or that it is a mere "honour" clause, would not create a legally enforceable contract, in Sri Lanka. [*Weeramantry,* p. 158].

Cf. the following English Cases:

(i) *Jones* v. *Vernon 's Pools Ltd.,* (1938) 2 All ER 628;

(ii) *Appleson* v. *Littlewood Ltd.,* (1939) 1 All ER 464.

Form

In Sri Lanka, writing is required for certain kinds of contract.

Following are the important examples:—

(a) Section 12, Prescription Ordinance (Cap. 68) – acknowledgment for the purpose of limitation.

(b) Sections 7, 8, 9 and 10, Contracts for Hire and Service Ordinance – contracts of hire or service of servant if made for a period exceeding one month (including contracts entered into in India) and contracts terminating such contracts.

(c) Section 10, Money Lending Ordinance (Cap. 80) – provision that a promissory note is void if it is not accompanied by a written agreement, separately setting out the principal amount and the rate of interest.

(d) Section 20(3), General Marriages Ordinance (Cap 112) – promise to marry.

(e) Section 2, Prevention of Frauds Ordinance No. 7 of 1840, discussed in the next paragraph.

Prevention of Frauds Ordinance

By section 2 of the Prevention of Frauds Ordinance No. 7 of 1840, the following classes of contract shall be of no force or avail in law, unless they are in writing and signed in the presence of a licensed notary public and two or more witnesses and attested:—

(a) sale, purchase transfer, etc. or mortgage of immovable property;

(b) any promise, bargain, agreement, etc. for effecting any such object or for establishing any security, interest or encumbrance, affecting immovable property;

(c) any contract, etc., for the future sale or purchase of immovable property.

Movable Property

Section 17 of the Registration of Documents Ordinance, (Cap. 117), provides that a pledge, mortgage or bill of sale of movables shall not be of any force in law or give the transferee any right, etc. unless—

(i) such property is actually delivered into the possession and custody of the pledge, etc., or

(ii) such pledge, etc., is created by a written and signed instrument and duly registered within 21 days, with the Registrar of Lands.

Consideration and *Causa*

The common law doctrine of "consideration" (return for a promise), as an essential component of the validity of a contract, is not prevalent in Sri Lanka, as a general rule. In the Roman Dutch law, (and in most continental systems based or the civil law) the simple requirement of "*just causa*" suffices [*Weeramantry*, pp. 219, 279-283].

This ensures that the promise is serious and deliberate. However, in respect of contracts governed by principles of English law (mainly because of statutory provisions) consideration may be required, *e.g.*, contracts for the sale of goods and bills of exchange (which are governed by English law).

As regards the doctrine of "*causa*" (operative generally in Sri Lanka), it is now well established. It means the ground, reason or object of a promise, giving such promise a binding effect in law. It has a much wider meaning than the English term "consideration" and comprises the motive or reason for the promise and also purely moral consideration. [Mr. Justice Wemdt in *Lipton* v. *Buchanan*, (1904) 8 NLR 49, confirmed in 10 NLR 158].

In particular, a moral obligation suffices to constitute "*causa*" [*Jayawickrema* v. *Amarasuriya*, (1918) 20 NLR 293 (294)].

This is in contrast with the common law, where (as a general rule) an existing moral obligation (which is not enforceable at law) does not constitute a good consideration [*Currie* v. *Misa*, (1875) LR 10 EX 153].

Lord Mansfield had in 1782 attempted to widen the scope "consideration" so as to take within its scope a pre-existing moral obligation [*Hawkes* v. *Saunders* (1782) 1 Cowp 289]. But this theory was rejected within half a century [*Eastwood* v. *Kenyan*, (1840) 9 LJQB 409].

It has been said by a very high authority that moral obligation is essentially subjective, while consideration (as known to the common law) is essentially objective [Lord Wright, "*Ought the Doctrine of Consideration to be Abolished from the Common Law*" (1936) 49 Harvard Law Review 1225, 1235].

It would seem that legal systems all over the world may be classified into the following four categories in this regard:—

(a) Countries requiring "consideration" for the validity of contract. Most countries in the common law fold belong to this group.

(b) Countries insisting on '*causa*', but without a statutory requirement to that effect. Sri Lanka belongs to this category. So also South Africa [*Robinson* v. *Rendfontein Esels G.M. Co.*, (1921) AD 236].

(c) Countries where *causa* is expressly and by statute required for the validity of a contract. Examples are – Dutch Civil Code of 1838, article 1356, Italian Civil Code of 1865, and Quebec Civil Code of 1858.

(d) Countries where the Civil Code requires *causa* but the requirement is not enforced in practice, *e.g.*, articles 1108, 1131 and 1135, French Civil Code.

See the following:—

(i) Newman *The doctrine of Causa or consideration in the Civil Law*, (1952) 30 Canadian Bar Review 662.

(ii) Von Mehren *Civil Law Analogues to Consideration*, (1959) 72 Harvard Law Review 1009.

(iii) Walton *Cause and Consideration in contracts*, (1925) 41 LQR 306.

(iv) *Weeramantry*, pp. 251, 265.

Factors Vitiating Consent

As in other legal systems certain factors can vitiate the quality of consent and thus make the agreement void or voidable. These are – (a) mistake, (b) misrepresentation (fraudulent or non fraudulent), and (c) undue influence and coercion. In principle, the law of Sri Lanka also talks of provision for these factors. As to mistake, an erroneous impression, it may (i) prevent agreement , or (ii) nullify the agreement. Though, in Sri Lanka the system of law operative is the Roman Dutch law, yet English cases seem to be often cited in this field. Moreover, the Evidence Ordinance of Sri Lanka closely follows the Indian Evidence Act, 1872, so that, in the light of section 92 of that Ordinance (and its various provisos) evidence is freely admitted of factors nullifying a transaction for want of consent.

Illegality

Illegality of a contract results on two consequences:

(a) the agreement is void; and

(b) a party cannot recover what he has parted with (or paid), upon the illegal contract (*Weeramantry*, p. 332).

Contracts may become illegal:—

(a) because they are in conflict with a statute, or

(b) because they are illegal at common law, or

(c) because they are opposed to public policy or morality (*Weeramantry*, p. 333).

Statutory Prohibition

Express statutory prohibition (in Sri Lanka) is illustrated by sections 11-12 Rubber Control Ordinance (Cap. 436), which render it illegal for any person to sell or purchase rubber in excess of the prescribed quantity, unless he is a licensed dealer. The Lotteries

Ordinance No. 8 of 1844 provides that all lotteries "shall be deemed and are hereby declared to be common nuisances and against law"

Common Law Prohibitions

As regards contracts which are illegal at common law, the principal categories are:—

(a) transactions in things *extra commerciom,* and

(b) contracts entered into with a fraudulent object (*Weeramantry,* p. 342, para 348).

As to things *extra commercium,* the Roman distinction between things *absolutely extra commercium* and things *relatively extra commercium* is recognised in modern Roman Dutch law. Some of the things *absolutely extra commercium* are the – (i) seashore, (ii) public streams, (iii) crown lands, (iv) minerals found thereon and public property. Amongst things *relatively extra commercium* are – opium, foreign currency, dangerous drugs and fire arms (for which a license is required).

As to fraud the classical statement is: "Fraud is not a thing that can stand even when robed in a judgment" [*Black on Judgments,* Vol. 1, section 292-293, cited by Bertram C.J., in *Suppramaniam* v. *Erampakurukal,* (1922) 23 NLR 417 (435) (FB)].

The most interesting aspect of Roman law is the Paulian Action, under which an alienation of property can be challenged, if it is fraudulent.

In Roman law, it was a collective action. In modern Sri Lanka, it is an action brought by an individual creditor who challenges fraudulent transfer by the debtor.

Public Policy

Agreements contrary to public policy (in the law of Sri Lanka) are grouped as follows: (*Weeramantry,* pp. 363 -364, para 365):

(a) Agreements conflicting with the interests of the State:

 (i) Agreements in conflict with the national security;

 (ii) Agreements in conflict with the the public service;

 (iii) Agreements in conflict with the the administration of justice;

(b) Agreements conflicting with considerations of morality;

(c) Agreements restraining individual freedom.

Administration of Justice

Agreements conflicting with the administration of justice [Category (a)(iii) above], are of particular interest from the point of view of comparative law. In the Sri Lankan context, the following appear to be the principal examples of agreements void under this category:—(*Weeramantry*, pp. 356-364):

(1) Stifling of criminal prosecutions;
(2) Agreements to give or suppress evidence for another person;
(3) Agreement to commit a crime;
(4) Maintenance and champerty;
(5) Intermeddling with suitors;
(6) Agreements ousting the jurisdiction of courts;
(7) Assignment of rights in a pending action;
(8) Abuse of the process of court.

Performance and Tender of Performance

Performance of a contract is a vast topic, covering time, place and manner of performance, payment appropriation and the like. Here, it is proposed to concentrate on one point which is of special interest in the context of Sri Lankan law, namely, "tender of performance". "Tender" means offer of performance. It must be made at the time and place agreed upon. The offer of performance must be unconditional. The importance of tender has been highlighted by the observation of one writer, that "tender is the instinctive resource of the oppressed, against the exactions of the relentless and it is for the person sought to be victimised to make proper use of this resource" [Harris on Tender, p. 1, cited by Mr. Justice Soertz in *Fernando* v. *Coomaraswamy*, (1940) 41 NLRR 466 (473)].

Where the obligation is to pay money, tender does not in itself discharge the obligation but precludes a claim for interest, either in English law or in Roman Dutch law (*Weeramantry*, p. 671). Tender must be made of the full amount due. Otherwise the creditor is not bound to accept. Tender should be unconditional. However, the law does not compel performance of that which has no utility avail (*lex non cogit ad inutilia*). Hence, where the creditor has in anticipation, already refused to accept payment from the debtor then no further tender is necessary. [*Sideek* v. *Sainambu Natchiya*, 55 NLR 367].

An interesting aspect of Roman Dutch law is the process of judicial deposit (consignate), offering effective protection to a debtor who wishes to pay, where the creditor refuses to accept payment. By this procedure a debtor who considers that the creditors claim is excessive or unwarranted can make a judicial deposit (*Weeramantry*, p. 675). The relevant provision is contained in section 409 of the Code of Civil Procedure of Sri Lanka, which covers deposits by the defendant as well as by the plaintiff. The object of a judicial deposit is to enable a debtor to protect himself against—(i) interest, (ii) costs, and (iii) other consequences of default. After the deposit is made, delay in court procedure does not affect the plaintiff, the maxim being *cursus curiae neminem gravabit*.

Damages for Breach of Contract

The main principle on which damages for breach of contract are awarded in Sri Lanka is that the sum to be awarded should, as nearly possible, be a sum which will put the wronged party in the position which he would have enjoyed if he had not sustained the wrong for which the award of damages is made and it should include both actual loss and loss of profit (*Weeramantry*, p. 888). Damages may be excluded by special clauses to that effect in the contract.

Damages may be:—

(a) general (*damnum commune*), or

(b) special (*damnum singulare*).

The former refers to direct loss which would be suffered by any person as a result of breach of the contract in question. The latter refers to losses which are personal and peculiar to the plaintiff being losses which other persons similarly placed would not have suffered. The distinction broadly corresponds to the common law distinction between "ordinary" damages and damages "specially contemplated" [Cf. *Radcliffe* v. *Evans*, (1892) 2 QB 524].

In regard to liquidated damages, the approach adopted in Sri Lanka seems to be substantially the same as in England (*Weeramantry*, pp. 912, 913). In English law, the court will regard the sum fixed by the parties as liquidated damages as the quantum to be awarded, even though the damages actually sustained are very different from this figure [*Swisse Atlantique etc.* v. *N.V. etc.*, 196, *Rotterdamasche etc.*, (1966) 2 All ER 61 (HL)].

In Sri Lanka also the court will not interfere with the mode of assessment adopted by the parties, unless the payment stipulated, is in reality a penalty (*Weeramantry*, pp. 912 to 916).

It should be mentioned that the Roman law did not distinguish between liquidated damages and penalty. But the distinction seems to have been adopted in Roman Dutch law particularly with the South African case of *Pearl Assurance Co.* v. *Union Government*, (1934) AD 560 (568) (PC).

It may, however, be mentioned that in South Africa, by the Conventional Penalties Act (15 of 1962), the legislature has ensured that liquidate damages and penalty clauses are both subject to judicial scrutiny. Courts in South Africa have a discretion to reduce a sum which is considered excessive, in both cases. At the same time "penalties" can also be recovered, subject to the above limitation (*Weeramantry*, p. 915). In other words, a contractual stipulation in South Africa can be judicially reviewed, whether it speaks of liquidated damages or penalty.

LAW OF LIMITATION IN SELECTED SAARC COUNTRIES

A COMPARATIVE PERSPECTIVE

The Background

Statutes of limitation prescribe periods during which certain actions can be brought, or certain rights can be enforced, through legal proceedings. After the period of time set out in the applicable statute has run out, no legal action can be brought. The bar created by such a statute is (subject to certain minor relaxations meant for special situations), mandatory, in the sense that hardship in individual cases does not constitute a ground for the court granting a relaxation.

The Juristic Rationale

The juristic rationale justifying such bars rests on several factors. First, the law assists the wakeful and not the sleeping or the indolent. The maxim is – *lex vigitantibus, non dormentibus, subvenit.* Secondly, after the lapse of a certain period of time, the memory of witnesses may fade; evidence may get lost; and documents may become unavailable. The law has to take into account all these factors. It therefore discourages the filing of stale claims before the courts.

Suits and Arbitration Claims

Pursuing this general approach, statutes of limitation seek to lay down periods within which suits may be instituted in court on various types of causes of action. And, since the considerations mentioned above are as much valid in regard to claims in arbitration, as in regard to claims in courts of law, the legal system extends the law of limitation to claims in arbitration also.

It is against this background, that it may be useful to examine what approach the statute law of selected SAARC Countries has actually adopted, when dealing with suits or claims based on arbitration. Attention can be focused on contractual causes of action, since arbitration proceedings mostly relate to such causes of action.

Issues for Consideration

For this purpose, certain issues have been chosen for a comparative study of the limitation statutes of selected countries. These issues are as under:

(1) the title of the applicable statutes;

(2) the normal periods of limitation, for suits based on contractual causes of action;

(3) statutory provisions for relaxation or extension (of the period of limitation) on specific grounds;

(4) date on which claim is deemed to have been made in arbitration (for the purpose of limitation);

(5) any other point that may be considered to be of special interest on the subject.

COMPARATIVE POSITION

The broad position as under:

India

In India, the earlier Act of 1908 – the Indian Limitation Act, 1908, has been repealed and re-enacted, as Limitation Act, 1963. This Act, constitutes the present enactment for determining the periods of limitation and the principles applicable for computing such periods, for civil suits and arbitrations.

Section 43(1) of the Arbitration and Conciliation Act, 1996 (26 of 1996), in force in India, provides that the provisions of the Limitation Act, 1963, apply to arbitrations, as they apply to suits.

Pakistan

In Pakistan, statute prescribing the limitation periods within which suits and actions can be instituted is the Limitation Act, 1908. The scheme of the Act (as in the Indian Act) is such, that whilst the rules relating to computation of time and regulating the course and manner for providing relief are contained in the main body of the Act (comprising various "sections"), the specific limitation periods within which suits and actions are required to be instituted, are contained in the First Schedule to the Act (comprising several articles).

Bangladesh

The Limitation Act, 1908, is the governing law in Bangladesh. The rules relating to computation of time, etc. are contained in the main body of the Act; and the specific limitation periods within which suits can be filed, are contained in the First Schedule to the Act.

Sri Lanka*

The Prescription Ordinance No. 22 of 1871, as amended by Ordinance No. 2 of 1889, governs the law on acquisitive prescription and limitation of all causes of action, subject to any special statutory provision to the contrary. The commencement of the period of the various causes of action is expressly laid down in the relevant sections of the ordinance.

PERIODS OF LIMITATION

India

In India, under the Limitation Act, 1963, the periods applicable to suits based on contract are as under:

(a) Specific performance of a contract – 3 years (article 54) (from the date fixed for performance, or, if no such date is fixed, then the date, when the plaintiff has noticed that performance is refused).

(b) Compensation for the breach of any contract – (not otherwise provided for) – 3 years from the date of breach (article 55).

Pakistan

In Pakistan, normal limitation period for suits and actions based on contractual causes of action is three years. Certain specific instances are mentioned below:

(a) Article 113 prescribes the limitation period for the specific performance of a contract to be three years, from the date fixed for the performance of the contract, or where no such date is fixed, then, from the date when the plaintiff has notice that performance has been refused.

(b) Article 114 prescribes the limitation period for the rescission of a contract to be three years, from the date on which the facts that entitle a plaintiff to rescind the contract first become known to him.

(c) Article 115 prescribes the limitation period for compensation for the breach of a contract (express or implied), not in writing, which is not registered (and not provided for in any other article). In such a case, the suit for compensation can be brought

* Sources for Sri Lankan Limitation Laws: Law of Contracts (Volume 2) by C.G. Weeramantry.

within a period of three years from the date when the contract is broken, or (where there are successive breaches), from the date when the breach in respect of which the suit is instituted occurs, or (where the breach is continuing) when it ceases.

(d) Article 116 prescribes the limitation period for compensation for breach of a contract in writing, which is registered to be six years. The period of limitation would begin to run from the same date as in the case of a suit brought on a similar contract not registered.

Bangladesh

In Bangladesh, the normal limitation period for suits based on contractual causes of action of action is three years, as elaborated below:

(1) The limitation period for a suit for specific performance of a contract is three years, from the date fixed for the performance of the contract (or where no such date is fixed), from the date when the plaintiff has notice that performance has been refused [article 113].

(2) The limitation period for a suit for the recession of a contract is three years, from the date when the facts that entitle a plaintiff to rescind the contract, first become known to him [article 114].

(3) The limitation period for s suit for compensation for the breach of a contract, express or implied, not in writing and not registered and not provided for in any other article is three years, from the date when the contract is broken, or (where there are successive breaches), the date when the breach in respect of which the suit is instituted occurs, or (where the breach is continuing), the date when it ceases [article 115].

(4) The limitation period for a suit for compensation for the breach of a contract in writing, which is registered, is to be six years from the date on which the period of limitation would begin to run in the case of a suit brought on a similar contract which is not registered [article 116].

Sri Lanka

Section 6 of the Ordinance provides that no action shall be maintainable

(a) upon any deed for establishing a partnership, or

(b) upon any promissory note or bill of exchange, or

(c) (i) upon any written promise contract, bargain or agreement, or

(ii) other written security not falling within the description of instruments set forth in section 5,

unless such action shall be brought within six years:

(a) from the date of the breach of such partnership deed or of such written promise contract bargain or agreement or other written security, or

(b) from the date when such note or bill shall have become due, or

(c) of the last payment of interest thereon.

Section 7 provides that no action shall be maintainable for the recovery of—

(a) any movable property, rent, or mesne profit, or

(b) for any money lent without written security, or

(c) for any money paid or expended by the plaintiff on account of the defendant, or

(d) for money received by the defendant for the use of the plaintiff, or

(e) for money due upon an account stated, or

(f) upon any unwritten promise, contract, bargain or agreement,

unless such action shall be commenced within three years from the time after the cause of action shall have arisen.

Where any given cause of action may appear to fall within the scope of more than one section of the Ordinance, courts would follow the principle that the particular enactment prevails over the general.

No special form of writing is required for the purpose of section 5 except that it should have a certain degree of formality.

RELAXATION OR EXTENSION OF THE PERIOD OF LIMITATION

India

In India, the main provisions of the Limitation Act, 1963, which provide for relaxation or extension of the time for filing a suit, etc., are as under:

(a) Legal disability of the plaintiff (minority, insanity or idiocy) [sections 6, 7 and 8].

(b) Exclusion of time taken in a proceeding prosecuted with due diligence in a court which, from defect of jurisdiction or other cause of a like nature, is unable to entertain it [section 14].

(c) Institution of a suit restrained by an injunction or order [section 15].

(d) Fraud or mistake [section 17].

(e) Acknowledgement of liability in writing [section 18]. (*See* note below).

(f) Payment on account of debt (or interest, etc. on a debt), evidenced in writing [section 19].

Note.—Acknowledgement of liability in respect of a property or right, in order that it may give a fresh starting point of limitation, must have been made in writing, before expiry of the limitation period and must be signed by the person against whom such property or right is claimed.

Pakistan

Section 19 of the Limitation Act in force in Pakistan provides that where, prior to the expiry of the period of limitation prescribed for bringing an action under the Act, there is an acknowledgement of liability, made in writing and signed by the party against whom the claim is made, a fresh period of limitation will start from the date of such acknowledgement.

The limitation period for a suit is also subject to relaxation, if the defendant has been out of the country. Section 13 of the Act in force in Pakistan states that in computing the period of limitation, any time spent by the defendant outside of Pakistan shall be excluded.

The limitation period is subject to relaxation, in cases where the plaintiff is subject to a legal disability. Section 6 of the Act in force in Pakistan provides that where the plaintiff is under a legal disability, the limitation period will start to run from the date the "disability has ceased". For the purposes of section 6, a minor, or an insane person, or an idiot, is a legally disabled person.

Under section 14 of the Pakistan Act, in computing the period of limitation prescribed by the Act, the time spent by the plaintiff in prosecuting with due diligence another civil proceeding shall be excluded from computation of the limitation period. The proceedings of the other suit should have been founded on the same cause of action and prosecuted in good faith in a court, which, from defect of jurisdiction, or other cause of a like nature, is unable to entertain the claim.

Section 18 of the Pakistan Act provides that where a person who has a right to institute a suit has, by means of fraud, been kept from the knowledge of such right, the limitation period will commerce when the fraud becomes known to him.

Bangladesh

Where, prior to the expiry of the period of limitation prescribed for bringing an action under the Act, there is an acknowledgement of liability, made in writing and signed by the party against whom the claim is made, a fresh period of limitation will start from the date of such acknowledgement [section 19].

In computing the period of limitation for any suit, any time spent by the defendant outside of Bangladesh shall be excluded [section 13].

Where the plaintiff is under a legal disability, the limitation period will start to from the date on which the "disability has ceased" under section 6. For the purposes of section 6, a minor, or and person insane, or an idiot, is a legally disabled person.

In computing the period of limitation prescribed by the Act, the time spent by the plaintiff in prosecuting, with due diligence, another civil proceeding shall be excluded. The proceedings of the other suit should have been founded on the same cause of action and prosecuted in good faith in a court, which, from defect of jurisdiction, or other cause of a like nature, is unable to entertain the claim [section 14].

Where a person who has a right to institute a suit has, by means of fraud, been kept from the knowledge of such right, the limitation period will commerce when the fraud becomes known to him.

Sri Lanka

In any forms of action referred to in sections 5, 6, 7, 8, 10 and 11* of the Ordinance, section 12 provides that no acknowledgement or promise by words only shall be deemed evidence of a new or continuing contract whereby to take the case out of the operation of the enactments contained in the said sections, or any of them, or to deprive any party the benefit thereof, unless such acknowledgement shall be made or contained in some writing signed by the party chargeable, or by an agent duly authorised to enter into such a contract on his behalf.

The acknowledgement should be unconditional or if conditional, the conditions should have been fulfilled.

---

* Section 5. Term is case of Mortgage debt or bond-ten years from date of instrument, last payment of interest or breach of condition.

Section 8. Term is case of goods sold, shop bill, book debt or work and labour-one year from the time debt became due.

Section 9. Term in case of loss, injury or damages – two years from the time when the cause of action arose.

Section 10. Term in cases not provided form three years from the tie the cause of action arose.

Section 11. Claims in reconvention not to be allowed where action is barred by any provision in the Ordinance.

The effect of a part-payment made in circumstances from which a promise to pay the balance may be inferred, is to take the case out of the operation of the Ordinance.

Payment of interest is regarded as implying not merely an acknowledgement of an existing debt, but a promise to pay it.

Disabilities

Section 14 of the Ordinance provides that if at any time the right of action in respect of any of the causes referred to in sections 5, 6, 7, 8, 10 and 11 shall accrue, the person so entitled to sue shall be subject to any of the following disabilities, namely:

(a) infancy,

(b) idiocy,

(c) unsoundness of mind,

(d) lunacy, or

(e) absence beyond the seas.

then the several grounds of limitation provided in the said sections shall not follow whichever shall first happen.

The disability therefore must exist at the time when the cause of action first accrues and subsequent disabilities are of no effect, and where a person suffering from any of the above mentioned disabilities dies, the period of limitation commences to run against him from the date of his death.

Fraud and Mistake

Prescription does not run in the case of concealed fraud or mistake until there is knowledge of the fraud or mistake or until the party defrauded or mistaken might by due diligence have come to know of it, as equitable principles of concealed fraud and mistake apply in Sri Lanka.

Mediation Board Act No. 72 of 1988, as amended by Act No. 15 of 1997

Section 17 of the above Act provides that, in computing the period of prescription in regard to any cause of action or offence, the period commencing on the date on which an application is made to the Chairman of the panel of mediators in respect of the dispute constituting such causes of action or such offence, as the case may be, and ending on the date of the certificate issued under section 14A in respect of that dispute or offence, shall be disregarded notwithstanding anything to the contrary in any other written law.

DATE OF INSTITUTION OF THE CLAIM IN ARBITRATION

India

In India, by virtue of section 43(2) of the Arbitration and Conciliation Act, 1996 the date of commencement of the arbitration (for the purposes of the Limitation Act, 1963 and the Arbitration and Conciliation Act, 1996) is the date mentioned in section 21 of the latter Act. Section 21 of latter Act provides that unless otherwise agreed by the parties, an arbitration shall be deemed to have commenced when the respondent receives request for reference of the dispute to arbitration.

Pakistan

Provisions of the Limitation Act, 1908 (Pakistan) apply to arbitrations as they apply to civil courts, under section 37 of the Arbitration Act, 1940. Under section 37(3) of the Arbitration Act, 1940, an arbitration shall be deemed to have commenced, when one party to the arbitration agreement serves on the other parties thereto, a notice, requiring the appointment of an arbitrator, or where the arbitration agreement provides that the reference shall be to a person named or designated in the agreement, requiring that the differences be submitted to the person so named or designated.

Bangladesh

Position in Bangladesh is substantially the same as in Pakistan in this regard.

Sri Lanka

In calculating the period of prescription for the purpose of any action the period that lapsed between the commencement of an arbitration and its completion, or termination as the case may be, shall be excluded. Arbitration proceedings are deemed to commence when a party to the agreement has received a notice after a dispute has arisen, to refer or concur in the reference of the dispute to arbitration or appoint an arbitrator or concur in the appointment of an arbitral tribunal.

OTHER POINTS OF SPECIAL INTEREST

India

In India, in the scheme of the Arbitration and Conciliation Act, 1996, an award of an arbitrator is not required to be filed in the court. It is given the status of a decree. Hence, so much of the law of limitation as was applicable to the filing of an award in court has now become obsolete.

Pakistan

Under article 178 of the First Schedule to the Limitation Act, 1908, in force in Pakistan, an award under the Arbitration Act, 1940 must be filed within 90 days of the date of service of notice of filing of the award.

Bangladesh

In Bangladesh, an arbitrator's award must be filed within 90 day of service of notice of filing of the award (Article 178, Limitation Act, 1940).

Sri Lanka

In Sri Lanka a party to an arbitration agreement should apply to court for the enforcement of an award within one year the expiry of fourteen days of the making of the award.

RULES OF ARBITRATION OF THE INDIAN COUNCIL OF ARBITRATION

ICA ARBITRATION CLAUSE

The Indian Council of Arbitration recommends to all parties desirous of making reference to arbitration by the Indian Council of Arbitration, the use of the following arbitration clause in writing in their contracts:

"Any dispute or difference whatsoever arising between the parties out of or relating to the construction, meaning, scope, operation or effect of this contract or the validity or the breach thereof, shall be settled by arbitration in accordance with the Rules of Arbitration of the Indian Council of Arbitration and the award made in pursuance thereof shall be binding on the parties."

DEFINITIONS

Rule 1

(i) These rules may be called the "Rules of Arbitration of the Indian Council of Arbitration."

(ii) These rules shall apply where parties have agreed in writing that (a) a dispute has arisen or (b) a dispute which may arise between them in respect of defined legal relationship whether contractual or not shall be settled under the Rules of Arbitration.

Rule 2

In these rules, the following words have the following meanings:

(i) "Arbitral Tribunal" means an arbitrator or arbitrators appointed for determining a particular dispute or difference.

(ii) "Arbitral Award" includes an interim award.

(iii) "Committee" means the Arbitration Committee of the Council as provided for hereinafter.

(iv) "Council" means the Indian Council of Arbitration.

(v) "Governing Body" means the Governing Body of the Council.

(vi) "Guidelines" means the guidelines for arbitrators and the parties to arbitration for expeditious conduct of the arbitration proceedings given in the Annexure to these Rules.

(vii) "International Commercial Arbitration" means an arbitration relating to disputes arising out of legal relationships, whether contractual or not, considered as commercial under the law in force in India and where at least one of the parties is (i) an individual who is a national of, or habitually resident in, any country other than India; or (ii) a body corporate which is incorporated in any country other than

India; or (iii) a company or an association or a body of individuals whose central management and control is exercised in any country other than India, or (iv) the Government of a foreign country.

(viii) "Party" means a party to an arbitration agreement. It shall include any individual, firm, company, Government, Government organisation or Government Undertaking.

(ix) "Panel" means the Panel of Arbitrators maintained by the Council.

(x) "Registrar" means the Registrar for the time being appointed by the Committee and includes such other persons as the Committee may nominate for carrying out the duties of the registrar under these rules.

(xi) "Rules" means the Rules of Arbitration of the Council,

(xii) "Rules of Conciliation" means the Rules of Conciliation of the Council.

(xiii) "Fast Track Arbitration" means arbitration in accordance with Rule 44.

(xiv) Words importing the singular number include, where the context admits or requires, the plural number and *vice versa*.

ARBITRATION COMMITTEE

Rule 3

(a) The Governing Body of the Council shall constitute an Arbitration Committee for performing the functions prescribed under these Rules. The Committee shall consist of the President of the Council, who shall be the ex-officio Chairman of the Committee and three members of the Governing Body of the Council elected by the Governing Body from amongst themselves. The Committee shall hold office for a year.

(b) The Committee may co-opt not more than two persons to be additional members of the Committee during its terms of office. Persons who are not members of the Governing Body may also be co-opted to be members of ihe Committee.

(c) The Committee or the Chairman of the Committee may delegate to the Registrar the power to take certain decisions provided that any such decision shall be reported to the Chairman or the Committee as the case may be.

RULES APPLICABLE

Rule 4

(a) Any dispute relating to any commercial matter including shipping, sale, purchase, banking, insurance, building construction, engineering, technical assistance, know-how, patents, trade marks, management consultancy, commercial agency, or labour, arising between two or more parties in India or a party or parties in India and a party or parties in a foreign country or between foreign parties who agree or have agreed for arbitration by the Council, or under the Rules of Arbitration of the Council, shall be determined and settled in accordance with these Rules.

(b) The Council shall also be competent to administer the conduct of arbitration in any dispute or difference relating to a commercial transaction between parties as mentioned in sub-clause (a) where they have agreed to have "their dispute arbitrated under any other Rules of Arbitration and have agreed to have such arbitration administered by the Council, wholly or in respect of some matters arising out of such arbitration.

(c) In case the parties have provided different procedure for appointment of arbitrator or schedule of cost including the arbitrator's fee, the Council shall not be bound to process the case unless both the parties agree to follow entire procedure of arbitration under Rules of Arbitration of the Council.

(d) The Council shall be competent to function as Appointing Authority as contemplated under the Arbitration Rules of the United Nations Commission on International Trade Law (UNCITRAL).

Rule 5

Wherever the Parties have provided or agreed for arbitration by the Indian Council of Arbitration or for arbitration under the Rules of Arbitration of the Council, these rules or any amendment thereof in the form obtaining at the time the dispute is referred to arbitration of the Council, shall apply.

Rule 6

If one or both of the parties to a dispute which is referred to arbitration by the Council belong to a country or countries other than India, in the absence of an agreement by the Parties on the substantive law to be applied, it will be determined by the arbitral tribunal. The procedural law shall be the laws of India and parties shall be deemed to have submitted to the jurisdiction of the Courts in India.

Rule 7

Any chamber of commerce, trade association or any arbitral or other organisation may adopt these Rules by making them generally available to its members or by applying them to any dispute in which any of its members may be parties or by normally conducting its arbitration under these Rules.

INTERPRETATION OF THE RULES

Rule 8

The decision of the Committee on any question relating to interpretation of these rules or any procedural matter thereunder shall be final and binding on the parties.

PANEL Of ARBITRATORS

Rule 9

A Panel of Arbitrators shall be appointed by the Committee from amongst persons who are qualified and possesses knowledge and experience in their respective field of profession and arbitration law & procedure and willing to serve as arbitrators generally or in specific fields and who are from time to time recommended by the members of the Council or any other person or organisation.

All the members of the Panel will carry equal status and parties will not have right to challenge the appointment of arbitrator on the ground that its nominee arbitrator has higher status than the Presiding Arbitrator.

Rule 10

The Registrar shall prepare and maintain an up-to-date Panel of Arbitrators together with adequate information as to their qualifications and experience. Separate lists may be kept and maintained of arbitrators included in the Panel for disputes in general and for each of the fields of international trade and/or business transactions in which the Governing Body decides that the Council will offer arbitration facilities under the Rules. The parties to a dispute or the Registrar where he appoints the arbitrator may choose any person from the panel with reference to any dispute. If any party appoints a foreigner/ person residing abroad, as arbitrator from the panel, that party will have to meet the travel & stay expenses of the person appointed as arbitrator from his country to the place of arbitration. The arbitral tribunal may, however, make any order in regard thereto in the award. The Panel of Arbitrators shall be open to inspection by all persons with the permission of the Registrar.

Rule 11

The Committee may at any time add the name of any person to the list of arbitrators included in the Panel or delete the name of any person from the panel.

Rule 12

The Chairman of the Committee may include the name of any person in the Panel, in case it is required in any particular case. His continuance in the Panel will be decided by the Committee.

Rule 13

The persons who have attained the age of more than 80 years will automatically cease to be member of the Panel of Arbitrators. In case a person who has been appointed as Arbitrator before attainment of the age of 80 years, his Panel membership will continue till the pronouncement of the Award in pending arbitration matter referred to him.

DUTIES OF THE REGISTRAR

Rule 14

(a) The Registrar shall receive applications for arbitration by the Council, receive payment of fees and deposits, appoint, in consultation with the Chairman of the Committee, and in his absence in consultation with the member of the Governing Body designated by him, an arbitrator or arbitrators as hereinafter provided. The Registrar shall also receive all communications made to the arbitral tribunal by the parties and communicate to them the orders and directions of the arbitral tribunal, keep a register of applications to the Council and of awards made by the arbitral tribunal, keep such other books or memoranda and make such other records or returns as the Committee shall from time to time require and generally carry out the directions of an arbitral tribunal so constituted under these rules and take such other steps as may be necessary to assist such arbitral tribunal in the carrying out of its functions.

(b) The Registrar may delegate to any officer of the Council, Chambers of Commerce or Trade Association at the premises of which the arbitration proceedings are taking place, to discharge such of the functions and administrative duties of the Registrar as are deemed proper and necessary from time to time, with reference to a particular case or cases.

INITIATION OF ARBITRATION

Rule 15

(i) Any Party wishing to commence arbitration proceedings under these rules (Claimant) shall give a notice of request for arbitration to the Registrar of ICA and to the Respondent,

(ii) The notice of request (application) for arbitration which is sent to the Registrar shall be accompanied by:—

(a) the names and full addresses of the parties to the dispute.

(b) statement of the claim and facts supporting the claim, points at issue and relief or remedies sought with other details of the claimant's case.

(c) original or duly certified copies of the arbitration agreement, any contract or agreement out of or in connection with which the dispute has arisen and such other documents and information relevant or relied upon.

(d) Registration fee of Rs. 2,500/- for claim upto Rs. One Crore and Rs. 5,000/- for claim more than Rs. One Crore.

(e) The Arbitration shall be deemed to have commenced on the day the application for arbitration, registration fee and statement of claim are received in the office of the Council.

Rule 16

If any Court makes an order directing that an arbitration be held under these Rules, in addition to the documents listed in Rules 15, the order of that Court or a copy thereof shall accompany the application for arbitration.

Rule 17

(a) On receipt of an application for arbitration, the Registrar shall have absolute discretion to accept or reject the said application. The Registrar is not bound to give reasons for the exercise of his discretion. Before deciding on the acceptability of an application for arbitration, the Registrar may ask the parties for further information and particulars of their claims,

(b) Similarly, if any information or particulars regarding the arbitration agreement furnished by claimant with the application for arbitration are found to be incorrect or false, at any time subsequently, the Registrar shall have a like power to reject the application for arbitration,

(c) Any Party aggrieved by the decision of the Registrar, in accepting or rejecting an application for arbitration as above, may apply to the Court for suitable directions.

DEFENCE STATEMENT

Rule 18

(a) On receipt of the application together with the claim statement, the Registrar shall send to the other Party (Respondent) a copy of claim statement and attached documents and ask such other party to furnish within thirty days or within any extended date, a defence statement setting out his case accompanied by all documents and information in support of or bearing on the matter.

(b) Any communication sent by the Registrar under Registered Post to the Respondent on the address appearing in the Arbitration Agreement/the contract between the parties, as per the information supplied to the Council, will be deemed to be duly served on the Respondent, if it is delivered to the addressee personally or at his place of business, habitual residence or mailing address last known, even if the Respondent refuses to accept the said communication or if it is returned to the Council by the postal authorities as unclaimed by the said party. The Registrar may proceed further with the arbitration proceedings as per the rules as if such communication had been duly served on the concerned party. The Registrar may in such cases make an additional communication to the Parties by Registered Letter or by other means which may provide a record of attempts to deliver it.

(c) A copy of the defence statement and all appended documents, if any, shall be sent to the Claimant for information.

(d) The communication is deemed to have been received on the day it is so delivered.

COUNTER-CLAIM AND REPLY TO COUNTER-CLAIM

Rule 19

(a) The Respondent may make a counter-claim against the Claimant provided the counter-claim arises under the same transaction as the original claim. He must submit the counter-claim with full details supported by all documents and information as in the case of the claim under Rule 15 within the period laid down for the defence statement to the claim and the Claimant may within twenty-one days of the notification of the counter claim or within such extended time submit a statement in reply to the counter-claim. The arbitral tribunal appointed to adjudicate upon the original claim shall also adjudicate upon the counter-claim and there will be no change in the number of members of arbitral tribunal already constituted on the basis of original claim.

(b) Copy of the reply of the Claimant to the counter-claim and all appended documents, if any, shall be sent to the Respondent for information.

COPIES OF STATEMENTS, ETC.

Rule 20

All statements, replies and other documents and papers submitted by the parties and all appended documents must be supplied in triplicate. Where there is more than one arbitrator or more than one opposing party, the parties shall within the time specified furnish to the Registrar such number of further copies as may be required by the Registrar.

CONSTITUTION OF THE ARBITRAL TRIBUNAL

Rule 21

On receipt of the application for arbitration, the Registrar shall take necessary steps to have the arbitral tribunal constituted for the adjudication of the dispute or difference as provided hereunder.

Rule 22

The number of arbitrators to hear a dispute shall be determined as under:

(a) Where the claim including determination of interest, if any, being claimed upto the date of commencement of arbitration in terms of Rule 15, does not exceed Rs. One crore and where the arbitration agreement does not specify three arbitrators, the reference shall be deemed to be to a sole arbitrator, unless the parties to the dispute agree to refer the dispute to three arbitrators within thirty days from the date of notification of request for arbitration.

(b) Where the claim including determination of interest, if any, being claimed upto the date of commencement of arbitration in terms of Rule 15 exceeds Rs. One crore the dispute will be heard and determined by three arbitrators, unless the parties to the dispute agree to refer the dispute to a sole arbitrator withir thirty days from the date of the notification of the request for arbitration.

(c) Where three arbitrators have to be appointed as per the above sub-rule and any of the parties to the dispute fails to make the necessary deposit towards the cost and expenses of arbitration, instead of three arbitrators, the Registrar may appoint a sole arbitrator, where the claim is upto one crore. Where the claim is for more than Rs, One crore, the Registrar may appoint arbitrator/s on behalf of the Respondent as well the as Presiding Arbitrator.

Rule 23

The appointment of sole arbitrator or three arbitrators shall be made in the following manner:

(a) In case a Sole Arbitrator has to be appointed, the Registrar shall call upon the parties to the dispute to forward the name of an agreed arbitrator from among the Panel of Arbitrators by a notice in writing, sent to them. The said notice shall specify the period within which the nomination shall be made which shall not be more than thirty days from the date of the said notice to the respective parties. If the parties fail to agree on the person to be appointed as sole arbitrator within the time granted by the Registrar, the Registrar in consultation with the Chairman of the Committee and in his absence in consultation with the member of the Governing Body designated by the Chairman, shall appoint the sole arbitrator from among the Panel of Arbitrators. If one of the parties is a national or resident of a country other than India, the sole arbitrator shall, as far as possible, be chosen or appointed by the Registrar from among the nationals of a country other than that of either of the parties. The sole arbitrator so nominated shall constitute the arbitral tribunal to hear the dispute and shall be appointed as such in writing by the Registrar. The Registrar shall give notice to the Parties of the constitution of the arbitral tribunal;

(b) Where the reference is to three arbitrators, the Registrar shall, in the first instance, call upon the parties to nominate one arbitrator each from among the Panel of Arbitrators by a notice in writing, sent to them. The said notice shall specify the period within which the nomination shall be made which shall not be more than thirty days from the date of the said notice to the respective Parties. If a Party to the dispute refuses or neglects to appoint an arbitrator on his behalf within the period specified or if he requests the Registrar to nominate an arbitrator on behalf of that party, the Registrar in consultation, with the Chairman of the Arbitration Committee and in his absence in consultation with the members of the Governing Body designated by the Chairman shall appoint the arbitrator from the Panel of Arbitrators on behalf of that party. On receipt of the nominations from the respective parties or on the appointment as aforesaid by the Registrar, the Registrar shall appoint another person as the Presiding Arbitrator of the arbitral tribunal in consultation with Chairman of the Committee and in his absence in consultation with members of the Governing Body designated by the Chairman, from among the panel of arbitrators to be additional arbitrator to act as Presiding Arbitrator of the arbitral tribunal,

(c) If one of the parties is a national or resident of a country other than India, the additional arbitrator shall, as far as possible, be chosen or appointed from among the nationals of a country other than that of either of the parties. The arbitrators so nominated or appointed shall constitute the arbitral tribunal and shall be appointed as such in writing by the Registrar. The additional arbitrator appointed by the Registrar shall act as Presiding Arbitrator of the arbitral tribunal. The Registrar shall give notice to the parties of the constitution of the arbitral tribunal.

Rule 24

The parties will obtain the consent from the persons nominated by them as arbitrator and intimate the Council accordingly. The Registrar will obtain the consent from person(s) nominated by him. After a person gives his consent for appointment as arbitrator, he will be duly intimated about his appointment to decide the dispute, by a Memo in writing under the hand of the Registrar about the constitution of the arbitral tribunal. The appointment of the arbitrator will take effect from the date of such intimation about the constitution of the arbitral tribunal.

Rule 25

Before accepting his nomination the prospective arbitrator shall disclose any circumstances such as financial or personal interest in the outcome of the award, likely to disqualify him as an impartial arbitrator. Upon receipt of such information, the Registrar shall disclose it to the parties, who if willing to proceed under the circumstances disclosed, shall advise the Registrar accordingly. If either party declines to waive the presumptive disqualification, the prospective arbitrator shall be disqualified from acting as arbitrator and the vacancy so created shall be filled, in accordance with the applicable provision of these Rules.

Rule 26

Any Party shall have the right to challenge the appointment of an arbitrator on receipt of the notice of his appointment for reasons which disqualify the arbitrator. The Challenge of an arbitrator shall be made within 30 days after his appointment has been communicated to the challenging party or within 30 days of his becoming aware of the reasons for which the challenge is made. Copies of the communication of challenge shall be sent to the other Parties and the arbitrators. The Committee shall be the sole judge of the grounds of challenge and its decision shall be final and binding on the Parties.

Rule 27

(a) If any appointed arbitrator resigns or dies or becomes incapable of acting or neglects or fails to act expeditiously, prior to or during the arbitration hearings, or if he fails to make the award within the prescribed time and the Parties do not agree to extend the time for making the award, the Registrar in consultation with the Arbitration Committee may terminate the authority of such an appointed arbitrator and inform him accordingly.

(b) In case of the resignation or death or termination of authority of an appointed arbitrator under Sub-Rule (a) above, a new arbitrator will be appointed in his place by the Registrar in case he had appointed the original arbitrator. Where the appointment was made by the Parties, the Registrar shall call upon the Party who had appointed the arbitrator to nominate another arbitrator in his place, If any Party refuses or neglects to nominate an arbitrator within 15 days of the date of notice requiring him to nominate the arbitrator or within such extended time, the Registrar shall nominate the arbitrator on behalf of that Party from among the Panel of Arbitrators.

(c) The arbitrator(s) appointed as above will be informed about the reconstitution of the arbitral tribunal and the reconstituted arbitral tribunal shall make the award expeditiously within the time prescribed under Rule 63 from the date when the reconstituted arbitral tribunal enters on the reference. The reconstituted arbitral tribunal shall proceed with the arbitration with the liberty to act on the record of evidence and proceedings as then existing or to commence the proceedings *de novo.*

DEPOSITS

Rule 28

The Registrar may require the Parties before passing the case on to the arbitrators under Rule 38, to deposit in advance in one or more instalments such sums of money as he deems necessary to defray expenses of the arbitration including the administrative charges and arbitrator's fee. As a general rule, the deposits shall be called for in equal shares from the Claimant(s) and the Defendant(s). The arbitral tribunal may during the course of the arbitration proceedings or in the arbitration award, require further sums to be deposited by the Parties or anyone of them to meet the expenses of the arbitration. When one of the Parties neglects or refuses to make the deposit, the Registrar or the arbitral tribunal as the case may be, may require such deposit whether in relation to a claim or a counter-claim to be made by the other Party to the dispute (Claimant or Defendant as the case may be). Should the whole or part of the deposit be not made by the Parties or any one of them, the Registrar shall inform the Parties or the Party concerned that the claim or counter-claim, as the case may be, will not be the subject-matter of the reference. The arbitral tribunal shall proceed only in respect of those claims or counter-claims for which the deposits has been duly paid to the Council and otherwise may order the suspension or termination of the arbitral proceedings.

All deposits towards costs and expenses shall be made with the Council and no payment shall be released lo the arbitrators directly by the parties. The deposit made shall be taken into account by the arbitral tribunal in apportioning the cost while making the award. Any deposit made in excess shall be refunded to such of parties as the arbitral tribunal may direct.

The Council shall have a lien for the arbitral award on any unpaid cost of the arbitration.

FEES AND EXPENSES

Rule 29

The arbitral tribunal shall be entitled to allow fees and expenses of witnesses, expenses connected with the selection and carriage of sample and examination of goods, Licensed Measure's Department charges, conveyance, hire, cost of legal or technical advice or proceedings in respect of any matter arising out of the arbitration incurred by the arbitral tribunal, and any other incidental expenses and charges in connection with or arising out of the reference or award as the arbitral tribunal shall, in its absolute discretion, think fit,

Rule 30

The costs of the reference and the award including charges, fees and other expenses shall be in the discretion of the arbitral tribunal, which may direct to and by whom, and in what proportion, such charges, fees and other expenses and any part there of shall be borne and paid, and may tax and settle the amount of costs to be so paid or any part thereof and may award costs to be paid as between solicitor and client. In the event, any administrative fees and expenses are due to the Council, the arbitral tribunal may award them in favour of the Council.

Rule 31

The fees, costs and expenses incidental to the reference and the award shall include the following:

(1) Registration Fee

The Registration fee shall be payable with regard to the amount in dispute in each case as under. The registration fee will not be refunded and becomes the property of the Council.

Rs. 2,500/- upto Rs. One Crore claim

Rs. 5,000/- more than Rs. One Crore claim

(2) Administrative Fee and Arbitrator's Fee

The Administrative fee (of ICA) and Arbitrator's fee (for each arbitrator) will be fixed separately withamount in dispute including determined interest in each case, as under:

Amount in Dispute	Arbitrator's Fee	Administrative Fee
Upto Rs. 5 lac (Rs. 5,00,000)	Rs. 30,000	Rs. 15,000
From Rs. 25 lac one to Rs. 1 crore (Rs. 2,500,001 to Rs. 10,000,000)	**Rs. 60,000** plus **Rs. 1,200** per lac or there of subject to a ceiling of Rs. 1,50,000	**Rs. 15,000** plus **Rs. 750** per lac or part thereof subject to a ceiling of Rs. 30,000.
From Rs. 1 crore one to Rs. 5 crore (Rs. 10,000,001 to Rs. 50,000,000)	**Rs. 1,50,000** plus **Rs. 22,500** per crore or part thereof subject to a ceiling of Rs. 2,40,000	**Rs. 75,000** plus **Rs. 11,250** per crore or part thereof subject to a ceiling of Rs. 1,20,000/-.
From Rs. 5 crore one to Rs. 10 crore (Rs. 50,000,001 to Rs. 100,000,000)	**Rs. 2,40,000** plus **Rs. 15,000** per crore or part thereof subject to a ceiling of Rs. 3,15,000.	**Rs. 1,20,000** plus **Rs. 8,000** per crore or part thereof subject to a ceiling of Rs. 1,60,000.
Over Rs.10 crore (Rs. 100,000,000)	**Rs. 3,15,000** plus **Rs. 12,000** per crore or part thereof.	**Rs. 1,60,000** plus **Rs. 6,000** per crore or part thereof.

(3) In addition to the above the ICA will be entitled to receive a Special Fee of Rs. 2500/- per hearing for providing facilities of hearing rooms, for arbitration hearings and secretarial assistance etc. at the arbitration hearing.

(4) Notwithstanding the provisions in Sub-Rule (2) of this Rule, the Committee/ Chairman of the Committee may prescribe the Arbitrator's fees and the Administrative fees of the Council at a figure higher than those prescribed in the said Sub-Rules, if in the exceptional circumstances of the case this appears to be necessary.

(5) Notwithstanding the provision in Sub-Rule (2) hereinabove, in arbitration cases to which Rule 39 applies, the Arbitrator's fee and the Administrative fee of the ICA will be fixed by computing the fee applicable to larger claim in addition to 60% of the applicable fees of all claims being tried jointly. Provided that the Committee will have power to prescribe the Arbitrator's Fee and Administrative Fee under this Sub-Rule in any other manner, having regard to the nature and facts of the matters under reference.

Rule 32

Other expenses : The arbitrator may be paid an amount of Rs. 750/- towards local conveyance for attending each arbitration hearing in the city of his residence. In respect of joint trial, the hearing will be treated as one irrespective of the number of cases. Any travelling and other expenses incurred by the arbitrator or the Registrar for attending the arbitration hearings in a city other than the place of residence, shall also be reimbursed to him as provided hereinafter. All the above expenses shall form part of the arbitration costs.

Rule 33

(1) An arbitrator who has to travel shall be paid travelling expenses by air or rail (air conditioned wherever available) or car (when neither air nor rail transport is available) at actuals. In addition, he may be paid out-of-pocket expenses at actuals for boarding, lodging and local transport subject to maximum of Rs. 6,000/- per day in metropolitan towns, Rs. 3,000/- in class A cities and Rs. 2,000/- in other cities. An arbitrator who makes his own arrangements for boarding, lodging, local transport etc. may be paid out of pocket expenses at the rate of Rs. 1,000/- per day, without production of vouchers. The limits for stay of the Registry officials will be of those applicable to arbitrators.

(2) The cost to be incurred on payment of expenses referred to in Sub-Rule (1) to an arbitrator nominated by a party will be borne and paid by the party nominating the arbitrator. However, if an appointed arbitrator changes his residence after his nomination by a party, he will not be entitled to reimbursement of any enhanced expenses for attending the arbitration hearing, unless the party nominating him agrees to reimburse the same to him. The expenses payable to the third arbitrator or sole arbitrator appointed by the Council under Rule 23(a) & (b) will be borne and paid by both the parties in equal proportion or in such other manner as may be determined by the Arbitral Tribunal.

Rule 34

Where the arbitration proceedings under an ad hoc arbitration or under the rules of arbitration of any other arbitral organisation or otherwise are administered by the Council wholly or in respect of some matters arising out of such arbitration, the Council may charge an appropriate fee for such administration and other services.

Rule 35

The amount of the claim shall be stated in the application by the party applying for arbitration. If the amount is stated in a currency other than the rupee, it shall be converted into Rupees, at the current official rate of exchange.

Rule 36

Where the sum under dispute is not stated or in arbitration proceedings where the relief claimed is other than a money claim, *viz.*, a declaratory claim, the Registrar and the Arbitral Tribunal under Rule 28, may require such deposits as may be deemed necessary to be paid by such of the parties as may be required subject to later adjustment.

Rule 37

The amount of interest wherever specified will be included in the claim amount for the purpose of calculation of administrative fee. Further, claims and counter-claims referred for arbitration shall be taken into consideration separately for the purpose of calculation of administrative fees under Sub Rule 31(2}.

SUBMISSION OF THE CASE TO THE ARBITRAL TRIBUNAL

Rule 38

The Registrar shall send copies of all papers relating to arbitration such as claim statement, defence statement, counter-claims, reply, statements, or other documents received from the parties to the dispute to the Arbitrator/ Arbitrators constituting the Arbitral Tribunal under Rule 22 with a request to proceed with the arbitration and the arbitral tribunal shall be deemed to have entered on the reference on the day on which applications, defence statement, counter-claims, replies, documents, etc. have been dispatched to the Arbitrator/Arbitrators. Intimation shall be given to the Parties of the day on which the Arbitral Tribunal is deemed to have entered on the reference. If the Claimant does not file all the requisite documents, papers, etc. or does not deposit the appropriate fees as per the Rules after having been given due opportunity for the purpose by the Registrar or the arbitral tribunal, the Registrar or the arbitral tribunal may dismiss/close the case on file for lack of pursual by the Claimant. Similarly, if the Respondent fails to produce any requisite documents, papers including the statement of defence or information or fails to deposit administrative fees, or arbitrators fees etc. after having been given due opportunity for the purpose by the Registrar or the arbitral tribunal, the Registrar or the arbitral tribunal may proceed further with the arbitration proceedings as per the Rules, notwithstanding such failure or refusal by the Respondent.

Rule 39

Where there are two or more applications for arbitration by the Council and the issue involved in the dispute arises out of the same transactions, the Registrar may, if he thinks proper to do so and with the consent of the Parties, fix the hearings of the disputes to be heard jointly or refer the applications to the same Tribunal. The awards, however, shall be given separately in each case.

NOTIFICATIONS AND/OR COMMUNICATIONS FROM THE REGISTRAR

Rule 40

All applications which the parties desire to make to the arbitral tribunal and all notices to be given to the Parties before or during the course of arbitration or otherwise in relation thereto shall be made through and sent by the Registrar who shall communicate the orders and directions of the Arbitral Tribunal thereon to the Parties.

AMENDMENT OF CLAIMS, ETC.

Rule 41

Amendments of the claim, defence statement, counter-claim or reply submitted to the Arbitral Tribunal must be formulated in writing by the Party so desiring. The Arbitral Tribunal will decide whether such amendments should be allowed or not. The Administrative fee and Arbitrator's fee (for each Arbitrator) shall get revised to the extent of increase for such additional claims/counter-claims. The party making such additional claim/counter-claim shall deposit the entire fees payable in respect of such increase of additional claim as set out in the schedule of fees in Rule 31(2).

PLACE OF ARBITRATION

Rule 42

The place or venue of arbitration shall be India. The Arbitration proceedings shall be held at such place or places in India as the Arbitral Tribunal may determine having regard to the convenience of the Arbitrators and the Parties. In a case in which one or both the Parties are from overseas, the Arbitration proceedings may also be held at any place outside India at the discretion of the Arbitral Tribunal.

PROCEEDINGS BEFORE THE ARBITRAL TRIBUNAL CONCILIATION

Rule 43

Optional Conciliation: The parties may opt for conciliation and request the arbitral tribunal before the commencement of the arbitration proceedings, unless they have already agreed otherwise, to settle their dispute through conciliation as per Rules of Conciliation of the Council.

FAST TRACK ARBITRATION

Rule 44

Fast Track Arbitration: The Parties may opt for Fast Track Arbitration and request the arbitral tribunal, before the commencement of the arbitration proceedings, to decide the reference in a fixed time frame of 3 to 6 months or any other time agreed between the Parties, according to the Fast Track Arbitration procedure, as under:

(1) The arbitral tribunal will be authorised to decide the dispute on the written pleadings, documents and written submissions filed by the Parties without any oral hearings.

(2) The arbitral tribunal shall have power to call for any further information/ clarification from the parties in addition to the pleading and documents filed by them.

(3) An oral hearing may be held if both the parties make a joint request or if the Arbitration tribunal considers an oral hearing necessary in any particular case.

(4) If an oral hearing is held, the arbitral tribunal may dispense with any technical formalities and adopt such procedure as it deems appropriate and necessary for economic and expeditious disposal of the case.

Rule 45

At a hearing, a party shall be entitled to appear by counsel, attorney, advocate or a duly authorised adviser or representative or personally. However, where the dispute is purely of a commercial nature, the parties shall have no right to be represented by lawyers except where, having regard to the nature or complexity of the dispute, the arbitral tribunal considers it necessary in the interest of justice that the parties should be allowed to be represented by counsel, attorney or advocate.

Rule 46

The arbitral tribunal may proceed with the reference notwithstanding any failure by a party to comply with any of the directions of the arbitral tribunal and may also proceed with the arbitral proceedings in the absence of any or both the Parties who fail or neglect to attend at the time and place appointed by the arbitral tribunal, inspite of due notice.

Rule 47

The parties shall do all acts necessary to enable the arbitral tribunal to make an award expeditiously and shall not do or cause or allow to be done, any act which will delay the proceedings or prevent the arbitral tribunal from making an award expeditiously, and if any party does cause or allow to be done any such act, that party shall pay such costs as the arbitral tribunal deems reasonable.

Rule 48

The arbitration session will go on as far as possible on a day-to-day basis from 10.30 a.m. to 4.30 p.m once the hearing begins after completion of all the formalities. The arbitral tribunal shall not ordinarily adjourn a hearing at the request of any party, except where the circumstances are beyond the control of the party and the arbitral tribunal is satisfied that reasons and circumstances for the adjournment are justified. While granting an adjournment, the arbitral tribunal may make such orders regarding payment of costs by one or both of the parties, as it deems fit and reasonable.

Rule 49

If the parties have agreed to submit their case to arbitration under these Rules and any party refuses or fails to take part in the arbitration proceedings, the arbitral tribunal may proceed with the arbitration notwithstanding such refusal or absence.

Rule 50

The arbitral tribunal may at its discretion at any time or times before making the final award and at the expense of the parties concerned, consult any person having special knowledge relating to the particular induslry, commodity, produce or branch of trade concerned in the reference or any expert or qualified accountant and may also at the like expenses of the Parties, consult solicitors, counsel or advocates upon any technical question of law, evidence, practice or procedure arising in the course of the reference, If the parties agree, the arbitral tribunal may, at the expense ot the Parties, appoint any expert, accountant, or lawyers to sit with as an assessor and take into account the advice of such assessor.

Rule 51

The Parties to the reference and any witness on their behalf shall, subject to the provisions of any law for the time being in force:

(a) submit to be examined by the arbitral tribunal on oath or affirmation in relation to the matters in dispute.

(b) produce before the arbitral tribunal all books, deeds, papers, accounts, writings and documents in their possession or power respectively which may be required or called for by the arbitral tribunal.

(c) Comply with the requirements of the arbitral tribunal as to the production or selection of samples, and

(d) generally do all other things which, during the pendency of the reference, the arbitral tribunal may require.

Rule 52

The arbitral tribunal will consider, as far as possible, to receive the evidence of witnesses by affidavit. Provided that the witness whose affidavit is admitted in evidence is made available for cross-examination at the request of the opposite Party.

The Arbitral Tribunal may:

(a) administer oath or affirmation to the Parties or witnesses appearing and giving evidence;

(b) make any award conditional or in the alternative;

(c) correct in any award any clerical mistake or error arising from or incidental to any slip or omission;

(d) administer to the Parties to the arbitration such interrogatories as it may consider necessary;

(e) decide all objections to its jurisdiction including any objection regarding the existence or validity of the arbitration clause or the arbitration agreement, without prejudice to the right of the parties to have the matter decided by the Court of law;

(f) decide the law governing:

(i) the contract or the matter in dispute,

(ii) the arbitration agreement, and

(iii) the arbitration procedure

(g) award interest including *pendent lite* interest.

Rule 53

When substantially the same dispute or questions of law and facts are likely to arise in more than one contract or agreement (Chain Contracts), the arbitral tribunal may invite all parties involved to agree to submit to an award in one arbitration between such two or more of the parties as are named for the purpose.

Rule 54

(i) The arbitral tribunal may by the award dismiss the application or claim:

(a) if the Claimant does not prosecute the arbitration proceedings or file the papers within the time granted.

(b) or neglects or refuses to pay the dues or deposits ordered to be paid by the arbitral tribunal or the Registrar,

(ii) The arbitral tribunal may make an *ex parte* award:

(a) if the Respondant neglects or refuses to appear or make his defence or fails to file the papers within the time granted.

(b) or neglects or refuses to pay the dues or deposits ordered to be paid by the arbitral tribunal or the Registrar.

Rule 55

The Registrar shall make necessary arrangements for a stenographic record of evidence whenever such record is required by a Party. The cost of the stenographic record and all transcripts thereof, if any, shall form part of the costs of the reference.

Rule 56

The language of the arbitration proceedings shall be English unless otherwise agreed by the parties. If any documents filed by a Party are in a language other than English, the Party filing such documents shall simultaneously furnish an English translation of the documents. The Registrar may make arrangements for the service of an interpreter at the request of one or more of the parties and costs thereof shall form part of the costs of the reference.

Rule 57

The arbitral tribunal may issue such orders or directions as it may deem necessary for safeguarding, interim custody, preservation, protection, storage, sale or disposal of the whole or part of the subject-matter of the dispute or for its inspection or sampling without prejudice to the rights of the Parties or the final determination of the dispute.

WAIVER OF RULES

Rule 58

Any party who proceeds with the arbitration with the knowledge that any provision or requirement of these rules has not been complied with and who fails to state his objection thereto in writing, shall be deemed to have waived his right to object.

RETURN OF DOCUMENTS

Rule 59

Unless required to be filed in a Court of law, the arbitral tribunal shall have full discretion to retain/or to return all books, documents or papers produced before it and may direct at any time that the books, documents or papers produced before it or any of them may be returned to the parties producing them on such terms and conditions as the arbitral tribunal may impose.

AWARD

Rule 60

No award shall be made by the arbitral tribunal unless the case of the party applying for arbitration has been brought to the notice of the other party and until after the lapse of such specified time within which he has been asked to submit his defence statement under Rule 18.

Rule 61

Whenever there is more than one arbitrator, the award of the majority shall prevail and be taken as the decision of arbitral tribunal. Failing a majority, the Presiding Arbitrator of the arbitral tribunal alone shall make the award.

Rule 62

Should the Parties arrive at a settlement of the dispute by common agreement before the Arbitral Tribunal and the Arbitral Tribunal is satisfied that such agreement is genuine and not to defeat the purpose of any law, the arbitral tribunal shall render an award as per agreement of the Parties. Otherwise, the arbitral tribunal shall make the award on the basis of the documents, evidence, etc. filed before it by the Parties.

Rule 63

The Arbitral Tribunal shall make the award as expeditiously as possible, preferably within six months according to the Guidelines from the date of the reference subject to a maximum limit of two years from the date of commencement of the arbitral proceedings. If necessary, the maximum limit of two years for making the award may be extended by agreement between the parties to the dispute or by the Committee.

Rule 64

The arbitral award shall state the reasons upon which it is based, unless:

(i) the parties have agreed that no reasons are to be given, or

(ii) the award is an arbitral award on agreed terms.

Rule 65

The arbitral award shall state its date and the place of arbitration and the award shall be deemed to have been made at that place.

Rule 66

The arbitral tribunal may make an interim award and may, by an award, determine and order what shall be done by either or any of the Parties, respecting the matters referred.

Rule 67

The arbitrators constituting the arbitral tribunal or the Presiding Arbitrator where Rule 61 is applicable, shall sign the award and the Registrar shall give notice in writing to the Parties of the making and signing thereof and of the amount of fees & charges payable in respect of the arbitration and the award. The arbitrators fee shall be payable by the Council on receipt of the award and requisite deposit made by the parties.

Rule 68

(a) When an award has been made, the Registrar shall furnish a true copy of the award to the parties by registered post provided the arbitration costs have been fully paid to the Council by the parties or by one of them.

(b) The Registrar may require either Party to notify him of the compliance with the award.

(c) The arbitral tribunal and the Registrar of the Council shall assist the parties in complying with any formalities that may be necessary for the enforcement of the award or for other purposes.

(d) The Council may print, publish or otherwise circulate any award made under its rules or under its auspices, in any arbitration journal, magazine, Report, etc. for the purpose of creating arbitration jurisprudence or precedents for the benefit and guidance of future arbitrations.

No party to the arbitration shall have any objection to the publication of awards as above, provided that the names and addresses of any Party to the dispute will be omitted from such publication and its identity duly concealed if so desired by such party.

Rule 69

Additional copies of the award certified true by the Registrar shall be made available to the parlies but to no one else, at all times at request and on payment as fixed by the Registrar.

Rule 70

A party shall in all things abide by and obey the award which shall be binding on the Parties and their respective representatives, notwithstanding the death of any party before or after the making of the award and such death shall not operate as revocation of the submission or reference. To avoid delays and further litigation, the arbitrators/ Registrar shall ask the Parties to agree that the award made by the arbitrators/s shall be final and binding on the Parties and neither Party shall be entitled to challenge it in the Court of law.

FILING OF AWARD

Rule 71

The Arbitral Tribunal shall, at the request of any of the Parties to the proceedings or of any person claiming under a Party, or if so directed by the Court and upon payment of fees and charges due in respect of the arbitration and award and of the costs and charges of filing the award, cause the award or a signed copy thereof together with the deposition or documents which may have been taken and proved before it to be filed before the Court.

Rule 72

A fee of Rs. 1.000/- plus incidental expenses at actuals in addition to the court fees, on the scale for the time being in force is payable by the party requiring the award to be filed.

STAMP DUTIES

Rule 73

Stamp duties are to be paid by the parties in equal share in all cases in accordance with the scale of stamp duties for the time being imposed by law.

COPIES OF PROCEEDINGS

Rule 74

No party is entitled as of right to copies of proceedings before the Arbitral Tribunal. In case the Registrar is required to furnish copies of depositions and/or documents which have been taken or proved before the arbitrator, a charge as demanded by the Registrar shall be paid by the party requiring such copies.

Rule 78

The Registrar shall, upon the written request of a party, furnish to such party at his expense certified facsimile of any documents filed in the arbitration proceedings.

CASES WITHDRAWN

Rule 76

When the party instituting a case desires to withdraw it before an Arbitral Tribunal has been constituted, the Registrar shall return to him any deposits made by him, under Rule 28, after deducting such charges as he might have incurred in connection with the cases. The registration fee, however, shall not be refundable.

Rule 77

If the arbitration is terminated by the act or default of any parties after constitution of the arbitral tribunal and before the award is made, any fees, charges and expenses incurred by the Council shall be paid by the parties in such proportion as per schedule of fees prescribed in the Rules of Arbitration of the Council.

INDEMNITY OF SECRETARIAT AND ARBITRATORS

Rule 78

The Council, the Arbitration Committee and officers of the Council shall not be liable for any act or omission in whatever capacity they may have acted in connection with or in relation to an arbitration under these Rules. Parties are themselves required to contest the proceedings regarding the validity of the arbitration agreement before the court.

Rule 79

No party shall bring or prosecute any suit or proceedings whatever against the arbitral tribunal, or any member thereof, for or in respect of any matter or thing purporting to be done under these Rules nor any suit or proceedings in respect thereof (save for enforcement of the award) against the other party.

AMENDMENT OF RULES

Rule 80

The Governing Body may revise, amend or alter these rules or the schedule of fees and other monies to be charged and paid as and when expedient and necessary.

Annexure

GUIDELINES FOR ARBITRATORS AND THE PARTIES FOR EXPEDITIOUS CONDUCT OF ARBITRATION PROCEEDINGS

1. The arbitrators and the parties to arbitration are expected to follow these guidelines to ensure economic and expeditious disposal of arbitration cases.

For Arbitrators

2. The arbitrators must take up the arbitration expeditiously on receipt of the request from the Council and should also complete the same with reasonable despatch. Serious efforts should be made to settle arbitration cases expeditiously within a period of 6 months where the amount of claim exceeds 1 crore and within a period of 4 months where the amount of claim is less than Rs. 1 crore.
3. When accepting his mandate, the arbitrator shall be able to perform his task with the necessary competence according to his professional qualifications.
4. When giving notice of his acceptance, the arbitrator shall disclose in writing in the printed format as under: any relationship with the parties or their counsel which may affect his independence and impartiality; any personal or economic interest, either direct or indirect, in the subject-matter of the dispute; any prejudice or reservation as to the subject-matter of the dispute which may affect his impartiality; Where necessary due to supervening facts, this Statement shall be repeated in the course of the entire arbitral proceedings until the award is filed.
5. Where facts that should have been disclosed are subsequently discovered, the arbitrator may either withdraw or be challenged or the Indian Council of Arbitration may refuse to appoint him in other arbitral proceedings on this ground.
6. The arbitrator may at all stages suggest the possibility of a settlement to the parties but may not influence their decision by indicating that he has already reached a decision on the dispute.
7. In the course of the arbitral proceedings, the arbitrator shall refrain from all unilateral contact with the parties or their counsel which is not notified to the Indian Council of Arbitration so that the ICA can inform the other parties and arbitrators.
8. The arbitrator shall refrain from giving the parties, either directly or through their counsel, notice of decisions in the evidence taking place or on the merits; notice of these decisions may be given exclusively by the ICA.
9. The arbitrator shall neither request nor accept any direct arrangement on costs or fees with the party which has designated him. The arbitrator is entitled to reimbursement of expenses and a fee as exclusively determined by the ICA according to its Schedule of Fees, which is deemed to be approved by the arbitrator when accepting his mandate.
10. The arbitrator shall encourage a serene and positive development of the arbitral proceedings. In particular, he shall decide on the date and manner of the hearings in such a way as to allow both parties to fully participate therein, in compliance with the principle of equal treatment and adversarial proceedings.
11. The first hearing of the arbitral tribunal should be convened within 15 days of the receipt of the complete reply of the respondent when the arbitral tribunal may issue necessary directions. Admission and denial of the documents may be got done by the Registrar. Issues if any to be framed, may be done at the same or at the next hearing. The arbitrators should hold arbitration hearings continuously on day-to-day basis during office hours.
12. The parties should be asked to furnish a list of their witness, if any, in advance and they should be asked to file affidavits of witness on the date fixed for evidence

preferably within a week of the settlement of issues, Cross-examination of such of the deponent's witnesses whose presence is demanded by the opposite party should be completed at a hearing to be fixed within 15 days.

13. Arguments preferably should be heard within 15 days of the completion of evidence, to be followed by submission of written arguments, if any.
14. Adjournments of duly fixed hearing should not be granted except for unavoidable reasons which should be spelt out in the adjournment order.
15. The Arbitrator should make the award expeditiously after the close of the hearings, preferably within 15 days.
16. The arbitrator who does not comply with the provisions of these guidelines may be replaced by the Committee. Where it is not appropriate to replace the arbitrator in order not to cause delay in the arbitral proceedings, the ICA may also take such action after the conclusion of the arbitral proceedings, by refusing to confirm him in subsequent arbitral proceedings.

For Parties

17. The claimant should file the applications or demand for arbitration to the Registrar of the Council with all the information and papers as per Rules, full statement of claim and copies of documents relied upon, in 3 sets in case of a Sole Arbitrator and in 5 sets in case of three arbitrators
18. The respondent should file his reply to the claim with complete information and documents relied upon, in 3 or 5 sets as above, as early as possible within the prescribed time. Fresh documentation/claims should not be entertained at a later stage of the proceedings unless the arbitral tribunal is satisfied about the reasons for granting such permission.
19. If any party to arbitration, particularly in cases where any arbitrator, advocate or any of the parties has to come from outstation to participate in arbitration proceedings, desires to seek adjournment on any valid ground, it must submit a written request to the Registrar at least 5 working days before more stating the grounds which compel it to request for postponement of the hearing so that the Council is in a position to take necessary steps to inform the Parties, Arbitrators and Advocates regarding postponement of the hearing. Parties seeking adjournment will have to pay cost as may be determined by the arbitral tribunal.
20. Parties should deposit arbitration and administrative fees with the Council (ICA) within the stipulated time, as per the Rules and no extension should be sought in this behalf except for compelling reasons.
21. To avoid excessive costs in arbitration proceedings, the parties are advised to choose their arbitrators from the Panel, as far as possible from the place where the arbitration hearings have to be held. In case, a party still chooses an arbitrator from a place other than the place of hearing, the concerned party will bear the entire extra cost to be incurred on stay, TA/DA etc. of the arbitrator nominated by it.

For Arbitration Committee

22. The Arbitration Committee of the Council may examine the arbitration case file, from time to time to evaluate the progress of the proceedings and to ascertain whether the arbitrators have granted adjournments only on reasonable grounds.
23. The Arbitration Committee shall be sole judge of the grounds of violation of the guidelines and its decision shall be final and binding on the arbitral tribunal as well as the parties.

ICA CODE OF CONDUCT

Preamble/Purpose/ Objective of the Code

The main objective of the Indian Council of Arbitration (ICA) is to promote amicable and quick settlement of industrial and trade disputes through arbitration. Its Rules of Arbitration have recently been revised keeping in mind the provisions of the Arbitration and Conciliation Act, 1996.These Rules comparable to international expectation, provide for a standard expected by the trade for quick and just settlement of their disputes. It maintains a panel of arbitrators consisting of people from all walks of life - Retired Judges, Advocates, Shipping Experts, Chartered Accountants, Chartered Engineers, Businessmen, Foreign Nationals and Executives having specialization in more than 20 fields. The Council has entered into arbitration service agreements with important foreign arbitral institutions in more than 40 countries to administer arbitration under their rules of arbitration if held in India.

The Council also provides arbitration services for settlement of maritime disputes arising out of charter party contracts and it has framed maritime arbitration rules for such disputes.

With a view to make arbitration Efficient, Simple, Just, User Friendly, Speedy, Trustworthy, Equitable, Serviceable and at relatively Low Cost, this Code aims to establish a set of standards for Arbitration Committee, Arbitrators, Parties and Counsel and they are expected to conform to such standards while discharging their respective duties under the auspices of the Indian Council of Arbitration.

This Code has been formulated in the wake of the fundamental principle that only an arbitral institution can guarantee the enforcement of such ethical norms, which is required at various stages of arbitration right from the appointment of an arbitrator till the rendering of an arbitration award. However, ad hoc arbitration can, as a self regulatory measure, adopt this Code of conduct to generate confidence in the institution of arbitration in general. As this Code evolves over the years, it would be a continuing objective to revise and update it from time to time to keep pace with International Standards.

The Code is set out in four parts:

Part I Code of Conduct for the Arbitration Committee.

Part II Code of Conduct for the Arbitrators.

Part III Code of Conduct for the parties

Part IV Code of Conduct for the Counsel.

Part I - Code of Conduct for the Arbitration Committee:

(1.1) The members of the Arbitration Committee cannot be appointed as arbitrators during their term of office.

(1.2) The Arbitration Committee, while appointing arbitrator/s in a case shall have regard to the following criteria:

(a) Nature of the dispute

(b) Availability of the Arbitrators,

(c) Identity of the parties

(d) Independence and impartiality of the arbitrator

(e) Any stipulation made in the Arbitration Agreement of the parties

(f) Past record of the Arbitrator

(1.3) The Arbitration Committee may, in case of non-availability of an arbitrator of required skills and experience, consider a non-panelist for appointment. The above stated criteria shall apply in such case as well.

Part II-Code of Conduct for the Arbitrators:

(2.1) This Code of Conduct shall apply to all Arbitrators on the Panel.

(2.2) Every person nominated as an arbitrator in a case shall make disclosures as specified in the Arbitrator's Declaration of Acceptance of Responsibility and Statement of Independence.

(2.3) The Arbitrators are expected to conduct themselves in a manner consistent with the rules and the policies of the ICA.

(2.4) The Arbitrator/s shall follow the Guidelines for expeditious conduct of Arbitration proceedings, annexed to the ICA Rules of Arbitration.

(2.2) Duties of Arbitrators:

(2.2.1) General:

(2.2.2) To act with honesty, integrity, diligence and dignity to which the profession of dispute resolution is associated: the arbitrator shall—

- Recognize a responsibility to the public, parties and to all other participants in the proceedings;
- not solicit appointment for himself;
- Accept appointment only if he believes that he is adequately competent and qualified, and can conduct the proceedings promptly;
- Refrain himself from entering into any kind of relationship with the parties or the counsel, while serving as an arbitrator, that is likely to affect his impartiality;
- Not accept any gift or substantial hospitality, directly or indirectly from any party to the arbitration.

(2.2.3) To disclose any interest or relationship with the parties: the Arbitrator shall have a continuing duty to—

- Disclose any direct or indirect financial or personal interest in the outcome of the arbitration;
- Disclose any existing or past relationship or interest that might affect his impartiality or might create a reasonable apprehension of bias.

(2.2.4) To be faithful to the relationship of trust and confidentiality inherent in his office: the arbitrator shall—

- Not, at any time, use confidential information acquired during the Arbitration Proceedings to gain personal advantage or advantage for others, or to affect adversely the interest of another;

- Keep all the information relating to the Proceedings confidential unless the parties otherwise agree or any law requires him to disclose.
- Not disclose the decision in advance of the time that is given to the parties.

(2.3) Conduct of Proceedings:

(2.3.1) To conduct the proceedings fairly and diligently: the arbitrator shall—

- Adhere to the concepts of fairness, patience, courteousness and equality;
- Ascertain from the parties about the method of record of proceedings;
- Afford full opportunity to other Arbitrators, if any, in the case to participate in all aspects of the proceedings;
- Act within the scope of authority set out in the arbitration agreement;
- Follow the procedure, if any, set out in the agreement;
- Not discuss the case with any party in the absence of the other party unless otherwise provided for in the agreement or if the circumstances require him to do so.

  Provided that due notice is served and the substance of such meeting is promptly conveyed to the other party.

(2.3.2) To conduct the proceedings as expeditiously as possible: the arbitrator shall—

- Prepare a time table consistent with the rules of ICA, at the first meeting along with the parties fixing the periods for submission of statements, evidence, hearing, award etc;
- Strictly adhere to such time table and no latitude or indulgence on such requirement should be entertained except for bona fide reasons to be recorded.
- Submit a performance statement reflecting the extent of conformity to the timetable, after the completion of every stage of proceedings.
- Not allow any lapse of time in between the steps to be taken inter se as also between conclusion of such steps and the commencement of hearing , and to have, as far as possible, continuous hearings day to day from Monday to Friday wherever required.

(2.4) Others

(2.4.1) **Regarding the fee:** the Arbitrator shall be governed by the pre- arranged fee structure of ICA, and shall not enter into any direct arrangement with the parties.

(2.4.2) **Decision-Making:** the Arbitrator shall decide all matters justly, exercising independent judgment and should not permit outside pressure to effect the decision. He shall also construct the award in a logical order, centered around the following principal elements:

- Brief summary of facts
- Disputes/issues referred to arbitration
- Averment of the parties on each of the issues
- Evidence led, if any.
- Statement, in respect of each point, of the applicable rule of Law and application of said rule to the issue being examined
- Reasons for the award

Part III - Code of Conduct for the parties:

(3.1) The parties shall maintain the dignity of Proceedings and shall act with honesty and diligence.

(3.2) The parties shall follow the Guidelines for Expeditious Conduct of Arbitration Proceedings annexed to the ICA Rules of Arbitration.

(3.3) The parties shall deposit the sum required by the Registrar within the stipulated time period.

(3.4) The parties shall respond in a timely manner to reasonable requests for information from the arbitrator or other party/ies.

(3.5) The parties shall strictly conform to the timetable (set out by the arbitrator in the first meeting) and submit all relevant documents and statements within the time period set out in the timetable.

(3.6) The parties shall not extend any hospitality, directly or indirectly to the Arbitrators.

(3.7) The parties shall pay the fees as agreed and their share of costs as specified in the Award.

(3.8) The parties shall follow all orders/ directions/rulings given by the arbitrator/s during the Proceedings.

(3.9) The parties shall avoid any kind of delaying tactics and shall make maximum/ best/all possible efforts for an expeditious resolution of the dispute.

Part IV - Code of conduct for the counsel:

(4.1) The Counsel shall fully co-operate with the parties and the Arbitrator/s during the Arbitration Proceedings.

(4.2) The Counsel shall be bound by the code of conduct prescribed by the Bar Council of India.

Indian Council of Arbitration

ARBITRATOR'S DECLARATION OF ACCEPTANCE OF RESPONSIBILITY AND STATEMENT OF INDEPENDENCE

Case No.___________

M/s.___________________________________(Claimant)

Vs.

M/s.________________________________(Respondent)

I, the undersigned,

Name________ Surname _____________

hereby declare that I accept to serve as arbitrator under the ICA Rules of Arbitration in the instant case and I do not have financial or personal interest in the outcome of the Award which is likely to disqualify me to act as an impartial or independent arbitrator.

I further declare that I am/ was not personally associated in any capacity with either of the parties. No circumstance exist which give rise to justifiable doubts about my independence or impartiality.

I have not rendered any opinion or advice in the matter in dispute to any party so far.

I shall act as an impartial and independent arbitrator and abide by the ICA Rules of Arbitration for expeditious conduct of the arbitration proceedings including:

(a) Preparing a timetable consistent with the ICA Rules of Arbitration and strictly adhere to it except for bona fide reasons.

(b) Holding Arbitration Proceedings continuously on day-to-day basis during office hours. (Para 11 of ICA Guidelines).

(c) Requiring the parties to file Affidavits of all witnesses and to complete cross-examination of the deponent's witnesses on day-to-day basis (Para 12 of ICA Guidelines).

(d) Requiring the parties to file written arguments after completion of the evidence to be followed by oral submissions (Para 13 of ICA Guidelines).

(e) Not allowing adjournments of duly fixed hearing except for unavoidable and sufficient reasons to be recorded in the adjournment order (Para 14 of ICA Guidelines).

(f) Making the Award within 15 days after the close of the hearings (Para 15 of ICA Guidelines)

DATE: (Signator)

PLACE: ADDRESS:

TELEPHONE................................FAX ......

MOBILE NO................................EMAIL

PAN/GIR..............................

RULES OF CONCILIATION OF THE INDIAN COUNCIL OF ARBITRATION

ICA CONCILIATION CLAUSE

For conciliation of contractual disputes

Parties to a contract who agree to resolve their contractual disputes in accordance with the ICA Rules of Conciliation and to have the ICA act as appointing authority and/or to provide administrative services, may use the following clause:

> "If a dispute arises out of or in connection with this contract, or in respect of any defined legal relationship associated therewith or derived therefrom, the parties agree to seek an amicable settlement of that dispute by conciliation under the ICA Rules of Conciliation.

The authority to appoint the conciliator/conciliators shall be the Indian Council of Arbitration.

The Indian Council of Arbitration will provide administrative services in accordance with the ICA Rules of Conciliation."

Note: Parties may wish to consider adding the following:

(a) The number of conciliator(s) shall be _____

(b) The language of the conciliation proceedings will be ___________

(c) Specific qualifications of the conciliator(s) including, but not limited to, language, nationality, technical qualifications and experience.

PRELIMINARY

1. Short title and scope.—(1) These rules may be called the ICA Rules of Conciliation.

(2) These rules shall apply where the parties have agreed in writing, that —

(a) a dispute which has arisen, or

(b) a dispute which may arise,

between them in respect of a defined legal relationship, whether contractual or not, should be resolved by amicable settlement under the ICA Rules of Conciliation.

(3) These rules shall not apply to disputes, which by virtue of any law for the time being in force, may not be submitted to conciliation.

2. Definitions.—In these rules, unless the context otherwise requires,—

(a) "Arbitration Committee" means the Arbitration Committee of the ICA;

(b) "Chairman" means the Chairman of the ICA Arbitration Committee;

(c) "Rules of Conciliation" or "rules" means the ICA Rules of Conciliation;

(d) "Governing Body" means the Governing Body of the ICA;

(e) "ICA" means the Indian Council of Arbitration, New Delhi;

(f) "Panel of conciliators" means the panel of persons approved by the Arbitration Committee to act as conciliators;

(g) "Party" means a party to the agreement referred to in rule 1(2);

(h) "Schedule" means the Schedule to these rules;

PART A

PROCEDURES FOR CONCILIATION PROCEEDINGS IN THE ICA

3. Commencement of conciliation proceedings.—(1) The party initiating conciliation shall send to the other party a written invitation to conciliate under these rules, briefly identifying the subject of the dispute.

(2) Conciliation proceedings shall commence when the other party accepts in writing the invitation to conciliate.

(3) If the other party rejects the invitation, there will be no conciliation proceedings.

(4) If the party initiating conciliation does not receive a reply within thirty days from the date on which he sends the invitation, or within such other period of time as specified in the invitation, he may elect to treat this as a rejection of the invitation to conciliate and inform the other party accordingly.

4. Number and appointment of conciliators.—(1) There shall be one conciliator unless the parties have agreed that there shall be two or three conciliators.

(2) The parties may agree to enlist the assistance of the ICA in connection with the appointment of conciliator, and in particular:—

(a) a party may request the ICA to recommend the names of suitable individuals to act as conciliator; or

(b) where the agreement between the parties provides for the appointment of conciliator by the ICA, a party may request the ICA in writing to appoint a conciliator.

(3) Where a request in pursuance of clause (a) or clause (b) of sub-rule (2) is made to the ICA, the party making the request shall send to the ICA.—

(a) a copy of the invitation to conciliate;

(b) a copy of the acceptance by the other party;

(c) a copy of the agreement, if any, between the parties providing for an amicable settlement of dispute between them by conciliation;

(d) any qualifications required of the conciliator;

(e) any additional information, if required, by the ICA.

(4) In recommending or appointing an individual to act as conciliator, the ICA will follow the procedure specified in rule 24 and will have regard to.—

(a) any qualifications required of the conciliator by the agreement of the parties;

(b) such considerations as are likely to secure the appointment of an independent and impartial conciliator; and

(c) where the parties are of different nationalities, the advisability of appointing a conciliator of a nationality other than the nationalities of the parties.

(5) A successor conciliator will be appointed in the manner in which his predecessor had been appointed.

5. Submission of statements to conciliator.—(1) The conciliator may, upon his appointment, request each party to submit to him and the ICA a brief statement in writing describing the general nature of the dispute, the points at issue and the amount, if any, of the claim. Each party shall send a copy of such statement to the other party.

(2) The conciliator may request each party to submit to him and the ICA a further statement in writing of his position and the facts and grounds in support thereof, supplemented by any documents and other evidence that such party deems appropriate. The party shall send a copy of such statement, documents and other evidence to the other party.

(3) At any stage of the conciliation proceedings, the conciliator may request a party to submit to him and the ICA such additional information as he deems appropriate.

6. Representation and assistance.—Each party shall advise, in writing, the other party and the conciliator of—

(a) the name and address of any person who will represent or assist him, and

(b) the capacity in which that person will represent.

7. Role of conciliator.—(1) The conciliator shall assist the parties in an independent and impartial manner in their attempt to reach an amicable settlement of the dispute.

(2) The conciliator shall be guided by principles of objectivity, fairness and justice, giving consideration to, among other things, the rights and obligations of the parties, the usages of the trade concerned and the circumstances surrounding the dispute, including any previous business practices between the parties.

(3) The conciliator may conduct the conciliation proceedings in such manner as he considers appropriate, taking into account the circumstances of the case, the wishes the parties may express, including any request by a party that the conciliator hear oral statements, and the need for a speedy settlement of the dispute.

(4) The conciliator may, at any stage of the conciliation proceedings, make proposals for a settlement of the dispute. Such proposals need not be in writing and need not be accompanied by a statement of the reasons therefor.

8. Administrative services.—The ICA will arrange the administrative services specified in Part B if.—

(a) the parties designate the ICA for arranging such services in the agreement to conciliate;

(b) the parties, or the conciliator with the consent of the parties, request the ICA to arrange such services.

9. Communication between conciliator and parties.—(1) The conciliator may invite the parties to meet him or may communicate with them orally or in writing. He may meet or communicate with the parties together or with each of them separately.

(2) Unless the parties have agreed upon the place where meetings with the conciliator are to be held, such place shall be determined by the conciliator, taking into consideration the circumstances of the conciliation proceedings:

Provided that where administrative assistance by the ICA is sought under Rule 8, the place where meetings with conciliator are to be held shall be determined in consultation with the ICA.

10. Disclosure of information.—When the conciliator receives factual information concerning the dispute from a party, he shall disclose the substance of that information to the other party in order that the other party may have the opportunity to present any explanation which he considers appropriate;

Provided that when a party gives any information to the conciliator subject to a specific condition that it be kept confidential, the conciliator shall not disclose that information to the other party.

11. Co-operation of parties with conciliator.—The parties shall in good faith co-operate with the conciliator and, in particular, shall endeavour to comply with requests by the conciliator to submit written materials, provide evidence and attend meetings.

12. Suggestions by parties for settlement of dispute.—Each party may, on his own initiative or at the invitation of the conciliator, submit to the conciliator suggestions for the settlement of the dispute.

13. Settlement agreement.—(1) When it appears to the conciliator that there exist elements of a settlement which may be acceptable to the parties, he shall formulate the terms of a possible settlement and submit them to the parties for their observations. After receiving the observations of the parties, the conciliator may reformulate the terms of a possible settlement in the light of such observations.

(2) If the parties reach agreement on a settlement of the dispute, they may draw up and sign a written settlement agreement. If requested by the parties, the conciliator may draw up, or assist the parties in drawing up, the settlement agreement.

(3) When the parties sign the settlement agreement, it shall be final and binding on the parties and persons claiming under them respectively.

(4) The conciliator shall authenticate the settlement agreement and furnish a copy thereof to each of the parties.

14. Confidentiality.—The conciliator and the parties shall keep confidential all matters relating to the conciliation proceedings. Confidentiality shall extend also to the settlement agreement, except where its disclosure is necessary for purposes of its implementation and enforcement.

15. Termination of conciliation proceedings.—(1) The conciliation proceedings shall be terminated—

(a) by the signing of the settlement agreement by the parties on the date of agreement; or

(b) by a written declaration of the conciliator, after consultation with the parties, to the effect that further efforts at conciliation are no longer justified, on the date of the declaration; or

(c) by a written declaration of the parties addressed to the conciliator to the effect that the conciliation proceedings are terminated, on the date of the declaration; or

(d) by a written declaration of a party to the other party and the conciliator, if appointed, to the effect that the conciliation proceedings are terminated, on the date of the declaration.

(2) The conciliator shall, upon termination of the conciliation proceedings, send an intimation thereof in writing to the ICA.

16. Resort to arbitral or judicial proceedings.—The parties shall not initiate, during the conciliation proceedings, any arbitral or judicial proceedings in respect of a dispute that is the subject-matter of the conciliation proceedings except that a party may initiate arbitral or judicial proceedings where, in his opinion, such proceedings are necessary for preserving his rights.

17. Costs.—(1) Upon termination of the conciliation proceedings, the conciliator shall fix the costs of the conciliation and give written notice thereof to the parties. The fee of the conciliator and any assistance provided pursuant to Rule 4(2)(b) and fee and charges for any administrative assistance pursuant to Rule 9 shall be fixed by the conciliator in accordance with the Schedule:

Provided that the ICA may, on request from the conciliator, fix the fee of the conciliator at a figure higher than that set out in the Schedule if, in exceptional circumstances of the case, this appears to be necessary.

(2) For the purpose of sub-rule (1), "costs" means costs relating to—

(a) the fee and expenses of the conciliator and witnesses requested by the conciliator with the consent of the parties;

(b) any expert advice requested by the conciliator with the consent of the parties;

(c) any assistance provided pursuant to Rule 4(2) and Rule 8;

(d) any other expenses incurred in connection with the conciliation proceedings and the settlement agreement.

(3) Where more than one conciliator is appointed, each conciliator shall be paid separately the fee set out in the Schedule.

(4) The costs shall be borne equally by the parties unless the settlement agreement provides for a different apportionment. All other expenses incurred by a party shall be borne by that party.

18. Deposits.—(1) The conciliator will, upon his appointment, in consultation with the ICA direct each party to deposit with the ICA an equal amount as an advance for the costs referred to in Rule 17(2) which he expects will be incurred.

(2) During the course of the conciliation proceedings, the conciliator may, in consultation with the ICA, direct supplementary deposits with the ICA in an equal amount from each party for the costs referred to in sub-rule (I).

(3) If the required deposits under sub-rules (1) and (2) are not made in full within thirty days, the conciliator will inform the parties in order that one or the other party may make the required deposit and if the required deposit is not made, the conciliator may suspend the proceedings, or may make a written declaration of termination of the proceedings to the parties, effective on the date of that declaration.

(4) Subject to any settlement agreement, upon termination of the conciliation proceedings, the ICA shall apply the deposits to the costs of the proceedings, render an accounting to the parties of the deposits received and applied and return any unexpended balance, to the parties.

19. Role of conciliator in other proceedings.—Unless otherwise agreed by the parties.—

(a) the conciliator shall not act as an arbitrator or as a representative or counsel of a party in any arbitral or judicial proceeding in respect of a dispute that is the subject-matter of the conciliation proceedings;

(b) the conciliator shall not be presented by the parties as a witness in any arbitral or judicial proceedings.

20. Admissibility of evidence in other proceedings.—The parties shall not rely on or introduce as evidence in arbitral or judicial proceedings, whether or not such proceedings relate to the dispute that is the subject-matter of the conciliation proceedings.—

(a) views expressed or suggestions made by the other party in respect of a possible settlement of the dispute;

(b) admissions made by the other party in the course of conciliation proceedings;

(c) proposals made by the conciliator;

(d) the fact that the other party had indicated his willingness to accept a proposal for settlement made by the conciliator.

21. Interpretation and application.—If any question arises as to the interpretation or application of these rules or any procedural matters thereunder, the decision of the Arbitration Committee shall be final and binding on the parties.

PART B

SERVICES FOR PROCEDURES UNDER THE RULES OF CONCILIATION

22. To facilitate the conduct of conciliation proceedings that the parties have agreed to conduct under the Rules of Conciliation, the ICA will—

(a) perform the functions of the appointing authority whenever-

(i) the ICA has been so designated by the parties in conciliation clause of their contract or in a separate agreement, or

(ii) the parties have agreed to submit a dispute to the ICA under the Rules of Conciliation without specifically designating it as the appointing authority; and

(b) provide the administrative services herein specified when required by the agreement, or when requested by all the parties, or by the conciliator with the consent of the parties.

23. Services as the registry.—(1) On receiving a request in pursuance of rule 4(2}(a) or 4(2)(b), the ICA will register the request and intimate in writing to the parties the registration number of the case which shall be quoted by the party while making any subsequent communication to the ICA.

(2) The ICA will scrutinise every request and the documents, make necessary entries in the register and prepare a file of the case.

24. Services as recommending or appointing authority.—(1) On receipt of a request in pursuance of Rule 4(2)(a), the ICA will communicate to the party making the request a list containing the names, addresses, nationalities and a description of qualifications and experience of at least three individuals from the panel of conciliators.

(2) On receipt of a request to appoint a conciliator in pursuance of Rule 4(2)(b), the ICA will follow the following procedure—

(i) the ICA will communicate to each party a list containing the names, addresses nationalities and a description of qualifications and experience of at least three individuals from the panel of conciliators;

(ii) within thirty days following the receipt of the list, a party may delete any name to which he objects and after renumbering the names in the order of his preference, return the list to the ICA.

(iii) on receipt of the list returned by the parties, the ICA will appoint the conciliator from the list taking into account the order of preference indicated by the parties;

(iv) if for any reason the appointment cannot be made according to the procedure specified in clauses (i) to (iii), the ICA may, unless the parties recommend the name of the conciliator to be appointed by the ICA, appoint the conciliator from the panel of conciliators.

(3) In recommending or appointing a conciliator the ICA will have regard to the matters referred to in Rule 4(4) and will carefully consider the nature of the dispute in order to include in the list, persons having appropriate professional or business experience, language ability and nationality.

(4) All appointments on behalf of the ICA will be made by the Arbitration Committee.

25. Administrative services.—(1) The ICA may provide the administrative services specified in this Part—

(a) upon the request of the parties;

(b) upon the request of the conciliator with the consent of the parties; or

(c) if the parties designate the ICA for providing such services.

(2) All oral or written communications from a party to the conciliator, except at meetings, may be directed to the ICA which will transmit them to the conciliator and, where appropriate, to the other party.

(3) Agreement by the parties that the ICA will provide the administrative services, constitutes consent by the parties that, for purposes of compliance with any time requirements of the rules, any written communications shall be deemed to have been received by the addressee when received by the ICA. When transmitting communications to a party, the ICA will do so to the addresses provided by each of them to the ICA for this purpose.

(4) The ICA will also assist in the exchange of information and of settlement proposals.

(5) The ICA will assist the conciliator to establish the dale, time and place of meetings and will give the parties advance notice of such meetings.

(6) The ICA will provide a meeting room for the conciliator and the parties or their counsel in the offices of the ICA on the charges set out in the Schedule. However, where these facilities are provided in any place other than the offices of the ICA, the charges will be determined by the ICA and billed separately in each case.

(7) Upon request, the ICA will make arrangements for reporter transcripts of meetings or hearings.

(8) Upon request, the ICA will make arrangements for the services of interpreters or translators. The cost of interpretation or translation will be determined by the ICA and billed separately and is not included in the fee for administrative services.

(9) (a) The ICA will hold advance deposits to be made towards the costs of the conciliation proceedings.

(b) On termination of the conciliation proceedings, the ICA will apply the proceeds of the advance deposits towards any of its unpaid administrative fee and charges and the costs of the conciliation proceedings and will render an accounting to the parties of the deposits received and applied and return any unexpended balance to the parties.

(10) (a) Upon request, the ICA will provide other appropriate administrative services the cost of which will be determined by the ICA and billed separately and are not included in the fee for administrative services,

(b) The kinds of services which can be provided are as follows:—

(i) long distance and local telephone access and telex and telecopier facilities;

(ii) photocopying and other usual office services.

(11) (a) The ICA may require the party requesting one or more of the services referred to in sub-rules (6), (7), (8) or (10) to deposit an amount specified by it as advance towards the cost of such services;

(b) The ICA may also require the parties to make supplementary deposits towards the costs of the services referred to in clause (a);

(c) If the required deposit under clause (a) or clause (b) is not made in full within the time specified by the ICA, the ICA may not provide the services requested for.

26. Fees and Expenses

A. Registration Fee

A registration fee of Rs. 5000/- shall be paid along with the application for reference to conciliation. The registration fee will not be refunded and will become the property of the Council.

B. Administrative Fee

(1) The fee of the ICA for appointing the conciliator and for providing administrative services, other than those specified in sub-rules (6), (7), (8) and (10) of Rule 25, is based upon the amount in dispute as disclosed when the statement of dispute is submitted to the ICA in pursuance of sub-rule (1) of Rule 5.

(2) Where the ICA is requested to act as appointing authority under Rule 4(2), the requesting party shall pay the ICA a sum of Rs. 2000/- as a non-refundable fee at the time of the request.

(3) The Rules of Conciliation provide that the costs of conciliation include the costs of the administrative and conciliators' fees. The Schedule of fee is given as under. These costs are borne equally by the parties unless the settlement agreement provides for a different apportionment Rule (17(4)).

Schedule of Fees

The Administrative fee (of ICA) and Conciliator's fee (for each conciliator), will be fixed separately with regard to the amount in dispute including determined interest in each case, as under:

Amount in Dispute	Arbitrator's Fee	Administrative Fee
Upto Rs. 5 lac (Rs.500,000)	Rs .30,000	Rs. 15,000
From Rs. 5 lac one to Rs. 25 lac (Rs. 500,001 to 2,500,000)	**Rs. 30,000** plus **Rs. 1,500** per lac or part thereof subject to a ceiling of Rs.60,000	**Rs. 15,000** plus **Rs. 750** per lac or part thereof subject to a ceiling of Rs. 30,000.
From Rs. 25 lac one to Rs. 1 crore (Rs. 2,500,001 to Rs. 10,000,000)	**Rs. 60,000** plus **Rs. 1,200** per lac or part thereof subject to a ceiling of Rs.1,50,000	**Rs. 30,000** plus **Rs. 600** per lac or part thereof subject to a ceiling of Rs. 75,000.
From Rs. 1 crore one to Rs. 5 crore	**Rs. 1,50,000** plus **Rs. 22,500** per crore	**Rs. 75,000** plus **Rs. 11,250** per crore or
Over Rs.10 crore (Rs. 100,000,000)	**Rs. 3,15,000** plus **Rs. 12,000** per crore or part thereof.	**Rs. 1,60,000** plus **Rs. 6,000** per crore or part thereof.
(Rs. 10,000,001 to Rs. 50,000,000)	or part thereof subject to a ceiling of Rs. 2,40,000	part thereof subject to a ceiling of Rs. 1,20,000.
From Rs. 5 crore one to Rs. 10 crore (Rs. 50,000,001 to Rs. 100,000,000)	**Rs. 2,40,000** plus **Rs. 15,000** per crore or part thereof subject to a ceiling of Rs. 3,15,000	**Rs. 1,20,000** plus **Rs. 8,000** per crore or part thereof subject to a ceiling of Rs. 1,60,000.
Over Rs. 10 crore (Rs. 100,000,000)	**Rs. 3,15,000** plus **Rs. 12,000** per crore or part thereof	**Rs. 1,60,000** plus **Rs. 6,000** per crore or part thereof.

In addition to the above, the ICA will be entitled to receive a Special Fee of Rs. 2500/ per hearing for providing facilities of hearing rooms and secretarial assistance etc. at the conciliation hearings.

(4) Notwithstanding the provisions in Sub-Rule (1) of this Rule, the Arbitration Committee/Chairman of the Arbitration Committee may prescribe the Conciliator's fees and the Administrative fees of the Council at a figure higher than those prescribed in the said Sub-Rules, if in the exceptional circumstances of the case this appears to be necessary.

Other expenses : The conciliator may be paid an amount of Rs. 750/- towards local conveyance for attending each conciliation hearing in the city of his residence. Any travelling and other expenses incurred by the conciliator or the Registrar for attending the conciliation hearings in a city other than the place of residence, shall also be reimbursed to him as provided hereinafter. All the above expenses shall form part of the conciliation costs.

A conciliator who has to travel shall be paid travelling expenses by air or rail (air conditioned wherever available) or car (when neither air nor rail transport is available) at actuals. In addition, he may be paid out-of-pocket expenses at actuals for boarding, lodging and local transport subject to maximum of Rs. 6,000/- per day in metropolitan towns, Rs. 3,000/- in class A cities and Rs. 2,000/- in other cities. A conciliator who makes his own arrangements for boarding, lodging, local transport etc, may be paid out of pocket expenses at the rate of Rs.1000/- per day, without production of vouchers. The limits for stay of the ICA officials will be of those applicable to conciliators.

Amendment of Rules

The Governing Body of the ICA may revise, amend or alter these Rules or the Schedule of Fees and other monies to be charged and paid as and when they think necessary.

NEPAL

NEPAL COUNCIL OF ARBITRATION RULES FOR DOMESTIC COMMERCIAL ARBITRATION PROCEEDINGS

GENERAL

1. Interpretation

1. In these Rules, terms and phrases have the same meanings as defined in or contemplated by the Nepal Arbitration Act.

In these Rules, "NEPCA" means the Nepal Council of Arbitration and "Act" means the Nepal Arbitration Act.

2. In these Rules, words signifying a male person include a female person and a corporation, words in the singular include the plural and words in the plural include the singular.

3. In these Rules, the required administrative expenses is to be ascertained from the schedule of administrative expenses established from time to time by NEPCA.

2. Time

In these Rules, where the time for doing an act falls or expires on a holiday, the time is extended to the next day following the holiday.

In these Rules, in the calculation of time, the first day shall be excluded and the last day included.

In these Rules, where the time for doing an act falls or expires on a day when the office is not open during regular business hours, the time is extended to the next day that the office is open.

3. Application

Where parties to a commercial agreement have agreed to submit present or future disputes arising out of such agreement to arbitration under the Rules of the Nepal Council of Arbitration those disputes shall be settled in accordance with these Rules in force at the time of commencement of the Arbitration.

4. Variation of Rules

The parties to a dispute to which these Rules apply may modify, vary or amend these Rules by agreement.

5. Communications Between Parties

Parties to an arbitration under these Rules agree that any written communications required or permitted under these Rules may be given by delivering the communication by mailing it by registered mail to a party's business address or mailing address. The communication is deemed to have been received on that date its receipt has been acknowledged or the date of the record of its attempted delivery. Except for the purpose of settling administrative details of the arbitration, there shall be no oral communication with respect to the substance of the dispute between the parties and the arbitrator other than at oral hearing or at a meeting in the presence of both parties or their representative. A copy of all written communications from a party to an arbitrator or to NEPCA shall be delivered by registered mail or by personal delivery to the other party at the time as is given to the arbitrator or NEPCA.

6. Waiver of Right to Object

A party who knows that any provision of, or requirement under, these Rules has not been complied with and yet proceeds with the arbitration without stating his objection shall be deemed to have waived his right to object.

INITIATION OF ARBITRATION

7. Initiation of Arbitration

1. Arbitration under Agreement – An arbitration under an arbitration clause or agreement may be commenced by the claimant giving a written notice of request to arbitrate to the respondent and to NEPCA. The notice of request to arbitrate shall contain:—

(a) the names and business or mailing addresses of the parties to the dispute, setting forth the nature of the dispute,

(b) a request that the described dispute be referred to arbitration,

(c) an estimate of the value of claim, if any,

(d) the remedy sought,

(e) the number and names of arbitrators agreed upon, if any,

(f) the required qualifications of the arbitrators, if any, and

(h) the required administrative Expenses.

Appended to the notice of request to arbitrate shall be a copy of the arbitration clause or agreement relied upon and a copy of the contract, if any, in relation to which the dispute has arisen.

2. Arbitration by Submission – Parties to a dispute may submit the same to arbitration by filing a notice of submission to arbitration with NEPCA. The notice of submission shall contain:—

(a) The names and business or mailing addresses of the parties or the parties to the dispute.

(b) A statement of the matter in dispute.

(c) An estimate of the value of the dispute or the amount of claim, if any.

(d) The remedy sought.

(e) The number and names of arbitrators agreed upon, if any.

(f) The required qualifications of the arbitrators, if any.

(g) The required administrative expenses.

The notice of submission shall be signed by the parties to the dispute. Appended to the notice of submission shall be a copy of the contract, if any, in relation to which the dispute has arisen.

8. NEPCA Review

Before an arbitrator has been appointed in an arbitration, NEPCA may review the documents initiating the arbitration and advise the parties whether or not it consider the matter in dispute to be arbitrable, but the parties are not bound by that advice.

9. Commencement Date

The arbitration is deemed to have commenced on the date the notice of request to arbitrate has been given to the respondent and or the notice of submission to arbitration has been filed with NEPCA.

APPOINTMENT OF ARBITRATOR

10. Number of Arbitrators

If the arbitration agreement does not specify the number of arbitrators, the dispute shall be heard and determined by a single arbitrator.

11. Appointment of Arbitrator

1. If the parties cannot agree on the single arbitrator within 30 days after the arbitration has commenced, a party may request NEPCA to appoint the single arbitrator.

2. Where the parties have agreed to appoint more than one arbitrator and a party or any other person fails to make a required appointment within the time agreed upon between the parties or, if no time is specified, within 30 days after the arbitration has commenced, a party may request NEPCA to make the required appointment.

3. Where the parties have agreed to appoint a Chairman/Umpire and if the Chairman/Umpire could not be appointed by following the procedure prescribed in the agreement within 15 days from the date of the appointment of last arbitrator, if no such procedure is fixed in the agreement, NEPCA shall appoint such Chairman/Umpire at the request of a party to the dispute.

4. Both parties may, at any time, request NEPCA to appoint an arbitrator.

12. Request to NEPCA

When a request is made to NEPCA to make an appointment, NEPCA shall be provided with a written list of the required qualifications of the arbitrators, if any, any additional information, NEPCA considers necessary to fulfill its function, and the required administrative expenses.

13. Description of Arbitrator

Where a person is proposed for his appointment as arbitrator, his full name and address and a description of his past and present professional positions, qualification and arbitration experience shall be given by the proposer to the other party and if NEPCA is the proposer, to all parties.

14. Method of Appointment by NEPCA

1. NEPCA shall appoint an arbitrator from its panel of arbitrators as promptly as possible after receiving a request. In making an appointment, NEPCA shall use the following procedure:

(a) It shall communicate to both parties an identical list containing at least 3 names.

(b) Within a period of 7 days following receipt of the list referred to in paragraph (a), each party shall return the list to NEPCA after having deleted the names if any to which he objects and number the remaining names on the list in order of his preference.

(c) After the expiration of 7 days period referred to in paragraph (b), NEPCA shall appoint the arbitrator from among the names approved on the lists returned to it and in accordance with order of preference indicated by the parties.

(d) If for any reason the appointment cannot be made according to this procedure, NEPCA may, in its sole discretion, appoint the arbitrator.

2. NEPCA may appoint an arbitrator at its discretion while making such appointment pursuant to clause 11.2.

3. NEPCA shall follow the procedure prescribed under sub-clause (1) while appointment a Chairman/Umpire of a arbitration tribunal.

4. In appointing an arbitrator, NEPCA will have due regard to the qualifications required of the arbitrator, the nature of the contract, the nature and circumstances of the dispute and any other considerations likely to secure the appointment of a qualified, independent and impartial arbitrator.

15. Substitution

1. If an arbitrator is unwilling or refuses to act or not entering into references forthwith, or is incapable of acting or resigns or is removed from office by order of the court or dies during the course of arbitral proceedings, NEPCA may, on submission of satisfactory evidence, declare the office vacant. A substitute arbitrator shall be appointed according to the provisions of these Rules that were applicable to the appointment of the arbitrator being replaced.

2. Where an arbitrator in sole arbitration or Umpire or Chairman is repalced, any hearings previously held shall be repeated. Where any other arbitrator is replaced, any hearings previously held may be repeated at the discretion of the arbitrators.

16. Independence and Impartiality of Arbitrator

1. An arbitrator shall be and remain at all times wholly independent and impartial and shall not act as an advocate for any party to the arbitration.

2. Every person shall before accepting an appointment as arbitrator, sign a statement declaring that there are no circumstances likely to give rise to justifiable doubts as to his independence or impartiality and that he will disclose any such circumstances to the parties if they should arise after that time and before the arbitration is concluded. A copy of the statement shall be filed with NEPCA if the person is appointed arbitrator.

17. Challenges

1. An arbitrator may be challenged if circumstances exist that give rise to justifiable doubts as to his independence or impartiality or if he does not possess the qualifications agreed to by the parties.

2. A party may challenge the arbitrator appointed by him only for reasons of which he becomes aware after the appointment has been made.

3. A party who intends to challenge an arbitrator shall, within 7 days after becoming aware of the appointment of a single arbitrator or of the constitution of the arbitral tribunal or after becoming aware of any circumstances mentioned in clause 16, send a written statement of the challenge and the reasons for the challenge to the single arbitrator or the arbitral tribunal.

4. If the arbitrator challenged withdraws from his office or the other party agrees to the challenge, the mandate of the arbitrator terminates.

5. In case of an arbitration with an arbitral tribunal, if the arbitrator challenged does not withdraw from his office nor does the other party agree to the challenge, the arbitral tribunal including the challenged arbitrator shall decide on the challenge.

6. If a challenge to an arbitrator in an arbitral tribunal is not successful, the challenging party may, on paying the required administrative expenses, request NEPCA, within 7 days having received notice of the decision of the challenge, to decide on the challenge.

7. If a single arbitrator or Chairman/Umpire who is challenged does not withdraw from office nor does the other party agree to the challenge, the challenging party may, on paying the required administrative expenses, request NEPCA, within 7 days after having advised the single arbitrator of the challenge, to decide on the challenge.

8. NEPCA shall decide on a challenge as soon as possible after receiving the request.

9. While a request to NEPCA is pending, the arbitrator, including the challenged arbitrator, may continue the arbitral proceedings and make an arbitral award.

CONDUCT OF THE PROCEEDING

18. Representation

The parties may be represented or assisted by any person during an arbitration. Where a party intends to be represented or assisted by a lawyer, that party shall, in writing, advise the other party of the lawyer's name and the capacity in which he is acting at least 5 days before any scheduled oral hearing or meeting.

19. Place of Arbitration

The place of arbitration shall be Kathmandu, Nepal, unless otherwise decided by the parties but the arbitrator may meet at any other place if considered necessary for consulation, to hear witnesses, experts or the parties or for inspection of documents, goods or other property.

20. Preliminary Hearing

1. At the request of any party or at the discretion of the arbitrator or the NEPCA, a preliminary hearing with the parties and/or their representatives and the arbitrator may be scheduled by the arbitrator within 15 days from the date of arbitrator's appointment or the constitution of arbitration tribunal to specify the issue to be resolved, to stipulate uncontested facts and to consider any other matters that will expedite the arbitration proceedings consistent with the expedited nature of arbitration, the arbitrator may, at the preliminary hearing, establish—

(i) the extent of and schedule for the production of relevant documents and other information,

(ii) the identification of any witness to be called, and

(iii) a schedule for further hearings to resolve the dispute.

2. The arbitrator shall record any agreements or consensus reached at the pre-arbitration meeting and shall, within 7 days of that meeting, send a copy of that document to each of the parties and file a copy with NEPCA.

21. Conduct of Arbitration

Subject to these Rules, the arbitrator may conduct the arbitration in the manner he considers appropriate but each party shall be treated fairly and shall be given full opportunity to present his case.

22. Exchange of Statements

1. Within 15 days after the pre-arbitration meeting or within 30 days after the arbitrator has been appointed or the arbitral tribunal has been constituted, the claimant shall send a written statement to the respondent, the arbitrator and to NEPCA outlining the facts supporting his claim, the points at issue and the relief or remedy sought.

2. Within 15 days after the respondent receives the claimant's statement, the respondent shall send a written statement outlining his defence to the particulars contained in the statements of claim and a written statement of his counterclaim, if any, to the claimant, the arbitrator and NEPCA. The respondent, by counterclaim, shall send a written statement to the claimant by counterclaim, the arbitrator and NEPCA outlining his defence to the counterclaim within 15 days after he receives the counterclaim.

3. Each party shall submit with his statement a list of the documents upon which he intends to rely. This list shall describe each document by specifying its document type, date, author, recipient and subject matter.

23. Amendment of or Supplement to Claim

The arbitrator may allow a party to amend or supplement his claim or counterclaim or defence during the course of the arbitration unless the arbitrator considers the delay in amending or supplementing the claim to be prejudicial to the other party or unless he considers that the amendment or supplement goes beyond the term of the arbitration agreement or submission to arbitrate.

24. Production of Documents

1. The arbitrator may, on application or on his own motion, order a party to produce any documents the arbitrator considers relevant to the arbitration within a time the arbitrator specifies and where such an order is made the other party may inspect those documents and take copies of them.

2. Each party shall make available to the other party for inspection and taking copies, any documents upon which the former party intends to rely.

25. Agreed Statement of Facts

The parties shall, within a period of time specified by the arbitrator , identify those facts which are not in dispute and submit to the arbitrator and file with NEPCA an agreed statement of facts.

26. Arbitration Hearings

1. The arbitrator shall set the dates for any oral hearings or meetings and shall give at least 7 days written notice or such hearing or meetings to the parties.

2. All oral hearings and meetings shall be in private and all written documents shall be kept confidential by the arbitrator, the parties and by NEPCA.

27. Evidence

1. Each party shall present the facts relied upon to support his claim or defence.

2. If a party is presenting evidence through a witness, the party shall, no later than 7 days before the commencement of the oral hearing, advise the arbitrator and the other party of the name and address of the witness and shall provide a brief summary of his evidence.

3. The arbitrator shall be the judge of the relevance and materiality of the evidence offered and conformity to legal rules of evidence shall not be necessary.

4. All oral evidence shall be taken in the presence of the arbitrator and all the parties except where any of the parties is absent in default or has waived the right to be present.

5. The parties shall prepare assemblies of all documents to be introduced at the oral hearing and shall submit those assemblies to the other party and to the arbitrator no later than 7 days before the commencement of the oral hearing. The parties agree that these documents assemblies shall be deemed to have been entered into evidence at the oral hearing without further proof and without being read out at the hearing but either party may challenge at the hearing the admissibility of any document so introduced.

6. The arbitrator may allow a party to introduce into evidence at the oral hearing a document which was not disclosed under section 22 if submitted 7 days before the commencement of the hearing under this Section but the arbitrator may take that failure into account at the time he fixes any costs under Section 40 and the applicable legislation, if any.

28. Examination of Parties

In an oral hearing, an arbitrator may order a party or a person claiming through a party to submit to being examined by the arbitrator under oath and to produce all documents that the arbitrator requires.

29. Witness

1. The arbitrator may determine the manner in which witness are to be examined and may require a witness, other than a party or the party's representative, to absent himself from an oral hearing during the testimony of another witness.

2. Where an arbitrator allow the evidence of a witness to be presented by written statement, the other party may require that the witness be present at an oral hearing for cross examination.

3. The arbitrator may call a witness on his own motion but where he is called the parties have the right to cross examine that witness and to call evidence in rebuttal.

30. Experts

1. The arbitrator may appoint one or more experts to report to the arbitrator on specific issues to be determined by the arbitrator and may require a party to give the expert any relevant information or to produce, or to provide access to, any relevant documents, goods or other property for his inspection.

2. The arbitrator shall communicate the expert's terms of reference to the parties. Any dispute between a party and an expert as to the-relevant of the required information or production of it shall be referred to the arbitrator for decision.

3. Upon receipt of the expert's report, the arbitrator shall communicate a copy of the report to the parties who shall be given the opportunity to express, in writting, their opinion on the report.

4. The expert shall, on the request of a party, make available to that party for examination all documents, goods or other property in the expert's possession with which he was provided in order to prepare his report and shall provide that party with a list of all documents, goods or other property not in the expert's possession, but with which he was provided in order to prepare his report, and a description of the location of those documents, goods or other property.

5. If a party so requests or if the arbitrator considers it necessary, the expert shall, after delivery of his written or oral report, be present at an oral hearing where the parties have the opportunity to cross examine him and to call evidence in rebuttal.

31. Default of a Party

1. Where a claimant, without sufficient casue, fails to communicate his statement of claim within the required time, under clause 22(1) the arbitrator may terminate the arbitration with respect to that claim by issuing an order to that effect.

2. Where the respondent, without sufficient cause fails to communicate his statement of defence within the required time under rule 22(2), the arbitrator shall order that arbitration proceeding continue. An award shall not be made solely on the default of the respondent and the arbitrator shall require the claimant to submit such evidence as the arbitrator may require for the making of an award.

3. Where a party, without sufficient cause, fails to appear at an oral hearing or to produce documentary evidence, the arbitrator may continue the arbitration. The arbitrator shall make an award based upon the evidence before him.

32. General Powers of Arbitrator

1. The arbitrator may—

(a) order an adjournment of the proceedings form time to time,

(b) make an interim award on any matter with respect to which he may make a final award, including an interim award for preservation of property which is subject matter of the dispute,

(c) order "on site" inspection of documents, exhibits or other property,

(d) order the taking down and recording of a transcription of any oral hearing, and

(e) at any time extend or abridge a period of time required in these Rules or fixed or determined by himself where he considers it just and appropriate in the circumstances.

33. Payment to NEPCA

1. A party may seek to mitigate liability for costs by paying money into the arbitation by sending a signed offer of settlement in a sealed envelope, a copy of the offer and a certified cheque payable to the offeree in the amount of the offer to NEPCA. On receipt, NEPCA shall advise the offeree, in writing, of the particulars of the offer and shall then hold the offer until it is accepted or until the arbitrator calls for it after he has been notified of its existence at the conclusion of the arbitration.

2. The arbitrator shall not be informed by NEPCA or any party of the fact that an offer has been made under this Rule unless the offer is not accepted, in which case the offerer may inform the arbitrator at the time of making any submission on the question of costs but not before. The arbitrator may then require NEPCA to give him the sealed offer and shall determine his finding on costs and the disposition of the certified cheque.

34. Deposits Against Costs

1. The arbitrator may, from time to time, require each party to deposit by cash or certified cheque to NEPCA in trust an equal amount as an advance for the anticipated costs of the arbitration including the arbitrator's fees.

2. If the required deposits are not made to NEPCA in trust within 15 days after receipt of the request from the arbitrator, the arbitrator shall inform the parties in order that another party may make the required payment.

3. If the required deposits are not made, the arbitrator may order the suspension or termination of the proceeding.

35. Payment out of Deposits

1. NEPCA may, from time to time, pay to the arbitrator from any deposit it holds under section 34 any amount it considers reasonable and appropriate for fees earned or expenses incurred by the arbitrator in the arbitration.

2. After the final award has been made, a settlement has been reached or the arbitration abandoned or otherwise finally disposed of, NEPCA shall apply any deposits it holds to the costs of the arbitration, including any required administrative expenses for holding and disbursing the deposits, render an accounting to the parties of the deposits received and applied and return any unexpended balance to the parties.

MAKING THE AWARD AND TERMINATING THE PROCEEDINGS

36. Legal Principles Apply

Subject to express authorization of the parties to decide otherwise an arbitrator shall decide the dispute in accordance with the law.

37. Closure of Hearings

1. Where the parties have, on inquiry, advised they have no further evidence to give or submissions to make, or the arbitrator considers further hearing to be unnecessary or inappropriate, the arbitrator may close the hearing.

2. On his own motion or on the application of a party, the arbitrator may, in exceptional circumstances, reopen the hearings at any time before the final award is made.

3. The parties may provide, by written agreement, for the waiver of oral hearings in any case, if the parties are unable to agree as to procedure, NEPCA shall specify a fair and equitable procedure.

38. Award

1. The arbitrator shall make his final award as soon as reasonably possible after the hearings have been closed and in no event shall the award be made later than 35 days after closure.

2. The final award of the arbitrator shall be in writing and state the reasons upon which it is based. The arbitrator shall give a signed copy of the award to each party. The parties are bound by the award and agree to comply with the award as soon as practicable.

3. Where the arbitral tribunal consists of more than 2 arbitrators, an award or any decision shall be made by a majority of the arbitrators. Where there is no majority decision, the decision of the Chairman/Umpire of the tribunal shall be the final decision.

4. The arbitrator shall file the original copy of the final award with NEPCA as soon as he has given a copy to each party, NEPCA shall supply a certified copy of the award to a party to that arbitration on request and after paying the required administrative expenses.

39. Interest

The arbitrator may order interest to be paid in the final award.

40. Costs

1. The arbitrator shall fix the costs of the arbitration in the final award and, on application made by a party within 30 days after being notified of the award, shall fix the costs of the arbitration.

2. Except for the cost of legal fees and legal expenses of the successful party, the costs of the arbitration unless otherwise agreed in writing by the parties shall be borne by the unsuccessful party unless the arbitrator considers it appropriate in the circumstances to apportion them between the parties.

3. The arbitrator may determine which party shall bear the cost of legal fees and legal expenses of the successful party and may apportion those costs if it is reasonable to do so. Where the arbitrator makes an order respecting legal fees and legal expenses or the manner of determining those amounts.

41. Amendments and Corrections to the Award

1. An arbitrator may, whether on the application of a party or on his own initiative, amend or vary an award to correct—

(a) a clerical or typographical error,

(b) an accidental error, slip, omission or other similar mistake, or

(c) an arithmetical error made in a computation.

2. An application by a party to amend or vary shall be made within 15 days after that party is notified of the award.

3. An amendment or variation shall not, without the consent of all parties, be made more than 30 days after all parties have been notified of the award.

4. An party may, within 15 days after being notified of the award, apply to the arbitrator for clarification of the award, and the arbitrator may amend the award where he considers that the amendment will clarify it.

5. A party may, within 30 days after receiving the award, apply to the arbitrator to make an additional award with respect to claims presented in the proceedings but omitted from the award.

42. Extension of Time

The parties may modify any period of time by mutual agreement. The NEPCA or the arbitrator may for good cause extend any period of time established by these rules, except the time for making the award. The NEPCA shall notify the parties of any extension.

43. Exercise of NEPCA's Authority

In these rules where NEPCA is required to act on any matter it shall do so through a person designated by the board of director's of NEPCA .

44. Commencement and Modification

1. These rules shall come in to force from 1st day of January 1992.

2. These rules may be amended from time to time by the board of director of NEPCA.

Schedule of Arbitrator's Fee

Sum of Dispute (Rs.)	Arbitrators Fee (Rs.)	
	Min.	Max
Upto 1,000,000	1000	3500
100,000 to 500,000	3500+3% of over 100,000	15,500
500,000 to 1,000,000	15,500+2.5% of over 500,000	28,000
1,000,000 to 2,500,000	28,000+2% of over 1,000,000	58,000
2,500,000 to 5,000,000	58,000+1.5% of over 2,500,000	95,500
5,000,000 to 10,000,000	95,500+1% of over 5,000,000	145,500
10,000,000 to 50,000,000	145,500+0.5% of over 10,000,000	345,500
Any amount over 50,000,000	345,000+0.2% of over 50,000,000	945,000

Note: The arbitrator's Fee is based on the assumption that there will be a panel of three arbitrators. However the fee may adjusted depending upon the number of arbitrators.

Schedule of Administrative Expenses

Sum of Dispute (Rs.)	Administrative Expenses (Rs.)	
	Min.	Max
Upto 100,000	1,000	1,500
100,000 to 500,000	1,500 + 1% of 400,000	5,500
500,000 to 1,000,000	5,500+0.8% of 500,000	9,500
1,000,000 to 2,500,000	9,500+0.6% of 1500,000	18,500
2,500,000 to 5,000,000	18,500+0.4% of 2500,000	28,500
5,000,000 to 10,000,000	28,500+0.3% of 5,000,000	43,500
10,000,000 to 50,000,000	43,500+0.15% of 40,000,000	103,500
Any amount over 50,000,000	103,500+0.1% of amount exceeding 50,000,000	

MODEL ARBITRATION CLAUSE

Any dispute, controversy or claim arising out of or relating to this contract, or the breach, termination or invalidity thereof, shall be decided by arbitration in accordance with Rules for Domestic Commercial Arbitration Proceedings of Nepal Council of Arbitration.

Note: Parties may wish to consider adding:

(a) The appointing authority shall be the Nepal Council of Arbitration .

(b) The number of Arbitrators shall be (one or three).

(c) The place of arbitration shall be (district or town)

(d) The language(s) to be used in the arbitration proceedings shall be.........

Address of the Nepal Council of Arbitration

The President,
Nepal Council of Arbitration,
Ramshah Path, Kathmandu,
G.P.O. Box : 6651.
Tel. 215725.

PAKISTAN

RULES AND REGULATION OF THE ARBITRATION TRIBUNAL

OF

THE FEDERATION OF PAKISTAN CHAMBERS OF COMMERCE AND INDUSTRY (SET UP UNDER SECTION 12 OF TRADE ORGANISATIONS ORDINANCE, 1961)

[APPROVED BY THE MINISTRY OF COMMERCE, GOVERNMENT OF PAKISTAN, VIDE LETTER NO. 1001(2) 1969 - DATED JANUARY 3, 1969]

Section 1

This Tribunal shall be called "The Arbitration Tribunal of the Federation of Pakistan Chambers of Commerce and Industry: hereinafter referred to as "The Tribunal".

Section 2

OFFICE - The office of the Tribunal shall be at the headquarters of the Federation of Pakistan Chamber of Commerce & Industry (hereinafter mentioned as "The Federation").

Section 3

OBJECTS - The objects of the Tribunal are:

(a) to determine, settle and/or adjust dispute arising between Member Bodies of the Federation or between any Member Body and its member of members,

(b) to determine the validity or propriety of any act or proceeding of any registered trade organisation or of the Executive Committee or other body thereof, or the constitution of, or election or appointment to such Committee or body questioned by any member of such trade organisation on an application made to the said Tribunal under section 12 of the Trade Organisations Ordinance, 1961 or under any other act or statute which may be in force,

(c) to discharge any other function or duty that may be assigned to the said Tribunal by the Central Government of Pakistan acting through the Ministry of Commerce as the Central Government may deem fit under the law.

Section 4

CONSTITUTION OF THE TRIBUNAL

Clause i - The Tribunal shall be constituted of not less than 3 or more than five such persons as are from time to time appointed by the Managing Committee of the Federation and who are willing to serve on the Tribunal. The Managing Committee of the Federation may at any time, if it thinks proper to do so, delete the name of any person or persons from the list of the members of the Tribunal and substitute any other person or persons as may be expedient or necessary.

Clause ii - The Managing Committee of the Federation shall appoint a Registrar of the Tribunal (hereinafter called only "the Registrar") for the general administration and management of the Tribunal. The Managing Committee of the Federation may also remove a person from the office of the Registrar and appoint another person in his place.

Clause iii - The duties of the Registrar shall be as follows:

> He shall by himself or his subordinate receive fees and costs, issue all necessary notices to the arbitrator or arbitrators (as provided hereinafter), issue notices of hearing to parties and all other necessary notices, keep a Register of Awards and Reconciliations, and such other books and memoranda and make such returns as the Tribunal shall from time to time require. He shall give such assistance to the arbitrator or arbitrators in an arbitration as he or they may properly require. The Registrar shall direct other officers of the Tribunal (if any) and shall generally carry out the instructions of the Managing Committee relating to the Tribunal.

Clause iv - If an Acting Registrar is appointed by the Managing Committee of the Federation he may, during the absence to the Registrar, perform the duties of the Registrar and at other times discharge such other duties as the Tribunal may direct.

Section 5

Clause i - In each case of a dispute between parties an application for arbitration together with the particulars required under Clause V of section 5 may be addressed by either or any of the parties to the Registrar.

Clause ii - The Registrar shall then inform the Managing Committee to constitute a Tribunal of not less than 3 or more than 5 persons to hear the dispute, who shall proceed to constitute a Tribunal for the purpose of hearing the said dispute.

Clause iii - If a person included in the Tribunal fails to act or dies the Registrar shall inform the President or if he is not available the Vice President to nominate a new member of the said Tribunal. The reconstituted Tribunal shall then proceed with full liberty to act on the record of proceedings and on the evidence, if any, then taken or to commence fresh proceedings.

Clause iv - Each party applying, for arbitration shall submit to the Registrar an application containing the names and addresses of the parties to the dispute and full details of the case and the original or certified copies of the relevant documents with four copies of the said application and every document submitted with it, and an extra copy for each party to the dispute.

Clause v - The Registrar shall then send to the other party along with an office notice, a copy of the above mentioned application and shall call upon the other party or parties to submit to him within the specified date a rejoinder with four copies and an extra copy for each party to the dispute detailing his or their case accompanied by the relevant documents. The Registrar may forward a copy of the rejoinder to the party or parties to the dispute who had first applied for arbitration and call upon him or them to submit any further statement relating to the case with relevant number of copies.

Clause vi - The Registrar shall then submit all statements, rejoinders documents; etc., relating to the case before the Tribunal constituted under section 5 Clause (ii), and (iii) and the Tribunal shall then proceed with its work.

Clause vii - Should any party refuse or fail to submit to arbitration within the appointed time the Tribunal shall proceed with the arbitration in the absence of such party.

Clause viii - No award shall be made by the Tribunal unless the case of the party applying for arbitration has been brought to the notice of the other party and until after the lapse of such specified time within which they have been asked to submit their replies under Clause (v) section 5. The party or parties shall be served with notice by registered letter or by telegram by the Registrar and he or they shall be deemed to have been duly notified.

Clause ix - All applications and notices relating to the dispute shall pass through the Registrar who shall communicate the orders and directions of the Tribunal thereon to the parties, unless the said application or notices are made or issued in the presence of the parties.

Clause x - The parties shall not wilfully act in a manner that may delay or prevent the Tribunal from making an award. If any party acts in a manner likely to delay or otherwise interfere with the lawful proceedings of the Tribunal, the Tribunal may make such orders as to costs as the Tribunal shall at its discretion deem fit.

Clause xi - The Tribunal shall have the discretion to call upon parties to submit any documents or things, other than those already submitted, in relation to the case. The Tribunal shall also have the discretion to appoint time and place for the hearing of reference and to take oral evidence.

Clause xii - The party or parties shall be entitled to appear by counsel, attorney, advocate or an authorized adviser or personally.

Clause xiii - Before making the final award the Tribunal shall have the discretion to procure, at the expense of parties concerned, the services in any form of any expert, lawyer or registered accountant, needed in the course of the reference.

Clause xiv - The parties to the dispute and the witnesses on their behalf shall (subject to the law in force)—

(a) submit to be examined by the Tribunal on oath or affirmation in relation to the matters in dispute,

(b) produce before the Tribunal when asked upon to do so by the Tribunal all relevant documents in their possession or power,

(c) comply with the rules and orders of the Tribunal and generally do anything lawful required by the Tribunal during the pendency of the reference.

Clause xv - The Tribunal may

(a) administer oath or affirmation to the parties or witnesses appearing or giving evidence,

(b) state a special case for the opinion of the Court or give its award in the form of a special case for the opinion of the Court,

(c) make any award conditional or, in the alternative,

(d) introduce any correction in the award and thus remove any clerical or patent error, and

(e) administer to the parties to the arbitration any Interrogatories it may deem necessary. All expenses arising out of a reference by the Tribunal of its motion by way of a special case for the opinion of the court shall be borne equally by the parties concerned.

Clause xvi - If a party wishes that any question arising in proceedings before the Tribunal be referred to the opinion of the court he shall apply in writing to the Registrar and pay with such application a fee prescribed from time to time. If the Tribunal decides that a point of law is involved it may accede to such request and the party applying shall be responsible for all costs incurred during such reference and incidental to the same and shall make such deposit on that account according to the direction given by the Tribunal.

Clause xvii - The Tribunal shall have the power to retain and/or return all documents produced before It in any proceedings. The Tribunal shall also have the discretion to return any or all of the documents to the party, or parties on such terms and conditions as it may deem fit.

Clause xviii - The Tribunal shall have the power to proceed with the reference notwithstanding any failure to comply with any of the directions of the Tribunal and may also proceed with the reference in the absence of any or both of the parties who, being entitled to appear under Clause xi or xii of section 5 refuse or neglect to attend at the time and place appointed under those clauses.

Section 6

AWARDS

Clause i - The award of the majority will be deemed as the decision of the Tribunal.

Clause ii - The Tribunal shall make its award in writing duly signed by all the Members of the Tribunal and the Registrar within one month from the date of closing the hearings or within such extended time as the parties may agree upon.

Clause iii - The Tribunal may make an interim award and may, by any award, order and determine what shall bo done by either or any of the parties, in respect of the matters under reference and as to costs.

Clause iv - The award shall be made available by the Registrar to each of the parties.

Clause v - The award shall be binding on the parties and their respective representatives notwithstanding the death of any party and such death shall not operate as arevocation of the submission or reference.

Clause vi - The costs of the reference and the award including costs, charges, fees and other expenses shall be in the discretion of the Tribunal which may direct to and by whom, and in what manner and in what proportion such charges, fees and other expenses or any part thereof shall be borne and paid, and may tax and settle the amount of cost to be so paid or any part thereof, and may award costs to be paid as between Solicitor and Client.

Section 7

FEES

Clause i - The Tribunal shall be entitled to charge fees and expenses of witnesses, legal or technical advice or proceedings in respect of any matter arising out of the arbitration incurred by the Tribunal, and any other incidental expenses and charges in connection with or arising out of the reference or award as the Tribunal shall in its absolute discretion think fit.

Clause ii - The fees, costs and charges incidental to the reference and the award shall be the following:

(i) Submission Fee: A fee of Pakistan Rs. 1500/- (rupees one thousand five hundred) by the party applying for arbitration to the Federation along with the application.

(ii) Certified Copies of awards: A fee of Pakistan Rs. 25/- (rupees twenty five) shall be payable for each certified copy of the award.

(iii) Stamp Duties: Stamp duties shall be payable in all cases according to the scale prescribed by law.

(iv) A fee of Pakistan Rs. 50/- (rupees fifty) to the Federation in addition to the court fees, on the scale in force under law, by the party requiring the award to bo filed.

(v) No party shall be entitled to copies of proceedings before arbitration.

(vi) In case where the party instituting a reference desire to withdraw it before a Tribunal has been constituted the Registrar shall return to that party half the submission fee.

SECURITY FOR ARBITRATORS

(vii) No party shall bring or prosecute any suit or proceeding whatever against the Tribunal or any member of the Tribunal for or in respect of any matter or thing purported to be done under these rules nor any suit or proceeding in respect thereof (except for the enforcement of the award) against the other party.

SRI LANKA

RULES OF THE ICLLP ARBITRATION CENTRE

(As adopted by the Council of Management of the Institute for the Development of Commercial Law and Practice and in force from the 29th of February 1996)

REQUEST FOR RESOLUTION BY ARBITRATION

1. A request for the resolution of a dispute by arbitration at the Centre shall be made by a party filing with the Centre a statement which shall include:

(a) the names and addresses of the parties to the dispute,

(b) the facts relevant to the dispute,

(c) the relief claimed by the claimant,

(d) together with a copy of the agreement on which the claim is based and a copy of the Arbitration Agreement, if the latter is not included in the former, and

(e) where applicable, the names and particulars of the arbitrator or arbitrators appointed by the Claimant.

PROCESSING OF REQUEST

2. Within three working days of the submission of the request to the Centre such request shall be submitted by the Secretary General to the Chairman of the Board.

3. On receipt of such request the Chairman shall expeditiously convene a meeting of the Board to consider such request.

4. (a) Where the Board is of the opinion that such request may be entertained by the Centre, the Board shall convey such opinion to the Secretary General for the Secretary General to take the further steps necessary in accordance with the Rules.

(b) Where the Board is of the opinion that the request cannot be entertained by the Centre for resolution under the ICLP Arbitration Centre Rules, the Board shall refer the request back to the Secretary General for action under section 9(2) of the Constitution.

NOTICE TO RESPONDENT

5.1. In the event that the Board decides that such request should be entertained under the Rules, the Secretary General shall within seven working days from such decision require the Respondent party to submit a reply to the Centre within the time period nominated by the Secretary General, which shall include-

(a) a statement commenting on the request made by the Claimant, and

(b) where applicable, a statement identifying the arbitrator or arbitrators appointed by the Respondent.

5.2. In the event that the Respondent wishes to raise any objection against the validity or concerning the applicability of the Arbitration Agreement, such objection shall be made in the reply together with the grounds therefor.

5.3. The Respondent may make a counter claim or plead a set-off. A statement to that effect shall be made in the reply, including the facts relevant to the dispute and the relief claimed. A counter claim or a plea by way of set-off must be within the scope of the Arbitration Agreement.

5.4. The Board may request the Respondent to be more comprehensive in the counter claim or plea for set-off. in the event that the Respondent fails to make a comprehensive counter claim or plea for a set-off upon the request of the Board such claim or plea maybe dismissed by the Board.

5.5. The reply of the Respondent shall be communicated to the Claimant by the Secretary General. The Claimant shall be given the opportunity to comment on any objections and pleas raised by the Respondent. Such comments shall be in a statement. A copy thereof shall be forwarded to the Respondent.

5.6. Failure bythe Respondent to submit a reply shall not prevent the continuance of the proceedings in the case.

6. In the event that the Centre has requested a party to perform any act within a specified time, such time limit may be extended by the Centre, on application by the parties or otherwise.

APPOINTMENT OF ARBITRATORS

7.1. Each party shall appoint an equal number of arbitrators who shall appoint a Chairman of the Tribunal. If the arbitrators are unable to appoint a Chairman in such an event the Board may make such appointment.

7.2. In the event that the parties have not agreed upon the number of arbitrators, the number shall be three.

7.3. In the event that the parties have agreed that the dispute shall be decided by a sole arbitrator but cannot agree on the person the appointment of such sole arbitrator shall be made by the Board.

7.4. In the event that the parties have so agreed the Board shall appoint all the arbitrators.

7.5. In the event that a party falls to appoint an arbitrator within the time prescribed by the Board, the Board shall make the appointment.

7.6. In the event of the death of an arbitrator appointed by a party, such appointing party shall appoint another arbitrator in place of the deceased arbitrator.

7.7. In the even to fan arbitrator resigning or being removed from office theBoard shall appoint another arbitrator provided however, that in the event that if the vacating arbitrator had been appointed by a party the Board shall make such appointment in concurrence with the party who appointed the arbitrator who vacated office.

7.8. In the event of the parties orthe Board failing to appoint arbitrators as above, a party may apply to the High Court to take necessary measures towards the appointment of the arbitrator/s.

DUTIES OF AN ARBITRATOR

8.1. A person who is requested to accept appointment as an arbitrator shall disclose any circumstances which is likely to affect the impartiality or independence, of such person.

8.2. An arbitrator shall, from the time of his appointment and during the arbitral proceedings, disclose without delay any such circumstances as are referred to in section 8.1, to the parties and to the other arbitrators.

CHALLENGE DISQUALIFICATION OF AN ARBITRATOR

9. A party wishing to challenge an arbitrator shall do so setting out the reasons therefore in writing and shall submit such writing to the Board, and copies thereof to the arbitrators and to each of the other parties.

10.1. The Board may decide that an arbitrator is disqualified, and upon the Board making such a decision it shall be conveyed to the arbitrators and the disqualified arbitrator shall be deemed to have been removed with effect from the date of such decision.

10.2. The Board may remove an arbitrator for failure to perform his duties in an adequate manner.

10.3. Before a decision of removal is made the Board shall ascertain the views of the parties and the arbitrators.

DUTIES OF THE BOARD

11. When the filing of written statements as required by the foregoing Rules has been concluded the Board shall, as applicable—

(a) appoint an arbitrator and/or arbitrators,and/or a Chairman of the Arbitral Tribunal,

(b) determine the place of arbitration having due regard to the wishes of the parties, and

(c) fix the amount of security and the time within which each party shall pay his share thereof.

12.1. The Board shall fix a sum which shall be paid to the Centre and which, together with the accrued interest, shall constitute security for the costs of the proceeding. The amount thereof shall be fixed in accordance with the regulations issued by the Centre. The Board may fix separate sums for a counterclaim and for a plea by way of set-off. After notification by the Arbitral Tribunal or on its own motion the Board may in the course of the arbitration proceedings increase the security.

12.2. In the event of a party failing to make payment as per rule 13.1 below, the Board shall afford the other party an opportunity to do so. In the event that the required payment Is not made, the case shall be wholly or partly dismissed or stayed by the Board.

12.3. As soon as the Arbitral Tribunal has been appointed and the security been provided, the Board shall refer the case to the Arbitral Tribunal.

PAYMENT OF SECURITY

13.1. Each party shall contribute half of such sums of money as are referred to in rule 12.1 above provided however, that one party may pay the entire sum if such party so desires.

13.2. The Secretariat may, in the course of the arbitration proceedings and thereafter, draw on the securityto payfees to the arbitrators and other costs of the proceedings.

1 3.3. The Board may decide that the security may partly consist of a bank guarantee or other security.

ARBITRAL PROCEEDINGS

14.1. The Arbitral Tribunal shall comply with the stipulations of the parties in the Arbitration Agreement, the rules and the wishes of the parties in determining the manner in which proceedings are to be conducted.

14.2. The Arbitral Tribunal shall deal with the case in an impartial, practical and expeditious manner. Each party shall be given a sufficient opportunity to present his case.

14.3. When the Arbitral Tribunal is composed of three or more members, the Chairman may, if the other arbitrators have so authorised him, decide questions of procedure on his own.

15. Unless the parties have agreed on the language or languages to be used in the proceedings, the Arbitral Tribunal shall make a determination in such respect.

16. The Arbitral Tribunal may require a party to be more comprehensive in any or all statements filed in accordance with the foregoing rules. The Arbitral Tribunal may dismiss the case if the Claimant fails to comply with such a requirement. In the event that the Respondent falis to do so, such failure shall not prevent the continuation of the proceedings in the case.

AMENDEMENT OF THE CLAIM OR DEFENCE

17.1. A party may amend his claim or defence in the course of the proceedings if his case, as amended, is still within the scope of the Arbitration Agreement and unless the Arbitral Tribunal considers it inappropriate having regard to the point of time at which the request is made, that prejudice may be caused to the other party or due to other circumstances.

17.2. The provisions of the preceding paragraph shall apply equally to the right of a party to introduce a plea for a set-off or a counterclaim.

ORAL HEARING

18.1. An oral hearing shall be held, guided by the wishes of the parties and the Arbitral Tribunal shall determine the time at which such a hearing shall take place, its duration and the manner in which oral evidence shall be presented thereat.

18.2. In the event that an arbitrator is replaced in the course of the proceedings, the newly composed tribunal shall decide whether and towhat extent a prior oral hearing shall be repeated.

EVIDENCE

19.1 At the request of the arbitral tribunal the parties have to state the evidence on which they wish to rely upon, specifying what they wish to prove thereby.

19.2. The parties shall produce as requested by the Arbitral Tribunal the documentary evidence on which they rely.

20. The Arbitral Tribunal may when it deems appropriate require the submission of written affidavits.

21. The Arbitral Tribunal may refuse to accept evidence offered to it if it considers that such evidence is not required or is irrelevant or that proof can be established more simply by other means on a particular matter.

22. Unless the parties agree otherwise, the Arbitral Tribunal may appoint an expert to give his opinion on a particular matter.

23. In the event that a party falls to appear at a hearing or otherwise to comply with an order of the Arbitral Tribunal and does not show valid cause for such failure, such failure shall not prevent the Arbitral Tribunal from proceeding with the case and/or rendering an award.

WAIVER

24. A party who falls during the proceedings to object within a reasonable time to any deviation from provisions of the Arbitration Agreement or other Rules applicable to the proceedings, shall be deemed to have waived his right to invoke such irregularity.

THE AWARD

25. An award shall be made not later than one year after the case has been referred to the Arbitral Tribunal. At the request of the Arbitral Tribunal, the Board may, however, if appropriate extend this period.

26. After having conscientiously considered and evaluated all aspects of the proceedings, the Arbitral Tribunal shall determine what has been proved in the case and make their award accordingly.

27. The majority opinion of the Arbitral Tribunal shall prevail. In the event that such a majority is not attained the opinion of the Chairman shall prevail.

28. A separate issue or part of the matter in dispute between the parties may, at the request of a party, be decided by a separate award. If any party objects, such an award may be rendered only if the Arbitral Tribunal deems that there are exceptional reasons therefor.

29. Where a party has partially admitted a claim, the Arbitral Tribunal may give a separate award on the part that has been admitted.

30.1. The award shall be rendered at the place of arbitration. The award shall contain an order or declaration and the reasons therefor and shall be signed by all the arbitrators. An award may be rendered even in the absence of the signature of an arbitrator provided that the award has been signed by a majority of the arbitrators and contains a verification by them that the arbitrator whose signature is absent took part in deciding the dispute.

30.2. An arbitrator may attach a dissenting opinion to the award.

30.3. In the event a settlement is made the Arbitral Tribunal may at the request of the parties confirm such settlement in an award.

31. An Arbitral Tribunal shall after the close of the proceedings submit to the Centre one copy of each award as well as a record of all the proceedings.

PAYMENT OF FEES OR COSTS

32.1 The Arbitral Tribunal shall decide in the award the amount of fees that are due to the Centre and the arbitrators, respectively.

32.2. The Parties shall be liable jointly and severally for the payment of all such sums.

32.3. The party against whom an award is made shall be ordered to pay such fees and costs as well as the fees and costs of the other party unless the circumstances call for a different result.

32.4. When a case is terminated before it has been referred to the Arbitral Tribunal, the Centre will determine the amount of compensation due to it. When a case is terminated before an award has been rendered, the Arbitral Tribunal may decide that the parties shall pay compensation to the Centre and the arbitrators.

33. An award may be rendered even if it deals only with costs.

34.1. The fees of arbitrators shall be reasonable in amount and shall be determined taking into account the time spent by the arbitrators, the complexity of the case, the amount in dispute and other circumstances.

34.2 The amount of fees due to the Centre will be determined in accordance with regulations issued by the Centre.

ARBITRATION STATUTES OF SELECTED SAARC COUNTRIES

BANGLADESH

THE ARBITRATION ACT, 2001

(1 of 2001)

[*24th January, 2001*]

An Act to enact the law relating to international commercial arbitration, recognition and enforcement of foreign arbitral award and other arbitrations.

WHEREAS it is expedient and necessary to enact the law relating to international commercial arbitration, recognition and enforcement of foreign arbitral award and other arbitrations. It is hereby enacted as follows:—

CHAPTER I

INTRODUCTORY

1. Short title, extent and commencement

(1) This Act may be called the Arbitration Act, 2001.

(2) It extends to the whole of Bangladesh.

(3) It shall come into force on such date as the Government shall, by notification in the official Gazette, appoint.

CHAPTER II

GENERAL PROVISIONS

2. Definitions

In this Act, unless there is anything repugnant in the subject or context,—

(a) "Legal representative" means a person who in law represents the estate of a deceased person, and includes any person who intermeddles with the estate of the deceased, and, where a party acts in a representative character, the person on whom the estate devolves on the death of the party so acting;

(b) "Court" means Court of District Judge and includes the Court of Additional District Judge appointed by the Government for discharging the functions of the Court of District Judge under this Act through Gazette notification;

(c) "International Commercial Arbitration" means an arbitration relating to disputes arising out of legal relationships, whether contractual or not, considered as commercial under the law in force in Bangladesh and where at least one of the parties is—

(i) an individual who is a national of, or habitually resident in, any country other than Bangladesh; or

(ii) a body corporate which is incorporated in any country other than Bangladesh; or

(iii) a company or an association or a body of individuals whose central management and control is exercised in any country other than Bangladesh; or

(iv) the Government of a foreign country;

(d) "Limitation Act" means Limitation Act, 1908 (IX of 1908);

(e) "Code of Civil Procedure" means Code of Civil Procedure, 1908 (Act V of 1908);

(f) "Specified State" means a specified state declared by the Government under section 47 of this Act;

(g) "Party" means a party to an arbitration agreement;

(h) "Chief Justice" means the Chief Justice of Bangladesh;

(i) "Rules" means any rules made under this Act;

(j) "Person" means a statutory or other organization, company and association and includes partnership firm;

(k) "Foreign arbitral award" means an award which is made in pursuance of an arbitration agreement in the territory of any state other than Bangladesh but does not include an award made in the territory of a specified state.

(1) "Evidence Act" means Evidence Act, 1872 (Act I of 1872);

(m) "Arbitration" means any arbitration whether or not administered by permanent institution;

(n) "Arbitration agreement" means an agreement by the parties to submit to arbitration all or certain disputes which have arisen or which may arise between them in respect of a defined legal relationship, whether contractual or not;

(o) "Arbitration tribunal" means a sole arbitrator or a panel of arbitrators;

(p) "Arbitral award" means a decision made by the tribunal on the issue in dispute;

(q) "High Court Division" means High Court Division of the Supreme Court of Bangladesh.

3. Scope

(1) This Act shall apply where the place of arbitration is in Bangladesh.

(2) Notwithstanding anything contained in sub-section (1) of this section, the provisions of sections 45, 46 and 47 shall also apply to the arbitration if the place of that arbitration is outside Bangladesh.

(3) This Act shall not affect any other law for the time being in force by virtue of which certain disputes may not be submitted to arbitration.

(4) Where any arbitration agreement is entered into before or after the enforcement of this Act, the provisions thereof shall apply to the arbitration proceedings in Bangladesh relating to the dispute arising out of that agreement.

4. Construction of Reference

(1) Where this Act, except section 36, leaves the parties free to determine a certain issue, that freedom shall include the right of the parties to authorise any person to determine that issue.

(2) Where this Act—

(a) refers to the fact that the parties have agreed or that they may agree, or

(b) in any other way refers to an agreement of the parties, that agreement shall include any arbitration rules referred to in that agreement.

(3) Where this Act, other than clause (a) of sub-section 3 of Section 35 or clause (a) of sub-section 2 of section 41, refers to a claim, it shall also apply to a counter-claim, and where it refers to a defence, it shall also apply to a defence to that counter-claim.

5. Receipt of written communications

(1) Unless otherwise agreed by the parties—

(a) any written communication, notice or summons is deemed to have been received if it is delivered to the addressee personally or at his place of business, habitual residence or mailing address, and

(b) if none of the places referred to in clause (a) can be found after making a reasonable inquiry, a written communication is deemed to have been received if it is sent to the addressee's last known place of business, habitual residence or mailing address by registered letter or by any other means which provides a record of the attempt to deliver it.

(2) The communication, notice or summons, as the case may be, shall be deemed to have been received on the day it is so delivered.

(3) This section does not apply to written communication, notice or summons, as the case may be, in respect of proceedings of any judicial authority.

6. Waiver of right to object

A party who knows that—

(a) any provision of this Act from which the parties may derogate, or

(b) any requirement under the arbitration agreement has not been complied with and yet proceeds with the arbitration without stating his objection to such non-compliance without undue delay or, if a time limit is provided therefor within such period of time, shall be deemed to have waived his right to so object.

7. Jurisdiction of Court in respect of matters covered by arbitration agreement

Notwithstanding anything contained in any other law for the time being in force, where any of the parties to the arbitration agreement files legal proceedings in a Court against the other party, no judicial authority shall hear any legal proceedings except in so far as provided by this Act.

8. Administrative assistance

In order to facilitate the conduct of the arbitral proceedings, the parties, or the arbitral tribunal with the consent of the parties, may arrange for administrative assistance by a suitable person.

CHAPTER III

ARBITRATION AGREEMENT

9. Form of arbitration agreement

(1) An arbitration agreement may be in the form of an arbitration clause in a contract or in the form of a separate agreement.

(2) An arbitration agreement shall be in writing and an arbitration agreement shall be deemed to be in writing if it is contained in—

(a) a document singed by the parties;

(b) an exchange of letters, telex, telegrams, fax, e-mail or other means of telecommunication which provide a record of the agreement; or

(c) an exchange of statement of claim and defence in which the existence of the agreement is alleged by one party and not denied by the other.

Explanation.—The reference in a contract of a document containing an arbitration clause constitutes an arbitration agreement if the contract is in writing and the reference is such as to make that arbitration clause part of the contract.

10. Arbitrability of the dispute

(1) Where any party to an arbitration agreement or any person claiming under him commences any legal proceeding against any other party to the agreement or any person claiming under him in respect of any matter agreed to be referred to arbitration, any party to such legal proceedings may, at any time before filing a written statement, apply to the Court before which the proceedings are pending to refer the matter to arbitration.

(2) Thereupon, the Court shall, if it is satisfied that an arbitration agreement exists, refer the parties to arbitration and stay the proceedings, unless the Court finds that the arbitral agreement is void, inoperative or is incapable of determination by arbitration.

(3) Notwithstanding that an application has been made under sub-section (1) and that the issue is pending before the judicial authority, arbitration may be commenced or continued and an arbitral award made.

CHAPTER IV

COMPOSITION OF ARBITRAL TRIBUNAL

11. Number of arbitrators

(1) Subject to the provisions of sub-section (3) below, the parties are free to determine the number of arbitrators.

(2) Failing the determination of a number referred to in sub-section (1) above the tribunal shall consist of three arbitrators.

(3) Unless otherwise agreed by the parties, where they appoint an even number of arbitrators, the appointed arbitrators shall jointly appoint an additional arbitrator who shall act as a Chairman of the tribunal.

12. Appointment of arbitrators

(1) Subject to the provisions of this Act, the parties are free to agree on a procedure for appointing the arbitrator or arbitrators.

(2) A person of any nationality may be an arbitrator, unless otherwise agreed by the parties.

(3) Failing any agreement referred to in sub-section—

(a) in an arbitration with a sole arbitrator, if the parties fail to agree on the arbitrator within thirty days from receipt of a request by one party from the other party to so agree the appointment shall be made upon request of a party—

(i) by the District Judge in case of arbitration other than international commercial arbitration; and

(ii) in case of international commercial arbitration, the Chief Justice or a Judge of the Supreme Court nominated by the Chief Justice.

(b) in an arbitration with three arbitrators, each party shall appoint one arbitrator, and the two appointed arbitrators shall appoint the third arbitrator who shall be the Chairman of the arbitral tribunal.

(4) If the appointment procedure in sub-section (3) applies and

(a) a party fails to appoint an arbitrator within thirty days of the receipt of a request to do so from the other party; or

(b) the appointed arbitrators fail to agree on the third arbitrator within thirty days of their appointment, the appointment shall be made, upon the application of the party;

(c) by the District Judge except in case of international commercial arbitration; and

(d) by the Chief Justice or by any other Judge of the Supreme Court designated by the Chief Justice in case of international commercial arbitration.

(5) The third arbitrator appointed under clause (b) of sub-section (4) shall be the chairman of the said tribunal.

(6) If more than one arbitrator are appointed under sub-section (4) the District Judge, or the Chief Justice or any other Judge of the Supreme Court designated by the Chief Justice, as the case may be, shall appoint one person from among the said arbitrators to be the chairman of the arbitral tribunal.

(7) Where, under an appointment procedure agreed upon by the parties—

(a) a party fails to act as required under such procedure; or

(b) the parties, or the arbitrators, fail to reach an agreement under the same procedure; or

(c) a person or any third party fails to perform any function assigned to him under that procedure, unless the agreement on the appointment procedure provides other means to take the necessary measure for securing the appointment, a party may apply to;

(d) the District Judge except in case of international commercial arbitration and the District Judge shall appoint the chairman of the tribunal along with the other arbitrators;

(e) the Chief Justice or any Judge of the Supreme Court designated by the Chief Justice in case of international commercial arbitration and the Chief Justice or the Judge of the Supreme Court as designated by the Chief Justice shall appoint the Chairman of the tribunal along with other arbitrators.

(8) The appointment of the arbitrator or arbitrators under sub-sections (3), (4) and (7) shall be made within sixty days from the receipt of the application thereof.

(9) The Chief Justice, or a Judge of the Supreme Court as designated by the Chief Justice, or the District Judge, as the case may be, in appointing an arbitrator under this section, shall have due regard to any qualifications required of the arbitrator under the agreement between the parties, and to such considerations as are likely to secure the appointment of an independent and impartial arbitrator.

(10) In the case of appointment of a sole arbitrator or third arbitrator in an international commercial arbitration, the Chief Justice or the Judge of the Supreme Court designated by the Chief Justice, as the case may be, may appoint an arbitrator of a nationality other than the nationalities of the parties where the parties belong to different nationalities.

(11) The Chief Justice or the District Judge, as the case may be, may make such scheme as he may deem appropriate for dealing with matters under this section.

(12) The decision under sub-sections (3), (4) and (7) of the Chief Justice or the Judge of the Supreme Court designated by the Chief Justice or the District Judge, as the case may be, shall be final.

(13) The Chief Justice may entrust a Judge with the duties for a particular case or cases or for discharging the entire duties and may fix up the tenure of that Judge for the purposes of this section.

Explanation.—In this section "District Judge" means that District Judge within whose local jurisdiction the concerned arbitration agreement has been entered into.

13. Grounds for challenge

(1) When a person is requested to accept appointment as an arbitrator, he shall first disclose any circumstances likely to give to justifiable doubts as to his independence or impartiality.

(2) An arbitrator shall, from the time of his appointment and throughout the arbitral proceedings, without delay, disclose to the parties any circumstances referred to in sub-section (1) unless they have already been so informed by him.

(3) An arbitrator may be challenged only if circumstances exist that give rise to justifiable doubts as to his independence or impartiality, or he does not posses the qualifications agreed to by the parties.

(4) A party may challenge an arbitrator appointed by him, or in whose appointment he has participated, only for reasons of which he becomes aware after the appointment has been made.

14. Challenge procedure

(1) Subject to sub-section (6), the parties shall be free to agree on a procedure for challenging an arbitrator.

(2) Failing any agreement referred to in sub-section (1), a party who intends to challenge an arbitrator shall, within thirty days after becoming aware of the circumstances referred to in sub section (3) of section 13, send a written statement of the reasons for the challenge to the arbitral tribunal.

(3) Unless the arbitrator challenged under sub-section (2), withdraws from his office or the other party agrees to the challenge, the arbitral tribunal shall decide on the challenge within thirty days from the date of filing the written statements referred to in sub-section 2.

(4) Any party aggrieved by the decision of the arbitral tribunal under sub-section (3), may prefer an appeal to the High Court Division within thirty days from the date of the said decision.

(5) The High Court Division shall decide the matter within ninety days from the date on which it is filed.

(6) If a challenge under any procedure agreed upon by the parties or under the procedures of sub section (3) or the appeal preferred against the decision is not successful, the arbitral tribunal shall continue the arbitral proceedings and make an award.

15. Termination of arbitrator's mandate

(1) The mandate of an arbitrator shall terminate, if—

(a) he withdraws himself from office;

(b) he dies;

(c) all the parties agree on the termination of his mandate; or

(d) he is unable to perform his functions of his office or for other reasons fail to act without undue delay and withdraws from his office or the parties agree on the termination of his mandate.

(2) If any arbitrator has incurred disqualifications referred to in clause (d) of sub-section (1) and fails to withdraw himself from his office and all the parties fail to agree on his termination, then on the application by any party within the prescribed period by rules—

(a) the District Judge, in case of arbitrations other than international commercial arbitration;

(b) the Chief Justice or a Judge of the Supreme Court designated by the Chief Justice in case of international commercial arbitration may terminate the said arbitrator.

(3) Where the parties are agreed upon, the termination shall be enforceable by the person agreed by the parties.

(4) If an arbitrator withdraws himself from his office or where all the parties agree on the termination of mandate of an arbitrator under the circumstances as referred to in clause (d) of sub-section (1), it shall not imply acceptance of the validity of any ground referred to in this clause or in sub-section (3) of section 13.

Explanation.—In this section "District Judge" means District Judge within whose local jurisdiction the concerned arbitration agreement has been entered into.

16. Substitution of an arbitrator whose mandate has been terminated

(1) Where the mandate of an arbitrator terminates, a substitute arbitrator shall be appointed according to the provisions applicable to the appointment of the arbitrator whose mandate has been terminated.

(2) In the absence of any agreement between the parties—

(a) the substitute arbitrator shall, at the discretion of the arbitral tribunal, continue the hearings from the stage at which the mandate of the arbitrator has been terminated,

(b) any order or decision of the arbitral tribunal shall not be invalid before the termination of the mandate of an arbitrator due to such termination.

CHAPTER V

JURISDICTION OF ARBITRAL TRIBUNALS

17. Competence of arbitral tribunal to rule on its own jurisdiction

Unless otherwise agreed by the parties, the arbitral tribunal may rule on its own jurisdiction on any questions including the following issues, namely—

(a) whether there is existence of a valid arbitration agreement;

(b) whether the arbitral tribunal is properly constituted;

(c) whether the arbitration agreement is against public policy;

(d) whether the arbitration agreement is incapable of being performed; and,

(e) what matters have been submitted to arbitration in accordance with the arbitration agreement.

18. Severability of agreement

An arbitration agreement which forms part of another agreement shall be deemed to constitute a separate agreement when ruling upon the validity of that arbitration agreement for the purpose of determining the jurisdiction of the arbitral tribunal.

19. Objection as to the jurisdiction of the arbitral tribunal

(1) An objection that the tribunal does not have jurisdiction shall be raised not later than the submission of the statement of defence.

(2) An objection during the course of the arbitral proceedings that the tribunal is exceeding the scope of its authority shall be raised as soon as the matter alleged to be beyond the scope of its authority is raised.

(3) The arbitral tribunal may in either of the cases referred to in sub-sections (1) and (2) admit a later plea if it considers the delay justified.

(4) The arbitral tribunal shall decide on an objection referred to in subsection (1) and (2) and where the arbitral tribunal takes a decision rejecting the plea, continue with the arbitral proceedings and make and arbitral award.

(5) A party shall not be precluded from raising such a plea merely because he has appointed, or has participated in the appointment of an arbitrator.

20. Powers of the High Court Division in deciding jurisdiction

(1) The High Court Division may, on the application of any of the parties to the arbitration agreement, after serving notice upon all other parties, determine any question as to the jurisdiction of the arbitral tribunal.

(2) No application under this section shall be taken into account, unless the High Court Division is satisfied that—

(a) the determination of the question is likely to produce substantial savings in costs;

(b) the application was submitted without any delay; and

(c) there is good reason why the matter should be decided by the Court.

(3) The application shall state the reasons on which the matter should be decided by the High Court Division.

(4) Unless otherwise agreed by the parties, where any application is pending before the High Court Division under this section, the arbitral tribunal shall continue arbitration proceedings and make an arbitral award.

21. Powers of the arbitration tribunal to make interim orders

(1) Unless otherwise agreed by the parties, the arbitral tribunal may, at the request of a party, order a party to take any interim measure of protection as the arbitral tribunal may consider necessary in respect of the subject-matter of the dispute, and no appeal shall lie against this order.

(2) The arbitral tribunal may require a party to provide appropriate security in connection with a measure ordered under sub-section (1).

(3) No order under this section shall be passed without giving a notice to the other parties:

Provided that the arbitral tribunal may, where it appears that the object of taking interim measure under this section would be defeated by the delay, dispense with such notice.

(4) An order of an arbitral tribunal requiring the taking of interim measures may be enforced by the court, on an application made therefor, by the party requesting the taking of such interim measures.

(5) The application filed before the Court for the enforcement of the interim measures under sub section (4) shall be deemed not to be incompatible with section 7 or with the arbitration agreement or a waiver of the agreement.

22. Settlement other than arbitration

(1) It shall not be incompatible with an arbitration agreement for an arbitral tribunal to encourage settlement of the dispute otherwise than by arbitration and, with the agreement of all the parties, the arbitral tribunal may use mediation, conciliation or any other procedures at any time during the arbitral proceedings to encourage settlement.

(2) If, during arbitral proceedings, the parties settle the dispute, the arbitral tribunal shall, if requested by the parties, record the settlement in the form of an arbitral award on agreed terms.

(3) An arbitral award on agreed terms shall be made in accordance with section 38 and shall state that it is an arbitral award on agreed terms.

(4) An arbitral award on agreed terms shall have the same status and effect as any other arbitral award made in respect of the dispute.

CHAPTER VI

CONDUCT OF ARBITRAL PROCEEDINGS

23. General Responsibilities of the arbitral tribunal

(1) The arbitral tribunal shall deal with any of the dispute submitted to it fairly and impartially and for this purpose—

(a) each party shall be given reasonable opportunity to present his case orally or in writing; or both, and

(b) each party shall be given reasonable opportunity to examine all the documents and other relevant materials filed by other party or any other person concerned before the tribunal.

(2) The arbitral tribunal shall deal with a dispute submitted to it as quick as possible.

(3) The arbitral tribunal in conducting proceedings shall act fairly and impartially in deciding procedure and evidence and in exercising other powers conferred on it.

24. The arbitral tribunal not bound by the Code of Civil Procedure and the Evidence Act

The arbitral tribunal shall not be bound to follow the provisions of the Code of Civil Procedure and the Evidence Act in disposing of a dispute under this Act.

25. Determination of rules of procedure

(1) Subject to this Act, the arbitration tribunal shall follow the procedure to be agreed on all or any by the parties in conducting its proceedings.

(2) In the absence of any agreement as to the procedure referred to in sub-section (1), the arbitral tribunal shall, subject to this Act, decide procedural and evidential matters in conducting its proceedings.

(3) Without prejudice to the powers of the parties to include by agreement, or of the arbitral tribunal to include, any other procedural and evidential matters, procedural and evidential matters include—

(a) time and place of holding the proceedings either in whole or in part;

(b) language of the proceedings and to supply translation of a document concerned;

(c) written statement of claim, specimen copy of defence, time of submission and range of amendment;

(d) publication of document and presentation thereof;

(e) the questions asked to the parties and replies thereof;

(f) written or oral evidence as to the admissibility, relevance and weight of any materials;

(g) power of the arbitral tribunal in examining the issue of fact and issue of law;

(h) submission or presentation of oral or documentary evidence.

(4) The arbitral tribunal may fix the time to enforce its orders and extend the time fixed by it.

26. Place of arbitration

(1) The parties shall be free to agree on the place of arbitration.

(2) Failing such an agreement referred to in sub-section (1), the place of arbitration shall be determined by the arbitral tribunal having regard to the circumstances of the case, including the convenience of the parties.

(3) Notwithstanding anything contained in sub-section(1), or sub-section(2), the arbitral tribunal may, unless otherwise agreed by the parties, meet at any place it consider appropriate for consultation among its members, for hearing witness, experts or the parties, or for inspection for documents, goods and other property.

27. Commencement of arbitral proceedings

Unless otherwise agreed by the parties, the proceedings shall be deemed to have commenced if—

(a) any dispute arises where the concerned arbitration agreement applies; and

(b) any party to the agreement—

(i) has received from another party to the agreement a notice requiring that party to refer, or to concur in the reference of, the dispute to arbitration; or

(ii) has received from another party to the agreement a notice requiring that party to appoint an arbitral tribunal or to join or concur in, or approve the appointment of, an arbitral tribunal in relation to the dispute.

28. Consolidation of proceedings and concurrent hearing

(1) The parties shall be free to agree upon in this respect that—

(a) any arbitration proceedings shall be consolidated with other arbitral proceedings;

(b) concurrent hearings shall be held on such terms as may be agreed.

(2) The arbitral tribunal shall have no power to consolidate the proceedings or concurrent hearings, unless the same is given by the parties on agreed terms to the tribunal.

29. Statement of claim and defence

(1) Within the period of time determined by the tribunal, and unless otherwise agreed by the parties, the claimant shall state the facts supporting his claim, the points at issue and the relief or remedy sought, and the respondent shall state his defence in respect of these particulars.

(2) The parties may submit with their statement all documents they consider to be relevant or may add a reference to the documents or other evidence they will submit in future.

(3) Unless otherwise agreed by the parties, either party may amend or supplement his claim or defence during the course of the proceedings, unless the tribunal considers

it inappropriate to allow the amendment or supplement for the sake of fairness or having regard to the delay in making it.

30. Hearings and proceedings

(1) Unless otherwise agreed by the parties, the tribunal shall decide whether to hold oral hearings for the presentation of evidence or for oral argument, or whether the proceedings shall be conducted on the basis of documents and other materials:

Provided that the tribunal shall hold oral hearings, at an appropriate stage of the proceedings, either on a request by a party, or of its own motion, unless the parties have agreed that no oral hearing shall be held.

(2) The parties shall be given sufficient advance notice of any hearing and of any meeting of the tribunal for the purposes of inspection of documents, goods or other property.

(3) All statements, documents or other information supplied to, or applications made to the tribunal by one party shall be communicated to the other party, and any expert report or evidentiary document on which the tribunal may rely in making its decision shall be communicated to the parties.

31. Legal or other representation

Unless otherwise agreed by the parties, a party to an arbitral proceedings may be represented in the proceedings by a lawyer or any other person nominated by him.

32. Power to appoint experts, Legal advisers or assessors

(1) Unless otherwise agreed by the parties, the arbitral tribunal may—

(a) appoint expert or legal adviser to report to it on specific issues to be determined by the tribunal; and

(b) appoint assessor to assist it on technical matters; and

(c) require a party to give the expert, legal adviser or the assessor, as the case may be, any relevant information or to produce, or to provide access to, any relevant documents, goods or other property for his inspection.

(2) Unless otherwise agreed by the parties—

(a) if a party or the arbitral tribunal so requests, the expert, legal adviser or the assessor, as the case may be, shall, after delivery of his written or oral report, participate in an oral hearing where the parties have the opportunity to put questions to him and to present expert witnesses in order to testify on the points at issue;

(b) the expert, legal adviser or the assessor, as the case may be, shall, on the request of a party, make available to that party all documents, goods or other property in the possession of him with which he was provided in order to prepare his report;

(c) the parties shall be given reasonable opportunity to comment on the report, information, opinion or advice submitted in the tribunal by the expert, legal adviser or the assessor.

33. Summons to witnesses

(1) The arbitral tribunal, or a party to the proceedings with the approval of the tribunal, may apply to the Court for issuing summons upon any person necessary for examining, or submitting materials or appearing, or producing before the tribunal for both the purpose, as the case may be, and the Court shall issue such summons.

(2) A person shall not be compelled under any summons issued under sub-section (1) to answer any question or produce any documents or materials which that person could not be compelled to answer or produce at the trial in an action before the Court.

(3) Persons failing to attend before the tribunal in accordance with such summons as issued under sub-section (1), or makes any other default, or refuses to perform, or is guilty of any contempt to the arbitral tribunal during the conduct of arbitral proceedings, shall, upon the representation of arbitral tribunal, be subject to the like punishments by order of the Court as they would incur for the like offences in suits tried before the Court.

34. Evidence before the arbitral tribunal

Unless otherwise agreed by the parties—

(a) evidence may be given before the arbitral tribunal orally or in writing or by affidavit,

(b) the arbitral tribunal may administer on oath or affirmation to a witness subject to his consent.

35. Powers of the arbitral tribunal in case of default of the parties

(1) The parties shall be free to agree on the powers of the arbitral tribunal in case of a party's failure to do something necessary for the proper and expeditious conduct of the arbitration.

(2) Where under sub-section (1) of section 29—

(a) any claimant fails to communicate his statement of claim, the tribunal shall terminate the proceedings; and

(b) the respondent fails to communicate his statement of defence,

the tribunal shall continue the proceedings without treating that failure in itself as an admission of the allegation by the claimant.

(3) If the arbitral tribunal is satisfied that there has been inordinate and inexcusable delay on the part of the claimant in pursuing his claim and that the delay—

(a) gives rise, or is likely to give rise, to a substantial risk that it is not possible to have a fair resolution of the issue in that claim, or

(b) has caused, or is likely to cause, serious prejudice to the respondent, the arbitral tribunal may make an award dismissing the claim.

(4) If without showing sufficient cause a party—

(a) fails to attend or be represented at an oral hearing of which due notice was given, or

(b) where matters are to be dealt with in writing fails, after due notice, to submit written evidence or make written submissions.

The arbitral tribunal may continue the proceedings in the absence of that party or, as the case may be, without any written evidence or submissions on his behalf, and may make an award on the basis of the evidence before it.

(5) If without showing sufficient cause a party fails to comply with any order or directions of the arbitral tribunal, the arbitral tribunal may make an order to comply with such order or directions within such time as it may deem fit.

(6) If a claimant fails to comply with an order of the arbitral tribunal to provide security for costs, the arbitral tribunal may make an award dismissing his claim.

(7) If a party fails to comply with any other kind of order not referred to in any of the sub-sections of this section, then the arbitral tribunal may—

(a) direct that the party in default shall not be entitled to rely upon any allegation or material which was the subject-matter of the order;

(b) draw such adverse inferences from the act of non-compliance as the circumstances justify;

(c) proceed to an award on the basis of such materials as have been properly provided to it; or

(d) make such order, as it thinks fit, as to the payment of costs of the arbitration incurred in consequence of the non-compliance.

CHAPTER VII

MAKING OF ARBITRAL AWARD AND TERMINATION OF PROCEEDINGS

36. Rules applicable to substance of dispute

(1) The arbitral tribunal shall decide the dispute in accordance with the rules of law as are designated by the parties as applicable to the substance of the dispute:

Provided that any designation by the parties of the law or legal system of a given country shall be construed, unless otherwise expressed, as directly referring to the substantive law of that country.

(c) whether the arbitration agreement is against public policy.

(d) whether the arbitration agreement is incapable of being performed, and,

(2) Failing any designation of the law under sub-section (1) by the parties, the arbitral tribunal shall apply the rules of law it considers to be appropriate given all the circumstances surrounding the dispute.

(3) The arbitral tribunal shall decide in accordance with the terms of the contract taking into account the usages of the concerned matter, if any, for ends of justice.

37. Decision making by panel of arbitrators

(1) Unless otherwise agreed by the parties, in arbitral proceedings with more than one arbitrator, any decision of the arbitral tribunal shall be made by a majority of all its members.

(2) Notwithstanding anything contained in sub-section (1), if authorized by the parties or all the members of the arbitral tribunal, questions of procedure may be decided by the Chairman of the arbitral tribunal.

38. Form and contents of arbitral award

(1) An arbitral award shall be made in writing and shall be signed by the arbitrator or arbitrators.

(2) In arbitral proceedings with more than one arbitrator, the signatures of the majority of all the members of the arbitral tribunal shall be sufficient so long as the reason for any omitted signature is stated.

(3) No reasons shall have to be stated by the arbitral tribunal where the parties have agreed that no reasons are to be given, or the award is an arbitral award on agreed terms under section 22.

(4) The arbitral award shall state its date and the place of arbitration as determined in accordance with section 26 and the award shall be deemed to have been made at the place.

(5) After the arbitral award is made, a copy signed by the arbitrator or arbitrators shall be delivered to each party.

(6) Unless otherwise agreed by the parties—

(a) where and in so for as an arbitral award is for the payment of money, the arbitral tribunal may include in the sum for which the award is made interest, at such rate as it deems reasonable, on the whole or any part of money, for the whole or any part of the period between the date on which the cause of action arouse and the date on which the award is made; and

(b) unless the award otherwise directs, the sum directed to be paid by an arbitral award shall carry interest at the rate of two percent (2%) per annum which is more than the usual Bank rate from the date of the award to the date of payment.

Explanation—"Bank Rate" under this sub-section means the rate of interest as determined by the Bangladesh Bank from time to time.

(7) Unless otherwise agreed by the parties—

(a) The costs of an arbitration shall be fixed by the arbitral tribunal.

(b) The arbitral tribunal shall specify—

(i) the party entitled to costs;

(ii) the party who shall pay the costs;

(iii) the amount of costs or method of determining that amount;

(iv) the manner in which the costs shall be paid.

Explanation.—Under this sub-section, "arbitration costs" includes reasonable costs relating to the fees and expenses of the arbitrators and witnesses, legal fees and expenses, any administration fees of the institution supervising the arbitration and any other expenses incurred in connection with the arbitral proceedings and the arbitral award.

39. Award to be final and binding

(1) An arbitral award made by an arbitral tribunal pursuant to an arbitration agreement shall be final and binding both on the parties and on any person claiming through or under them.

(2) Notwithstanding anything contained in sub-section (1), the right of a person to challenge the arbitral award in accordance with the provisions of this Act shall not be affected.

40. Correction and interpretation of awards etc.

(1) Within fourteen days from the receipt of the arbitral award, unless another period of time has been agreed upon by the parties—

(a) a party with notice to the other party—

(j) may request the arbitral tribunal to correct any computation error, any clerical or typographical error or any other error of a similar nature occurring in the award;

(k) may request the arbitral tribunal to any divisible part of the award which has not been sent to the tribunal or if sent it does not affect the arbitral award on the matters sent to the tribunal.

(b) if so agreed by the parties, a party with notice to the other party, may request the arbitral tribunal to give an interpretation of a party or a specific point of the arbitral award.

(2) If the arbitral tribunal considers the request made under sub-section (1) to be justified, it shall make the correction, or give the interpretation as the case may be, within fourteen days from the receipt of the request or where the parties agree upon the longer

period of time on the request of the arbitral tribunal, within that agreed longer period of time.

(3) The arbitral tribunal may correct any computation errors, any clerical or typographical errors or any other errors of similar nature occurring in the award referred to in clause (a) of sub-section (1) within fourteen days from the date of the arbitral award.

(4) Under this section any correction, modification or interpretation, as the case may be, shall form part of the arbitral award.

(5) Unless otherwise agreed by the parties, a party with a notice to the other party, may request, within fourteen days from the receipt of the arbitral award, the arbitral tribunal to make an additional arbitral award as to claims presented in the arbitral proceedings but omitted from the arbitral award.

(6) If the arbitral tribunal considers the request made under sub-section (5) to be justified, it shall make the additional arbitral award within sixty days from the date of receipt of such request.

(7) The provisions of sections 38 and 39 shall apply to a correction, modification or interpretation of the arbitral award or to an additional arbitral award made under this section.

41. Termination of proceedings

(1) The arbitral proceedings shall be terminated by the final arbitral award or by an order of the arbitral tribunal under sub-section (2).

(2) The arbitral tribunal shall issue an order for the termination of the arbitral proceedings where—

- (a) the claimant withdraws his claim, unless the respondent objects to the order and the arbitral tribunal recognises a legitimate interest on his part in obtaining a final settlement of the dispute;
- (b) the parties agree on the termination of the proceedings; or
- (c) the arbitral tribunal finds that the continuation of the proceedings has for any other reason become unnecessary or impossible.

(3) Subject to the provisions of section 40, the mandate of the arbitral tribunal shall terminate with the termination of the arbitral proceedings.

CHAPTER VIII

RECOURSE AGAINST ARBITRAL AWARD

42. Application for setting aside arbitral award

(1) The Court may set aside any arbitral award under this Act other than an award made in an international commercial arbitration on the application of a party within sixty days from the receipt of the award.

(2) The High Court Division may set aside any arbitral award made in an international commercial arbitration held in Bangladesh on the application of a party within sixty days from the receipt of the award.

43. Grounds for setting aside arbitral tribunal

(1) An arbitral award may be set aside if—

- (a) the party making the application furnishes proof that—
  - (i) a party to the arbitration agreement was under some incapacity;
  - (ii) the arbitration agreement is not valid under the law to which the parties have subjected it;

(iii) the party making the application was not given proper notice of the appointment of an arbitrator or of the arbitral proceedings or was otherwise unable due to some reasonable cause to present his case;

(iv) the arbitral award deals with a dispute not contemplated by or not falling within the terms of the submission to arbitration, or it contains decision on matters beyond the scope of the submission to arbitrators: Provided that, if the decisions on matters submitted to arbitration can be separated from those not so submitted, only that part of the arbitral award which contains decisions on matters not submitted to arbitration may be set aside;

(v) the composition of the arbitral tribunal or the arbitral procedure was not in accordance with the agreement of the parties, unless such agreement was in conflict with the provisions of this Act, or, in the absence of such agreement, was not in accordance with the provisions of this Act.

(b) the court or the High Court Division, as the case may be, is satisfied that—

(i) the subject matter of the dispute is not capable of settlement by arbitration under the law for the time being in force in Bangladesh;

(ii) the arbitral award is prima facie opposed to the law for the time being in force in Bangladesh;

(iii) the arbitral award is in conflict with public policy of Bangladesh; or

(iv) the arbitral award is induced or affected by fraud or corruption.

(2) Where an application is made to set aside an award, the court or the High Court Division, as the case may be, may order that any money payable by the award shall be deposited in the Court or the High Court Division, as the case may be, or otherwise secured pending the determination of the application.

Explanation.—The expression "Court", in this section means the Court within the local limits of whose jurisdiction the arbitral award has been finally made and signed.

CHAPTER IX

ENFORCEMENT OF ARBITRAL AWARDS

44. Enforcement of arbitral award

Where the time for making an application to set aside the arbitral award under section 42 has expired, or such application having been made, it has been refused, the award shall be enforced under the Code of Civil Procedure, in the same manner as if it were a decree of the Court.

Explanation.—The expression "Court", in this section means the Court within the local limits of whose jurisdiction the arbitral award has been finally made and signed.

CHAPTER X

RECOGNITION AND ENFORCEMENT OF CERTAIN FOREIGN ARBITRAL AWARDS

45. Recognition and enforcement of foreign arbitral awards

(1) Notwithstanding anything contained in any law for the time being in force, subject to the provisions of section 46—

(a) any foreign award which would be enforceable shall be treated as binding for all purposes on the persons as between whom it was made, and may accordingly be relied on by any of those persons by way of defence, set-off or otherwise in any legal proceedings in Bangladesh;

(b) a foreign arbitral award shall, on the application being made to it by any party, be enforced by execution by the Court under the Code of Civil Procedure, in the same manner as if it were a decree of the Court.

(2) An application for the execution of a foreign arbitral award shall be accompanied by—

(a) the original arbitral award or a copy thereof, duly authenticated in the manner required by the law of the country in which it was made;

(b) the original agreement for arbitration or a duly certified copy thereof; and

(c) such evidence as may be necessary to prove that the award is a foreign award.

(3) If the award or agreement to be produced under sub-section (2) is in English or in any other language excluding Bangla, the party seeking to enforce the award under sub-section (1), shall produce a translation in English certified as correct by a diplomatic or consular agent of the country to which that party belongs or certified as correct in such other manner as may be sufficient according to the law in force in Bangladesh.

Explanation.—The expression "Court" shall mean the District Judge's Court exercising the jurisdiction within the district of Dhaka for the purpose of his section.

46. Grounds for refusing recognition or execution of foreign arbitral awards

(1) Recognition or execution of foreign arbitral award may be refused only on the following grounds, namely—

(a) if the party against whom it is invoked furnished proof to the Court that—

(i) a party to the arbitration agreement was under some incapacity;

(ii) the arbitration agreement is not valid under the law to which the parties have subjected it;

(ii) the party against whom the award is invoked was not given proper notice of the appointment of the arbitrator or of the arbitral proceedings or was otherwise unable due to some reasonable causes to present his case; or

(iv) the concerned foreign arbitral award contains decisions on matters beyond the scope of the submission to arbitration:

Provided that, if the decisions on matters submitted to arbitration can be separated from those not so submitted, that part of the award which contains decisions on matters submitted to arbitration may be recognised and enforced;

(v) the composition of the arbitral tribunal or the arbitral procedure was not in accordance with the agreement of the parties or, failing such agreement, was not in accordance with the law of the country where the arbitration took place;

(vi) the award has not yet become binding on the parties, or has been set aside or suspended by a competent authority of the country in which, or under the law of which, that award was made; or

(b) the court in which recognition or execution of the foreign arbitral award is sought, finds that—

(i) the subject matter of the dispute is not capable of settlement by arbitration under the law for the time being in force in Bangladesh; or

(ii) the recognition and execution of the foreign arbitral award is in conflict with the public policy of Bangladesh.

(2) If an application for the setting aside or suspension of the enforcement of the foreign arbitral award has been made to a competent authority referred to in sub-clause (v) of clause (a) of subsection (1) the Court may, if it considers it proper, adjourn the decision on the enforcement of the foreign arbitral award and may also, on the application of the party claiming enforcement of the foreign award, order the other party to give suitable security.

47. Power of Government to declare specified state

For the purposes of this chapter, the Government may, by notification in the official Gazette, declare a state as a specified state.

CHAPTER XI

APPEALS

48. Appeals

An appeal shall lie from the following orders of the Court to the Appellate Division, namely—

(a) setting aside or refusing to set aside an arbitral award under sub-section (1) of section 42;

(b) refusing to enforce that arbitral award under section 44;

(c) refusing to recognize or enforce any foreign arbitral award under section 45.

CHAPTER XII

MISCELLANEOUS

49. Deposit of costs etc.

(1) The arbitral tribunal may fix the amount of the deposit as an advance for the costs referred to in sub-section (7) of section 38, which it expects will be incurred in respect of the claim submitted to it:

Provided that where, apart from the claim, a counter-claim has been submitted to the arbitral tribunal, it may fix separate amount of deposit for the claim and counter-claim.

(2) The deposit referred to in sub-section (1) shall be payable in equal shares by the parties:

Provided that where one party fails to pay his share of the deposit, the other party may pay that share:

Provided further that where the other party also does not pay the aforesaid share in respect of the claim or the counter-claim, the arbitral tribunal may terminate the arbitral proceedings in respect of such claim or counter claim or refuse to make an award to the parties.

(3) Upon termination of the arbitral proceedings, the arbitral tribunal shall render an accounting to the parties of the deposits received and shall return any unexpended balance to the party or parties, as the case may be.

50. Dispute as to arbitrator's remuneration or costs

(1) If in any case an arbitral tribunal refuses to deliver its award except on payment of the costs demanded by it, the court may, on an application in this behalf, order that—

(a) the arbitral tribunal shall deliver the award to the applicant on payment into court by the applicant of the costs demanded, and

(b) the Court shall, after such inquiry, if any, as it thinks fit, further order that out of the money so paid into Court there shall be paid to the arbitral tribunal by way of costs such sum as the court may consider reasonable and that the balance of the money if any, shall be refunded to the applicant.

(2) An application under sub-section (1) may be made by any party under the fees demanded have been fixed by written agreement between him and the arbitral tribunal, and the tribunal shall be entitled to appear and be heard on any such application.

(3) The Court may make such orders as it thinks fit respecting the costs of the arbitration where any question arises respecting such costs and the arbitral award contains no sufficient provision concerning them.

(4) Subject to the provisions of sub-section (1) and to any provision to the contrary in the arbitration agreement, the arbitral tribunal shall have a lien on the arbitral award for any unpaid costs of the arbitration.

51. Arbitration agreement not to be discharged by death of parties there to

(1) Unless otherwise agreed by the parties—

(a) an arbitration agreement shall not be discharged by the death of any party thereto, but shall in such event be enforceable by or against the legal representative of the deceased;

(b) the mandate of an arbitrator shall not be affected by the death of any party by whom he was appointed.

(2) Nothing in this section shall affect the operation of any law by virtue of which any right of action is extinguished by the death of a person.

52. Provision in case of bankruptcy

(1) Where it is provided by a term in a contract to which an insolvent is a party that any dispute arising thereout or in connection therewith shall be submitted to arbitration, the said term shall, if the receiver adopts the contract, be enforceable by or against him so far as it relates to any such dispute.

(2) Where a person who has been adjudged insolvent had, before the commencement of the insolvency proceedings, become a party to an arbitration agreement, and any matter to which the agreement applies is required to be determined in connection with, or for the purpose of, the bankruptcy proceedings,

(a) then, if the case is one to which sub-section (1) does not apply, any other party or the receiver may apply to the judicial authority having jurisdiction in the bankruptcy proceedings for an order directing that the matter in question shall be submitted to arbitration in accordance with the arbitration agreement; and

(b) the Bankruptcy Court may, if it is of opinion that, having regard to all the circumstances of the case, the matter ought to be determined by arbitration, make an order accordingly.

Explanation.—In this section "Bankruptcy Act" means "Bankruptcy Act, 1997" (Act No. X of 1997) and "Receiver" means the receiver as explained in clause (4) of section 2 of the Bankruptcy Act.

53. Jurisdiction

Notwithstanding anything contained elsewhere in this Act, or in any other law for the time being in force, where with respect to an arbitration agreement any application under this Act has been made in a Court—

(a) that court alone shall have jurisdiction over the arbitral proceedings, and

(b) all subsequent applications arising out of that agreement and the arbitral proceedings shall be made in that court and in no other court.

54. Application of this Act to other laws providing for arbitration

Nothing of this Act shall apply to the Industrial Relations Ordinance, 1969 (XXIII of 1969) or to any other law making special provisions for arbitration.

55. Limitations

(1) Subject to the provisions of this Act, the Limitation Act, shall apply to arbitrations under this Act as they apply to proceedings in Court.

(2) For the purposes of this section and the Limitation Act, an arbitration shall be deemed to have commenced on the date referred to in section 27.

(3) Where an arbitration agreement to submit future dispute to arbitration provided that any claim to which the agreement applies shall be barred unless some step to commence arbitral proceedings is taken within a time fixed by the agreement, the court may, on such terms, if any, as the justice of the case may require, extend the time for such period as it thinks proper.

(4) Where the court orders that an arbitral award be set aside, the period between the commencement of the arbitration and the date of the order of the court shall be excluded in computing the time prescribed by the Limitation Act.

56. Publication of a text in English

After the commencement of this Act, the Government shall, by notification in the official Gazette, publish an Authentic text in English which shall be known as the Authentic English Text of this Act:

Provided that in the event of any conflict between this Act and the English text, this Act shall prevail.

57. Power of the Government to make rules

Subject to the provisions of section 58, the Government may, by notification in the official Gazette, make rules for carrying out the provisions of this Act.

58. Power of the Supreme Court to make rules in certain cases

The Supreme Court may, with the approval of the President, make rules consistent with this Act, for regulating the proceedings of the High Court Division or the Court under this Act.

CHAPTER XIV
REPEALS AND SAVINGS

59. Repeal and savings

(1) The Arbitration (Protocol and Convention) Act, 1937; The Arbitration Act, 1940, hereinafter mentioned as Acts, are hereby repealed.

(2) Notwithstanding such repeal, the provisions of the enactments as referred to in sub-section (1) shall apply to all arbitral proceedings which commenced before this Act came into force unless otherwise agreed by the parties, as if this Act were not promulgated.

INDIA

THE ARBITRATION AND CONCILIATION ACT, 1996

(26 of 1996)

[*16th August, 1996*]

An Act to consolidate and amend the law relating to domestic arbitration, international commercial arbitration and enforcement of foreign arbitral awards as also to define the law relating to conciliation and for matters connected therewith or incidental thereto.

WHEREAS the United Nations Commission on International Trade Law (UNCITRAL) has adopted the UNCITRAL Model Law on International Commercial Arbitration in 1985;

AND WHEREAS the General Assembly of the United Nations has recommended that all countries give due consideration to the said Model Law, in view of the desirability of uniformity of the law of arbitral procedures and the specific needs of international commercial arbitration practice;

AND WHEREAS the UNCITRAL has adopted the UNCITRAL Conciliation Rules in 1980;

AND WHEREAS the General Assembly of the United Nations has recommended the use of the said Rules in cases where a dispute arises in the context of international commercial relations and the parties seek an amicable settlement of that dispute by recourse to conciliation;

AND WHEREAS the said Model Law and Rules make significant contribution to the establishment of a unified legal framework for the fair and efficient settlement of disputes arising in international commercial relations;

AND WHEREAS it is expedient to make law respecting arbitration and conciliation, taking into account the aforesaid Model Law and Rules;

BE it enacted by Parliament in the Forty-seventh Year of the Republic as follows:—

PRELIMINARY

1. Short title, extent and commencement.—(1) This Act may be called the Arbitration and Conciliation Act, 1996.

(2) It extends to the whole of India:

Provided that Parts I, III and IV shall extend to the State of Jammu and Kashmir only in so far as they relate to international commercial arbitration or, as the case may be, international commercial conciliation.

Explanation.—In this sub-section, the expression "international commercial conciliation" shall have the same meaning as the expression "international commercial arbitration" in clause (f) of sub-section (1) of section 2, subject to the modification that for the word "arbitration" occurring therein, the word "conciliation" shall be substituted.

(3) It shall come into force on such date as the Central Government may, by notification in the official Gazette, appoint.

PART I

ARBITRATION

CHAPTER I

GENERAL PROVISIONS

2. Definitions.—(1) In this Part, unless the context otherwise requires,—

(a) "arbitration" means any arbitration whether or not administered by permanent arbitral institution;

(b) "arbitration agreement" means an agreement referred to in section 7;

(c) "arbitral award" includes an interim award;

(d) "arbitral tribunal" means a sole arbitrator or a panel of arbitrators;

(e) "Court" means the principal Civil Court of original jurisdiction in a district, and includes the High Court in exercise of its ordinary original civil jurisdiction, having jurisdiction to decide the questions forming the subject-matter of the arbitration if the same had been the subject-matter of a suit, but does not include any civil court of a grade inferior to such principal Civil Court, or any Court of Small Causes;

(f) "international commercial arbitration" means an arbitration relating to disputes arising out of legal relationships, whether contractual or not, considered as commercial under the law in force in India and where at least one of the parties is—

(i) an individual who is a national of, or habitually resident in, any country other than India; or

(ii) a body corporate which is incorporated in any country other than India; or

(iii) a company or an association or a body of individuals whose central management and control is exercised in any country other than India; or

(iv) the Government of a foreign country;

(g) "legal representative" means a person who in law represents the estate of a deceased person, and includes any person who intermeddles with the estate of the deceased, and, where a party acts in a representative character, the person on whom the estate devolves on the death of the party so acting;

(h) "party" means a party to an arbitration agreement.

Scope

(2) This Part shall apply where the place of arbitration is in India.

(3) This Part shall not affect any other law for the time being in force by virtue of which certain disputes may not be submitted to arbitration.

(4) This Part except sub-section (1) of section 40, sections 41 and 43 shall apply to every arbitration under any other enactment for the time being in force, as if the arbitration were pursuant to an arbitration agreement and as if that other enactment were an arbitration agreement, except in so far as the provisions of this Part are inconsistent with that other enactment or with any rules made thereunder.

(5) Subject to the provisions of sub-section (4), and save in so far as is otherwise provided by any law for the time being in force or in any agreement in force between

India and any other country or countries, this Part shall apply to all arbitrations and to all proceedings relating thereto.

Construction of references

(6) Where this Part, except section 28, leaves the parties free to determine a certain issue, that freedom shall include the right of the parties to authorise any person including an institution, to determine that issue.

(7) An arbitral award made under this Part shall be considered as a domestic award.

(8) Where this Part—

(a) refers to the fact that the parties have agreed or that they may agree, or

(b) in any other way refers to an agreement of the parties, that agreement shall include any arbitration rule referred to in that agreement.

(9) Where this Part, other than clause (a) of section 25 or clause (a) of sub-section (2) of section 32, refers to a claim, it shall also apply to a counter-claim, and where it refers to a defence, it shall also apply to a defence to that counter-claim.

3. Receipt of written communications.—(1) Unless otherwise agreed by the parties,—

(a) any written communication is deemed to have been received if it is delivered to the addressee personally or at his place of business, habitual residence or mailing address, and

(b) if none of the places referred to in clause (a) can be found after making a reasonable inquiry, a written communication is deemed to have been received if it is sent to the addressee's last known place of business, habitual residence or mailing address by registered letter or by any other means which provides a record of the attempt to deliver it.

(2) The communication is deemed to have been received on the day it is so delivered.

(3) This section does not apply to written communications in respect of proceedings of any judicial authority.

4. Waiver of right to object.—A party who knows that—

(a) any provision of this Part from which the parties may derogate, or

(b) any requirement under the arbitration agreement, has not been complied with and yet proceeds with the arbitration without stating his objection to such non-compliance without undue delay or, if a time limit is provided for stating that objection, within that period of time, shall be deemed to have waived his right to so object.

5. Extent of judicial intervention.—Notwithstanding anything contained in any other law for the time being in force, in matters governed by this Part, no judicial authority shall intervene except where so provided in this Part.

6. Administrative assistance.—In order to facilitate the conduct of the arbitral proceedings, the parties, or the arbitral tribunal with the consent of the parties, may arrange for administrative assistance by a suitable institution or person.

CHAPTER II
ARBITRATION AGREEMENT

7. Arbitration agreement.—(1) In this Part, "arbitration agreement" means an agreement by the parties to submit to arbitration all or certain disputes which have arisen or which may arise between them in respect of a defined legal relationship, whether contractual or not.

(2) An arbitration agreement may be in the form of an arbitration clause in a contract or in the form of a separate agreement.

(3) An arbitration agreement shall be in writing.

(4) An arbitration agreement is in writing if it is contained in—

(a) a document signed by the parties;

(b) an exchange of letters, telex, telegrams or other means of telecommunication which provide a record of the agreement; or

(c) an exchange of statements of claim and defence in which the existence of the agreement is alleged by one party and not denied by the other.

(5) The reference in a contract to a document containing an arbitration clause constitutes an arbitration agreement if the contract is in writing and the reference is such as to make that arbitration clause part of the contract.

8. Power to refer parties to arbitration where there is an arbitration agreement.—(1) A judicial authority before which an action is brought in a matter which is the subject of an arbitration agreement shall, if a party so applies not later than when submitting his first statement on the substance of the dispute, refer the parties to arbitration.

(2) The application referred to in sub-section (1) shall not be entertained unless it is accompanied by the original arbitration agreement or a duly certified copy thereof.

(3) Notwithstanding that an application has been made under sub-section (1) and that the issue is pending before the judicial authority, an arbitration may be commenced or continued and an arbitral award made.

9. Interim measures, etc. by Court.—A party may, before or during arbitral proceedings or at any time after the making of the arbitral award but before it is enforced in accordance with section 36, apply to a court—

(i) for the appointment of a guardian for a minor or a person of unsound mind for the purposes of arbitral proceedings; or

(ii) for an interim measure of protection in respect of any of the following matters, namely:—

(a) the preservation, interim custody or sale of any goods which are the subject-matter of the arbitration agreement;

(b) securing the amount in dispute in the arbitration;

(c) the detention, preservation or inspection of any property or thing which is the subject-matter of the dispute in arbitration, or as to which any question may arise therein and authorising for any of the aforesaid purposes any person to enter upon any land or building in the possession of any party, or authorising any sample to be taken or any observation to be made, or experiment to be tried, which may be necessary or expedient for the purpose of obtaining full information or evidence;

(d) interim injunction or the appointment of a receiver;

(e) such other interim measure of protection as may appear to the court to be just and convenient, and the Court shall have the same power for making orders as it has for the purpose of, and in relation to, any proceedings before it.

CHAPTER III
COMPOSITION OF ARBITRAL TRIBUNAL

10. Number of arbitrators.—(1) The parties are free to determine the number of arbitrators, provided that such number shall not be an even number.

(2) Failing the determination referred to in sub-section (1), the arbitral tribunal shall consist of a sole arbitrator.

11. Appointment of arbitrators.—(1) A person of any nationality may be an arbitrator, unless otherwise agreed by the parties.

(2) Subject to sub-section (6), the parties are free to agree on a procedure for appointing the arbitrator or arbitrators.

(3) Failing any agreement referred to in sub-section (2), in an arbitration with three arbitrators, each party shall appoint one arbitrator, and the two appointed arbitrators shall appoint the third arbitrator who shall act as the presiding arbitrator.

(4) If the appointment procedure in sub-section (3) applies and—

(a) a party fails to appoint an arbitrator within thirty days from the receipt of a request to do so from the other party; or

(b) the two appointed arbitrators fail to agree on the third arbitrator within thirty days from the date of their appointment, the appointment shall be made, upon request of a party, by the Chief Justice or any person or institution designated by him.

(5) Failing any agreement referred to in sub-section (2), in an arbitration with a sole arbitrator, if the parties fail to agree on the arbitrator within thirty days from receipt of a request by one party from the other party the appointment shall be made, upon request of a party, by the Chief Justice or any person or institution designated by him.

(6) Where, under an appointment procedure agreed upon by the parties,—

(a) a party fails to act as required under that procedure; or

(b) the parties, or the two appointed arbitrators, fail to reach an agreement expected of them under that procedure; or

(c) a person, including an institution, fails to perform any function entrusted to him or it under that procedure,

a party may request the Chief Justice or any person or institution designated by him to take the necessary measure, unless the agreement on the appointment procedure provides other means for securing the appointment.

(7) A decision on a matter entrusted by sub-section (4) or sub-section (5) or sub-section (6) to the Chief Justice or the person or institution designated by him is final.

(8) The Chief Justice or the person or institution designated by him, in appointing an arbitrator, shall have due regard to—

(a) any qualifications required of the arbitrator by the agreement of the parties; and

(b) other considerations as are likely to secure the appointment of an independent and impartial arbitrator.

(9) In the case of appointment of sole or third arbitrator in an international commercial arbitration, the Chief Justice of India or the person or institution designated by him may appoint an arbitrator of a nationality other than the nationalities of the parties where the parties belong to different nationalities.

(10) The Chief Justice may make such scheme as he may deem appropriate for dealing with matters entrusted by sub-section (4) or sub-section (5) or sub-section (6) to him.

(11) Where more than one request has been made under sub-section (4) or sub-section (5) or sub-section (6) to the Chief Justices of different High Courts or their designates, the Chief Justice or his designate to whom the request has been first made under the relevant sub-section shall alone be competent to decide on the request.

(12) (a) Where the matters referred to in sub-sections (4), (5), (6), (7), (8) and (10) arise in an international commercial arbitration, the reference to "Chief Justice" in those sub-sections shall be construed as a reference to the "Chief Justice of India".

(b) Where the matters referred to in sub-sections (4), (5), (6), (7), (8) and (10) arise in any other arbitration, the reference to "Chief Justice" in those sub-sections shall be construed as a reference to the Chief Justice of the High Court within whose local limits the principal Civil Court referred to in clause (e) of sub-section (1) of section 2 is situate and, where the High Court itself is the Court referred to in that clause, to the Chief Justice of that High Court.

12. Grounds for challenge.—(1) When a person is approached in connection with his possible appointment as an arbitrator, he shall disclose in writing any circumstance likely to give rise to justifiable doubts as to his independence or impartiality.

(2) An arbitrator, from the time of his appointment and throughout the arbitral proceedings, shall, without delay, disclose to the parties in writing any circumstance referred to in sub-section (1) unless they have already been informed of them by him.

(3) An arbitrator may be challenged only if—

(a) circumstances exist that give rise to justifiable doubts as to his independence or impartiality, or

(b) he does not possess the qualifications agreed to by the parties.

(4) A party may challenge an arbitrator appointed by him, or in whose appointment he has participated, only for reasons of which he becomes aware after the appointment has been made.

13. Challenge procedure.—(1) Subject to sub-section (4), the parties are free to agree on a procedure for challenging an arbitrator.

(2) Failing any agreement referred to in sub-section (1), a party who intends to challenge an arbitrator shall, within fifteen days after becoming aware of the constitution of the arbitral tribunal or after becoming aware of any circumstance referred to in sub-section (3) of section 12, send a written statement of the reasons for the challenge to the arbitral tribunal.

(3) Unless the arbitrator challenged under sub-section (2) withdraws from his office or the other party agrees to the challenge, the arbitral tribunal shall decide on the challenge.

(4) If a challenge under any procedure agreed upon by the parties or under the procedure under sub-section (2) is not successful, the arbitral tribunal shall continue the arbitral proceedings and make an arbitral award.

(5) Where an arbitral award is made under sub-section (4), the party challenging the arbitrator may make an application for setting aside such an arbitral award in accordance with section 34.

(6) Where an arbitral award is set aside on an application made under sub-section (5), the Court may decide as to whether the arbitrator who is challenged is entitled to any fees.

14. Failure or impossibility to act.—(1) The mandate of an arbitrator shall terminate if—

(a) he becomes *de jure* or *de facto* unable to perform his functions or for other reasons fails to act without undue delay; and

(b) he withdraws from his office or the parties agree to the termination of his mandate.

(2) If a controversy remains concerning any of the grounds referred to in clause (a) of sub-section (1), a party may, unless otherwise agreed by the parties, apply to the Court to decide on the termination of the mandate.

(3) If, under this section or sub-section (3) of section 13, an arbitrator withdraws from his office or a party agrees to the termination of the mandate of an arbitrator, it shall not imply acceptance of the validity of any ground referred to in this section or sub-section (3) of section 12.

15. Termination of mandate and substitution of arbitrator.—(1) In addition to the circumstances referred to in section 13 or section 14, the mandate of an arbitrator shall terminate—

(a) where he withdraws from office for any reason; or

(b) by or pursuant to agreement of the parties.

(2) Where the mandate of an arbitrator terminates, a substitute arbitrator shall be appointed according to the rules that were applicable to the appointment of the arbitrator being replaced.

(3) Unless otherwise agreed by the parties, where an arbitrator is replaced under sub-section (2), any hearings previously held may be repeated at the discretion of the arbitral tribunal.

(4) Unless otherwise agreed by the parties, an order or ruling of the arbitral tribunal made prior to the replacement of an arbitrator under this section shall not be invalid solely because there has been a change in the composition of the arbitral tribunal.

CHAPTER IV

JURISDICTION OF ARBITRAL TRIBUNALS

16. Competence of arbitral tribunal to rule on its jurisdiction.—(1) The arbitral tribunal may rule on its own jurisdiction, including ruling on any objections with respect to the existence or validity of the arbitration agreement, and for that purpose,—

(a) an arbitration clause which forms part of a contract shall be treated as an agreement independent of the other terms of the contract; and

(b) a decision by the arbitral tribunal that the contract is null and void shall not entail *ipso jure* the invalidity of the arbitration clause.

(2) A plea that the arbitral tribunal does not have jurisdiction shall be raised not later than the submission of the statement of defence; however, a party shall not be precluded from raising such a plea merely because he has appointed, or participated in the appointment of, an arbitrator.

(3) A plea that the arbitral tribunal is exceeding the scope of its authority shall be raised as soon as the matter alleged to be beyond the scope of its authority is raised during the arbitral proceedings.

(4) The arbitral tribunal may, in either of the case referred to in sub-section (2) or sub-section (3), admit a later plea if it considers the delay justified.

(5) The arbitral tribunal shall decide on a plea referred to in sub-section (2) or sub-section (3) and, where the arbitral tribunal takes a decision rejecting the plea, continue with the arbitral proceedings and make an arbitral award.

(6) A party aggrieved by such an arbitral award may make an application for setting aside such an arbitral award in accordance with section 34.

17. Interim measures ordered by arbitral tribunal.—(1) Unless otherwise agreed by the parties, the arbitral tribunal may, at the request of a party, order a party to take any interim measure of protection as the arbitral tribunal may consider necessary in respect of the subject-matter of the dispute.

(2) The arbitral tribunal may require a party to provide appropriate security in connection with a measure ordered under sub-section (1).

CHAPTER V

CONDUCT OF ARBITRAL PROCEEDINGS

18. Equal treatment of parties.—The parties shall be treated with equality and each party shall be given a full opportunity to present his case.

19. Determination of rules of procedure.—(1) The arbitral tribunal shall not be bound by the Code of Civil Procedure, 1908 (5 of 1908) or the Indian Evidence Act, 1872 (1 of 1872).

(2) Subject to this Part, the parties are free to agree on the procedure to be followed by the arbitral tribunal in conducting its proceedings.

(3) Failing any agreement referred to in sub-section (2), the arbitral tribunal may, subject to this Part, conduct the proceedings in the manner it considers appropriate.

(4) The power of the arbitral tribunal under sub-section (3) includes the power to determine the admissibility, relevance, materiality and weight of any evidence.

20. Place of arbitration.—(1) The parties are free to agree on the place of arbitration.

(2) Failing any agreement referred to in sub-section (1), the place of arbitration shall be determined by the arbitral tribunal having regard to the circumstances of the case, including the convenience of the parties.

(3) Notwithstanding sub-section (1) or sub-section (2), the arbitral tribunal may, unless otherwise agreed by the parties, meet at any place it considers appropriate for consultation among its members, for hearing witnesses, experts or the parties, or for inspection of documents, goods or other property.

21. Commencement of arbitral proceedings.—Unless otherwise agreed by the parties, the arbitral proceedings in respect of a particular dispute commences on the date on which a request for that dispute to be referred to arbitration is received by the respondent.

22. Language.—(1) The parties are free to agree upon the language or languages to be used in the arbitral proceedings.

(2) Failing any agreement referred to in sub-section (1), the arbitral tribunal shall determine the language or languages to be used in the arbitral proceedings.

(3) The agreement or determination, unless otherwise specified, shall apply to any written statement by a party, any hearing and any arbitral award, decision or other communication by the arbitral tribunal.

(4) The arbitral tribunal may order that any documentary evidence shall be accompanied by a translation into the language or languages agreed upon by the parties or determined by the arbitral tribunal.

23. Statement of claim and defence.—(1) Within the period of time agreed upon by the parties or determined by the arbitral tribunal, the claimant shall state the facts supporting his claim, the points at issue and the relief or remedy sought, and the respondent shall state his defence in respect of these particulars, unless the parties have otherwise agreed as to the required elements of those statements.

(2) The parties may submit with their statements all documents they consider to be relevant or may add a reference to the documents or other evidence they will submit.

(3) Unless otherwise agreed by the parties, either party may amend or supplement his claim or defence during the course of the arbitral proceedings, unless the arbitral tribunal considers it inappropriate to allow the amendment or supplement having regard to the delay in making it.

24. Hearings and written proceedings.—(1) Unless otherwise agreed by the parties, the arbitral tribunal shall decide whether to hold oral hearings for the presentation of evidence or for oral argument, or whether the proceedings shall be conducted on the basis of documents and other materials:

Provided that the arbitral tribunal shall hold oral hearings, at an appropriate stage of the proceedings, on a request by a party, unless the parties have agreed that no oral hearing shall be held.

(2) The parties shall be given sufficient advance notice of any hearing and of any meeting of the arbitral tribunal for the purposes of inspection of documents, goods or other property.

(3) All statements, documents or other information supplied to, or applications made to the arbitral tribunal by one party shall be communicated to the other party, and any expert report or evidentiary document on which the arbitral tribunal may rely in making its decision shall be communicated to the parties.

25. Default of a party.—Unless otherwise agreed by the parties, where, without showing sufficient cause,—

(a) the claimant fails to communicate his statement of claim in accordance with sub-section (1) of section 23, the arbitral tribunal shall terminate the proceedings;

(b) the respondent fails to communicate his statement of defence in accordance with sub-section (1) of section 23, the arbitral tribunal shall continue the proceedings without treating that failure in itself as an admission of the allegations by the claimant;

(c) a party fails to appear at an oral hearing or to produce documentary evidence, the arbitral tribunal may continue the proceedings and make the arbitral award on the evidence before it.

26. Expert appointment by arbitral tribunal.—(1) Unless otherwise agreed by the parties, the arbitral tribunal may—

(a) appoint one or more experts to report to it on specific issues to be determined by the arbitral tribunal, and

(b) require a party to give the expert any relevant information or to produce, or provide access to, any relevant documents, goods or other property for his inspection.

(2) Unless otherwise agreed by the parties, if a party so requests or if the arbitral tribunal considers it necessary, the expert shall, after delivery of his written or oral report, participate in an oral hearing where the parties have the opportunity to put questions to him and to present expert witnesses in order to testify on the points at issue.

(3) Unless otherwise agreed by the parties, the expert shall, on the request of a party, make available to that party for examination all documents, goods or other property in the possession of the expert with which he was provided in order to prepare his report.

27. Court assistance in taking evidence.—(1) The arbitral tribunal, or a party with the approval of the arbitral tribunal, may apply to the Court for assistance in taking evidence.

(2) The application shall specify—

(a) the names and addresses of the parties and the arbitrators;

(b) the general nature of the claim and the relief sought;

(c) the evidence to be obtained, in particular,—

(i) the name and address of any person to be heard as witness or expert witness and a statement of the subject-matter of the testimony required;

(ii) the description of any document to be produced or property to be inspected.

(3) The Court may, within its competence and according to its rules on taking evidence, execute the request by ordering that the evidence be provided directly to the arbitral tribunal.

(4) The Court may, while making an order under sub-section (3), issue the same processes to witnesses as it may issue in suits tried before it.

(5) Persons failing to attend in accordance with such process, or making any other default, or refusing to give their evidence, or guilty of any contempt to the arbitral tribunal during the conduct of arbitral proceedings, shall be subject to the like disadvantages, penalties and punishments by order of the Court on the representation of the arbitral tribunal as they would incur for the like offences in suits tried before the Court.

(6) In this section the expression "Processes" includes summons and commissions for the examination of witnesses and summons to produce documents.

CHAPTER VI

MAKING OF ARBITRAL AWARD AND TERMINATION OF PROCEEDINGS

28. Rules applicable to substance of dispute.—(1) Where the place of arbitration is situate in India,—

(a) in an arbitration other than an international commercial arbitration, the arbitral tribunal shall decide the dispute submitted to arbitration in accordance with the substantive law for the time being in force in India;

(b) in international commercial arbitration,—

(i) the arbitral tribunal shall decide the dispute in accordance with the rules of law designated by the parties as applicable to the substance of the dispute;

(ii) any designation by the parties of the law or legal system of a given country shall be construed, unless otherwise expressed, as directly referring to the substantive law of that country and not to its conflict of laws rules;

(iii) failing any designation of the law under clause (a) by the parties, the arbitral tribunal shall apply the rules of law it considers to be appropriate, given all the circumstances surrounding the dispute.

(2) The arbitral tribunal shall decide *ex aequo et bono* or as *amiable compositeur* only if the parties have expressly authorised it to do so.

(3) In all cases, the arbitral tribunal shall decide in accordance with the terms of the contract and shall take into account the usages of the trade applicable to the transaction.

29. Decision making by panel of arbitrators.—(1) Unless otherwise agreed by the parties, in arbitral proceedings with more than one arbitrator, any decision of the arbitral tribunal shall be made by a majority of all its members.

(2) Notwithstanding sub-section (1), if authorised by the parties or all the members of the arbitral tribunal, questions of procedure may be decided by the presiding arbitrator.

30. Settlement.—(1) It is not incompatible with an arbitration agreement for an arbitral tribunal to encourage settlement of the dispute and, with the agreement of the parties, the arbitral tribunal may use mediation, conciliation or other procedures at any time during the arbitral proceedings to encourage settlement.

(2) If, during arbitral proceedings, the parties settle the dispute, the arbitral tribunal shall terminate the proceedings and, if requested by the parties and not objected to by the arbitral tribunal, record the settlement in the form of an arbitral award on agreed terms.

(3) An arbitral award on agreed terms shall be made in accordance with section 31 and shall state that it is an arbitral award.

(4) An arbitral award on agreed terms shall have the same status and effect as any other arbitral award on the substance of the dispute.

31. Form and contents of arbitral award.—(1) An arbitral award shall be made in writing and shall be signed by the members of the arbitral tribunal.

(2) For the purposes of sub-section (1), in arbitral proceedings with more than one arbitrator, the signatures of the majority of all the members of the arbitral tribunal shall be sufficient so long as the reason for any omitted signature is stated.

(3) The arbitral award shall state the reasons upon which it is based, unless—

(a) the parties have agreed that no reasons are to be given, or

(b) the award is an arbitral award on agreed terms under section 30.

(4) The arbitral award shall state its date and the place of arbitration as determined in accordance with section 20 and the award shall be deemed to have been made at that place.

(5) After the arbitral award is made, a signed copy shall be delivered to each party.

(6) The arbitral tribunal may, at any time during the arbitral proceedings, make an interim arbitral award on any matter with respect to which it may make a final arbitral award.

(7) (a) Unless otherwise agreed by the parties, where and in so far as an arbitral award is for the payment of money, the arbitral tribunal may include in the sum for

which the award is made interest, at such rate as it deems reasonable, on the whole or any part of the money, for the whole or any part of the period between the date on which the cause of action arose and the date on which the award is made.

(b) A sum directed to be paid by an arbitral award shall, unless the award otherwise directs, carry interest at the rate of eighteen per centum per annum from the date of the award to the date of payment.

(8) Unless otherwise agreed by the parties,—

(a) the costs of an arbitration shall be fixed by the arbitral tribunal;

(b) the arbitral tribunal shall specify—

(i) the party entitled to costs,

(ii) the party who shall pay the costs,

(iii) the amount of costs or method of determining that amount, and

(iv) the manner in which the costs shall be paid.

Explanation.—For the purpose of clause (a), "costs" means reasonable costsrelating to—

(i) the fees and expenses of the arbitrators and witnesses,

(ii) legal fees and expenses,

(iii) any administration fees of the institution supervising the arbitration, and

(iv) any other expenses incurred in connection with the arbitral proceedings and the arbitral award.

32. Termination of proceedings.—(1) The arbitral proceedings shall be terminated by the final arbitral award or by an order of the arbitral tribunal under sub-section (2).

(2) The arbitral tribunal shall issue an order for the termination of the arbitral proceedings where—

(a) the claimant withdraws his claim, unless the respondent objects to the order and the arbitral tribunal recognises a legitimate interest on his part in obtaining a final settlement of the dispute,

(b) the parties agree on the termination of the proceedings, or

(c) the arbitral tribunal finds that the continuation of the proceedings has for any other reason become unnecessary or impossible.

(3) Subject to section 33 and sub-section (4) of section 34, the mandate of the arbitral tribunal shall terminate with the termination of the arbitral proceedings.

33. Correction and interpretation of award; additional award.—(1) Within thirty days from the receipt of the arbitral award, unless another period of time has been agreed upon by the parties—

(a) a party, with notice to the other party, may request the arbitral tribunal to correct any computation errors, any clerical or typographical errors or any other errors of a similar nature occurring in the award;

(b) if so agreed by the parties, a party, with notice to the other party, may request the arbitral tribunal to give an interpretation of a specific point or part of the award.

(2) If the arbitral tribunal considers the request made under sub-section (1) to be justified, it shall make the correction or give the interpretation within thirty days from the receipt of the request and the interpretation shall form part of the arbitral award.

(3) The arbitral tribunal may correct any error of the type referred to in clause (a) of sub-section (1), on its own initiative, within thirty days from the date of the arbitral award.

(4) Unless otherwise agreed by the parties, a party with notice to the other party, may request, within thirty days from the receipt of the arbitral award, the arbitral tribunal to make an additional arbitral award as to claims presented in the arbitral proceedings but omitted from the arbitral award.

(5) If the arbitral tribunal considers the request made under sub-section (4) to be justified, it shall make the additional arbitral award within sixty days from the receipt of such request.

(6) The arbitral tribunal may extend, if necessary, the period of time within which it shall make a correction, give an interpretation or make an additional arbitral award under sub-section (2) or sub-section (5).

(7) Section 31 shall apply to a correction or interpretation of the arbitral award or to an additional arbitral award made under this section.

CHAPTER VII
RECOURSE AGAINST ARBITRAL AWARD

34. Application for setting aside arbitral award.—(1) Recourse to a Court against an arbitral award may be made only by an application for setting aside such award in accordance with sub-section (2) and sub-section (3).

(2) An arbitral award may be set aside by the Court only if—

(a) the party making the application furnishes proof that—

(i) a party was under some incapacity, or

(ii) the arbitration agreement is not valid under the law to which the parties have subjected it or, failing any indication thereon, under the law for the time being in force; or

(iii) the party making the application was not given proper notice of the appointment of an arbitrator or of the arbitral proceedings or was otherwise unable to present his case; or

(iv) the arbitral award deals with a dispute not contemplated by or not falling within the terms of the submission to arbitration, or it contains decisions on matters beyond the scope of the submission to arbitration:

Provided that, if the decisions on matters submitted to arbitration can be separated from those not so submitted, only that part of the arbitral award which contains decisions on matters not submitted to arbitration may be set aside; or

(v) the composition of the arbitral tribunal or the arbitral procedure was not in accordance with the agreement of the parties, unless such agreement was in conflict with a provision of this Part from which the parties cannot derogate, or, failing such agreement, was not in accordance with this Part; or

(b) the Court finds that—

(i) the subject-matter of the dispute is not capable of settlement by arbitration under the law for the time being in force, or

(ii) the arbitral award is in conflict with the public policy of India.

Explanation.—Without prejudice to the generality of sub-clause (ii) it is hereby declared, for the avoidance of any doubt, that an award is in conflict with the public policy of India if the making of the award was induced or affected by fraud or corruption or was in violation of section 75 or section 81.

(3) An application for setting aside may not be made after three months have elapsed from the date on which the party making that application had received the arbitral award or, if a request had been made under section 33, from the date on which that request had been disposed of by the arbitral tribunal:

Provided that if the Court is satisfied that the applicant was prevented by sufficient cause from making the application within the said period of three months it may entertain the application within a further period of thirty days, but not thereafter.

(4) On receipt of an application under sub-section (1), the Court may, where it is appropriate and it is so requested by a party, adjourn the proceedings for a period of time determined by it in order to give the arbitral tribunal an opportunity to resume the arbitral proceedings or to take such other action as in the opinion of arbitral tribunal will eliminate the grounds for setting aside the arbitral award.

CHAPTER VIII

FINALITY AND ENFORCEMENT OF ARBITRAL AWARDS

35. Finality of arbitral awards.—Subject to this Part an arbitral award shall be final and binding on the parties and persons claiming under them, respectively.

36. Enforcement.—Where the time for making an application to set aside the arbitral award under section 34 has expired, or such application having been made, has been refused, the award shall be enforced under the Code of Civil Procedure, 1908 (5 of 1908) in the same manner as if it were a decree of the Court.

CHAPTER IX

APPEALS

37. Appealable orders.—(1) An appeal shall lie from the following orders (and from no others) to the Court authorised by law to hear appeals from original decrees of the Court passing the order, namely:—

(a) granting or refusing to grant any measure under section 9;

(b) setting aside or refusing to set aside an arbitral award under section 34.

(2) An appeal shall also lie to a Court from an order granting of the arbitral tribunal.—

(a) accepting the plea referred in sub-section (2) or sub-section (3) of section 16; or

(b) granting or refusing to grant an interim measure under section 17.

(3) No second appeal shall lie from an order passed in appeal under this section, but nothing in this section shall affect or take away any right to appeal to the Supreme Court.

CHAPTER X

MISCELLANEOUS

38. Deposits.—(1) The arbitral tribunal may fix the amount of the deposit or supplementary deposit, as the case may be, as an advance for the costs referred to in sub-section (8) of section 31, which it expects will be incurred in respect of the claim submitted to it:

Provided that where, apart from the claim, a counter-claim has been submitted to the arbitral tribunal, it may fix separate amount of deposit for the claim and counter-claim.

(2) The deposit referred to in sub-section (1) shall be payable in equal shares by the parties:

Provided that where one party fails to pay his share of the deposit, the other party may pay that share:

Provided further that where the other party also does not pay the aforesaid share in respect of the claim or the counter-claim, the arbitral tribunal may suspend or terminate the arbitral proceedings in respect of such claim or counter-claim, as the case may be.

(3) Upon termination of the arbitral proceedings, the arbitral tribunal shall render an accounting to the parties of the deposits received and shall return any unexpended balance to the party or parties, as the case may be.

39. Lien on arbitral award and deposits as to costs.—(1) Subject to the provisions of sub-section (2) and to any provision to the contrary in the arbitration agreement, the arbitral tribunal shall have a lien on the arbitral award for any unpaid costs of the arbitration.

(2) If in any case an arbitral tribunal refuses to deliver its award except on payment of the costs demanded by it, the Court may, on an application in this behalf, order that the arbitral tribunal shall deliver the arbitral award to the applicant on payment into Court, by the applicant of the costs demanded, and shall, after such inquiry, if any, as it thinks fit, further order that out of the money so paid into Court there shall be paid to the arbitral tribunal by way of costs such sum as the Court may consider reasonable and that the balance of the money, if any, shall be refunded to the applicant.

(3) An application under sub-section (2) may be made by any party unless the fees demanded have been fixed by written agreement between him and the arbitral tribunal, and the arbitral tribunal shall be entitled to appear and be heard on any such application.

(4) The Court may make such orders as it thinks fit respecting the costs of the arbitration where any question arises respecting such costs and the arbitral award contains no sufficient provision concerning them.

40. Arbitration agreement not to be discharged by death of party thereto.—(1) An arbitration agreement shall not be discharged by the death of any party thereto either as respects the deceased or as respects any other party, but shall in such event be enforceable by or against the legal representative of the deceased.

(2) The mandate of an arbitrator shall not be terminated by the death of any party by whom he was appointed.

(3) Nothing in this section shall affect the operation of any law by virtue of which any right of action is extinguished by the death of a person.

41. Provisions in case of insolvency.—(1) Where it is provided by a term in a contract to which an insolvent is a party that any dispute arising therefrom or in connection therewith shall be submitted to arbitration, the said term shall, if the receiver adopts the contract, be enforceable by or against him so far as it relates to any such dispute.

(2) Where a person who has been adjudged as an insolvent had, before the commencement of the insolvency proceedings, become a party to an arbitration agreement, and any matter to which the agreement applies is required to be determined in connection with, or for the purposes of, the insolvency proceedings, then, if the case is one to which sub-section (1) does not apply, any other party or the receiver may apply

to the judicial authority having jurisdiction in the insolvency proceedings for an order directing that the matter in question shall be submitted to arbitration in accordance with the arbitration agreement, and the judicial authority may, if it is of opinion that, having regard to all the circumstances of the case, the matter ought to be determined by arbitration, make an order accordingly.

(3) In this section the expression "receiver" includes an Official Assignee.

42. Jurisdiction.—Notwithstanding anything contained elsewhere in this Part or in any other law for the time being in force, where with respect to an arbitration agreement any application under this Part has been made in a Court, that Court alone shall have jurisdiction over the arbitral proceedings and all subsequent applications arising out of that agreement and the arbitral proceedings shall be made in that Court and in no other Court.

43. Limitations.—(1) The Limitation Act, 1963 (36 of 1963), shall apply to arbitrations as it applies to proceedings in Court.

(2) For the purposes of this section and the Limitation Act, 1963 (36 of 1963), an arbitration shall be deemed to have commenced on the date referred to in section 21.

(3) Where an arbitration agreement to submit future disputes to arbitration provides that any claim to which the agreement applies shall be barred unless some step to commence arbitral proceedings is taken within a time fixed by the agreement, and a dispute arises to which the agreement applies, the Court, if it is of opinion that in the circumstances of the case undue hardship would otherwise be caused, and notwithstanding that the time so fixed has expired, may on such terms, if any, as the justice of the case may require, extend the time for such period as it thinks proper.

(4) Where the Court orders that an arbitral award be set aside, the period between the commencement of the arbitration and the date of the order of the Court shall be excluded in computing the time prescribed by the Limitation Act, 1963 (36 of 1963), for the commencement of the proceedings (including arbitration) with respect to the dispute so submitted.

PART II
ENFORCEMENT OF CERTAIN FOREIGN AWARDS

CHAPTER I

NEW YORK CONVENTION AWARDS

44. Definition.—In this Chapter, unless the context otherwise requires, "foreign award" means an arbitral award on differences between persons arising out of legal relationships, whether contractual or not, considered as commercial under the law in force in India, made on or after the 11th day of October, 1960—

(a) in pursuance of an agreement in writing for arbitration to which the Convention set forth in the First Schedule applies, and

(b) in one of such territories as the Central Government, being satisfied that reciprocal provisions have been made may, by notification in the Official Gazette, declare to be territories to which the said Convention applies.

45. Power of judicial authority to refer parties to arbitration.—Notwithstanding anything contained in Part I or in the Code of Civil Procedure, 1908 (5 of 1908), a judicial authority, when seized of an action in a matter in respect of which the parties have made an agreement referred to in section 44, shall, at the request of one of the parties or any person claiming through or under him, refer the parties to arbitration, unless it finds that the said agreement is null and void, inoperative or incapable of being performed.

46. When foreign award binding.—Any foreign award which would be enforceable under this Chapter shall be treated as binding for all purposes on the persons between whom it was made, and may accordingly be relied on by any of those persons by way of defence, set off or otherwise in any legal proceeding in India and any reference in this Chapter for enforcing a foreign award shall be construed as including references for relying on an award.

47. Evidence.—(1) The party applying for the enforcement of a foreign award shall, at the time of the application, produce before the court—

(a) the original award or a copy thereof, duly authenticated in the manner required by the law of the country in which it was made;

(b) the original agreement for arbitration or a duly certified copy thereof; and

(c) such evidence as may be necessary to prove that the award is a foreign award.

(2) If the award or agreement to be produced under sub-section (1) is in a foreign language, the party seeking to enforce the award shall produce a translation into English, certified as correct by a diplomatic or consular agent of the country to which that party belongs or certified as correct in such other manner as may be sufficient according to the law in force in India.

Explanation.—In this section and all the following sections of this Chapter, "Court" means the principal Civil Court of original jurisdiction in a district, and includes the High Court in exercise of its ordinary original civil jurisdiction, having jurisdiction over the subject-matter of the award if the same had been the subject-matter of a suit, but does not include any civil court of a grade inferior to such principal Civil Court, or any Court of Small Causes.

48. Conditions for enforcement of foreign awards.—(1) Enforcement of a foreign award may be refused, at the request of the party against whom it is invoked, only if that party furnishes to the court proof that—

(a) the parties to the agreement referred to in section 44 were, under the law applicable to them, under some incapacity, or the said agreement is not valid under the law to which the parties have subjected it or, failing any indication thereon, under the law of the country where the award was made; or

(b) the party against whom the award is invoked was not given proper notice of the appointment of the arbitrator or of the arbitral proceedings or was otherwise unable to present his case; or

(c) the award deals with a difference not contemplated by or not falling within the terms of the submission to arbitration, or it contains decisions on matters beyond the scope of the submission to arbitration:

Provided that, if the decisions on matters submitted to arbitration can be separated from those not so submitted, that part of the award which contains decisions on matters submitted to arbitration may be enforced; or

(d) the composition of the arbitral authority or the arbitral procedure was not in accordance with the agreement of the parties, or, failing such agreement, was not in accordance with the law of the country where the arbitration took place; or

(e) the award has not yet become binding on the parties, or has been set aside or suspended by a competent authority of the country in which, or under the law of which, that award was made.

(2) Enforcement of an arbitral award may also be refused if the Court finds that—

(a) the subject-matter of the difference is not capable of settlement by arbitration under the law of India; or

(b) the enforcement of the award would be contrary to the public policy of India.

Explanation.—Without prejudice to the generality of clause (b) of this section, it is hereby declared, for the avoidance of any doubt, that an award is in conflict with the public policy of India if the making of the award was induced or affected by fraud or corruption.

(3) If an application for the setting aside or suspension of the award has been made to a competent authority referred to in clause (e) of sub-section (1) the Court may, if it considers it proper, adjourn the decision on the enforcement of the award and may also, on the application of the party claiming enforcement of the award, order the other party to give suitable security.

49. Enforcement of foreign awards.—Where the Court is satisfied that the foreign award is enforceable under this Chapter, the award shall be deemed to be a decree of that Court.

50. Appealable orders.—(1) An appeal shall lie from the order refusing to—

(a) refer the parties to arbitration under section 45;

(b) enforce a foreign award under section 48,

to the court authorised by law to hear appeals from such order.

(2) No second appeal shall lie from an order passed in appeal under this section, but nothing in this section shall affect or take away any right to appeal to the Supreme Court.

51. Saving.—Nothing in this Chapter shall prejudice any right which any person would have had of enforcing in India of any award or of availing himself in India of any award if this Chapter had not been enacted.

52. Chapter II not to apply.—Chapter II of this Part shall not apply in relation to foreign awards to which this Chapter applies.

CHAPTER II
GENEVA CONVENTION AWARDS

53. Interpretation.—In this Chapter "foreign award" means an arbitral award on differences relating to matters considered as commercial under the law in force in India made after the 28th day of July, 1924,—

(a) in pursuance of an agreement for arbitration to which the Protocol set forth in the Second Schedule applies, and

(b) between persons of whom one is subject to the jurisdiction of some one of such Powers as the Central Government, being satisfied that reciprocal provisions have been made, may, by notification in the Official Gazette, declare to be parties to the Convention set forth in the Third Schedule, and of whom the other is subject to the jurisdiction of some other of the Powers aforesaid, and

(c) in one of such territories as the Central Government, being satisfied that reciprocal provisions have been made, may, by like notification, declare to be territory to which the said Convention applies,

and for the purposes of this Chapter an award shall not be deemed to be final if any proceeding for the purpose of contesting the validity of the award is pending in the country in which it was made.

54. Power of judicial authority to refer parties to arbitration.—Notwithstanding anything contained in Part I or in the Code of Civil Procedure, 1908 (5 of 1908), a judicial authority, on being seized of a dispute regarding a contract made between persons to whom section 53 applies and including an arbitration agreement, whether referring to present or future differences, which is valid under that section and capable of being carried into effect, shall refer the parties on the application of either of them or any person claiming through or under him to the decision of the arbitrators and such reference shall not prejudice the competence of the judicial authority in case the agreement or the arbitration cannot proceed or becomes inoperative.

55. Foreign awards when binding.—Any foreign award which would be enforceable under this Chapter shall be treated as binding for all purposes on the persons between whom it was made, and may accordingly be relied on by any of those persons by way of defence, set off or otherwise in any legal proceeding in India and any reference in this Chapter for enforcing a foreign award shall be construed as including references for relying on an award.

56. Evidence.—(1) The party applying for the enforcement of a foreign award shall, at the time of application, produce before the Court—

(a) the original award or a copy thereof duly authenticated in the manner required by the law of the country in which it was made;

(b) evidence proving that the award has become final; and

(c) such evidence as may be necessary to prove that the conditions mentioned in clauses (a) and (c) of sub-section (1) of section 57 are satisfied.

(2) Where any document requiring to be produced under sub-section (1) is in a foreign language, the party seeking to enforce the award shall produce a translation into English, certified as correct by a diplomatic or consular agent of the country to which that party belongs or certified as correct in such other manner as may be sufficient according to the law in force in India.

Explanation.—In this section and all the following sections of this Chapter, "Court" means the principal Civil Court of original jurisdiction in a district, and includes the High Court in exercise of its ordinary original civil jurisdiction, having jurisdiction over the subject-matter of the award if the same had been the subject-matter of a suit, but does not include any civil court of a grade inferior to such principal Civil Court, or any Court of Small Causes.

57. Conditions for enforcement of foreign awards.—(1) In order that a foreign award may be enforceable under this Chapter, it shall be necessary that—

(a) the award has been made in pursuance of a submission to arbitration which is valid under the law applicable thereto;

(b) the subject-matter of the award is capable of settlement by arbitration under the law of India;

(c) the award has been made by the arbitral tribunal provided for in the submission to arbitration or constituted in the manner agreed upon by the parties and in conformity with the law governing the arbitration procedure;

(d) the award has become final in the country in which it has been made, in the sense that it will not be considered as such if it is open to opposition or appeal or if it is proved that any proceedings for the purpose of contesting the validity of the award are pending;

(e) the enforcement of the award is not contrary to the public policy or the law of India.

Explanation.—Without prejudice to the generality of clause (e), it is hereby declared, for the avoidance of any doubt, that an award is in conflict with the public policy of India if the making of the award was induced or affected by fraud or corruption.

(2) Even if the conditions laid down in sub-section (1) are fulfilled, enforcement of the award shall be refused if the Court is satisfied that—

(a) the award has been annulled in the country in which it was made;

(b) the party against whom it is sought to be used has not been given notice of the arbitration proceedings in sufficient time to enable him to present his case; or that, being under a legal incapacity, he was not properly represented;

(c) the award does not deal with the differences contemplated by or falling within the terms of the submission to arbitration or that it contains decisions on matters beyond the scope of the submission to arbitration:

Provided that if the award has not covered all the differences submitted to the arbitral tribunal, the Court may, if it thinks fit, postpone such enforcement or grant it subject to such guarantee as the Court may decide.

(3) If the party against whom the award has been made proves that under the law governing the arbitration procedure there is a ground, other than the grounds referred to in clauses (a) and (c) of sub-section (1) and clauses (b) and (c) of sub-section (2) entitling him to contest the validity of the award, the Court may, if it thinks fit, either refuse enforcement of the award or adjourn the consideration thereof, giving such party a reasonable time within which to have the award annulled by the competent tribunal.

58. Enforcement of foreign awards.—Where the Court is satisfied that the foreign award is enforceable under this Chapter, the award shall be deemed to be a decree of the Court.

59. Appealable orders.—(1) An appeal shall lie from the order refusing—

(a) to refer the parties to arbitration under section 54; and

(b) to enforce a foreign award under section 57,

to the court authorised by law to hear appeals from such order.

(2) No second appeal shall lie from an order passed in appeal under this section, but nothing in this section shall affect or take away any right to appeal to the Supreme Court.

60. Saving.—Nothing in this Chapter shall prejudice any rights which any person would have had of enforcing in India of any award or of availing himself in India of any award if this Chapter had not been enacted.

PART III
CONCILIATION

61. Application and scope.—(1) Save as otherwise provided by any law for the time being in force and unless the parties have otherwise agreed, this Part shall apply to conciliation of disputes arising out of legal relationship, whether contractual or not and to all proceedings relating thereto.

(2) This Part shall not apply where by virtue of any law for the time being in force certain disputes may not be submitted to conciliation.

62. Commencement of conciliation proceedings.—(1) The party initiating conciliation shall send to the other party a written invitation to conciliate under this Part, briefly identifying the subject of the dispute.

(2) Conciliation proceedings shall commence when the other party accepts in writing the invitation to conciliate.

(3) If the other party rejects the invitation, there will be no conciliation proceedings.

(4) If the party initiating conciliation does not receive a reply within thirty days from the date on which he sends the invitation, or within such other period of time as specified in the invitation, he may elect to treat this as a rejection of the invitation to conciliate and if he so elects, he shall inform in writing the other party accordingly.

63. Number of conciliators.—(1) There shall be one conciliator unless the parties agree that there shall be two or three conciliators.

(2) Where there is more than one conciliator, they ought, as a general rule, to act jointly.

64. Appointment of conciliators.—(1) Subject to sub-section (2),—

(a) in conciliation proceedings with one conciliator, the parties may agree on the name of a sole conciliator;

(b) in conciliation proceedings with two conciliators, each party may appoint one conciliator;

(c) in conciliation proceedings with three conciliators, each party may appoint one conciliator and the parties may agree on the name of the third conciliator who shall act as the presiding conciliator.

(2) Parties may enlist the assistance of a suitable institution or person in connection with the appointment of conciliators, and in particular,—

(a) a party may request such an institution or person to recommend the names of suitable individuals to act as conciliator; or

(b) the parties may agree that the appointment of one or more conciliators be made directly by such an institution or person:

Provided that in recommending or appointing individuals to act as conciliator, the institution or person shall have regard to such considerations as are likely to secure the appointment of an independent and impartial conciliator and, with respect to a sole or third conciliator, shall take into account the advisability of appointing a conciliator of a nationality other than the nationalities of the parties.

65. Submission of statements to conciliator.—(1) The conciliator, upon his appointment, may request each party to submit to him a brief written statement describing the general nature of the dispute and the points at issue. Each party shall send a copy of such statement to the other party.

(2) The conciliator may request each party to submit to him a further written statement of his position and the facts and grounds in support thereof, supplemented by any document and other evidence that such party deems appropriate. The party shall send a copy of such statement, documents and other evidence to the other party.

(3) At any stage of the conciliation proceedings, the conciliator may request a party to submit to him such additional information as he deems appropriate.

Explanation.—In this section and all the following sections of this Part, the term "conciliator" applies to a sole conciliator, or two or three conciliators as the case may be.

66. Conciliator not bound by certain enactments.—The conciliator is not bound by the Code of Civil Procedure, 1908 (5 of 1908) or the Indian Evidence Act, 1872 (1 of 1872).

67. Role of conciliator.—(1) The conciliator shall assist the parties in an independent and impartial manner in their attempt to reach an amicable settlement of their dispute.

(2) The conciliator shall be guided by principles of objectivity, fairness and justice, giving consideration to, among other things, the rights and obligations of the parties, the usages of the trade concerned and the circumstances surrounding the dispute, including any previous business practice between the parties.

(3) The conciliator may conduct the conciliation proceedings in such a manner as he considers appropriate, taking into account the circumstances of the case, the wishes the parties may express, including any request by a party that the conciliator hear oral statements, and the need for a speedy settlement of the dispute.

(4) The conciliator may, at any stage of the conciliation proceedings, make proposals for a settlement of the dispute. Such proposals need not be in writing and need not be accompanied by a statement of the reasons therefor.

68. Administrative assistance.—In order to facilitate the conduct of the conciliation proceedings, the parties, or the conciliator with the consent of the parties, may arrange for administrative assistance by a suitable institution or person.

69. Communication between conciliator and parties.—(1) The conciliator may invite the parties to meet him or may communicate with them orally or in writing. He may meet or communicate with the parties together or with each of them separately.

(2) Unless the parties have agreed upon the place where meetings with the conciliator are to be held, such place shall be determined by the conciliator, after consultation with the parties, having regard to the circumstances of the conciliation proceedings.

70. Disclosure of information.—When the conciliator receives factual information concerning the dispute from a party, he shall disclose the substance of that information to the other party in order that the other party may have the opportunity to present any explanation which he considers appropriate:

Provided that when a party gives any information to the conciliator subject to a specific condition that it be kept confidential, the conciliator shall not disclose that information to the other party.

71. Co-operation of parties with conciliator.—The parties shall in good faith co-operate with the conciliator and, in particular, shall endeavour to comply with requests by the conciliator to submit written materials, provide evidence and attend meetings.

72. Suggestions by parties for settlement of dispute.—Each party may, on his own initiative or at the invitation of the conciliator, submit to the conciliator suggestions for the settlement of the dispute.

73. Settlement agreement.—(1) When it appears to the conciliator that there exist elements of a settlement which may be acceptable to the parties, he shall formulate the terms of a possible settlement and submit them to the parties for their observations. After receiving the observations of the parties, the conciliator may reformulate the terms of a possible settlement in the light of such observations.

(2) If the parties reach agreement on a settlement of the dispute, they may draw up and sign a written settlement agreement. If requested by the parties, the conciliator may draw up, or assist the parties in drawing up, the settlement agreement.

(3) When the parties sign the settlement agreement, it shall be final and binding on the parties and persons claiming under them, respectively.

(4) The conciliator shall authenticate the settlement agreement and furnish a copy thereof to each of the parties.

74. Status and effect of settlement agreement.—The settlement agreement shall have the same status and effect as if it is an arbitral award on agreed terms on the substance of the dispute rendered by an arbitral tribunal under section 30.

75. Confidentiality.—Notwithstanding anything contained in any other law for the time being in force, the conciliator and the parties shall keep confidential all matters relating to the conciliation proceedings. Confidentiality shall extend also to the settlement agreement, except where its disclosure is necessary for purposes of implementation and enforcement.

76. Termination of conciliation proceedings.—The conciliation proceedings shall be terminated—

(a) by the signing of the settlement agreement by the parties on the date of the agreement; or

(b) by a written declaration of the conciliator, after consultation with the parties, to the effect that further efforts at conciliation are no longer justified, on the date of the declaration; or

(c) by a written declaration of the parties addressed to the conciliator to the effect that the conciliation proceedings are terminated, on the date of the declaration; or

(d) by a written declaration of a party to the other party and the conciliator, if appointed, to the effect that the conciliation proceedings are terminated, on the date of the declaration.

77. Resort to arbitral or judicial proceedings.—The parties shall not initiate, during the conciliation proceedings, any arbitral or judicial proceedings in respect of a dispute that is the subject-matter of the conciliation proceedings except that a party may initiate arbitral or judicial proceedings where, in his opinion, such proceedings are necessary for preserving his rights.

78. Costs.—(1) Upon termination of the conciliation proceedings, the conciliator shall fix the costs of the conciliation and give written notice thereof to the parties.

(2) For the purpose of sub-section (1), "costs" means reasonable costs relating to—

(a) the fee and expenses of the conciliator and witnesses requested by the conciliator with the consent of the parties;

(b) any expert advice requested by the conciliator with the consent of the parties;

(c) any assistance provided pursuant to clause (b) of sub-section (2) of section 64 and section 68;

(d) any other expense incurred in connection with the conciliation proceedings and the settlement agreement.

(3) The costs shall be borne equally by the parties unless the settlement agreement provides for a different apportionment. All other expenses incurred by a party shall be borne by that party.

79. Deposits.—(1) The conciliator may direct each party to deposit an equal amount as an advance for the costs referred to in sub-section (2) of section 78 which he expects will be incurred.

(2) During the course of the conciliation proceedings, the conciliator may direct supplementary deposits in an equal amount from each party.

(3) If the required deposits under sub-sections (1) and (2) are not paid in full by both parties within thirty days, the conciliator may suspend the proceedings or may make a written declaration of termination of the proceedings to the parties, effective on the date of that declaration.

(4) Upon termination of the conciliation proceedings, the conciliator shall render an accounting to the parties of the deposits received and shall return any unexpended balance to the parties.

80. Role of conciliator in other proceedings.—Unless otherwise agreed by the parties,—

(a) the conciliator shall not act as an arbitrator or as a representative or counsel of a party in any arbitral or judicial proceeding in respect of a dispute that is the subject of the conciliation proceedings;

(b) the conciliator shall not be presented by the parties as a witness in any arbitral or judicial proceedings.

81. Admissibility of evidence in other proceedings.—The parties shall not rely on or introduce as evidence in arbitral or judicial proceedings, whether or not such proceedings relate to the dispute that is the subject of the conciliation proceedings,—

(a) views expressed or suggestions made by the other party in respect of a possible settlement of the dispute;

(b) admissions made by the other party in the course of the conciliation proceedings;

(c) proposals made by the conciliator;

(d) the fact that the other party had indicated his willingness to accept a proposal for settlement made by the conciliator.

PART IV

SUPPLEMENTARY PROVISIONS

82. Power of High Court to make rules.—The High Court may make rules consistent with this Act as to all proceedings before the Court under this Act.

83. Removal of difficulties.—(1) If any difficulty arises in giving effect to the provisions of this Act, the Central Government may, by order published in the Official Gazette, make such provisions, not inconsistent with the provisions of this Act as appear to it to be necessary or expedient for removing the difficulty:

Provided that no such order shall be made after the expiry of a period of two years from the date of commencement of this Act.

(2) Every order made under this section shall, as soon as may be after it is made, be laid before each House of Parliament.

84. Power to make rules.—(1) The Central Government may, by notification in the Official Gazette, make rules for carrying out the provisions of this Act.

(2) Every rule made by the Central Government under this Act shall be laid, as soon as may be, after it is made before each House of Parliament while it is in session, for a total period of thirty days which may be comprised in one session or in two or more successive sessions, and if, before the expiry of the session immediately following the session or the successive sessions aforesaid, both Houses agree in making any modification in the rule or both Houses agree that the rule should not be made, the rule shall thereafter have effect only in such modified form or be of no effect, as the case may be; so, however, that any such modification or annulment shall be without prejudice to the validity of anything previously done under that rule.

85. Repeal and savings.—(1) The Arbitration (Protocol and Convention) Act, 1937 (6 of 1937), the Arbitration Act, 1940 (10 of 1940) and the Foreign Awards (Recognition and Enforcement) Act, 1961 (45 of 1961) are hereby repealed.

(2) Notwithstanding such repeal,—

(a) the provisions of the said enactments shall apply in relation to arbitral proceedings which commenced before this Act came into force unless otherwise agreed by the parties but this Act shall apply in relation to arbitral proceedings which commenced on or after this Act comes into force;

(b) all rules made and notifications published, under the said enactments shall, to the extent to which they are not repugnant to this Act, be deemed respectively to have been made or issued under this Act.

86. Repeal of Ordinance 27 of 1996 and Saving.—(1) The Arbitration and Conciliation (Third) Ordinance, 1996 (27 of 1996) is hereby repealed.

(2) Notwithstanding such repeal, any order, rule, notification or scheme made or anything done or any action taken in pursuance of any provision of the said Ordinance, shall be deemed to have been made, done or taken under the corresponding provisions of this Act.

THE FIRST SCHEDULE

(*See* section 44)

CONVENTION ON THE RECOGNITION AND ENFORCEMENT OF FOREIGN ARBITRAL AWARDS

Article I

1. This Convention shall apply to the recognition and enforcement of arbitral awards made in the territory of a State other than the State where the recognition and enforcement of such awards are sought, and arising out of differences between persons, whether physical or legal. It shall also apply to arbitral awards not considered as domestic awards in the State where their recognition and enforcement are sought.

2. The term "arbitral awards" shall include not only awards made by arbitrators appointed for each case but also those made by permanent arbitral bodies to which the parties have submitted.

3. When signing, ratifying or acceding to this Convention, or notifying extension under article X hereof, any State may on the basis of reciprocity declare that it will apply the Convention to the recognition and enforcement of awards made only in the territory of another Contracting State. It may also declare that it will apply the Convention only to differences arising out of legal relationships, whether contractual or not, which are considered as commercial under the national law of the State making such declaration.

Article II

1. Each Contracting State shall recognise an agreement in writing under which the parties undertake to submit to arbitration all or any differences which have arisen or which may arise between them in respect of defined legal relationship, whether contractual or not, concerning a subject-matter capable of settlement by arbitration.

2. The term "agreement in writing" shall include an arbitral clause in a contract or an arbitration agreement, signed by the parties or contained in an exchange of letters or telegrams.

3. The court of a Contracting State, when seized of an action in a matter in respect of which the parties have made an agreement within the meaning of this article, shall, at the request of one of the parties, refer the parties to arbitration, unless it finds that the said agreement is null and void, inoperative and incapable of being performed.

Article III

Each Contracting State shall recognize arbitral awards as binding and enforce them in accordance with the rules of procedure of the territory where the award is relied upon, under the conditions laid down in the following articles. There shall not be imposed substantially more onerous conditions or higher fees or charges on the recognition or enforcement of arbitral awards to which this Convention applies than are imposed on the recognition or enforcement of domestic arbitral awards.

Article IV

1. To obtain the recognition and enforcement mentioned in the preceding article, the party applying for recognition and enforcement shall, at the time of the application, supply—

(a) the duly authenticated original award or a duly certified copy thereof;

(b) the original agreement referred to in article II or a duly certified copy thereof.

2. If the said award or agreement is not made in an official language of the country in which the award is relied upon, the party applying for recognition and enforcement of the award shall produce a translation of these documents into such language. The translation shall be certified by an official or sworn translator or by a diplomatic or consular agent.

Article V

1. Recognition and enforcement of the award may be refused, at the request of the party against whom it is invoked, only if that party furnishes to the competent authority where the recognition and enforcement is sought, proof that—

(a) the parties to the agreement referred to in article II were, under the law applicable to them, under some incapacity, or the said agreement is not valid under the law to which the parties have subjected it or, failing any indication thereon, under the law of the country where the award was made; or

(b) the party against whom the award is invoked was not given proper notice of the appointment of the arbitrator or of the arbitration proceedings or was otherwise unable to present his case; or

(c) the award deals with a difference not contemplated by or not falling within the terms of the submission to arbitration, or it contains decisions on matters beyond the scope of the submission to arbitration; provided that, if the decisions on matters submitted to arbitration can be separated from those not so submitted, that part of the award which contains decisions on matters submitted to arbitration may be recognised and enforced; or

(d) the composition of the arbitral authority or the arbitral procedure was not in accordance with the agreement of the parties, or, failing such agreement, was not in accordance with the law of the country where the arbitration took place; or

(e) the award has not yet become binding on the parties, or has been set aside or suspended by a competent authority of the country in which, or under the law of which, that award was made.

2. Recognition and enforcement of an arbitral award may also be refused if the competent authority in the country where recognition and enforcement is sought finds that—

(a) the subject-matter of the difference is not capable of settlement by arbitration under the law of that country; or

(b) the recognition or enforcement of the award would be contrary to the public policy of that country.

Article VI

If an application for the setting aside or suspension of the award has been made to a competent authority referred to in article V(1)(e), the authority before which the award is sought to be relied upon may, if it considers it proper, adjourn the decision on the enforcement of the award and may also, on the application of the party claiming enforcement of the award, order the other party to give suitable security.

Article VII

1. The provisions of the present Convention shall not affect the validity of multilateral or bilateral agreements concerning the recognition and enforcement of arbitral awards entered into by the Contracting States nor deprive any interested party of any right he may have to avail himself of an arbitral award in the manner and to the extent allowed by the law or the treaties of the country where such award is sought to be relied upon.

2. The Geneva Protocol on Arbitration Clauses of 1923 and the Geneva Convention on the Execution of Foreign Arbitral Awards of 1927 shall cease to have effect between Contracting States on their becoming bound and to the extent that they become bound by this Convention.

Article VIII

1. This Convention shall be open until 31st December, 1958 for signature on behalf of any Member of the United Nations and also on behalf of any other State which is or hereafter becomes member of any specialised agency of the United Nations, or which is or hereafter becomes a party to the Statute of the International Court of Justice, or any other State to which an invitation has been addressed by the General Assembly of the United Nations.

2. This Convention shall be ratified and the instrument of ratification shall be deposited with the Secretary-General of the United Nations.

Article IX

1. This Convention shall be open for accession to all States referred to in article VIII.

2. Accession shall be effected by the deposit of an instrument of accession with the Secretary-General of the United Nations.

Article X

1. Any State may, at the time of signature, ratification or accession, declare that this Convention shall extend to all or any of the territories for the international relations of which it is responsible. Such a declaration shall take effect when the Convention enters into force for the State concerned.

2. At any time thereafter any such extension shall be made by notification addressed to the Secretary-General of the United Nations and shall take effect from the ninetieth day after the day of receipt by the Secretary-General of the United Nations of this notification, or from the date of entry into force of the Convention for the State concerned, whichever is the later.

3. With respect to those territories to which this Convention is not extended at the time of signature, ratification or accession, each State concerned shall consider the

possibility of taking the necessary steps in order to extend the application of this Convention to such territories, subject, where necessary for constitutional reasons, to the consent of the Governments of such territories.

Article XI

In the case of a federal or non-unitary State, the following provisions shall apply:—

(a) with respect of those articles of this Convention that come within the legislative jurisdiction of the federal authority, the obligations of the federal Government shall to this extent be the same as those of Contracting States which are not federal States;

(b) with respect to those articles of this Convention that come within the legislative jurisdiction of constituent States or provinces which are not, under the constitutional system of the federation, bound to take legislative action, the federal Government shall bring such articles with a favourable recommendation to the notice of the appropriate authorities of constituent States or provinces at the earliest possible moment;

(c) a federal State Party to this Convention shall, at the request of any other Contracting State transmitted through the Secretary-General of the United Nations, supply a statement of the law and practice of the federation and its constituent units in regard to any particular provision of this Convention, showing the extent to which effect has been given to that provision by legislative or other action.

Article XII

1. This Convention shall come into force on the ninetieth day following the date of deposit of the third instrument of ratification or accession.

2. For each State ratifying or acceding to this Convention after the deposit of the third instrument of ratification or accession, this Convention shall enter into force on the ninetieth day after deposit by such State of its instrument of ratification or accession.

Article XIII

1. Any Contracting State may denounce this Convention by a written notification to the Secretary-General of the United Nations. Denunciation shall take effect one year after the date of receipt of the notification by the Secretary-General.

2. Any State which has made a declaration or notification under article X may, at any time thereafter, by notification to the Secretary-General of the United Nations, declare that this Convention shall cease to extend to the territory concerned, one year after the date of the receipt of the notification by the Secretary-General.

3. This Convention shall continue to be applicable to arbitral awards in respect of which recognition or enforcement proceedings have been instituted before the denunciation takes effect.

Article XIV

A Contracting State shall not be entitled to avail itself of the present Convention against other Contracting States except to the extent that it is itself bound to apply the Convention.

Article XV

The Secretary-General of the United Nations shall notify the States contemplated in article VIII of the following:—

(a) signatures and ratifications in accordance with article VIII;

(b) accessions in accordance with article IX;

(c) declarations and notifications under articles I, X and XI;

(d) the date upon which this Convention enters into force in accordance with article XII;

(e) denunciations and notifications in accordance with article XIII.

Article XVI

1. This Convention, of which the Chinese, English, French, Russian and Spanish texts shall be equally authentic, shall be deposited in the archives of the United Nations.

2. The Secretary-General of the United Nations shall transmit a certified copy of this Convention to the States contemplated in article XIII.

THE SECOND SCHEDULE

(*See* section 53)

PROTOCOL ON ARBITRATION CLAUSES

The undersigned, being duly authorised, declare that they accept, on behalf of the countries which they represent, the following provisions:—

1. Each of the Contracting States recognises the validity of an agreement whether relating to existing or future differences between parties subject respectively to the jurisdiction of different Contracting States by which the parties to a contract agree to submit to arbitration all or any differences that may arise in connection with such contract relating to commercial matters or to any other matter capable of settlement by arbitration, whether or not the arbitration is to take place in a country to whose jurisdiction none of the parties is subject.

   Each Contracting State reserves the right to limit the obligation mentioned above to contracts which are considered as commercial under its national law. Any Contracting State which avails itself of this right will notify the Secretary-General of the League of Nations in order that the other Contracting States may be so informed.

2. The arbitral procedure, including the constitution of the Arbitral Tribunal, shall be governed by the will of the parties and by the law of the country in whose territory the arbitration takes place.

   The Contracting States agree to facilitate all steps in the procedure which require to be taken in their own territories, in accordance with the provisions of their law governing arbitral procedure applicable to existing differences.

3. Each Contracting State undertakes to ensure the execution by its authorities and in accordance with the provisions of its national laws of arbitral awards made in its own territory under the preceding articles.

4. The Tribunals of the Contracting Parties, on being seized of a dispute regarding a contract made between persons to whom Article I applies and including an Arbitration Agreement whether referring to present or future differences which is valid by virtue of the said article and capable of being carried into effect, shall refer the parties on the application of either of them to the decision of the Arbitrators.

Such reference shall not prejudice the competence of the judicial tribunals in case the agreement or the arbitration cannot proceed or becomes inoperative.

5. The present Protocol, which shall remain open for signature by all States, shall be ratified. The ratification shall be deposited as soon as possible with the Secretary-General of the League of Nations, who shall notify such deposit to all the Signatory States.
6. The present Protocol will come into force as soon as two ratifications have been deposited. Thereafter it will take effect, in the case of each Contracting State, one month after the notification by the Secretary-General of the deposit of its ratification.
7. The present Protocol may be denounced by any Contracting State on giving one year's notice. Denunciation shall be effected by a notification addressed to the Secretary-General of the League, who will immediately transmit copies of such notification to all the other Signatory States and inform them of the date on which it was received. The denunciation shall take effect one year after the date on which it was notified to the Secretary-General, and shall operate only in respect of the notifying State.
8. The Contracting States may declare that their acceptance of the present Protocol does not include any or all of the under-mentioned territories: that is to say, their colonies, overseas possessions or territories, protectorates or the territories over which they exercise a mandate.

   The said States may subsequently adhere separately on behalf of any territory thus excluded. The Secretary-General of the League of Nations shall be informed as soon as possible of such adhesions. He shall notify such adhesions to all Signatory States. They will take effect one month after the notification by the Secretary-General to all Signatory States.

   The Contracting States may also denounce the Protocol separately on behalf of any of the territories referred to above. Article 7 applies to such denunciation.

THE THIRD SCHEDULE

(*See* section 53)

CONVENTION OF THE EXECUTION OF FOREIGN ARBITRAL AWARDS

Article 1

(1) In the territories of any High Contracting Party to which the present Convention applies, an arbitral award made in pursuance of an agreement, whether relating to existing or future differences (hereinafter called "a submission to arbitration") covered by the Protocol on Arbitration Clauses opened at Geneva on September 24th, 1923, shall be recognised as binding and shall be enforced in accordance with the rules of the procedure of the territory where the award is relied upon, provided that the said award has been made in a territory of one of the High Contracting Parties to which the present Convention applies and between persons who are subject to the jurisdiction of one of the High Contracting Parties.

(2) To obtain such recognition or enforcement, it shall, further, be necessary—

(a) that the award has been made in pursuance of a submission to arbitration which is valid under the law applicable thereto;

(b) that the subject-matter of the award is capable of settlement by arbitration under the law of the country in which the award is sought to be relied upon;

(c) that the award has been made by the Arbitral Tribunal provided for in the submission to arbitration or constituted in the manner agreed upon by the parties and in conformity with the law governing the arbitration procedure;

(d) that the award has become final in the country in which it has been made, in the sense that it will not be considered as such if it is open to opposition, appeal or *pourvoi en cassation* (in the countries where such forms of procedure exist) or if it is proved that proceedings for the purpose of contesting the validity of the award are pending;

(e) that the recognition or enforcement of the award is not contrary to the public policy or to the principles of the law of the country in which it is sought to be relied upon.

Article 2

Even if the conditions laid down in Article 1 hereof are fulfilled, recognition and enforcement of the award shall be refused if the court is satisfied—

(a) that the award has been annulled in the country in which it was made;

(b) that the party against whom the award is sought was not given notice of the arbitration proceedings in sufficient time to enable him to present his case; or that, being under a legal incapacity, he was not properly represented;

(c) that the award does not deal with the differences contemplated by or falling within the terms of the submission to arbitration or that it contains decisions on matters beyond the scope of the submission to arbitration.

If the award has not covered all the questions submitted to the arbitral tribunal, the competent authority of the country where recognition or enforcement of the award is sought can, if it thinks fit, postpone such recognition or enforcement or grant it subject to such guarantee as that authority may decide.

Article 3

If the party against whom the award has been made proves that, under the law governing the arbitration procedure, there is a ground, other than the grounds referred to in Article 1(a) and (c), and Article 2(b) and (c), entitling him to contest the validity of the award in a Court of Law, the Court may, if it thinks fit, either refuse recognition or enforcement of the award or adjourn the consideration thereof, giving such party a reasonable time within which to have the award annulled by the competent tribunal.

Article 4

The party relying upon an award or claiming its enforcement must supply, in particular—

(1) the original award or a copy thereof duly authenticated, according to the requirements of the law of the country in which it was made;

(2) documentary or other evidence to prove that the award has become final, in the sense defined in Article 1(d), in the country in which it was made;

(3) when necessary, documentary or other evidence to prove that the conditions laid down in Article 1, paragraph (1) and paragraph (2) (a) and (c), have been fulfilled.

A translation of the award and of the other documents mentioned in this Article into the official language of the country where the award is sought to be relied upon may be demanded. Such translations must be certified as correct by a diplomatic or consular agent of the country to which the party who seeks to rely upon the award belongs or by a sworn translator of the country where the award is sought to be relied upon.

Article 5

The provisions of the above Articles shall not deprive any interested party of the right of availing himself of an arbitral award in the manner and to the extent allowed by the law or the treaties of the country where such award is sought to be relied upon.

Article 6

The present Convention applies only to arbitral awards made after the coming into force of the Protocol on Arbitration Clauses opened at Geneva on September 24th, 1923.

Article 7

The present Convention, which will remain open to the signature of all the signatories of the Protocol of 1923 on Arbitration Clauses, shall be ratified.

It may be ratified only on behalf of those Members of the League of Nations and Non-Member States on whose behalf the Protocol of 1923 shall have been ratified.

Ratification shall be deposited as soon as possible with the Secretary-General of the League of Nations, who will notify such deposit to all the signatories.

Article 8

The present Convention shall come into force three months after it shall have been ratified on behalf of two High Contracting Parties. Thereafter, it shall take effect, in the case of each High Contracting Party, three months after the deposit of the ratification on its behalf with the Secretary-General of the League of Nations.

Article 9

The present Convention may be denounced on behalf of any Member of the League or Non-Member State. Denunciation shall be notified in writing to the Secretary-General of the League of Nations, who will immediately send a copy thereof, certified to be in conformity with the notifications, to all the other Contracting Parties, at the same time informing them of the date on which he received it.

The denunciation shall come into force only in respect of the High Contracting Party which shall have notified it and one year after such notification shall have reached the Secretary-General of the League of Nations.

The denunciation of the Protocol on Arbitration Clauses shall entail, *ipso facto,* the denunciation of the present Convention.

Article 10

The present Convention does not apply to the colonies, protectorates or territories under suzerainty or mandate of any High Contracting Party unless they are specially mentioned.

The application of this Convention to one or more of such colonies, protectorates or territories to which the Protocol on Arbitration Clauses opened at Geneva on September 24th, 1923, applies, can be effected at any time by means of a declaration addressed to the Secretary-General of the League of Nations by one of the High Contracting Parties.

Such declaration shall take effect three months after the deposit thereof.

The High Contracting Parties can at any time denounce the Convention for all or any of the Colonies, Protectorates or territories referred to above. Article 9 hereof applies to such denunciation.

Article 11

A certified copy of the present Convention shall be transmitted by the Secretary-General of the League of Nations to every Member of the League of Nations and to every Non-Member State which signs the same.

NEPAL

ARBITRATION ACT, 1999

Preamble

Whereas it is expedient to update the current legal provisions relating to arbitration, now therefore, the parliament has enacted this law in the 27th year of the reign of His Majesty King Birendra Bir Bikram Shah Dev.

CHAPTER 1

PRELIMINAY

1. Short Title and Commencement

This law may be called the Arbitration Act, 1999.

It shall come into force at once.

2. Definitions

Unless otherwise meant with reference to the subject or context, in this act,

(a) Agreement means a written agreement reached between the concerned parties for settlement through arbitration of any dispute concerning any specific legal issue that has arisen or may arise in the future under a contract or otherwise.

> *Explanation.*—For the purposes of this clause, the concerned parties shall be deemed to have entered into a written agreement in case any of the following documents exists:
>
> Any contract containing provisions for arbitration also, or any separate agreement signed in that connection.
>
> Letters, telex, telegram or telefax messages, or any other similar messages exchanged through communication media whose records can be maintained in a written form, between the concerned parties parties which provide for referring their disputes to arbitration.
>
> In case any party has presented a claim for referring any dispute to arbitration, the objection to that claim submitted by the party objecting to that claim without rejecting the proposal for referring the dispute to arbitration.

(b) Party means any party connected with arbitration.

(c) District Court means the District Court of the place prescribed in the agreement as the the place of arbitration, if any, and if no such place has been prescribed, the District Court of the place where the dispute has arisen or where the arbitration proceedings have been conducted and decisions taken, or the District Court with territorial jurisdiction over the place where any party generally resides.

(d) Appellate Court means the Appellate Court of the place prescribed in the agreement as the place of arbitration, if any, and if no such place has been prescribed, the Appellate Court of the place where the dispute has arisen or where the arbitration proceedings have been conducted and decisions taken, or the Appellate Court with territorial jurisdiction over the place where any party generally resided.

(e) Dispute means a dispute which can be settled through arbitration under this act.

(f) Counter-claim means a claim made by the objecting party on the party which has made the claim.

(g) Rejoinder means the objection made by the party which has made the claim to the counter-claim.

(h) Arbitrator means an arbitrator appointed for the settlement of a dispute; the term includes a panel of arbitrators.

CHAPTER 2

SETTLEMENT OF DISPUTES THROUGH ARBITRATION

3. Disputes to be settled through arbitration

In case any agreement provides for the settlement of disputes through arbitration, the disputes connected with that agreement or with issues coming under that agreement shall be settled through arbitration according to the procedure prescribed in that agreement, if any, and if not, according to this act.

Notwithstanding anything contained in sub-section (1), in case of concerned parties to a civil suit of a commercial nature which has been filed in a court and which may be settled through arbitration according to current law, file an application for its settlement through arbitration, such dispute shall also be settled through arbitration.

4. Cancellation of Records of Suits

The court may order the cancellation of the records of a suit filed in connection with a dispute which (the concerned parties) have sought to settle through arbitration under sub-section (2) of section 3. Notwithstanding anything contained in sub-section (1), the court of a suit in the following circumstances:

In case it is deemed necessary to pronounce a decision on any issue which cannot be arbitrated together with an issue which can be arbitrated, or

In case there appears any appropriate reason why the dispute cannot be settled through arbitration.

CHAPTER 3

APPOINTMENT OF ARBITRATORS AND THEIR OFFICE

5. Number of Arbitrators

As many arbitrators as specified in the agreement shall be appointed. In case the agreement does not specify the number of arbitrators, there shall ordinarily be three arbitrators.

In case the number of arbitrators appointed under the agreement is an even one, it shall be turned into an odd one by designating an additional arbitrator chosen by them.

6. Appointment of Arbitrator

Except when otherwise provided for in the agreement, the process of appointing arbitrators must be started within 30 days from the date when the reason for the settlement of a dispute through arbitration arises.

In case the agreement mentions the names of arbitrators, they themselves shall be recognised as having been appointed as arbitrators. In case the agreement has made any separate provision for the appointment of arbitrators, arbitrators shall be appointed accordingly. Except when otherwise provided for in the agreement, each party shall appoint one arbitrator each and the arbitrators so appointed shall appoint the third arbitrator who shall work as the chief arbitrator. Appointment of Arbitrators by Court. Either party may submit an application to the Appellate Court pleading for the appointment of arbitrators in the following circumstances:

In case no arbitrator can be appointed according to the provision contained in the agreement.

In case the agreement does not mention anything about the appointment of arbitrators.

The application to be filed under sub-section (I) must explicitly mention the full names, addresses, occupations and the fields of specialisation of at least Ihree persons who can be appointed as arbitrators, and also be accompanied by a copy of the agreement.

On receipt of an application under sub-section (1), the appellate court shall notify all the parties and appoint as arbitrators the persons proposed by them in case they reach a consensus in that connection, and in case they fail to reach a consensus in that connection, the persons deemed appropriate by it, within 60 days from the date of receipt of the agreement. The decision taken by the court in that manner shall be final.

Appointment of Arbitrators in Vacant Posts in Special Circumstances

In case the position of an arbitrator appointed for the purpose of arbitration falls vacant by reason of his resignation or refusal to function in that capacity or of his death or for any other reason, it shall be filled up by appointing another arbitrator ordinarily within 30 days from the date when the vacancy has occurred in the manner in which the arbitrator had originally been appointed.

In case the position of an arbitrator which has fallen vacant be filled up within the time limit mentioned in sub-section (1), either party may apply to the appellate Court within 15 days from the date of expiry of that time limit. In case such an application is filled, the appellate court shall appoint an arbitrator subject to section 7 ordinarily within 15 days.

Before starting the proceedings of arbitration, the arbitrator must affix his signature on two copies of a written oath as indicated in the schedule regarding impartiality and honesty and send one copy thereof of the Appellate Court and keep the other copy in the case-file.

Before taking oath under sub-section (1), the arbitrator must make clear matters, if any, which raise a reasonable doubt about his impartiality or independence in respect to the dispute which he has to settle.

Qualifications of Arbitrators

The following persons shall not be qualified for appointment as arbitrators:

Those are disqualified for entering into contracts under current law.

Those who have been punished by a court on criminal charges involving moral turpitude.

Those who have become insolvent or been declared bankrupt.

Those who have any personal interest in the dispute which has to be settled through arbitration.

Those who do not possess any specific qualification specified in the agreement for becoming eligible for appointment as an arbitrator.

7. Power to Remove Arbitrators

The circumstances in which an arbitrator may be removed and the procedure to be followed for the purpose shall be as mentioned in the agreement.

In case the circumstances (in which an arbitrator may be removed) and the working procedure (to be followed for the purpose) have got been mentioned in the agreement as mentioned in sub-section (1), any party may, in any of the following circumstances, submit an application to the arbitrator requesting for permission to remove an arbitrator within 15 days from the date of his appointment or from the date when the party learns that the concerned arbitrator has failed to act according to the provisions of this sub-section:

In case any arbitrator is clearly seen to have shown a bias toward or discriminated against any party instead of working in an impartial manner;

In case any arbitrator engages in improper actions or commits fraud in the course of arbitration;

In case any arbitrator frequently commits mistakes or irregularities in the course of arbitration;

In case any arbitrator does not attend arbitration meetings or refuses to take part in arbitration proceedings for more than three times without furnishing satisfactory reasons with the objective of prolonging or delaying the arbitration proceedings in an improper manner;

In case any arbitrator takes any action which is opposed to the principles or rules of natural justice; or

In case any arbitrator is found to be lacking the necessary qualifications, or to have ceased to be qualified.

In case an application is received under sub-section (2), and in case the arbitrator whose removal has been demanded does not relinquish his post voluntarily, or in case the other party does not agree with grounds on which his removal has been demanded the arbitrator must take a decision on the matter within 30 days from the date of application.

An appeal may be filed with the Appellate Court against the decision taken under sub-section (3), and the decision taken by the Appellate Court on the application shall be final.

12. Location of Office of the Arbitrator

The office of the arbitrator shall be located at the following place:

At the place specified in the agreement, if any.

If the agreement does not specify the location of the arbitrator's office, at the place selected by the concerned parties.

In case the concerned parties do not select such place within 15 days from the date of appointment of the arbitrator, or in case the concerned parties fail to reach an agreement in that connection, at the place specified by the arbitrator in the light of all the relevant circumstances.

Notwithstanding anything contained elsewhere in this section, the arbitrators may, except when any other arrangement has been made by the concerned parties, designate through mutual consultations the location of their office at any other appropriate place which is convenient for them to record the statements of witnesses, obtain the opinion of experts, and inspect any document, object or place.

13. Language to be Used by Arbitrators in their Proceedings

The language to be used by the arbitrators in the course of their proceedings shall be as specified in the agreement, if any. In case the agreement does not specify any such language, they shall use the language determined by them through mutual consultations. In case the arbitrators fail to determine the language to be used by them, the language used in the agreement shall be the language to be used by the arbitrators.

CHAPTER 4

ARBITRATION PROCEEDINGS AND POWERS OF ARBITRATORS

14. Submission of Claims, Counter-Claims, objections or Rejoinders

(1) The party making a claim shall submit its claim to the arbitrator in writing explicitly mentioning the details of the subject-matter of difference and the remedy sought, along with evidence, and also supply a copy thereof to the other party within the time limit mentioned in the agreement , if any, and within three months from the date when a dispute requiring arbitration has arisen in case only the name of the arbitration has arisen in case only the name of the arbitration has been mentioned in the agreement without mentioning any time limit, and from the date of appointment of the arbitrator in case the arbitrator has been appointed after the dispute has arisen.

(2) After a claim is filed under sub-section (1), the other party shall submit its objection to it within 30 days from the date of receipt of the claim, unless otherwise provided for in the agreement.

(3) The other party shall submit its objection, as well as its counter-claim, if any, in that connection within the time limit mentioned in sub-section (2). In case it submits a counter-claim also, the arbitrator must provide a time limit of 15 days to arbitrator must provide a time limit of 15 days of the party making the claim to submit its rejoinder over such counter-claim. In case a rejoinder is submitted in that manner, a copy thereof must be supplied to the party making the counter claim.

(4) In case any party fails to submit its claim, objection, or rejoinder within the time limit mentioned in sub-section (2) or (3) due to circumstances beyond its control, it may submit an application to the arbitrator for an extension of the time limit within 15 days from the date of expiry of the time limit, explicitly mentioning satisfactory reasons for its failure to do so. The arbitrator may, if he finds the reasons mentioned in the application to be satisfactory, extend the time limit for not more than seven days.

(5) While submitting claims, counter-claims, objections or rejoinders under this section, all documents, as well as evidence substantiating them, if any, must also be submitted. In case the parties wish to substantiate any point through witnesses, they must mention the full names and addresses of such witnesses in their claims, counter claims, objections or rejoinders, and they shall themselves be responsible for presenting such witnesses before the arbitrator on the day prescribed by him.

(6) Each party submitting documents to the arbitrator in connection with arbitration proceedings under this act must supply copies thereof to the other party.

15. Circumstances in which Arbitration Proceedings shall Terminate or Continue

Except when otherwise provided for by the parties, arbitration proceedings shall terminate or continue in the following circumstances:

(a) The arbitration proceedings shall terminate in case the claimant does not submit his claim within the time- limit mentioned in section 14(1).

(b) Even if no objection is submitted within the time limit mentioned in Section 14(2), this alone shall not be taken as the acceptance by the party not submitting its counter-claim to the claim made by the claimant, and the arbitrator shall continue his proceedings in such a manner as to evaluate the claimant's claim and the evidence submitted to substantiate the claim.

(c) The arbitrator may pronounce his decision on the basis of the evidence that has been submitted in case any party does not present itself or does not submit any written evidence at the time of hearing prescribed by the arbitrator. He must send a copy of the decision to the party not submitting its objection as well.

16. Power of the Arbitrator to Determine Jurisdiction

(1) In case any party wishes to make a claim that the arbitrator has no jurisdiction over the dispute which has been referred to him for settlement, or that the contract because of which the dispute has emerged is itself illegal or mull and void, it may do so before the arbitrator. The arbitrator must before starting proceeding on the matter referred to him, take a decision on his jurisdiction or the validity or effectiveness of the contract.

(2) Any part which is not satisfied with the decision taken under sub-section (2) may file an appeal with the Appellate Court within 30 days from the date of decision, and the decision taken by that court on the matter shall be final.

(3) For the purpose of taking a decision on the validity or effectiveness of a contract under sub section (1), in case the contract contains provisions for the settlement of disputes through arbitration as its integral part, such provisions shall be taken as a separate agreement, and even if the arbitrator takes a decision holding the contract as null and void, such provisions shall not be held to be legally null and void for that reason alone.

(4) No claim may be made under sub-section (1) after the expiry of the time limit for submitting objections prescribed under sub-section (2) of section 14.

(5) No party shall be deemed to have been deprived of the opportunity to make a claim under sub section (1) simply for the reason of having appointed an arbitrator on its behalf, or participated in or agreed to the appointment of the arbitrator.

(6) The filling of a petition with the Appellate Court under sub-section (2) shall not be deemed to have prejudiced the power of the arbitrator to continue his proceedings and pronounce his decision before the petition is finally disposed of by the court.

17. Working Procedure to be Adopted by Arbitrators

(1) The procedure to be adopted by the arbitrator while taking a decision on a dispute shall be as mentioned in the agreement, and in case no such procedure has been mentioned in the agreement, it shall be as laid down in this act:

Provided that the procedure not laid down in the act shall be as prescribed by the arbitrator with the consent of the parties, and in case the parties fail to reach an agreement in that connection, it shall be as prescribed by the arbitrator himself.

(2) The arbitrator must start arbitration proceedings immediately after receiving all such claims, objections, counter-claims or rejoinders as need to be received by him.

(3) The arbitrator must inform the parties about the type of proceedings to be held, and the day and time fixed for the purpose and also keep records thereof in the concerned case file.

(4) In respect to a dispute which has been referred to three or more arbitrators, the arbitrators who are present may conduct all arbitration proceedings other than taking the final decision or issuing the final order.

(5) The arbitrator may continue arbitration proceedings and pronounce his decision on the basis of the available evidence even if any party does not present itself on the day and at the time of arbitration proceedings after receiving a notice under sub-section (3).

(6) After the completion of the process of hearing, the arbitrator shall issue an order or the effect that the hearing has concluded and keep a record thereof in the case file.

Evidence may not be examined or the parties heard thereafter.

(7) Except when otherwise provided for in the agreement, the arbitrator must read out his written decision within 30 days from the date of issue of an order under sub-section (6)

18. Substantive Law to be applied by Arbitrators

(1) The Nepal Law shall be the substantive law to be applied by the arbitrator, except when otherwise provided for in the agreement.

(2) The arbitrator may settle the dispute according to the principle of ex acta et bono or amiable compositor only when explicity authorised by the parties to do so.

(3) Notwithstanding anything contained elsewhere in this act, the arbitrator shall settle the dispute according to the conditions stipulated in the concerned contract. While doing so, he shall also pay attention to the commercial usages applicable to the concerned transaction.

19. Arbitration Hearings to be held *in camera*

Except when otherwise desired by the parties. Arbitration proceedings shall be held *in camera.*

20. Delivery of Notices and Summonses

(1) Notwithstanding anything contained in current law, any notice to be furnished in connection with arbitration, or any notice or summons to be furnished in the name of any party residing within or outside the Kingdom of Nepal in connection with the hearing by the arbitrator, or with the dispute under the consideration of the arbitrator, may be delivered directly to the concerned party or sent to its telex, telefax or telegram address or to the address of any other communication media whose printed records can be maintained, if such address is mentioned in the agreement, or if the concerned parties have supplied such address to each other or to their respective arbitrators after signing the agreement , except when otherwise provided for in the agreement. In case the address of such communication media or any other address has not been supplied, such notices or summonses shall be delivered at the place of business or permanent residence of the concerned party. Notices or summonses so sent shall be deemed to have been duly delivered:

Provided that notices or summonses to be sent by post shall be sent only after registering them.

(2) Notwithstanding anything contained in sub-section (1), this provision shall have no prejudicial impact on the functions and proceedings of the court.

21. Power of the Arbitrator

(1) The powers of the arbitrator shall be as follows, except when otherwise provided for in the agreement:

(a) To direct the concerned parties to appear before him and submit documents, and record their statements according to need.

(b) To record statements of witnesses.

(c) To appoint experts and seek their opinions or have them examine any specific issue.

(d) In case any of the parties is a foreign national so that the decision pronounced by the arbitrator is not likely to be implemented, to obtain a bank guarantee or any other appropriate guarantee as prescribed by the arbitrator.

(e) To inspect the concerned place, object, product, structure, production process or any other related matter which are connected with the dispute on the request of the parties or on his own initiative if he so deems appropriate, and in case there is any material or object which is likeiy to be destroyed or damaged, to sell them in consultation with the parties, and keep the sale proceeds as a deposit.

(f) To exercise any specific power conferred on him by the parties.

(g) To issue preliminary orders, or interim or provisional orders in respect to any matter connected with the dispute on the request of any party, or take a conditional decision.

(h) To issue certified copies of documents.

(i) To exercise the other power conferred by this act.

(2) Any party which is not satisfied with the order issued by the arbitrator under clause (g) of sub section (1) may appeal to the appellate court within 15 days, and the decision taken by the Appellate Court in the connection shall be final.

22. Parties to have Equal Opportunities

(1) In the arbitration proceedings, each party shall be provided with an equal and adequate opportunity to present its case subject to this act.

(2) Any party may attend the arbitration proceedings either personally or by proxy, and also designate a legal practitioner on its behalf.

23. Assistance of the Court May be Sought to Examine Any Evidence

Notwithstanding anything contained in current law, in case the arbitrator requires the assistance of the court to examine any evidence concerning a dispute which is under his consideration, the arbitrator himself may, on his own or on the request of any party, request the District Court for such assistance. In case any such request is received, the District Court shall provide assistance in examining the evidence according to current law.

CHAPTER 5

DECISION OF ARBITRATORS AND IMPLEMENTATION THEREOF

24. Period Within Which Decision Must Be Taken

Except when otherwise provided for in the agreement, the arbitrator must pronounce his decision ordinarily within 120 days from the date of submission of documents under section 14 subject to subsection (7) of Section 17.

25. Circumstances in Which Decisions Must Not Be Taken

(1) In case any issue requiring arbitration is found to be inextricably linked with any other issue on which the arbitrator cannot pronounce his decision, he shall not pronounce any decision on that issue.

(2) In the event of a situation in which the arbitrator cannot take a decision under sub-section (1), he must inform the concerned parties accordingly.

(3) The concerned parties may file a complaint with the Court within 35 days from the date of receipt of a notice under sub-section (2), Notwithstanding anything contained in current law.

26. Decision of Arbitrator

(1) In case there are three and more arbitrators, the decision of the majority shall be deemed to be the decision of arbitration.

(2) In case the arbitrators have divergent opinions so that the majority (opinion) cannot be ascertained, the opinion of the chief arbitrator shall be deemed to be the decision of arbitration, except when otherwise provided for in the agreement.

(3) Every arbitrator must affix his signature on the decision subject to sub-section (4): Provided that in case there is any special reason why any arbitrator cannot affix his signature on the decision, the other arbitrators shall affix their signatures explicitly mentioning the matter.

(4) In case any arbitrator does not agree with the decision of arbitration, he may express his dissident opinion.

27. Matters to be Indicated in Decision

The arbitrator must explicitly indicate the following matters in his decision, except when otherwise provided for in the agreement:

(a) Brief particulars of the matter referred to for arbitration.

(b) In case any party had questioned the jurisdiction of arbitration, grounds for deciding that the matter came under the jurisdiction of arbitration.

(c) The arbitrator's decision, and the reasons and grounds for reaching that decision.

(d) Claims which must be realised or amounts which must be compensated.

(e) Interest on amount to be realized, and the additional rate of interest to be charged after the expiry of the time limit for implementing the decision of the arbitrator in the event of the limit mentioned in section 31.

(f) Place and date of decision.

28. Decision to be Read Out

The arbitrator shall read out the decision in the presence of the concerned parties, hand over a copy of that decision to each party, and keep evidence thereof in the case file. In case any party is absent at the time fixed for reading out the decision or refuses to accept a copy of the decision even after being present at the time fixed for reading out the decision, a notice shall be furnished to it along with a copy of the decision after indicating the same.

29. Prohibition to Review Decision

(1) Except when the Appellate Court has issued an order under Section 30, the arbitrator must not take another decision on the matter referred to him for arbitration after once reading out his decision on the matter, except correcting arithmetic, printing, typing or similar other minor mistakes and inserting omitted particulars without prejudice to the substance of the decision.

(2) In case any party feels that any mistake contained in the decision of the arbitrator needs to be corrected under sub section (1) it must submit an application to the arbitrator within 30 days from the date of receipt of a copy of the decision. In case the arbitrator

deems it appropriate to correct such mistakes or insert any omitted particulars, he may prepare a separate note thereof and have the omitted particulars inserted or mistakes corrected within 15 days from the date of receipt of the application. In case the arbitrator himself deems it appropriate to make such corrections, he must do so by preparing a note thereof and informing the parties accordingly within 30 days from the date of decision.

(3) Notwithstanding anything contained elsewhere in this section, in case the arbitrator has not taken a decision on any point from among the points contained in the claims made by any party, the concerned party may submit an application for a decision on the point to the extent of the matter covered by it after securing the approval of the other party within 30 days from the date of decision by the arbitrator. In case such an application is received, a supplementary decision may be taken by confining it to the matter covered by the point within 45 days from the date of application.

(4) If the parties so agree, any party may, by notifying the other party, request the arbitrator to explain any point contained in or any part of the arbitrator's decision which is not clear within 30 days from the date of decision. In case any such request is received, the arbitrator may explain and clarify any unclear point within 45 days.

30. Circumstances in which decision may be invalidated

(1) Any party which is dissatisfied with the decision taken by the arbitrator may, if the wishes to have the decision invalidated, file a petition to the appellate court along with the related documents and a copy of the decision within 35 days from the date when it heard the decision or received a notice thereof under this act. It must also supply a copy of that petition to the arbitrator and the other party.

(2) In case a petition is filed under sub-section (1) the Appellate Court may, in case the petitioner proves that the arbitration decision contains any of the following matters, invalidate that decision or issue an order to have a fresh decision taken according to need:

(a) In case any party to the agreement was incompetents for any reason to sign an agreement at the time of signing the agreement, or in case the agreement is not valid under the laws of the nation which exercises jurisdiction over the parties, or in case such laws are not clear, under the laws of Nepal.

(b) In case the party which has submitted the petition was not given a notice to appoint an arbitrator or about the arbitration proceedings according to rules in time.

(c) In case the decision has been taken on a matter connected with the dispute which had not be referred to the arbitrator, or in a manner contrary to the conditions prescribed for the arbitrator, or by acting beyond the jurisdiction prescribed for the arbitrator.

(d) Except when an agreement has been signed contrary to the laws of Nepal, in case the procedure of designation of arbitrators or their functions and actions do not conform to the agreement signed between the parties, or to this act in case no such agreement has been signed.

(3) Notwithstanding anything contained in sub-section (2), the Appellate Court may invalidate the decision of the arbitrator in the following circumstances in case a petition is filed under subsection (1):

(a) In case the dispute in respect to which the arbitrator has taken a decision cannot be settled through arbitration under the laws of Nepal.

(b) In case the decision taken by the arbitrator is likely to be prove detrimental to the public interests or policies.

31. Implementation of Decision

The concerned parties shall be under obligation to implement has decision taken by the arbitrator within 45 days from the date when they receive a copy thereof.

32. Implementation of Decision by Court

In case a decision cannot be implemented within the time limit prescribed in section 31 of this act, the concerned party may file a petition to the District Court within 30 days from the date of expiry of the time limit prescribed for the purpose for having the arbitration decision implemented. In case such a petition is filed, the District Court shall implement the decision ordinarily within 30 days as if its was its own judgement.

33. Interest to be paid

Except when otherwise provided for in the agreement in case the arbitrator has taken a decision providing for the payment of any amount by one party to another, the concerned party must also pay interest at the rate prescribed by the arbitrator in the light also of the nature of the business connected with the dispute and by ensuring that it is not higher than the rate of interest currently charged by commercial banks in respect to similar transactions:

Provided that no interest shall be payable for the period between the date of decision by the arbitrator and the time limit prescribed for the implementation of the decision under this act.

34. Implementation of Decision Taken in Foreign Countries

(1) Any party which wishes to have a decision taken in a foreign country implemented in the Kingdom of Nepal must submit an application to the Appellate Court along with the following documents:

(a) The original document of the arbitrators decision or a certified copy thereof.

(b) The original document of the agreement, or a certified copy thereof.

(c) In case the arbitrators decision is not in the Nepali Language, an official translation thereof in the Nepali language.

(2) In case Nepal is a party to any treaty which provides for recognition and implementation of decisions taken by arbitrators in foreign countries, any decision taken by an arbitrator after the commencement of this act within the area of the foreign country which is a party to that treaty shall be recognised and implemented in the Kingdom of Nepal in the following circumstances subject to the provisions of that treaty and the conditions mentioned at the time of becoming a party to it:

(a) In case the arbitrator has been appointed and decision taken according to the laws and procedure mentioned in the agreement.

(b) In case the parties had been notified about the arbitration proceedings in time.

(c) In case the decision has been taken according to the conditions mentioned in the agreement or by confining only to the subject- matters referred to the arbitrator.

(d) In case the decision has become final and binding on the parties according to the laws of the country where the decision has been taken.

(e) In case the laws of the country of the person who has applied for the implementation of an arbitrator's decision, or the laws of Ihe country where arbitration proceedings have been conducted, do not contain provisions under which arbitration decisions taken in the Kingdom of Nepal cannot be implemented.

(f) In case the application has been filed for the implementation of the decision within 90 days from the date of decision.

(3) In case the Appellate Court is satisfied that the conditions mentioned in sub-section (2) have been fulfilled by an application filed under sub section (1) it shall forward the decision to the District court for its implementations.

(4) Notwithstanding anything contained elsewhere in this section, no decision taken by an arbitrator in a foreign country shall be implemented in the following circumstances.

(a) In case the dispute after settling which the decision has been taken is a dispute which cannot be settled through arbitration according to the laws of Nepal.

(b) In case the implementation of the decision is detrimental to the public policy.

CHAPTER VI

35. Cost of Arbitration Proceedings

(1) Except when otherwise provided for in the agreement, the parties seeking arbitration must pay to the arbitrator the amount fixed by him in consultation with them for conducting the arbitration proceedings.

(2) Except when otherwise provided for in the agreement, each party must bear the expenses required for conducting the arbitration proceedings in the proportion prescribed by the arbitrator in the light of the relevant circumstances.

36. Arbitrator's Remuneration

(1) The arbitrator's remuneration shall be as prescribed in the agreement.

(2) In case the arbitrator's remuneration is not mentioned in the agreement, the concerned parties must pay the remuneration fixed by the arbitrator in consultation with them. Such remuneration must be paid either in a lump sum or in the form of an advance payment as ordered by the arbitrator in consultation with the concerned parties.

37. Arbitrator To Refund Payments

In case no hearing can be made on the dispute referred to the arbitrator, or the position of the arbitrator falls vacant for any reason, the concerned arbitrator, if he has already received payment of remuneration under section 36, must refund the balance left after deducting

PAKISTAN

THE ARBITRATION ACT, 1940

(X of 1940)

[11th March, 1940]

An Act consolidate and amend the law relating to Arbitration

Preamble

WHEREAS it is expedient to consolidate and amend the law relating to arbitration in Pakistan. It is hereby enacted as follows:—

CHAPTER I

INTRODUCTORY

1. Short title, extent and commencement

(1) This Act may be called the Arbitration Act, 1940.

(2) It extends to the whole of Pakistan.

(3) It shall come into force on the 1st day of July, 1940.

2. Definitions

In this Act, unless there is anything repugnant in the subject or context,—

(a) "arbitration agreement" means a written agreement to submit present or future differences to arbitration, whether an arbitrator is named therein or not;

(b) "award" means an arbitration award;

(c) "Court" means a Civil Court having jurisdiction to decide the question forming the subject-matter of reference if the same had been the subject-matter of a suit, but does not, except for the purpose of arbitration proceedings under section 21, include a Small Cause·Court;

(d) "legal representative" means a person who in law represents the estate of a deceased person, and includes any person who intermeddles with the estate of the deceased, and where a party acts in representative character, the person on whom the estate devolves on the death of the party so acting;

(e) "reference" means reference to arbitration.

CHAPTER II

ARBITRATION WITHOUT INTERVENTION OF A COURT

3. Provisions implied in arbitration agreement

An arbitration agreement, unless a different intention is expressed therein, shall be deemed to include the provisions set out in the First Schedule in so far as they are applicable to the reference.

4. Agreement that arbitrators be appointed by third party

The Paries to an arbitration agreement may agree that any reference thereunder shall be to an arbitrator or arbitrators to be appointed by a person designated in the agreement either by name or as the holder for the time being of any office or appointment.

5. Authority of appointed arbitrator or umpire irrevocable except by leave of Court

The authority of an appointed arbitrator or umpire shall not be revocable except with the leave of the Court, unless a contrary intention is expressed in the arbitration agreement.

6. Arbitration agreement not to be discharged by death of party thereto

(1) An arbitration agreement shall not be discharged by the death of any party thereto, either as respects the deceased or any other party, but shall in such event by enforceable by or against the legal representative of the deceased.

(2) The authority of an arbitrator shall not be revoked by the death of any party by whom he was appointed.

(3) Nothing in this section shall affect the operation of any law by virtue of which any right of action is extinguished by the death of a person.

7. Provisions in case of insolvency

(1) Where it is provided by a term in a contract to which an insolvent is a party that any difference arising thereout or in connection therewith shall be referred to arbitration, the said term shall if the receiver adopts the contract, be enforceable by or against him so far as it relates to any such differences.

(2) Where a person who has been adjudged an insolvent had, before the commencement of the insolvency proceedings, become a party to an arbi-tration agreement and any matter to which the agreement applies is required to be determined in connection with, or for the purposes of the insolvency proceedings, then, if the case is one to which sub-section (1) does not apply, any other party to the agreement or the receiver may apply to the Court having jurisdiction in the insolvency proceedings for an order directing that the matter in question shall be referred to arbitration in accordance with the agreement and the Court may, if it is of opinion that, having regard to all the circum-stances of the case, the matter ought to be determined by arbitration, make an order accordingly.

(3) In this section the expression "receiver" includes an Official Assignee.

8. Power of Court to appoint arbitrator or umpire

(1) In any of the following cases—

(a) where an arbitration agreement provides that the reference shall be to one or more arbitrators to be appointed by consent of the parties, and all the parties do not, after difference have arisen, concur, in the appointment or appointments; or

(b) if any appointed arbitrator or umpire neglects or refuses to act, or is incapable of acting, or dies, and the arbitration agreement does not show that it was intended that the vacancy should not be supplied; and the parties or the arbitrators, as the case may be, do not supply the vacancy; or

(c) where the parties or the arbitrators are required to appoint an umpire and do not appoint him; any party may serve the other parties or the arbitrators, as the case may be, with a written notice to concur in the appointment or appointments or in supplying the vacancy.

(2) If the appointment is not made within fifteen clear days after the service of the said notice, the Court may, on the application of the party who gave notice and after giving the other parties an opportunity of being heard, appoint an arbitrator or arbitrators or umpire, as the case may be, who shall have like power to act in the reference and to make an award as if he or they had been appointed by consent of all parties.

9. Power to party to appoint new arbitrator or, in certain cases, a sole arbitrator

Where an arbitration agreement provides that a reference shall be to two arbitrators, one to be appointed by each party, then, unless a different intention is expressed in the agreement—

(a) if either of the appointed arbitrator, neglects or refuses to act, or is incapable of acting, or dies, the party who appointed him may appoint a new arbitrator in his place;

(b) if one party fails to appoint an arbitrator, either originally or by way of substitution as aforesaid, for fifteen clear days, after the service by the other party of a notice in writting to make the appointment, such other party having appointed his arbitrator before giving the notice, the party who has appointed an arbi-trator may appoint that arbitrator to act as sole arbitrator in the reference, and his award shall be binding on both parties as if he had been appointed by consent:

Provided that the Court may set aside any appointment as sole arbi-trators made under clause (b) and either, on sufficient cause being shown, allow further time to the defaulting party to appoint an arbitrator or pass such other order as it thinks fit.

Explanation: The fact that an arbitrator or umpire, after request by either party to enter on proceed with the reference, does not within one month comply with the request may constitute a neglect or refusal to act within the meaning of section 8 and this section.

10. Provisions as to appointment of three or more arbitrators

(1) Where an arbitration agreement provides that a reference shall be to three arbitrators, one to be appointed by each party and the third by the two appointed arbitrators, the agreement shall have effect as if it provided for the appointment, of an umpire, and not for the appointment of a third arbitrator, by the two arbitrators appointed by the parties.

(2) Where an arbitration agreement provides that a reference shall be to three arbitrators to be appointed otherwise than as mentioned in sub-section (1), the award of the majority shall, unless the arbi-tration agreement otherwise provides, prevail.

(3) Where an arbitration agreement provides for the appointed of more arbitrators than three, the award of the majority, or if the arbi-trators are equally divided in their opinions, the award of the umpire shall, unless the arbitration agreement otherwise provides, prevail.

11. Power of Court to remove arbitrators or umpire in certain circumstances

(1) The Court may, on the application of any party to reference, remove an arbitrator or umpire who fails to use all reasonable dispatch in entering on and proceeding with the reference and making an award.

(2) The Court may remove an arbitrator or umpire who has misconducted himself or the proceedings.

(3) Where an arbitrator or umpire is removed under this section, he shall not be entitled to receive any remuneration in respect of his services.

(4) For the purposes of this section the expression "proceeding with the reference" includes, in a case where reference to the umpire be-comes necessary, giving notice of that fact to the parties and to the umpire.

12. Power of Court where arbitrator is removed or his authority revoked

(1) Where the Court removes an umpire who has not entered on the reference or one or more arbitrators (not being all the arbitrators), the Court may, on the application of any party to the arbitration agreement, appoint persons to fill the vacancies.

(2) Where the authority of an arbitrator or arbitrators or an umpire is revoked by leave of the Court, or where the Court removes an umpire who has entered on the reference or a sole arbitrator or all the arbi-trators, the Court may, on the application of any party to the arbitration agreement, either—

(a) appoint a person to act as sole arbitrator in the place of the person or persons displaced, or

(b) order that the arbitration agreement shall cease to have effect with respect to the difference referred.

(3) a person appointed under this section as an arbitrator or umpire shall have the like power to act in the reference and to make an award as if he had been appointed in accordance with the arbitration agreement.

13. Powers of arbitrator

The arbitrators or umpire shall, unless a different intention is expressed in the agreement, have power to—

(a) administer oath to the parties and witnesses appearing;

(b) state a special case for the opinion of the Court on any question of law involved, or state the award, wholly or in part, in the form of a special case of such question for the opinion of the Court;

(c) make the award any clerical or in the alternative;

(d) correct in an award any clerical mistake or error arising from any accidential slip or omission;

(e) administer to any party to the arbitration such interrogatories as may, in the opinion of the arbitrators or umpire, be necessary.

14. Award to be signed and filed

(1) When the arbitrators or umpire have made their award, they shall sign it and shall give notice in writing to the parties of the making and signing thereof and of the amount of fees and charges payable in respect of the arbitration and award.

(2) The arbitrators or umpire shall, at the request of any party to the arbitration agreement or any person claiming under such party or if so directed by the Court and upon payment of the fees and charges due in respect of the arbitration and award and of the costs and charges of filing the award, cause the award or signed copy of it, together with any depositions and documents which may have been taken and proved before them, to be filed in Court, and the Court shall thereupon give notice to the parties of the filing of the award.

15. Power of Court to modify award

The Court may by order modify or correct an award—

(a) where it appears that a part of the award is upon a matter not referred to arbitration and such part can be separated from the other part and does not affect the decision on the matter referred; or

(b) where the award is imperfect in form, or contains any obvious error which can be amended without effecting such decision; or

(c) where the award contains clerical mistake or an error arising from an accidental slip or omission.

16. Power to remit award

(1) The Court may from time to time remit the award or any matter referred to arbitration to the arbitrators or umpire for reconsideration upon such terms as it thinks fit—

(a) where the award has left undetermined any of the matters referred to arbitration, or where it determines any matter not referred to arbitration and such matter cannot be separated without affecting the determination of the matters referred; or

(b) where the award is so indefinite as to be incapable of execution; or

(c) where an objection to the legality of the award is apparent upon the face of it.

(2) Where an award is remitted under sub-section (1) the Court shall fix the time within which te arbitrator or umpire shall submit his decision to the Court:

Provided that any time so fixed may be extended by subsequent order of the Court.

(3) An award is remitted under sub-section (1) shall become void on the failure of the arbitrator or umpire to reconsider it and submit his decision within the time fixed.

17. Judgment in terms of award

Where the Court sees no cause to remit the award or any of the matters referred to arbitration for consideration or to set aside the award has expired, or such application having been made, after refusing it, proceed to pronounce judgement according to the award, and upon the judgement so pronounced a decree shall follow, and no appeal shall lie from such decree except on the ground that it is in excess of, or not otherwise in accordance with, the award.

18. Power of Court to pass interim order

(1) Notwithstanding anything contained in section 17, at any time after the filing of the award, whether notice of the filing has been served or not, upon being satisfied by affidavit or otherwise that a party has taken or is about to take steps to defeat, delay or obstruct the execution of any decree that may be passed upon the award, or that speedy execution of the award is just and necessary, the Court may pass such interim orders as it deems necessary.

(2) Any person against whom such interim orders have been passed may show cause against such orders, and the Court, after hearing the parties, may pass such further orders as it deems necessary and just.

19. Power to supersede arbitration where award becomes void or is set aside

Where an award has become void under sub-section (3) of section 16 or has been set aside, the Court may by order supresede the reference and shall there upon order that the arbitration agreement shall cease to have effect with respect to the difference referred.

CHAPTER III

ARBITRATION WITH INTERVENTION OF A COURT WHERE THERE IS NO SUIT PENDING

20. Application to file in Court arbitration agreement

(1) Where any person have entered into an arbitration agreement before the institution of any suit with respect to the subject-matter of the agreement or any part of it, and

where a difference has arisen to which the agreement applies, they or any of them, instead of proceeding under Chapter II, may apply to a Court having jurisdiction in the matter to which the agreement relates, that the agreement be filed in the Court.

(2) The application shall be in writing and shall be numbered and registered as a suit between one or more of the parties interested or claiming to be interested as plaintiff or plaintiffs and the remainder as defendant or defendants, if the application has been presented by all the parties, or, if otherwise, between the applicant as plaintiff and the other parties as defendants.

(3) On such application being made the Court shall direct notice thereof to be given to all parties to the agreement other than the applicants, requiring them to show cause within the time specified in the notice why the agreement should not be filed.

(4) Where no sufficient cause is shown, the Court shall order the agreement to be filed, and shall make an order of reference to the arbitrator appointed by the parties, whether in the agreement or otherwise, or, where the parties cannot agree upon an arbitrator, to an arbitrator appointed by the Court.

(5) Thereafter the arbitration shall proceed in accordance with, and shall be governed by, the other provisions of this Act so far as they can be made applicable.

CHAPTER IV
ARBITRATION IN SUITS

21. Parties to suit may apply for order of reference

Where in any suit all the parties interested agree that any matter in difference between them in the suit shall be referred to arbitration, they may at any time before judgement is pronounced apply in writing to the Court for an order of reference.

22. Appointment of arbitrator

The arbitrator shall be appointed in such manner as may be agreed upon between the parties.

23. Order of reference

(1) The Court shall, by order, refer to the arbitrator the matter in difference which he is required to determine, and shall in the order specify such time as it thinks reasonable for the making of the award.

(2) Where a matter is referred to arbitration the Court shall not, save in the manner and to the extent provided in this Act, deal with such matter in the suit.

24. Reference to arbitration by some of the parties

Where some only of the parties to a suit apply to have the matters in difference between them referred to arbitration in accordance with, and in the manner provided by section 21 the Court may, if it thinks fit so, refer such matters to arbitration by section 21 the Court may, if it thinks fit so, refer such matters to arbitration (provided that the manner provided in that section, but the suits shall continue so far as it relates to the parties who have not joined in the said application and to matters not contained in the said reference as if no such application had been made, and an award made in pursuance of such a reference shall be binding only on the parties who have joined in the application.

25. Provisions applicable to arbitrations under this Chapter

The provisions of the other Chapters shall, so far as they can be made applicable, apply to arbitrations under this Chapter:

Provided that the Court may, in any of he circumstances mentioned in sections 8, 10, 11 and 12, instead of filling up the vacancies or making the appointment, make an order superseding the arbitration and proceed with the suit, and where the Court makes an order superseding the arbitration under section 19, it shall proceed with the suit.

CHAPTER V
GENERAL

26. Application of Chapter

Save as otherwise provided in this Act, the provision of this Chapter shall apply to all arbitrations.

***26A. Award to set out reasons**

(1) The arbitrator or umpire shall state in the award the reasons for the award in sufficient detail to enable the Court to consider, any question of law arising out of the award.

(2) Where the award not state the reasons in sufficient detail, the Court shall remit the award to the arbitrators or umpire and fix the time within which the arbitrator or umpire shall submit the award together with the reasons in sufficient detail.

Provided that any time so fixed may be extended by subsequent order of the Court.

(3) An award remitted under sub-section (2) shall become void on the failure of the arbitrator or umpire to submit it in accordance with the direction of the Court.

27. Power of arbitrators to make an interim award

(1) Unless a different intention appears in the arbitration agreement, the arbi-trators or umpire may, if they think fit, make an interim award.

(2) All references in this Act to an award shall include references to an interim award made under sub-section (1).

28. Power to Court only to enlarge time for making award

(1) The Court may, if it thins fit, whether the time for making the award has expired or not and whether the award has been made or not, enlarge from time to time the time for making the award.

(2) Any provision in an arbitration agreement whereby the arbitrators or umpire may, except with the consent of all the parties to the agreement, enlarge the time for making the award, shall be void and of no effect.

29. Interest on awards

Where and in so far as an award is for the payment of money the Court may in the decree order interest, from the date of the decree at such rate as the court deems reasonable, to be paid on the principal sum as adjusted by the award and confirmed by the decree.

30. Grounds for setting aside award

An award shall not be set aside except on one or more of the following grounds, namely:—

(a) that in arbitrator or umpire has misconducted himself or the proceedings;

(b) that an award has been made after the issue of an order by the Court superseding the arbitration or after arbitration proceedings have become invalid under section 35;

(c) that an award has been improperly procured or is otherwise invalid.

---

* Section 26A Ins. by Arbitration (Amendment) Ordinance, XV of 1981.

31. Jurisdiction

(1) Subject to the provisions of this Act, an award may be filed in any Court having jurisdiction in the matter to which the reference relates.

(2) Notwithstanding anything contained in any other law for the time being in force and save as otherwise provided in this Act, all questions regarding the validity, effect or existence of an award or an arbitration agreement between the parties to the agreement or persons claiming under them shall be decided by the Court in which the award under the agreement has been, or may be, filed, and by no other Court.

(3) All application regarding the conduct of arbitration proceedings or otherwise arising out of such proceedings shall be made to the Court where award has been, or may be, and to no other Court.

(4) Notwithstanding anything contained elsewhere in this Act or in any other law for the time being in force, where in any reference any application under this Act has been made in a Court competent to entertain it, that Court alone shall have jurisdiction over the arbitration proceedings and all subsequent application arising out of that reference and the arbitration proceedings shall be made in that Court and in no other Court.

32. Bar to suit contesting arbitration agreement or award

Notwithstanding any law for the time being in force, no suit shall lie on any ground whatsoever for a decision upon the existence, effect, or validity of an arbitration agreement or award, nor shall any arbitration agreement or award be set aside, amended, modified or in any way affected otherwise than as provided in this Act.

33. Arbitration agreement or award to be contested by application

Any party to an arbitration agreement or any person claiming under him desiring to challenge the existence or validity of an arbitration agreement or an award or to have the effect of either determined shall apply to the Court and the Court shall decide the question on affidavits:

Provided that where the Court deems it just and expedient, it may set down the application for hearing on other evidence also, and it may pass such orders for the discovery and particulars as it may do in a suit.

34. Power to stay legal proceedings where there is an arbitration agreement

Where any party to an arbitration agreement or any person claiming under him commences any legal proceedings against any other party to the agreement or any person claiming under him in respect of any matter agreed to be referred, any party to such legal proceedings may, at any time before filing a written statement or taking any other steps in the proceedings, apply to the judicial authority before which the proceeding: and if satisfied that there in no sufficient reason why the matter should not be referred in accordance with the arbi-tration agreement and that the applicant was, at the time when the proceedings were commenced, and still remains, ready and willing to do all things necessary, to the proper conduct of the arbitration such authority may make an order staying the proceedings.

35. Effect of legal proceedings on arbitration

(1) No refernece nor award shall be rendered invalid by reason only of the commencement of legal proceedings upon the subject-matter of the reference, but when legal proceedings upon the whole of the subject-matter of the reference have been commenced between all the parties to the reference and a notice thereof has been given to the arbitrators or umpire, all further proceedings in a pending reference shall, unless a stay of proceedings is granted under section 34, be invalid.

(2) In this section the expression "parties to the referenece" includes any person claiming under any of the parties and litigating under the same title.

36. Power of Court, where arbitration agreement is ordered not to apply to a particular difference, to order that a provision making an award a condition precedent to a action shall not apply to such difference

Where it is provided (whether in the arbitration agreement or otherwise) that an arbitration agreement shall be a condition precedent to the bringing of an action with respect to any matter to which the agreement applies, the Court, if it orders (whether under this Act or any other law) that the agreement shall cease to have effect as regards any particular difference may further order that the said provision shall also cease to have effect as regards that difference.

37. Limitations

(1) All the provisions of the Limitation Act, 1908, shall apply to arbitrations as they apply to proceedings in Court.

(2) Notwithstanding any term in an arbitration agreement to the effect that no cause of action shall accrue in respect of any matter required by the agreement to be referred until an award is made under the agreement, a cause of any such matter at the time when it would have accrued but for that term in the agreement.

(3) For the purposes of this section and of the Limitation Act, 1908, an arbitration shall be deemed to be commenced when one party to the arbitration agreement serves on the other parties thereto a notice requiring the appointment of an arbitrator, or where the arbitration agreement provides that the reference shall be to a person named or designated in the agreement, requiring that the difference be submitted to the person so named or designated.

(4) When the terms of an agreement to refer future differences to arbitration provide that any claims to which the agreement applies shall be barred unless notice to appoint arbitrator is given or an arbitrator is appointed or some other step to commence arbitration proceedings is taken within a time fixed by the agreement, and a difference arises to which the agreement applies, the Court, if it is of opinion that in the circumstances of the case undue hardship would otherwise be caused, and notwithstanding that the time so fixed has expired, may on such terms, if any, as the justice of the case may require, extend the time for such period as it thinks proper.

(5) Where the Court orders that an award be set aside or orders, after the commencement of an arbitration, that the arbit have effect with respect to the difference referred, the period between the commence-ment of the arbitration and the date of the order of the Court shall be excluded in computing the time prescribed by the Limitation Act, 1908, for the commencement of the proceeding (including arbitration) with respect to the difference referred.

38. Disputes as to arbitrator's remuneration or costs

(1) If in any case an arbitrator or umpire refuses to deliver his award except on payment of the fees demanded by him, the Court may, on an application in this behalf, order that the arbitrator or umpire shall deliver the award to the applicant on payment into Court by the applicant of the fees demanded, and shall, after such inquiry, if any, as it thinks fit, further order that out of the money so paid into Court there shall be paid to the arbitrator or umpire by way of fees sum as the Court may consider reasonable and that the balance of the money, if any, shall be refunded to the applicant.

(2) An application under sub-section (1) may be made by any party to the reference unless the fees demanded have been fixed by written agreement between him and the

arbitrator or umpire, and the arbitrator or umpire shall be entitled to appear and be heard on any such application.

(3) The Court may make such orders as it thinks fit respecting the costs of an arbitration where any question arises respecting such costs and the award contains no sufficient provision concerning them.

CHAPTER VI
APPEALS

39. Appealable orders

(1) An appeal shall lie from the following orders passed under this Act (and from no others) to the Court authorised by law to hear appeals from original decrees of the Court passing the order:

An order—

(i) superseding an arbitration;

(ii) on an award stated in the form of a special case;

(iii) modifying or correcting award;

(iv) filing or refusing to file an arbitration agreement;

(v) staying or refusing to stay legal proceedings where there is an arbitration agreement;

(vi) setting aside or refusing to set aside an award:

Provided that the provisions of this section shall not apply to any order passed by a Small Cause Court.

(2) No second appeal shall lie from an order passed in appeal under this section, but nothing in this section affect or take away any right to appeal to the Supreme Court.

CHAPTER VII
MISCELLANEOUS

40. Small Cause Court not to have jurisdiction over arbitrations save arbitration in suits before it

A Small Court shall have no jurisdiction over any arbitration proceedings or over any applicaiton arising save on application made under section 21.

41. Procedure and powers of Court

Subject to the provisions of this Act and of rules made thereunder—

(a) the provisions of the Code of Civil Procedure, 1908, shall apply to all proceedings, before the Court, to all appeals, under this Act, and

(b) the Court shall have, for the purpose of, and in relation to, arbitration proceedings, the same power of making orders in respect of any of the matters set out in the Second Schedule as it has for the purpose of, and in relation to, any proceedings before the Court:

Provided that nothing in clause (b) shall be taken to prejudice any power which may be vested in an arbitrator or umpire for making orders with respect to any of such matters.

42. Service of notice by party or arbitrator

Any notice required by this Act to be served otherwise than through the Court by a party to an arbitration agreement or by an arbitrator or umpire shall be served in the manner provided in the arbitration agreement, or if there is no such provision, either—

(a) by delivering it to the person on whom it is to be served, or

(b) by sending it by the post in a letter addressed to that person at his usual or last known place of abode or business in Pakistan and registered under Chapter VI of the Post Office Act, 1898.

43. Power of Courts issue processes for appearance before arbitrator

(1) The Court shall issue the same processes to the parties and wit-nesses whom the arbitrator or umpire desires to examine as the Court may issue in suits tried before it.

(2) Persons failing to attend in accordance with such process, or making any other default, or refusing to give their evidence, of guilty or any contempt to the arbitration or umpire during the investigation of the reference, shall be subject to the like dis-advantages, penalties and punishments by order of the Court on the representation of the arbitrator or umpire as they would incur for the like offences in suits tried before the Court.

(3) In this section the expression "process" includes summonses and commissions for the examination of witnesses and summonses to produce documents.

44. Power of High Court to make rules

The High Court may make reules consistent with this Act as to—

(a) the filing of awards and all proceedings consequent thereon or incidental thereto;

(b) the filing and hearing of special cases and all proceedings conse-quent thereon or incidental thereto;

(c) the staying of any suit or proceeding in contravention of an arbi-tration agreement;

(d) the forms to be used for the purposes of this Act;

(e) generally all proceedings in Court under this Act.

45. Government to be bound

The provisions of this Act shall be binding on the Government.

46. Application of Act to statutory arbitrations

The provisions of this Act, except sub-section (1) of section 6 and sections 7, 12, 36 and 37, shall apply to every arbitration under any other enactment for the time being in force, as if the arbitration were pursuant to an arbitration agreement and as if that other enactment were an arbitration agreement, except in so far as this Act is inconsistent with that other enactment or with any rules made thereunder.

47. Act to apply to all arbitrations

Subject to the provisions of Section 46, and save in so far as is otherwise provided by any law for the time being in force, the provisions of this Act shall apply to all arbitraitons and to all proceedings thereunder:

Provided that an arbitration award otherwise obtained may with the consent of all the parties interested be taken into consideration as a compromise or adjustment of a suit by any Court before which the suit is pending.

48. Saving for pending references

The provisions of this Act shall not apply to any reference pending at the commencement of this Act, to which the law in force immediately before the commencement of this Act shall, notwithstanding any repeal affected by this Act, continue to apply.

49. Repeals and Amendment

[*Rep. by the Repealing and Amending Act, 1945 (VI of 1945), Sec. 2 and First Schedule.*]

THE FIRST SCHEDULE

(*See* section 3)

IMPLIED CONDITIONS OF ARBITRATION AGREEMENTS

1. Unless otherwise expressly provided, the reference shall be to a sole arbitrator.
2. If the reference is to an even number of arbitrators, the arbitrators shall appoint an umpire not later than one month from the latest date of their respective appointments.
3. The arbitrators shall make their award within four months after entering on the reference or after having been called upon to act by notice in writing from any party to the arbitration agreement or within such extended time as the Court may allow.
4. If the arbitrators have allowed their time to expire without making an award or have delivered to any party to the arbitration agreement or to the umpire a notice in writing stating that they cannot agree, the umpire shall forthwith enter on the reference in lieu of the arbitrators.
5. The umpire shall make his award within two months of entering on the reference or within such extended time as the Court may allow.
6. The parties to the reference and all persons claiming under them shall subject to the provisions of any law for the time being in force, submit to be examined by the arbitration or umpire on oath or affirmation in relation to the matters in difference and shall, subject as aforesaid, produce before the arbitrators or umpire all books, deeds, papers, accounts, writings and documents within their possession or power respectively, which be required or called for, and do all other things which, during the proceedings on the reference, the arbitrators or umpire may require.
7. The award shall be final binding on the parties and persons claiming under them respectively.
8. The cost of the reference and award shall be in the discretion of the arbitrators or umpire who may direct to, and by whom, and in what manner, such costs or any part thereof shall be paid, and may tax or settle the amount of costs to be so paid or any part thereof and may award costs to be paid as between legal practitioner and client.

THE SECOND SCHEDULE

(*See* section 41)

POWERS OF COURT

1. The preservation, interim custody or sale of any goods which are subject-matter of the reference.
2. Securing the amount in difference in the reference.
3. The detention, preservation or inspection of any property or thing which is the subject of the reference or as to which any question may arise therein and authorising for any of the aforesaid purposes any person to enter upon or into any land or building in the possession or any party to the refernece, or authorising any

samples to be taken or any observation to be made or experiment to be tried, which may be necessary or expedient for the purpose of obtaining full information or evidence.

4. Interim injunctions or the appointment of a receiver.
5. The appointment of a guardian for a minor or person of unsound mind for the purposes of arbitration proceedings.

THE THIRD SCHEDULE & THE FOURTH SCHEDULE

[*Rep. by the Repealing and Amending Act, 1945 (VI of 1945), Sec. 2 and First Schedule.*]

SRI LANKA

ARBITRATION ACT, 1995

(No. 11 of 1995)

[30th March, 1995]

An Act to provide for the conduct of Arbitration proceedings; to give effect to the convention on the recognition and enforcement of foreign arbitral awards; to repeal the Arbitration Ordinance (Chapter 93) and certain sections of the Civil Procedure Code (Chapter 101); and to provide for matters connected therewith or incidental thereto.

WHEREAS it is necessary to make comprehensive legal provision for the conduct of arbitration proceedings and the enforcement of awards made thereunder:

AND WHEREAS it is necessary to make legal provision to give effect to the principles of the Convention on the Recognition and Enforcement of Foreign Arbitral Awards of 1958;

BE It therefore enacted by the Parliament of the Democratic Socialist Republic of Sri Lanka as follows:—

1. Short title and date of the "operation date"

This Act may be cited as the Arbitration Act, No. 11 title and of 1995 and shall come into operation on such date of as the Minister may appoint by Order published in the operation Gazette (hereinafter referred to as "appointed date").

PART I

PRELIMINARY

2. Application

(1) The provisions of this Act shall, subject to the provisions of section 48, apply to all arbitration proceedings commenced in Sri Lanka after the appointed date, whether the arbitration proceedings are commenced, was entered into before or after the appointed date.

(2) Where arbitration proceedings were commenced prior to the appointed date, the law in force prior to the appointed date, shall, unless the parties otherwise agree, apply to such arbitration proceedings.

PART II

ARBITRATION AGREEMENT

3. Form of arbitration agreement

(1) An arbitration agreement may be in the form of arbitration an arbitration clause in a contract or in the form agreement of a separate agreement.

(2) An arbitration agreement shall be in writing. An agreement shall be deemed to be in writing if its is contained in a document signed by the parties or in an exchange of letters, telexes, telegrams of other means of telecommunication which provide a record of the agreement.

4. Arbitrability submit of the dispute

Any dispute which the parties have agreed to submit of the to arbitration under an arbitration agreement may be dispute determined by arbitration unless the matter in respect of which the arbitration unless the matter in respect of which the arbitration agreement is entered into is contrary to public policy or, is not capable of determination by arbitration.

5. Jurisdiction insitutes of Court in respect of dispute covered by to arbitration such agreement

Where a party to an arbitration agreement legal proceedings in a court against another party such agreement in respect of a matter agreed to be submitted for arbitration under such agreement, the Court shall have no jurisdiction to hear and determine such matter if the other party objects the court exercising jurisdiction in respect of matter.

PART III

COMPOSITION OF THE ARBITRAL TRIBUNAL

6. Number of arbitrators

(1) The parties shall be free to determine the number arbitrators of arbitrators of an arbitral tribunal subject to the provisions of sub-section (3) of this section.

(2) Where no such determination is made, the number of arbitrators shall be three.

(3) Where the parties appoint an even number of arbitrators, the arbitrators so appointed shall jointly appoint an additional arbitrator who shall act as Chairman.

7. Appointment of arbitrators

(1) The parties shall be free to agree on a of arbitrators procedure for appointing the arbitrators, subject to the provisions of this Act.

(2) In the absence of such agreement—

(a) in an arbitration with a sole arbitrator if the parties are unable to agree on the arbitrator that arbitrator shall be appointed, on the application of a party by the High Court;

(b) in an arbitration with three arbitrators, each party shall appoint one arbitrator, and the two arbitrators thus appointed shall appoint the third arbitrator; if a party fails to appoint that arbitrator within sixty days of recepit of a request to do so from the other party, or if the two arbitrators fall to agree on the third arbitrator whithin sixty days of their appointment, the appointment shall be made, upon the application of a party, by the High Court.

(3) Where, under an appointment procedure agreed upon by the parties—

(a) a parties, fails to act as required under such procedure; or

(b) the parties, or the arbitrators, are unable to reach an agreement required of them under such procedure; or

(c) a third party, including an institution, fails to perform any function assigned to such third party under such procedure.

any party may apply to the High Court to take necessary measures towards the appointment of the arbitrator or arbitrators.

(4) The High Court shall in appointing an arbitrator, have due regard to any qualifications required of an arbitrator under the agreement between the parties and to such considerations as are likely to secure the appointment of an independent and impartial arbitrator.

8. Termination of Arbitrator's mandate and removal of Arbitrator

(1) The mandate of an arbitrator shall terminate if arbitrator becomes unable to perform the functions of that office or for any other reason fails to not without under delay, or dies, or withdraws from office or the parties agree on the termination.

(2) Where an arbitrator unduly delays in discharging the duties of his office the High Court may upon the application of a party, remove such arbitrator and appoint another arbitrator in his place:

Provided however that where the parties have so agreed, such removal and appointment shall be made by an arbitral institution.

(3) Where the mandate of an arbitrator is terminated, proceedings shall not be had de-novo unless the parties otherwise agree.

9. Appointment of substitute arbitrator

Where the mandate of an arbitrator terminates under section 8, a substitute arbitrator shall beappointed in the manner applicable to the appointment of the arbitrator whose mandate has terminated.

10. Grounds for challenge

(1) Where a person is requested to accept appointment as an arbitrator, he shall first rise to disclose any circumstances likely to give justifiable doubts as to his impartiality or independence, and shall, from the time of his appointment and throughout the arbitral proceedings, disclose without delay any circumstances referred to in this subsection to all the parties aid to the other arbitrators, unless they have already been so informed by the arbitrator.

(2) An arbitrator may be challenged only if circumstances exist that give rise to justifiable doubts as to his impartiality or independence. A party may challenge an arbitrator appointed by him, or in whose appointment he has participated, only for reasons of which be becomes aware after the appointment was made.

(3) A party who seeks to challenge an arbitrator shall, unless the parties have decided that the decision shall be taken by some other person, first do so before the arbitral tribunal, within thirty days of his becoming aware of the circumstances which give rise to doubts about the arbitrators' impartiality or independence.

(4) Where a party who makes an application to an arbitral tribunal under this section, is dissatisfied with the order of the tribunal on such application, he may within thirty days of the receipt of the decision, appeal from that order to the High Court.

PART IV

JURISDICTION OF THE ARBITRAL TRIBUNAL

11. Competences of Arbitral

(1) An Arbitral tribunal may rule on its Arbitral, jurisdiction including any question, with respect Tribunal. to the existence or validity of the arbitration agreement or as to whether such agreement is contrary to public policy or is incapable of being performed; but any party to the arbitral proceedings may apply to the High Court for a determination of any such question.

(2) Where an application has been made to the High Court under subsection (1) the arbitral tribunal may continue the arbitral proceedings pending the determination of such question by the High Court.

12. Severability

An arbitration agreement which forms part of another of agreement, agreement shall be deemed to constitute a separate agreement when ruling upon the validity of that arbitration agreement for the purpose of determining the jurisdiction of the arbitral tribunal.

13. Interim measures of protection

(1) An arbitral tribunal may, at the request of a party, order any other party to take such interim measures as it may consider necessary to protect or secure the claim which forms the subject matter of the dispute. The arbitral tribunal may also order the party making such request to provide the party ordered to take such interim measures, with security for any expense, loss or damage that may be caused in taking such interim measures:

Provided however that other than in exceptional cases no such order shall be made except after hearing the other parties.

(2) An order of an arbitral tribunal requiring the taking of interim measures may be enforced by the High Court, on an application made therefor, by the party requesting the taking of such interim measures.

(3) An application to the High Court, under subsection (a), for the enforcement of interim measures, shall be deemed not to be incompatible with sector 5 or the arbitration agreement or a waiver of the agreement.

14. Settlement

(1) It shall not be incompatible with arbitration proceedings for an arbitral tribunal to encourage settlement arbitral tribunal may use mediation, conciliation of any other procedure at any time during the arbitral proceedings to encourage settlement.

(2) If, during arbitral proceedings the parties settle the dispute, the arbitral tribunal shall if requested by the parties, record the settlement in the form of an arbitral award on agreed terms.

(3) An arbitral award on agreed terms shall be made in accordance with section 25 and shall state that it is an arbitral award on agreed terms.

(4) An arbitral award on agreed terms has the same status and effect as any other arbitral award made in respect of the dispute.

PART V

CONDUCT OF ARBITRATION PROCEEDINGS

15. Duties of Arbitral tribunal

(1) An arbitral tribunal shall deal with any dispute submitted to it for arbitration in an impartial, practical and expeditious manner.

(2) An arbitral tribunal shall afford all the parties an opportunity, of presenting their respective cases in writing or orally and to examine all documents and other material furnished to it by the other parties or any other person. The arbitral tribunal may, at the request of a party, have an oral hearing before determining any question before it.

(3) An arbitral tribunal may, notwithstanding the failure of a party without reasonable cause, to appear before it, or to comply with any order made by it, continue the arbitral proceedings and determine the dispute on the material available to it.

(4) Parties may, introduce new prayers for relief provided that such prayers for relief fall within the scope of the arbitration agreement and it is not inappropriate to accept them having regard to the point of time at which they are introduced and to other circumstances. During the course of such proceedings, either party may, on like condition, amend or supplement prayers for relief introduced earlier and rely on new circumstances in support of their respective cases.

16. Place of arbitration

(1) The parties to an arbitration proceeding shall be free to agree on the place of arbitration. Failing such agreement, the place of arbitration shall be determined by the arbitral tribunal having regard to the circumstances of the case, including the convenience of the parties.

(2) Notwithstanding the provisions of subsection (1) providing for the place of arbitration, the arbitral tribunal may, unless otherwise agreed upon by the parties, meet at any place it considers appropriate for consultation among its members, for hearing witnesses, experts or the parties, or for inspection of goods, other property or documents.

17. Determination of rules of procedures

Subject to the provisions of this Act, the parties shall be free to agree on the procedure to be followed by the arbitral tribunal inconducting the proceedings. The power conferred upon the arbitral tribunal shall include the power to determine the admissibility, relevance, and weight of any evidence.

18. Commencement of arbitral proceedings

An arbitration shall be deemed to have been commenced if—

(a) a dispute to which the relevant arbitration agreement applies has arisen; and

(b) a party to the agreement—

(i) has received from another party to the agreement a notice requiring that party to refer, or to concur in the reference of, the dispute to arbitration; or

(ii) has received from another party to the agreement a notice requiring that party to appoint an arbitral tribunal or to join or concur on or approve the appointment of, an arbitral tribunal in relation to the dispute.

19. Manner in which decision are made

(1) Unless a contrary intention is expressed in the arbitration agreement, any decision made in the course of arbitral proceedings, by a majority of the are made arbitrators and failing a majority, the decision of the arbitrator appointed by the other arbitrators, or where in terms of the arbitration agreement or this Act, there is a Chairman, the decision of such Chairman, shall be binding.

(2) Where there is a Chairman of an arbitral tribunal, the Chairman shall have the power to administer the conduct of the arbitral proceedings.

20. Parties may obtain summons

(1) Any party to an arbitration agreement having obtained the prior consent in writting of the arbitral tribunal may apply to the High Court for summons requiring a person to attend for examination before the tribunal and to produce to the tribunal any document or thing specified in the summons.

(2) A person shall not be compelled under any summons issued in accordance with subsection (1) to answer any question or produce any document or thing which that person could not be compelled to answer or produce at the trial in an action before court.

21. Refusal or failure to before arbitral tribunal

(1) Unless otherwise agreed upon by the parties, where any person not a party to the arbitration agreement -arbitral

(a) refuses or fails to attend before the arbitral tribunal tribunal for examinations when required under summons or by the arbitral tribunal to do so;

(b) appearing as a witness before the arbitral tribunal—

(i) refuses or fails to take an oath or make an affirmation of affidavit when required by the arbitral tribunal to do so; or

(ii) refuses or fails to answer a question that the witness is required by the arbitral tribunal to answer; or

(iii) refuses or fails to produce a document that he is required under summons or by the arbitral tribunal to produce; or

(c) refuses or fails to do any other thing which the arbitral tribunal may require; or the High Court may order the defaulter to appear before the Court for examination or to produce to the Court the relevant document or thing or to do any relevant thing if a party to the arbitration proceedings makes an application to Court in that behalf.

(2) No such application shall be made except after notice to the other parties and with the prior sanction or consent of the arbitral tribunal and no order shall be made under subsection (1), unless the court after hearing the defaulter considers that it is necessary in the circumstances to make such order.

(3) Where the court makes an order under subsection (1) it shall, in addition make an order for the transmission to the arbitral tribunal of—

(a) a record of any evidence given pursuant to an order made under subsection (1);

(b) any document or thing produced pursuant to an order under subsection (1) or a copy of any such document ; or

(c) particulars of anything done pursuant to an order under subsection

(1) and any such evidence, document or thing shall be deemed to have been given, produced or done, as the case may be, in the course of the arbitration proceeding.

22. Evidence before arbitral tribunal

(1) Unless otherwise agreed upon by the parties, evidence before the arbitral tribunal may be given orally, in writing or by affidavit.

(2) Unless otherwise agreed upon by the parties, an arbitral tribunal may administer an oath or affirmation or take an affidavit for the purposes of proceedings under the agreement.

(3) Unless otherwise agreed upon by the parties, an arbitral tribunal in conducting proceedings in pursuance of an arbitration agreement shall not be bound by the provisions of the Evidence Ordinance.

23. Representation

Unless otherwise agreed in writing by the parties to the arbitration agreement, a party to an arbitration agreement—

(a) may appear before the arbitral tribunal personally or, where the party is a body of persons, whether corporate or unincorporate by an officer, employee or agent of that body ; and

(b) may be represented by an attorney-at-law if the party so desires.

24. Law applicable to the substance of system dispute

(1) And arbitral tribunal shall decide the dispute in accordance with such rules of law as are chosen to by the parties as applicable to the substance of the substance of dispute. Any designation of the law or legal system dispute.of a given State shall be construed, unless otherwise expressed as referring to the substantive law of that State and not to its conflict of laws rules.

(2) Failing any designation by the parties to any arbitration agreement, the arbitral tribunal shall apply the law determined by the conflict of laws rules which it considers applicable.

(3) The provisions of subsections (1) and (2) shall apply only to the extent agreed to by the parties.

(4) The arbitral tribunal shall decide according to considerations of general justice and fairness or trade usages only if the parties have expressly authorised it to do so.

PART VI
AWARDS

25. Form and content of award

(1) The award shall be made in writing and shall be signed by the arbitrators constituting the arbitral tribunal. In arbitral proceedings with more than one arbitrator, the signatures of the majority of the members of the arbitral tribunal shall suffice, provided that the reason for any omitted signature is stated.

(2) The award shall state the reasons upon which it is based, unless the parties have agreed that no reasons are to be given or the award is an award on agreed terms under section 14.

(3) The award shall state its date and place of arbitration as determined in accordance with section 16. The award shall be deemed to have been made at that place.

(4) After the award is made, a copy signed by the arbitrators constituting the arbitral tribunal in accordance with subsection (1) of this section shall be delivered to each party.

26. Award to final

Subject to the provisions of Part VII of this Act, the award made by the arbitral tribunal shall be final and binding on the parties to the arbitration agreement.

27. Correction

(1) Within fourteen days of receipt of the award, and unless another period of time has been agreed upon interpretation by the parties, whether at the request of the award; arbitral tribunal or otherwise -Additional awards.

(a) a party, with notice to the other party, may request the arbitral tribunal—

(i) to correct in the award any errors in computation, any clerical or typographical errors or omissions or any errors of a similar nature; or

(ii) to modify the award where a part of the award is upon a matter not referred to arbitration, provided such part can be separated from the other part and does not affect the decision on the matter referred;

(b) if so agreed upon by the parties, a party, with notice to the other party, may request the arbitral tribunal to give an interpretation of a specific point or part of the award.

(2) If the arbitral tribunal considers the request to be justified, it shall make the correction, modification or give the interpretation within fourteen days of the receipt of

the request, or such longer period as the parties may agree to, at the request of the arbitral tribunal. The interpretation shall form part of the award.

(3) The arbitral tribunal may correct any error of the type referred to in sub-paragraph (i) of paragraph (a) of subsection (1) of this section, on its own motion within fourteen days of the date of the award.

(4) Unless otherwise agreed upon by the parties, a party, with notice to the other party, may request the arbitral tribunal within fourteen days of receipt of the award to make an additional award as to claims presented in the arbitral proceedings but omitted from the award. If the arbitral tribunal after hearing the other parties, considers the request to be justified, it shall make the additional award within thirty days of conclusion of the hearing.

(5) The provisions of section 26 shall apply to a correction, modification or interpretation of the award or to an additional award.

28. Interest

Unless otherwise agreed upon by the parties where an arbitral tribunal makes an award for the payment of money (whether on a claim for a liquidated or unliquidated amount), the arbitral tribunal may in the award, order interest, at the rate agreed upon between the parties in the arbitration agreement or in the absence of any such agreement, at the legal interest prevailing at the time of making the arbitral award, to be paid on the principal sum awarded, from the date of commencement of arbitral proceedings to the date of the award, in addition to any interest awarded on such principal sum for any period prior to the institution of arbitral proceedings, with further interest at the aforesaid rate on the aggregate sum so awarded from the date of the award to the date of payment or such earlier date as the arbitral tribunal thinks fit.

29. Compensation

(1) The parties shall be jointly and severally of arbitrators, liable for the payment of reasonable compensation to the arbitrators constituting the arbitral tribunal for their work and disbursements:

Provided however that when the arbitral tribunal declares in its award that it has no jurisdiction to decide the dispute, the party who did not request the arbitration shall be liable for such payment only if there are exceptional circumstances which warrant such payment by him.

(2) The final award shall order the payment of compensation to each of the arbitrators consituting the arbitral tribunal in such sum, and within such period, as may be specified in the award, with legal interest on each such sum calculated with effect iron the date of expiration of a period of one month from the date on which the award was delivered.

(3) The arbitral tribunal may order the payment of deposit of security by the parties, for the payment of the compensation of the arbitrators constituting the arbitral tribunal, in such sum and within such period as may be specified in the order. Separate deposits of security may be ordered in respect of each prayer for relief.

(4) Where a party fails to pay his share of the deposit of security ordered by the arbitral tribunal within the period specified in the order for payment of deposit of security, the other party or parties may pay the whole of the deposit of security ordered.

(5) Where none of the parties pay the deposit of security ordered by the arbitral tribunal, within the period specified in the order for the payment of the deposit of security, the arbitral tribunal may terminate the arbitral proceedings.

(6) The arbitrators consituting the arbitral tribunal may, during the course of arbitral proceedings, draw on such deposit or security, for the purpose of meeting their expenses.

30. Award not to be withheld arbitral

An arbitral tribunal shall not withhold delivering its award pending the payment of the compensation payable to the arbitrators constituting the arbitral tribunal.

PART VII

31. Application to Courts Relating to Awards (Including Recognition and Enforcement of Foreign Awards Application for filing and enforcement of award

(1) A party to an arbitration agreement pursuant to which an arbitral award is made may, within one year after the expiry of fourteen days of the making of the award, apply to the High Court for the award, of award apply to the High Court for the enforcement of the award.

(2) An application to enforce the award shall be accompanied by —

(a) the original arbitration agreement under which the award purports to have been made or a duly certified copy of such agreement.

For the purposes of this subsection a copy of an award or of the arbitration agreement shall be deemed to have been duly certified if —

(i) it purports to have been certified by the arbitral tribunal on by a member of that tribunal, and it has not been shown to the Court that it was not in fact so certified; or

(ii) it has been otherwise certified to the satisfaction of the court.

(3) If a document or part of a document produced under subsection (2) is written in a language other than the official language of the court or other than in English, these shall be produced with the document a translation in such official language, or in the English language, of that document or that part, as the case may be, certified to be a correct translation.

(4) For the purposes of subsection (2), a translation shall be certified by an official or a sworn translator or by a diplomatic or a consular agent in Sri Lanka of the country in which the award was made or otherwise to the satisfaction of the Court.

(5) A document produced to the court in accordance with this section may upon its production be received by the Court as sufficient evidence of the matters to which it relates.

(6) Where an application is made under subsection (1) of this section and there is no application for the setting aside of such award under section 32 or the court sees no cause to refuse the recognition and enforcement of such award under the provisions contained in sections 33 and 34 of this Act, it shall on a day of which notice shall be given to the parties, proceed to file the award and give judgment according to the award. Upon the judgment so given a decree shall be entered.

32. Application

(1) An arbitral award made in an arbitration held in for setting Sri Lanka may be set aside by the High Court, on aside arbitral application made therefor, within sixty days of the award, receipt of the award—

(a) where the party making the application furnishes proof that—

(i) a party to the arbitration agreement was under some incapacity or the said agreement is not valid under the law to which the parties have subjected it or, failing any indication on that question under the law of Sri Lanka; or

(ii) the party making the application was not given proper notice of the appointment of an arbitrator or of the arbitral proceedings or was otherwise unable to present his case; or

(iii) the award deals with a dispute not contemplated by or not falling within the terms of the submission to arbitration, or contains decisions on matters beyond the scope of the submission to arbitration:

Provided however that, if the decision on matters submitted to arbitration can be separated from those not so submitted, only that part of the award which contains decisions on matters not submitted to arbitration may be set aside ; or

(iv) the composition of the arbitral tribunal or the arbitral procedure was not in accordance with the agreement of the parties, unless such agreement was in conflict with the provisions of this Act, or, in the absence of such agreement, was not in accordance with the provisions of this Act : or where the High Court finds that—

the subject matter of the dispute is not capable of settlement by arbitration under the law of Sri Lanka : or (ii) the arbitral award is in conflict with the public policy of Sri Lanka.

(2) Where an application is made to set aside an award, the High Court may order that any money made payable by the award shall be brought into Court or otherwise Kcured pending the determination of the application.

33. Recognition and enforcement of foreign arbitral awards

A foreign arbitral award irrespective of the country in which it was made shall subject to the provisions of section 34 be recognised as binding and, upon application by a party under section 31 arbitral to the High Court, be enforced by filing the award in accordance with the provisions of that section.

34. Grounds for refusing recognition or enforcement

(1) Recognition or enforcement of a foreign arbitral for refusing award, irrespective of the country in which it wasmade, may be refused only

(a) on the objection of the party against whom it is invoked, if that party furnishes to the Court where recognition or enforcement is sought, proof that—

(i) a party to the arbitration agreement was under some incapacity, or the said agreement is not valid under the law to which the parties have subjected it, or failing any indication as to the law to which the parties have subject such agreement, under the law of the country where the award was made; or

(ii) the party against whom the award is invoked was not given proper notice of the appointment of an arbitrator or of the arbitral proceeding or was otherwise unable to present his case; or

(iii) the award deals with the dispute not contemplated by or not falling within the terms of the submission to arbitration, or it contains decisions on matters beyond the scope of the submission to arbitration:

Provided, however that, if the decision on matters submitted to arbitration can be separated from those not so submitted, that part of the award which contains a decision on matter submitted to arbitration, may be recognised and enforced; or

(iv) the composition, of the arbitral tribunal or the arbitral procedure was not in accordance with the agreement of the parties or, in the absence of such agreement, was not in accordance with the law of the country where the arbitration took place; or

(v) the award has not yet become binding on the parties or has been set aside or suspended by a court of the country in which, or under the law of which, that award was made; or

(b) If the Court finds that—

(i) the subject-matter of the dispute is not capable of settlement by arbitration under the law of Sri Lanka; or

(ii) the recognition or enforcement of the award would be contrary to the public policy of Sri Lanka.

(2) If an application for setting aside or suspension of an award has been made to a court on the ground referred to in sub-paragraph

(v) of paragraph (a) of subsection (1) of this section, the court where recognition or enforcement is sought may, if it considers it proper, adjourn its decision and may also, on the application of the party claiming recognition or enforcement of the award, order the other party to provide appropriate security.

35. Power to consolidate a application to set aside with an under application for filing of an award

(1) Where applications filed in court to enforce an award and to set aside an award are pending, the court shall consolidate the applicationswith an

(2) Where an application to set aside the award section 32 has been refused, the court shall not permit a party to an arbitration to object to the enforcement of the award on any of the grounds specified in section 34.

36. Remissions to arbitral as tribunal

(1) The High Court may order the staying of an application to set aside an award for such period it may consider necessary to enable the arbitral tribunal to resume arbitral proceedings or to take such measures as may be necessary to eliminate the grounds for invalidating the award.

(2) No order shall be made by the High Court under sub-section (1) unless—

(a) all the parties to the arbitration request the making of such order and the Court is satisfied that there are grounds for invalidating the award.

37. Appeals

(1) Subject to subsection (2) of this section, noappeal or revision shall lie in respect of any order, judgment or decree of the High Court in the exercise of its jurisdiction under this Act except from an order, judgment or decree of the High Court under this Part of this Act.

(2) An appeal shall lie from an order, judgment or decree of the High Court referred to in subsection (1) to the Supreme Court only on a question of law and with the leave of the Supreme Court first obtained.

(3) The Supreme Court may in the exercise of its jurisdiction under subsection (2) of this section affirm, reverse or vary the order, judgment or decree of the High Court, subject to the provisions of this Act.

(4) The parties to an arbitration agreement may agree in writing (hereinafter referred to as an "exclusion agreement") to exclude any right to appeal in relation to an award.

38. Exclusion agreement

(1) The Supreme Court shall not in any event grant leave to appeal under subsection (2) of section 37 if there is in force an exclusion agreement between the parties to the arbitration agreement in relation to the award appealed against.

(2) An exclusion agreement may be expressed so as to relate to a particular award, to awards under a particular aribitration agreement or to any other description of awards, whether arising out of the same arbitration agreement or not.

(3) An agreement may be an exclusion agreement for the purposes of this section whether it is entered into before or after the appointed date and whether it forms part of an arbitration agreement or not.

39. Delay in prosecuting

(1) It shall be an implied term of the arbitration agreement that in the event of a dispute arising to which the agreement applies, it shall be the duty of the claimant to exercise due dilligence in the prosecution of a claim.

(2) Where there has been undue delay by a claimant in instituting or prosecuting a claim pursuant to an arbitration agreement, then on the application of any party to the dispute, the arbitral tribunal may make an order terminating the arbitration proceedings.

(3) The arbitral tribunal shall not make an order under subsection (2) unless it is satisfied—

(a) that the delay has been intentional or inordinate ; or

(b) that the delay will give rise to a substantial risk of it not being possible to have a fair determination of the issues in the arbitration proceedings or in such as is likely to cause or to have caused serious prejudice to the other parties to the arbitration proceedings either as between themselves and the claimant or between each other or between them and a third party.

(4) A party aggrieved by any order of the arbitral tribunal made on an application under subsection

(2) may appeal to the High Court.

PART VIII

PROCEEDINGS BEFORE THE HIGH COURT

40. Procedure

(1) Every application to the High Court under the provisions of this Act, whether by way of appeal or otherwise, shall be by way of petition and affidavit and all parties to the arbitration other than the petitioner or petitioners shall be named as respondents to such petition and shall be given notice of the same.

(2) Upon the petition and affidavit being presented to the court it shall by order appoint a day for the determination of the matter of the petition and grant the parties named as respondents to the petition a date to state their objections, if any, in writing supported by affidavit, and making available a copy thereof to the petitioners.

(3) In proceedings before the High Court evidence shall be given by affidavit. But where the court think it right so to do, it may take evidence viva voce in addition to evidence by affidavit.

(4) The High Court shall do with every application under sub-section (1) and deliver its determination thereon as expeditiously as possible.

41. Enforcement

Where a judgment is given according to an award and a decree entered under the provisions of section 31(6) it may be enforced in the same manner as a decree entered under the provisions of the Civil Procedure Code (Chapter 101) and accordingly the provisions of that Code relating to the execution of decrees shall, mutatis mutandis, apply to, such enforcement.

42. Service of

Where under this Act notice or summons is required notices and or permitted to be served on any person, the notice summons, or summons may be served in or out of Sri Lanka—

(a) by sending it by registered post addressed to that person to be served at the usual or last known place of residence or business of that person ;

(b) if there is no appearance by that person on the date stated therein, by serving it personally on him through the Fiscal; and

(c) if that person deliberately avoids accepting the notice or summons, by substituted service in accordance with the provisions of the Civil Procedure Code (Chapter 101).

43. Rules of Supreme Court

The Supreme Court may make rules with respect to —

(a) any application or appeal made to any Court under this Act and the costs of such application or appeal; and

(b) the payment of money into and out of the Court in satisfaction of a claim to which the arbitration agreements apply and the investment of such money;

44. Calculation of time

In calculating the period of prescription for the purpose of any action, the period that elapsed between the commencement of an arbitration and its completion, or termination as the case may be, shall be excluded.

PART IX

GENERAL PROVISIONS AS TO ABRITRATION

45. Liability of Arbitrator

An arbitrator shall not be liable for negligence respect of anything done or omitted to be done by him in the capacity of arbitrator but shall be liable for fraud in respect of anything done or omitted to be done in that capacity.

46. Death of party

(1) Unless a contrary intension is expressed in the arbitration agreement, where a party to an arbitration the mandate of the arbitrators constituting the arbitral tribunal shall not be revoked by the death of that party but the agreement Shall be enforceable by or against the legal representative of the estate of the deceased.

(2) Nothing in subsection (1) shall be taken to affect this operation of any enactment or rule of law by virtue of which a right of action is extinguished by the death of person.

47. Repeals

(1) The Arbitration Ordinance (Chapter 98) it hereby repealed.

(2) Section 693 to 698 of the Civil Procedure code (Chapter 101) are hereby repealed.

48. Application to other laws providing for Arbitration

For the avoidance of doubts, it is hereby declared that nothing in this Act shall apply to arbitral proceeding conducted under the Industrial Disputes Act or any other law, other than the Board of Investment of Sri Lanka Law No. 4 of 1973, making special provision for arbitration.

49. Sinhala text to revail in case of inconsistancy

In the event of any inconsistancy between the Sinhala and Tamil texts of this Act, the Sinhala text shall prevail.

50. Interpretation

(1) In this Act, unless the context otherwise requires—

"Arbitration Agreement" means an agreement by the parties to submit to arbitration all or certain disputes which have arisen or which may arise between them in respect of a defined legal relationship whether contractual or not;

"arbitration" means any arbitration whether or not administered by a permanent arbitral institution;

"arbitral tribunal" means a panel of one or more arbitrators;

"award" means a decision of the arbitral tribunal on the substance of the dispute;

"foreign arbitral award" means an award made in an arbitration conducted outside Sri Lanka; "High Court" means the High Court of Sri Lank, holden in the judicial zone of Colombo or holden in such other zone, as may be, designated by the Minister with the Concurrence of the Chief Justice, by Order published in the Gazette '

"legal interest" means interest at the rate specified in an Order made under section 192 of the Civil Procedure Code and for the time being in force.

CASE LAW ON UNCITRAL MODEL LAW ON INTERNATIONAL COMMERCIAL ARBITRATION*

The Secretariat of UNCITRAL publishes abstracts of court decisions and arbitral awards that are relevant to the interpretation or application of a text resulting from the work of UNCITRAL. For authoritative information, these abstracts may either be obtained from the UNCITRAL Secretariat or accessed through the UNCITRAL Home Page on the Internet (http://www.UNCITRAL.ORG). The copies of complete texts of court decisions and arbitral awards, in the original language, reported in the context of CLOUT, are available with the UNCITRAL Secretariat. This collection of "Case Law on UNCITRAL Texts" (CLOUT) contains decisions on the Model Law on International Commercial Arbitration. These readily available documents allow any judge, arbitrator, counsel or party to see how the Model Law is being applied worldwide—thus contributing to further harmonization in the real world of day-to-day application and interpretation.

With a view to making this emerging case law (CLOUT) available and in order to foster uniform interpretation, compilation of the abstracts of cases under each article of the UNCITRAL Model Law on International Commercial Arbitration (MAL)has been made and given below. Next to each article of Model Law, reference has been made to the corresponding provisions of the Indian Arbitration and Conciliation Act, 1996 and mention has been made wherever Indian law deviates from the Model Law.

This work should assist the professionals, judiciary, businessmen and all concerned in the arbitration community SAARC countries: in developing the arbitration law and process in line with other jurisdictions in the world.

This work aims at bringing to the reader interpretation that has been adopted by the courts and Arbitral bodies in applying the texts of the UNCITRAL Model Law in various parts of the world. In presenting the corresponding provision of the Indian statute side by side with the decisions given by various courts and Arbitral Tribunals, it is hoped that the various extracts will help the courts and Arbitral Tribunals to appreciate the provisions better while applying the said provisions in a given case. Needless to say, they will not have any binding effect. But their pursuasive effect will certainly be great.

---

* All abstracts of cases have been reproduced from documents entitled "CASE LAW ON UNCITRAL TEXTS"(CLOUT) published by the UNCITRAL secretariat and available on the internet www.uncitral.org.

CHAPTER I

GENERAL PROVISIONS

Article 1. Scope of application**

(1) This Law applies to international commercial** arbitration, subject to any agreement in force between this State and any other State or States.

(2) The provisions of this Law, except articles 8, 9, 35 and 36, apply only if the place of arbitration is in the territory of this State.

(3) An arbitration is international if:

(a) the parties to an arbitration agreement have, at the time of the conclusion of that agreement, their places of business in different States; or

(b) one of the following places is situated outside the State in which the parties have their places of business:

(i) the place of arbitration if determined in, or pursuant to the arbitration agreement;

(ii) any place where a substantial part of the obligations of the commercial relationship is to be performed or the place with which the subject-matter of the dispute is most closely connected; or

(c) the parties have expressly agreed that the subject-matter of the \arbitration agreement relates to more than one country.

(4) For the purposes of paragraph (3) of this article:

(a) if a party has more than one place of business, the place of business is that which has the closest relationship to the arbitration agreement;

(b) if a party does not have a place of business, reference is to be made to his habitual residence.

(5) This Law shall not affect any other law of this State by virtue of which certain disputes may not be submitted to arbitration or may be submitted to arbitration only according to provisions other than those of this Law.

†Indian Act—sections 1(2), 2(1)(f), 2(2) and 2(3)

#Case 13: MAL Articles 1(2); 5; 16

Canada: Ontario District Court, York Judicial District (Mandel, J.)

27 October, 1989

(Deco Automotive Inc. v. *G.P.A. Gesellschaft für Pressenautomation mbH Original in English,*

Where an arbitration occurs outside of Canada, pursuant to article 1(2), articles 5 and 16 will not apply. GPA (a German corporation) entered into a contract with Mareda (a U.S.

** Article headings are for reference purposes only and are not to be used for purposes of interpretation.

*** The term "commercial" should be given a wide interpretation so as to cover matters arising from all relationships of a commercial nature, whether contractual or not. Relationships of a commercial nature include, but are not limited to, the following transactions: any trade transaction for the supply or exchange of goods or services; distribution agreement; commercial representation or agency; factoring; leasing; construction of works; consulting; engineering; licensing; investment; financing; banking; insurance; exploitation agreement or concession; joini venture and other forms of industrial or business co-operation; carriage of goods or passengers by air. sea, rail or road.

† "Indian Act" refers to The Arbitration and Concilation Act, 1996 (26 of 1996).

Case numbers mentioned in this Chapter are as per citation of UNCITRAL.

company) to design, manufacture, deliver and put into operation a transfer system. This contract contained references to general conditions (ECE 188), which contained a clause referring disputes to arbitration. The arbitration terms provided for reference of any dispute to the International Chamber of Commerce for resolution through the application of the arbitration conditions of the Economic Commission for Europe (ECE). Mareda assigned the contract to Deco, a Canadian company. Deco refused to pay following disputes with GPA and sued in court for damages. GPA moved to have the action stayed. The court dismissed the motion finding that the reference to arbitration in the ECE rules did not cover the areas in dispute between the parties. Furthermore, the court ruled that where the arbitration is in Canada, then the matter may proceed as set out in Article 16, but where it is not (as in the present case) then article 16 does not apply by virtue of article 1(2). Also based on article 1(2), article 5 of the Model Law restricting judicial intervention does not apply because the place of arbitration is not in Canada.

Indian Act—Compare section 2(2)

Case 16: MAL 1; 5; 23(1); 34, especially 34(2)(a)(iii)

Canada: British Columbia Court of Appeal (Hutcheon, Proudfoot and Giggs, JJ.A)

24 October, 1990

Quintette Coal Limited v. *Nippon Steel Corp. et al.*

Published in English: 1 Western Weekly Reports, 1991, 219".

Commented on by: Tetley in [1993] Lloyd's Maritime and Commercial Law Quarterly, 238.

Commented on by: Paterson in Williamette Law Review, Vol. 27, 573.

Published in English and French: Canada Supreme Court Reports 1990 volume 2

The appropriate standard of review of arbitral awards is one which preserves the autonomy of the forum chosen by the parties and minimizes judicial intervention.

Quintette, a Canadian company, agreed to supply coal to the respondent, a Japanese company, Their agreement provided that any contract disputes would be submitted to binding arbitration under British Columbia Law. Accordingly, a dispute concerning the interpretation of a contract clause outlining a pricing mechanism was referred to arbitration and an award rendered. Quintette, relying on sections 5 and 34 of the Model Law as enacted by the International Commercial Arbitration Act, Statutes of British Columbia, 1986, c. 14 sought to set aside the award on the grounds that the arbitrators had exceeded their jurisdiction by dealing with a matter not contemplated by or falling within the scope of the submission to arbitration.

The Court of Appeal upheld the lower court's affirmation of the award. The Court noted the world-wide trend towards restricting the scope of judicial intervention into commercial arbitration. The award could be justified under the terms of the contract so the Court was prevented from intervening under article 34(2)(a)(iv) of the British Columbia Act (which is the same as article 34(2)(a)(iii) of the Model Law).

(The Supreme Court of Canada denied leave to appeal from the British Columbia Court of Appeal judgment on 13 December, 1990).

Indian Act—Compare section 5

Case 20: MAL l(3)(b)(ii); 3; 8; 10; 11; 16

Hong Kong: High Court of Hong Kong (Kaplan J.)

29 October, 1991

Fung Sang Trading Limited v. *Kai Sun Sea Products and Food Company Limited*

Original in English

Excerpts of judgement in Doyles dispute resolution practice: Asia Pacific in 1 volume. North Ryde, N.S.W.: CCH.

International, c1990-Tab 80-036, p.80, 661-80 and in: Yearbook Commercial Arbitration, (Deventer, Netherlands, Kluwer) vol. XVII, 1992, p. 289-303.

Commented on in: Doyles ADR update 5: 4-5, 28 February, 1992, and by Pryles, World Arbitration and Mediation Report 2:12:329 (December 1991).

Summary published: Yearbook XVIII-1992, International Council for Commercial Arbitration, 11.

Summarized and commented on by Kaplan, Spruce and Moser in Hong Kong and China Arbitration, cases and Materials, Butterworths, 1994.

Excerpts published in [1992] 1 Hong Kong Reports (HKLR), 40. (Abstract prepared by the UNCITRAL Secretariat) The plaintiff, a Hong Kong company, asked the court to appoint a second arbitrator, relying on a contract with another Hong Kong company that contained an arbitration clause. The contract was for the sale of soyabean extraction meal FOB Dalian; Dalian, which is in China, was stated to be the place of delivery. The defendant, asserting that there was no valid contract since the person who had signed had no authority to bind it, contended that an arbitrator had no jurisdiction to rule on whether or not a contract had been concluded. Even if an arbitration agreement existed, the arbitration would be domestic and thus have to be conducted by a sole arbitrator.

The court determined the arbitration to be international pursuant to article 1(3)(b)(ii) of the Model Law as enacted by the Hong Kong Arbitration (Amendmentl (No.2) Ordinance, 1989. It regarded delivery (which was to take place outside Hong Kong) as "a substantial part of the obligations of the commercial relationship", without ignoring that payment and nomination of the vessel (which were to take place in Hong Kong) were also important obligations in a contract of sale.

The court refused to deal with the question of whether a valid contract had been concluded since, according to article 16 MAL, it was first for the arbitral tribunal to decide on its jurisdiction. Recognizing the autonomy or separability of the arbitration clause except in the case of *ab initio* illegality of the contract (with references to English law], the court stated that the decision of the arbitral tribunal was neither final nor exclusive but subject to immediate review under article 16(3) MAL.

In making the appointment under article 11(5) MAL, the court deemed it important that when "appointing on behalf of the defaulting appointing party, it should go out of its way to ensure that no sense of grievance is felt, however unreasonable that attitude might appear to others".

Indian Act—sections 2(1)(f), 15(1)(b) and 16

Case 28: MAL 1(2); 8

Canada: Saskatchewan Court of Queen's Bench (MacPherson C.J.Q.B.)

19 March, 1993

BWV Investments Ltd. v. *Saskferco Products Inc.*, UHDE-GmbH, *et al.*

Original in English Unpublished

The parties entered into a series of contractual relationships concerning the construction of a fertilizer plant for Saskferco. The subcontract between UHDE and BWV for the construction contained an arbitration clause requiring that the arbitration take place in Zurich and the interpretation, application and performance of the sub-contract be governed by Swiss law. BWV sued the defendants in court for monies owing on the contract. UHDE applied to have the proceedings stayed in order that the case might be resolved by arbitration. In issue was the application of MAL to this dispute.

The court, stating that despite the provision in article 1(2) only articles 8, 9, 35 and 36 of MAL apply to arbitration agreements where the place of arbitration is outside the state, found that it could refer to the definitions in MAL by virtue of s. 2(2) of the International Commercial Arbitration Act, Statutes of Saskatchewan 1988-89, c.1-10.2, which enacts MAL. This section provides that all terms used in the Act will have the same meaning as in MAL. The court found that the agreement in question was an international commercial arbitration agreement within the meaning of the Act. The court found that the agreement was void as it conflicted with the Builders' Lien Act, Statutes of Saskatchewan 1984-85-86, c. B-7.1. The agreement would have rendered inapplicable the rights of several lien holders who would not be involved in an arbitration. The court declared the arbitration agreement void and did not grant a stay of proceedings.

Indian Act—contrast sections 8(1) and 16(1)

Case 39: MAL 1(3) (b) (ii), 9

Hong Kong: High Court of Hong Kong (Kaplan J.)

Katran Shipping Co. Ltd. v. Kenven Transportation Ltd.

Published in English: 1992, Hong Kong Law Digest, G9

Summarized and commented on by Kaplan, Spruce and Moser in Hong Kong and China Arbitration, Cases and Materials, Butterworths, 1994.

Commented on by Kaplan in Asia Law, January-February, 1995, 23.

Reported on in English: |1992| the Arbitration and Dispute Resolution Law Journal (ADRLJ) 235, [1992] ADRLJ 240, [1993] ADRJL 100 and [1994] ADRJL 49, 295, 307, 291, 290, 298 respectively.

(Abstract prepared by Kaplan).)

The defendant, a Hong Kong company, sought to have set aside a Mareva injunction that the court had granted the plaintiff, also a Hong Kong company. The issue before the court was whether it had jurisdiction to grant such an interim measure of protection, in view of the fact that a charter-party agreement entered by the plaintiff and the defendant contained an arbitration clause which provided that "any dispute will be settled before Hong Kong Arbitrators and under British Maritime law ...".

The court, relying on article 1(3)(b)(ii) MAL and its decision on *Fung Sang Trading* v. *Kai Sun Sea Products and Food Co. Ltd.* [see A/CN.9/SER.C/ABSTRACTS/1, case 20], found that MAL covered this dispute, since a substantial part of the obligations provided in the charter-party was to be performed outside Hong Kong.

The court held that the interim measure of protection referred to in article 9 MAL was wide enough to cover a Mareva injunction. "The protection afforded by a Mareva injunction" was held to be "the reduction in the risk of the amount of the claim, or part of it, being dissipated or otherwise put out of the plaintiff's reach before the resolution of the dispute".

The court concluded that it had jurisdiction to grant a Mareva injunction in support of a domestic arbitration carried out in Hong Kong, both under article 9 MAL and s. 14(6) of the Arbitration Ordinance which were identical in regard to domestic arbitration.

Indian Act—section 9(ii)(a)(b). The judgment is important as clarifying the legal position regarding Mareva injunction

Case 58; MAL 1(3)(b)(ii)

Hong Kong: High Court of Hong Kong (Kaplan J.)

22 June and 12 July 1993; appeal pending

Ananda Non-Ferrous Metals Ltd. v. *China Resources Metal and Minerals Co. Ltd.*

Excerpts published in [1993] 2 Hong Kong Law Reports (HKLR), 348

(Abstract prepared by the UNCITRAL Secretariat)

The plaintiff, a Hong Kong company, agreed to sell to the defendant, also a Hong Kong company, 40 metric tonnes of cadmium c.i.f. Rotterdam. Upon arrival in Rotterdam, the goods were inspected and the defendant contended that they did not comply with the description contained in the contract: The issue was submitted to arbitration and the arbitral tribunal in an interim award found in favour of the defendant. The plaintiff sought leave from the court to appeal against that interim award. The defendant argued that an international arbitration was involved, to which MAL applied, and that under MAL there was no right to appeal. It was agreed that the court should first deal with the issue whether it had jurisdiction depending on whether a domestic or international arbitration was involved. The plaintiff argued that the arbitration was domestic since both parties were Hong Kong companies and that, even if it were international, the defendant was estopped from raising that defence or had waived such a defence since the circumstances and the conduct of the parties indicated thai a domestic arbitration was involved.

The court, applying article 1(3)(b)(ii) MAL and citing its ruling on Fung Sang Trading Limited etc. [case 20], held that an international arbitration was involved since a substantial part of the obligations of the commercial relationship was to be performed outside Hong Kong. It was found that the documents submitted by the plaintiff and the circumstances did not indicate that the parties had agreed to opt into the domestic regime. It was also found that the defendant was not estopped from raising the defence that an international arbitration was involved since there was no representation by the defendant on which the plaintiff might have acted to its detriment; nor did the defendant waive such defence since the fact that the arbitration was international was never an issue in the arbitration proceedings and the defendant could not have waived a right of which he was not aware. The court dismissed the application.

Indian Act—contrast section 2(1)(f)

Case 75: MAL 1(3)(b)(ii)

Hong Kong: High Court of Hong Kong (Kaplan J.)

7 July, 1994

China Resources Metal and Minerals Co. Ltd. v. *Ananda Non-Ferrous Metals Ltd.*

Original in English Unpublished

(Abstract prepared by the UNCITRAL Secretariat)

The plaintiff applied to the court *ex parte* for leave to enforce a final arbitral award against the defendant. The leave was granted subject to the usual stay in order to give the defendant an opportunity to oppose. The defendant requested the court to set the *ex parte* order aside on the grounds that the appointment of the arbitrator, or alternatively, the arbitration agreement was void because of mutual mistake on the part of both parties who acted in the belief that the arbitration was a domestic one to which MAL did not apply.

The court dismissed the defendant's application holding that it was *res judicata* and the defendant was estopped from now raising arguments that were not raised before the same court (case 58) and the Court of Appeal. In any case, the court was convinced that there was no mutual mistake of the parties since, as it had previously held (case 58), the parties did not sufficiently focus on whether the arbitration they agreed upon was a domestic or an international one; and that even if there were a mutual mistake, it would be one of law and not of fact, and one that did not go to the root of the agreement to arbitrate so as to lead to its annulment.

Indian Act—see section 20-Indian Contract Act, 1872 as to mutual mistake

Case 77: MAL 1(1) and (3)(a); 5; 9; 27

Hong Kong: High Court of Hong Kong (Kaplan J.)

15 August, 1994

Vibroflotation A.G. v. *Express Builders Co. Ltd.*

Original in English, Unpublished, (Abstract prepared by the UNCITRAL Secretariat)

The plaintiff, a sub-contractor, appealed against an order of the Master of the court setting aside a subpoena issued by the plaintiff against a third party, the main contractor, for the production of certain documents before the arbitral tribunal (subpoena duces tecum], which was considering the plaintiff's claim against the defendant, sub-contractor, for breach of contract.

The court held that it had jurisdiction to grant subpoenas in order to assist arbitral tribunals in taking evidence on the grounds that an international arbitration covered by MAL was involved since the parties had their places of business in different States (article 1(1) and (3}(a) MAL); and that, while subpoenas could not be characterized as interim measures of protection falling under article 9 MAL, they could be granted under article 27 MAL, if requested, by the arbitral tribunal or by a party with the approval of the arbitral tribunal, since the domestic law of Hong Kong provided for subpoenas.

The court was satisfied that in the present case the subpoena had been issued in accordance with article 27 MAL and with the approval of the arbitral tribunal, which was implied by the fact that the tribunal fixed a date for the production of documents that "appeared to be relevant to one of the key issues to this arbitration". The court however dismissed the plaintiff's application on the grounds that it was not timely, since such a subpoena for the production of documents could only be applied for in relation to an evidential hearing and the parties to this arbitration were "months, if not years, away from the main evidential hearing in this arbitration".

Indian Act—section 27

Case 101: MAL 1(3); 11(3)(a)

Hong Kong: High Court of Hong Kong (Leonard J.)

27 January, 1995

Private Company "Triple V" Inc. Ltd. v. *Star (Universal) Co. Ltd. and Sky Jade Enterprises Group Ltd.*

Original in English, Unpublished, (Abstract prepared by the Secretariat)

The plaintiff, a Russian company, bought from the defendants, two Hong Kong companies, a number of television sets and microwaves. Pursuant to the contract, delivery was to be made in Russia. The contract provided for arbitration in Hong Kong. The plaintiff alleged that the television sets were not delivered at all and the microwaves delivered were defective. The parties failed to agree on a procedure for appointing the arbitrator and the plaintiff requested the court to make the appointment pursuant to article 11(3)(a) MAL, The second defendant argued that it was not part of the contract.

The court found that an international arbitration, as defined in article 1(3) MAL, was involved and that there was *prima facie* evidence of a dispute between the parties, and appointed a sole arbitrator. As to the second defendant, who in fact had not signed the contracl, the court found that it was represented by the first defendant and ruled that, in any event, it was at the discretion of the second defendant to challenge the jurisdiction of the arbitrator in accordance with article 16(1) and (3).

◆ ◆ ◆ ◆ ◆

Case 108: MAL l(3)(b)(H); 8(1)

Hong Kong: High Court of Hong Kong (Leonard }.)

4 May, 1995

D. Heung & Associates, Architects & Engineers v. *Pacific Enterprises (Holdings) Company Limited*

Original in English Unpublished

(Abstract prepared by N. Kaplan, Q.C.)

The plaintiff, a Hong Kong company, appointed by the defendant, also a Hong Kong company, as the architect for the entire design of a project in Dongshan Island, China, sued claiming agreed professional fees due by the defendant. The defendant sought a stay of the court proceedings under article 8 MAL and submission of the dispute to arbitration, since their agreement contained an arbitration clause.

The issue was whether, despite the fact that both parties were Hong Kong companies and that the contract was to be partly performed in Hong Kong, an "international arbitration agreement" in the meaning of article l(3)(b)(ii) was involved. The court found that the subject-matter of the dispute was most closely connected to the project in Dongshan, China, and that a substantial part of the defendant's duties related to the entire design and supervision of that project.

The court, noting that article 8(1) MAL was mandatory in its nature, stayed the proceedings, since no party had suggested that the arbitration agreement was *null and void* or inoperative or incapable of being performed, and in view of the fact that the plaintiff's claim was disputed by the defendant.

Indian Act— section 8(1)

Article 2. Definitions and rules of interpretation

For the *purposes* of this Law:

(a) "arbitration" means any arbitration whether or not administered by a permanent arbitral institution;

Indian Act—section 2(b), 2(1)(b)

(b) "arbitral tribunal" means a sole arbitrator or a panel of arbitrators;

Indian Act—section 2(1)(d)

(c) "court" means a body or organ of the judicial system of a State;

Indian Act—section 2(1)(e)

(d) where a provision of this Law, except article 28, leaves the parties free to determine a certain issue, such freedom includes the right of the parties to authorize a third party, including an institution, to make that determination; Indian Act—section 2(6)

(e) where a provision of this Law refers to the fact that the parties have agreed or that they may agree or in any other way refers to an agreement of the parties, such agreement includes any arbitration rules referred to in that agreement;

Indian Act—section 2(8)

(f) where a provision of this Law, other than in articles 25(a) and 32(2)(a), refers to a claim, it also applies to a counter-claim, and where it refers to a defence, it also applies to a defence to such counter-claim.

Indian Act—section 2(9)

Case 29: MAL 2;35;36

Canada: Ontario Court, General Division (While J.)

30 January, 1992

Kanto Yakin Kogyo Kabushiki-Kaisha v. *Can-Eng Manufacturing Ltd.*

Published in English: 7 Ontario Reports (3d), 779

Commented on by Tetley in (1993] Lloyd's Maritime and Commercial Law Quarterly, 238

Concluding an agreement prior to the existence of legislation implementing MAL will not mean that MAL will not apply to arbitrations taking place pursuant lo the agreement. The parties concluded an agreement which contained an arbitration clause and provided that arbitration would take place in Tokyo. Arbitration of an issue arising out of the agreement was held and an award was made. Kanto Yakin sought to enforce the award in Ontario. The court found that, despite the fact that the agreement was concluded prior to the coming into force of the International Commercial Arbitration Act, Revised Statutes of Ontario, 1990, c. 1.9, which enacts MAL, the agreement was still an arbitration agreement governed by the Act and was enforceable as such.

Indian Act—contrast section 85

Article 3. Receipt of written communications

(1) Unless otherwise agreed by the parties:

(a) any written communication is deemed to have been received if it is delivered to the addressee personally or if it is delivered at his place of business, habitual residence or mailing address; if none of these can be found after making a reasonable inquiry, a written communication is deemed to have been received if it is sent to the addressee's last-known place of business, habitual residence or mailing address by registered letter or any other means which provides a record of the attempt to deliver it;

(b) the communication is deemed to have been received on the day it is so delivered.

(2) The provisions of this article do not apply to communications in court proceedings.

Indian Act—section 3

Case 20: MAL 1(3)(b)(ii); 3; 8; 10; 11; 16

Hong Kong: High Court of Hong Kong (Kaplan J.)

29 October, 1991

Fung Sang Trading Limited v. *Kai Sun Sea Products and Food Company Limited*

Original in English

Excerpts of judgement in Doyles dispute resolution practice: Asia, Pacific in 1 volume. North Ryde, N.S.W.: CCH International, 1990-Tab 80-036, p.80, 661-80 and in: Yearbook Commercial Arbitration, (Deventer, Netherlands, Kluwer) vol. XVII, 1992, p. 289-303.

Commented on in: Doyles ADR update 5: 4-5, 28 February, 1992, and by Pryles, World Arbitration and Mediation Report 2:12:329 (December 1991.

Summary published: Yearbook XVIII-1992, International Council for Commercial Arbitration, 11.

Summarized and commented on by Kaplan, Spruce and Moser in Hong Kong and China Arbitration, Cases and Materials, Butterworths, 1994.

Excerpts published in [1992] 1 Hong Kong Reports (HKLR), 40.

(Abstract prepared by the UNCITRAL Secretariat)

The plaintiff, a Hong Kong company, asked the court to appoint a second arbitrator, relying on a contract with another Hong Kong company that contained an arbitration clause. The contract was for the sale of soyabean extraction meal FOB Dalian; Dalian, which is in China, was stated to be the place of delivery. The defendant, asserting that there was no valid contract since the person who had signed had no authority to bind it, contended that an arbitrator had no jurisdiction to rule on whether or not a contract had been concluded. Even if an arbitration agreement existed, the arbitration would be domestic and thus have to be conducted by a sole arbitrator.

The court determined the arbitration to be international pursuant to article 1(3)(b)(ii) of the Model Law as enacted by the Hong Kong Arbitration (Amendment) (No. 2) Ordinance, 1989. It regarded delivery (which was to take place outside Hong Kong) as "a substantial part of the obligations of (he commercial relationship", without ignoring that payment and nomination of the vessel (which were to take place in Hong Kong) were also important obligations in a contract of sale.

The court refused to deal with the question of whether a valid contract had been concluded since, according to article 16 MAL, it was first for the arbitral tribunal to decide on its jurisdiction. Recognizing the autonomy or separability of the arbitration clause except in the case of ab initio illegality of the contract (with references to English law), the court stated that the decision of the arbitral tribunal was neither final nor exclusive but subject to immediate review under article 16(3) MAL.

In making the appointment under article 11(5) MAL, the court deemed it important that when "appointing on behalf of the defaulting appointing party, it should go out of its way to ensure that no sense of grievance is felt, however unreasonable that attitude might appear to others".

Indian Act—contrast section 2(1)(f)

Article 4. Waiver of right to object

A *party who knows that* any *provision of this Law from which the parties may derogate or any requirement under the arbitration agreement has not been complied with and yet proceeds with the arbitration without stating his objection to such non-compliance without undue delay or, if a time-limit is provided therefor, within such period of time, shall be deemed to have waived his right to object,*

Indian Act—section 4. Note that section 4, like MAL covers "every requirement"

Article 5. Extent of court intervention

In matters governed by this Law, no court shall intervene except where so *provided in this Law.*

Indian Act—section 5. It emphatically begins with the words "Notwithstanding anything".

Case 13; MAL Articles 1(2); 5; 16

Canada: Ontario District Court, York Judicial District (Mandel, J.)

27 October, 1989

Deco Automotive Inc. v. C.P.A. Gesellschaft für Pressenautomation mbH Original in English

Where an arbitration occurs outside of Canada, pursuant to article 1(2), articles 5 and 16 will not apply.

GPA (a German corporation) entered into a contract with Mareda (a U.S.A. company) to design, manufacture, deliver and put into operation a transfer system. This contract contained references to general conditions (ECE 188), which contained a clause referring disputes to arbitration. The arbitration terms provided for reference of any dispute to the International Chamber of Commerce for resolution through the application of the arbitration conditions of the Economic Commission for Europe (ECE). Mareda assigned the contract to Deco, a Canadian company. Deco refused to pay following disputes with GPA and sued in court for damages. GPA moved to have the action stayed.

The court dismissed the motion finding that the reference to arbitration in the ECE rules did not cover the areas in dispute between the parties, Furthermore, the court ruled that where the arbitration is in Canada, then the matter may proceed as set out in Article 16, but where it is not (as in the present case) ihen article 16 does not apply by virtue of article 1(2). Also based on article 1(2), article 5 of the Model Law restricting judicial intervention does not apply because the place of arbilration is not in Canada.

Indian Act—See section 2(2)

Case 16: MAL 1; 5; 23(1); 34, especially 34(2)(a)(iii)

Canada: British Columbia Court of Appeal (Hutcheon, Proudfoot and Giggs,) JJ.)

24 October, 1990

Quintette Coal Limited v. *Nippon Steel Corp. et al.*

Published in English and French: Canada Supreme Court Reports 1990 volume 2 English: 1 Western Weekly Reports, 1991, 219.

Commented on by Tetley in 1993 Lloyd's Maritime and Commercial Law Quarterly, 238.

Commented on by Paterson in Williamette Law Review, Vol. 27, 573.

The appropriate standard of review of arbitral awards is one which preserves the autonomy of the forum chosen by the parties and minimizes judicial intervention.

Quintette, a Canadian company, agreed to supply coal to the respondent, a Japanese company. Their agreement provided that any contract disputes would be submitted to binding arbitration under British Columbia Law. Accordingly, a dispute concerning the interpreting of a contract clause outlining a pricing mechanism was referred to arbitration and an award rendered. Quintette, relying on sections 5 and 34 of the Model Law as enacted by the International Commercial Arbitration Act, Statutes of British Columbia, 1986, c. 14 sought to set aside the award on the grounds that the arbitrators had exceeded their jurisdiction by dealing with a matter not contemplated by or falling within the scope of the submission to arbitration.

The Court of Appeal upheld the lower court's affirmation of the award. The Court noted the world-wide trend toward restricting the scope of judicial intervention into commercial arbitration. The award could be justified under the terms of the contract so the Court was prevented from intervening under article 34(2)(a)(iv) of the British Columbia Act (which is the same as article 34(2)(a)(iii) of the Model Law).

(The Supreme Court of Canada denied leave to appeal from the British Columbia Court of Appeal judgment on 13 December, 1990.)

Indian Act—see sections 5 and 34

Case 18: MAL 5; 8; 16

Canada: Ontario Court of Justice - General Division (Henry J.)

1 March, 1991

Rio Algom Limited v. *Sammi Steel Co.*

Original in English

The interaction of articles 8 and 16 restricts the court's role in arbitrations to determining whether the arbitration clause is *null and void*. Any determination of the arbitrator's jurisdiction is made by the arbitrator pursuant to article 16.

The parties agreed that Sammi would purchase Rio's steel manufacturing business in Ontario, Quebec and New York State. The agreement provided that the parties each prepare a Closing Date Balance Sheet as soon as possible after closing. Arbitration was provided for if the parties could not resolve any dispute arising out of the Closing Date Balance Sheets. Such a dispute did arise, Sammi followed the required procedure and submitted the matter to an arbitrator. Rio commenced an action in court challenging the jurisdiction of the arbitrator and seeking an order staying the arbitration proceedings. The Chambers judge granted the order finding that the arbitrator's jurisdiction is a threshold issue of contract construction to be decided by the court. Leave to appeal the Chambers judge's order was sought.

The court granted leave to appeal. It found that the Chambers judge's decision had been erroneously based on principles of the domestic arbitration act rather than those found in the Model Law as enacted by the International Commercial Arbitration Act, Statutes of Ontario, 1988, c.30. In particular the court cited article 16 which provides the arbitral tribunal with the power to rule on its own jurisdiction. The court further noted article 8 which restricts court involvement to a determination of whether the arbitration agreement is *null and void*.

Indian Act—sections 8 and 16

Case 182: MAL 5; 16; 34

Canada: Superior Court of Quebec (Tellier J.)

9 September, 1994

International Civil Aviation Organization (ICAO) v. *Tripal Systems Pvt. Ltd.*

Original in French

Published in French: Recueil de jurisprudence du Quebec (1994) 2560

In February 1990, ICAO entered into a contract with Tripal for the conception, construction and installation of an airport in Hanoi, Vietnam. The contract included an arbitration clause as well as a clause that preserved any immunity that might accrue to ICAO. Following the commencement of arbitral proceedings to resolve a dispute between the parties, ICAO raised its immunity to contest the arbitral tribunal's competence. Considering that the issue was one of mixed fact and law, the arbitral tribunal, in order to rule on the objection, decided to hear all evidence. ICAO then asked the Superior Court of Quebec to declare that it enjoyed an absolute immunity from judicial process of any kind. Tripal responded with its own motion for dismissal on the grounds that only the arbitral tribunal was competent at that stage of the proceedings.

The Superior Court granted the motion for dismissal of the declaratory motion, having decided that the arbitral tribunal alone was competent to decide the immunity issue. To this end, the Superior Court examined the conditions regulating judiciary intervention in the arbitral process (articles 16 and 34 MAL) and concluded that these were not met. The Superior Court refused to intervene on the basis of article 5 MAL. However, it noted that once the arbitral tribunal had declared itself competent, the Superior Court would be competent to review this decision in accordance with article 16(31 MAL, should a party so request.

Indian Act—sections 8 and 16. As to immunity, see section 86, Code of Civil Procedure, 1908

Article 6. Court or other authority for certain functions of arbitration assistance and supervision

The functions referred to in articles 11(3), 11(4), 13(3), 14, 16(3) and 34(2) shall be performed by ... [Each State enacting this model law specifies the court, courts or, where referred to therein, other authority competent to perform these functions.]

Indian Act—sections 9 and 27

CHAPTER II

ARBITRATION AGREEMENT

Article 7. Definition and form of arbitration agreement

(1) "Arbitration agreement" is an agreement by the parties to submit to arbitration all or certain disputes which have arisen or which may arise between them in respect of a defined legal relationship, whether contractual or not. An arbitration agreement may be in the form of an arbitration clause in a contract or in the form of a separate agreement.

(2) The arbitration agreement shall be in writing. An agreement is in writing if it is contained in a document signed by the parties or in an exchange of letters, telex, telegrams or other means of telecommunication which provide a record of the agreement, OF in an exchange of statements of claim and defence in which the existence of an agreement is alleged by one party and not denied by another. The reference in a contract to a document containing an arbitration clause constitutes an arbitration agreement provided that the contract is in writing and the reference is such as to make that clause part of the contract.

Indian Act—sections 2(1)(b) and 7

Case 32: MAL 7; 8

Canada; Ontario Court, General Division (Zelinski].)

30 April, 1992

Mind Star Toys Inc. v. *Samsung Co. Ltd.*

Published in English: 9 Ontario Reports (3d), 374

Agreements containing both an arbitration clause and a right to sue will still be subject to article 8 MAL, depending on the particular agreement.

Mind Star was a licensee of a product which it sub-licensed to Samsung. The sub-licensing agreement contained an arbitration clause and also a clause providing Mind Star with the right to sue should Samsung fail to perform any of its obligations. Mind Star claimed that Samsung had fundamentally breached the agreement and that Mind Star was entitled to claim damages. The parties agreed that the arbitration clause in the agreement qualified as an arbitration agreement pursuant to article 7 MAL as enacted by the International Commercial Arbitration Act, Revised Statutes of Ontario, 1990, c.1.9.

The court concluded that the right to sue did not qualify ihe duty to arbitrate. Even disputes concerning the clause creating the right to sue were subject to arbitration. The court found this "consistent with the requirement that the arbitrator will, in the first instance, determine its own jurisdiction, and the scope of its authority." The arbitration clause was operative and as such article 8 MAL required that the parties be referred to arbitration.

Indian Act—sections 8 and 16

Case 40: MAL 7; 11(4)

Hong Kong: High Court of Hong Kong (Kaplan J.)

30 July 1992

Pacific International Lines (PTE) Ltd. & Another v. *Tsinlien Metals and Minerals Co. Ltd.*

Published in English: 1992, Hong Kong Law Digest, G5; excerpts of judgement in The Arbitration and Dispute Resolution Law Journal, Part 4, December 1992, 240

Summarized and commented on by Kaplan, Spruce and Moser in Hong Kong and China Arbitration, Cases and Materials, Butterworths, 1994.

(Abstract prepared by Kaplan).)

The plaintiff, owner and manager of a vessel which was chartered to the defendant, sought payment of damages or breach of the charter-party with the defendant. When the defendant failed to pay, the plaintiff appointed an arbitrator pursuant to an arbitration clause contained in Ihe charter-party. The defendant failed to appoint a second arbitrator and the plaintiff applied in accordance with article 11(4) MAL for the court to appoint a second arbitrator.

Although the charter-party was not signed by both parties, the court found that there was a charter-party between the plaintiff and the defendant, since there was no doubt from the facts and the pre-voyage communications that the defendant had chartered the vessel of the plaintiff and had paid also certain sums to the plaintiff in accordance with that charter-party. The court concluded that article 7 MAL requiring a written agreement to arbitrate had been complied with and gave the defendant seven days to appoint a second arbitrator, otherwise the court was to appoint him.

Compare case No. 64, infra Indian Act—sections 7(3) and 7(4) and compare decisions on earlier Act, to the same effect—Jugal Kishore* v. *Goolbau, AIR 1955 SC 812 and Banarsi Das* v. *Cane Commissioner AIR 1963 SC 141

Case 43: MAL 7(2) MAL

Hong Kong: High Court of Hong Kong (Mayo J.)

8 September, 1992

Hissan Trading Co. Ltd. v. *Orkin Shipping Corporation*

Published in English; 1992, Hong Kong Law Digest, H8

Summarized and commented on by Kalplan, Spruce and Moser in Hong Kong and China Arbitration, Cases and Materials, Butterworths, 1994.

Commented on by Kaplan in Asia Law January/February 1995, 23.

(Abstract prepared by Kaplan J.)

The plaintiff, sub-charterer, filed an action against the defendant, ship-owner, for loss of cargo occasioned by the vessel's sinking. The claim was made under a bill of lading subject to Japanese law, which incorporated the arbitration clause of a charter-party to which neither the plaintiff nor the defendant were parties. The bill of lading itself contained an exclusive jurisdiclion clause in favour of the Tokyo District Court. At the commencement of the action the plaintiff obtained an injunction against the defendant with regard to the proceeds of the insurance policy on the vessel.

The defendant applied for a stay of court proceedings on the ground of the arbitration clause, alternatively on the basis of the exclusive jurisdiction clause, contained in the bill of lading. The defendant also sought to have the injunction set aside,

The court found that, since the bill of lading was not signed by both parties, there was no written agreement to arbitrate contained in a document signed by both parties, as required by article 7(2) MAL. The correspondence between the parties was held to be insufficient as article *7(2)* MAL precluded the adoption of memoranda being relied upon, which were issued after the conclusion of the agreement to arbitrate [see, however, A/CN.9/SER.C/ABSTRACTS/2, case 44]. In addition, the court could not apply the relevant arbitration clause, even if it were a written agreement in the meaning of article 7(2) MAL, since it was not clear whether the parties had agreed to resolve their disputes through arbitration or through court proceedings before the Tokyo District Court. In order to apply the arbitration clause the court would have to manipulate the language of the agreement of the parties in a substantial and, thus, impermissible way. The court dismissed the application for a stay of proceedings.

Contrast Case No. 44 infra

The court dismissed also the defendant's application to have the injunction set aside. The court held that there was sufficient evidence that the main asset of the defendants, the proceeds of the insurance policy on the vessel, might be dissipated, as the defendant was a one-ship-owning Panamanian company which was unlikely to continue trading after the vessel had sunk.

Indian Act—sections 7(1) and 9

Case 44: MAL 7(2); 8

Hong Kong: High Court of Hong Kong (Kaplan J.)

17 February, J993

William Company v. *Chu Kong Agency Co. Ltd. and Guangzhou Ocean Shipping Company*

Published in English; 1993, Hong Kong Law Digest, B7

Summarized and commented on by Kaplan, Spruce and Moser in Hong Kong and China Arbitration, Cases and Materials, Butterworth, 1994.

Commented on by Kaplan in Asia Law January/February 1995, 23.

(Abstract prepared by the UNCITRAL Secretariat)

The plaintiff filed a suit against the defendants requesting damages for loss and damage to its cargo carried under a bill of lading issued by the first defendant in Hong Kong. The bill of lading, which was subject to the Hague- Visby Rules contained an arbitration clause providing for arbitration in China under Chinese law and an exclusive jurisdiction clause in favour of Chinese courts.

The defendants sought a stay of proceedings in favour of arbitration in China, alternatively a stay on the grounds of the Chinese exclusive jurisdiction clause and/or on the grounds of forum non conveniens.

The court found that the arbitration clause constituted a valid written agreement to arbitrate. Declining to follow a previous High Court decision to the contrary, namely *Hissan Trading Co Ltd.* v. *Orkin Shipping Corporation* [see A/CN.9/SER.C ABSTRACTS/2, case 43], the court held that, although the bill of lading was not signed by both parties and the arbitration clause contained therein could not be said to be a written agreement to arbitrate in the sense of article 7(2) MAL, material addressed by one party to the other after the conclusion of the agreement to arbitrate could provide a record of the agreement to arbitrate. In this case it was shown conclusively through the presentation of such material that the parties had agreed on arbitration in China.

As the bill of lading contained both an arbitration and an exclusive jurisdiction clause, the court addressed the question whether the arbitration clause was void. It was held that the claimant had a choice, either to seek arbitration or litigation in China. As the plaintiff opted for a method of dispute resolution not foreseen in the bill of lading, namely litigation in Hong Kong, it was open to the defendants to exercise that choice. By applying for a stay of proceedings pursuant to article 8 MAL, the defendants opted for arbitration in China. The court granted the stay of proceedings.

Contrast Case No. 43 supra Indian Act—sections 7 and 9

Case 62: MAL 7(2); 11

Hong Kong: High Court of Hong Kong (Kaplan J,)

2 February 1994

Oonc Lines Limited v. *Sino-American Trade Advancement Co. Ltd.*

Original in English

Commented on by Kaplan in Asia Law January/February 1995, 23.

Reported on in English: [1992] The Arbitration and Dispute Resolution Law Journal (ADRLJ) 235, [1992] ADRLJ 240, (1993) ADRLJ 240, (1993) ADRLJ 100 and (1994) ADRLJ 49, 295, 291, 290, 298 respectively.

(Abstract prepared by the UNCITRAL Secretariat)

The plaintiff requested the court to appoint an arbitrator on behalf of the defendant pursuant to article 11 MAL The defendant objected on the ground that article 7(2) MAL was not complied with since the defendant never signed the charterparty which contained in a rider the arbitration agreement invoked by the plaintiff.

The court found that, although the charterparty was not signed by either party, a number of communications exchanged between the parties provided a sufficient record in writing of their agreement to arbitrate. The court appointed an arbitrator on behalf of the defendant.

Indian Act—sections 7 and 11

Case 64: MAL 7

Hong Kong: High Court of Hong Kong (Kaplan J.)

13 May, 1994

H. Small Limited v. *Goldroyce Garment Limited*

Original in English

Commented on by Kaplan in Asia Law January/February 1995, 23.

Reported on in English: (1992) The Arbitration and Dispute Resolution Law Journal (ADRLJ) 235, (1992) ADRLJ 240, (1993) ADRLJ 240, (1993) ADRLJ 100 and (1994) ADRLJ 49, 295, 291, 290, 298 respectively.

(Abstract prepared by the UNCITRAL Secretariat)

The plaintiff, who had previous dealings with the defendant, sent to the defendant a purchase order, which, in its general conditions, contained an arbitration clause. The goods were delivered and a dispute arose as to their quality.

The defendant made an offer for compensation. The plaintiff rejected it and sought the appointment of an arbitrator by the court on behalf of the defendant pursuant to s. 12 of the Hong Kong Arbitration Ordinance, on the ground that the defendant failed to appoint an arbitrator.

The plaintiff was not able to produce a copy of the purchase order signed by the defendant but stated that a former employee of the defendant told them that the defendant had signed the purchase order and had kept the signed copy. The plaintiff argued that the evidence met the threshold of article 7 MAL requiring an arbitration agreement in writing. The plaintiff further argued that it was clearly beyond doubt that a contract existed between the parties and that the contract contained an arbitration clause.

The court, citing its ruling on Pacific International Lines etc. (case 40), found that the evidence produced by the plaintiff was hearsay, which, in the absence of a testimony from the former employee of the defendant, could not be held to meet the threshold of article 7 MAL. As to the second argument of the plaintiff, the court held that the arbitration agreement was separable from the contract of the parties and its existence could not be assumed on the basis of the conduct of the parties, but had to be either in a writing signed by the parties or in another document which provides a record of the agreement. The court decided in favour of the defendant and dismissed the plaintiff's application.

Compare Case No. 49, supra

Case 78; MAl 7(2)

Hong Kong; High Court of Hong Kong (Kaplan J.)

18 August 1994

Astel-Peiniger Joint Venture v. *Argos Engineering & Heavy Industries Co. Ltd. Original in English*

Reported on in English: [1992] The Arbitration and Dispute Resolution Law Journal (ADRLJ) 235, [1992] ADRLJ 240, [1993] ADRLJ 240, [1993] ADRLJ 100 and [1994] ADRLJ 49, 295, 291, 290, 298 respectively. (Abstract prepared by the UNCITRAL Secretariat)

The plaintiff, a sub-subcontractor entrusted with the paint works foreseen in an assembly subcontract concluded between the main contractor and the defendant as a subcontractor, filed a claim in court. At issue was which of them was responsible under the sub-subcontract for the supply and construction of mobile paint sheds. The sub-subcontract was on a "back-to-back-basis" and "proportional" to the subcontract, and the plaintiff was given a copy of the subcontract well before the conclusion of the sub-subcontract, without raising any objections. The defendant sought a stay of the proceedings and referral of the dispute to arbitration on the grounds that the sub-subcontract incorporated by reference the terms and conditions of the subcontract, including an arbitration clause. The court referred to the travaux preparatoiresof MAL (A/CN.9/264 and A/40/17) and held, contrary to the plaintiff's arguments, that under article 7(2) MAL the document containing the arbitration clause did not have to be between the same parties as the contract into which the arbitration clause was incorporated by reference. The court stayed the proceedings and referred the matter to arbitration, holding that the provision in the sub-subcontract that it would be "back to back" with the subcontract sufficiently demonstrated the intention of the parties to incorporate the arbitration clause into the sub-subcontract; and that the provision that the sub-subcontract should be "proportional" to the subcontract indicated that some modifications would have to be made to the arbitration clause so that it would be capable of being performed in the context of the sub-subcontract.

This point is of great importance in the Indian context

Case 87: MAL 7(2)

Hong Kong: High Court of Hong Kong (Kaplan J.)

17 November, 1994

Gay Constructions PTY Ltd. and Spaceframe Buildings (North Asia) Ltd. v. *Caledonian Techmore (Building) Limited and Hanison Construction Co. Ltd. (as a third party) Original in English Unpublished*

(Abstract prepared by the UNCITRAL Secretariat)

Hanison, the main contractor in a construction project, applied as a third party for a stay of court proceedings instituted by Gay Constructions and Spaceframe Buildings, the sub-subcontractors, against Caledonian, the subcontractor. The contract between the plaintiff and the defendant was in writing. It contained an arbitration clause but, while it was signed by Hanison, it was not signed by Caledonian.

At issue was the question whether the letters exchanged between Hanison and Caledonian provided a record of the contract, including the arbitration clause and whether there is an exchange of a statement of claim and defence in which the existence of the arbitration agreement is alleged and not denied (article 7(2) MAL).

The court held that the letters exchanged between the parties provided a record of their contract in the sense of article 7(2) MAL, despite the fact that no explicit reference was made in the letters to the arbitration clause contained in the contract. In addition, the court found that Caledonian had submitted to Hanison a claim called "contractual claim for loss and expense" on the basis of the contract and held that this claim constituted either a letter or, alternatively, a claim under article 7(2), in which the existence of the arbitration agreement was alleged by Caledonian and not denied by Hanison. The court noted that the phrase "statements of claim and defence" in article 7(2) MAL was not defined and found no reason why it should be interpreted as referring "only to pleadings in the formal sense once an arbitration has commenced". The court stayed the court proceedings under section 6 of the Hong Kong Arbitration Ordinance.

Indian Act—section 7(2)(c)

Case 147: MAL 7(2), 16(1)(3)

Russian Federation: Moscow City Court

13 December, 1994

Original in Russian

Unpublished

The plaintiff appealed to the court on the grounds that the arbitral tribunal had found that as no arbitration agreement existed between the parties, the tribunal had no competence to examine the dispute that had arisen between them.

The court confirmed the right of the arbitral tribunal under article 16(1) MAL to rule on its own jurisdiction. The court found that the question of whether or not a written agreement existed between the parties regarding the procedure for examining disputes had been thoroughly investigated by the arbitral tribunal. The arbitral tribunal had found that at the time of conclusion of the contract, which gave rise to the dispute and which contained an arbitration clause, the person signing the contract on behalf of the defendant did not possess the necessary powers to do so. On these grounds, the court upheld the ruling of the arbitral tribunal, namely that no arbitration agreement existed in writing between the plaintiff and the defendant.

Indian Act—sections 16 and 34(2)

Case 177: MAL 7, 10

India: Supreme Court of India

18 November, 1996

MMTC v. *Sterlite Industries (India) Ltd.*

Published in English: Judgments Today [1996] 10 S.C. 390

(Abstract prepared by the UNCITRAL Secretariat)

The case concerned an arbitration clause contained in a contract entered into by the parties.

The clause provided for the appointment of one arbitrator by each parly and an umpire to be jointly appointed by those arbitrators.

The appellant sought to rely on the arbitration clause after a dispute arose between the parties. After the respondent claimed that the arbitration clause could not be resorted to, and, therefore, refused to name an arbitrator, the appellant brought an action in the High Court. The High Court rejected the respondent's contention that the arbitration clause was invalid in light of section 10 of the new 1996 Arbitration and Conciliation Act (adapted from article 10 MAL). The aforementioned provision in the Act states that parties are free to determine the number of arbitrators, provided that such number shall not be an even number. Special leave was given to appeal to the Supreme Court.

The Supreme Court held that the relevant provision to determine the validity of an arbitration agreement is section 7 of the 1996 Act (adapted from article 7 MAL), which contains the writing requirement. As there is no reference to the number of arbitrators within this provision, the Supreme Court concluded that the validity of an arbitration clause does not depend on the number of arbitrators specified therein. The arbitration clause was therefore held to be valid.

Article 8. Arbitration agreement and substantive claim before court

(1) *A court* before *which an action is brought in a matter which is the subject of an arbitration agreement shall, if a party so requests not later than when submitting his first statement on the substance of the dispute, refer the parties to arbitration unless it finds that the agreement is* null and void, *inoperative or incapable of being performed.*

(2) *Where an action referred to in paragraph (1) of this article has been brought, arbitral proceedings may nevertheless be commenced or continued, and an award may be made, while the issue is pending before the court.*

Indian Act—section 8

Case 9: MAL 8

Canada: Federal Court of Canada, Trial Division (Denault, I)

2 November, 1987

Coopers and Lybrand Limited (Trustee) for BC Navigation S.A. (Bankrupt) v. *Canpotex Shipping Services Limited*

Published in English: 16 Federal Trial Reporter, 79

Commented on by Tetley in [1993] Lloyd's Martitime and Commercial Law Quarterly, 238.

Commented on by Paterson in Williamette Law review, Vol. 27, 573.

Where a valid arbitration agreement exists and a party requests a transfer of the dispute to the arbitration tribunal at the first opportunity, article 8 MAL obliges the court to refer the matter to arbitration.

The charter-party agreement executed by the parties contained an arbitration clause. After Coopers and Lybrand commenced an action against the Canpotex in court, Canpotex filed a conditional appearance objecting to the jurisdiction of the court and sought a stay of proceedings in order to allow the objection to be made, Canpotex also sought an order pursuant to section 50(1)(b) of the Federal Court Act seeking a stay of proceedings.

The court granted Canpotex's motion. Pursuant to article 8 of the Model Law, which is enacted by the Commercial Arbitration Act, R.S.C.1985, c.C-34.6, the court was obliged to refer the matter to arbitration. A valid arbitration agreement existed and Canpotex had requested a transfer of the dispute to the arbitration tribunal at the first opportunity. In the alternative, the court would have granted a stay pursuant to section 50 of the Federal Court Act.

This case was followed in Case No. 19, infra

Case 11; MAL 8; 9

Canada: Federal Court of Canada, Trial Division (Pinard, J.)

19 February, 1988

Relais Nordik v. *Secunda Marine Services Limited*

Published in English and French: 24 Federal Trial Reporter, 256

A mandatory interim injunction requiring compliance with the terms of a charter party is not an interim measure within the scope of article 9 MAL.

Relais Nordik applied pursuant to article 9 of the Model Law which is enacted by the Commercial Arbitration Act, Revised Statutes of Canada, 1985, c.C-34.6 for a mandatory interim injunction to force Secunda Marine to comply with the terms of a charter-party signed by both parties.

The Court dismissed the application for an injunction on the grounds that the applicant had not made out a strong *prima facie* case for an injunction. As well, damages would compensate any loss suffered by the applicant. Moreover, the court held that the remedy sought was not an interim measure within article 9 MAL. The applicant was seen as attempting to have the court rather than the arbitrators resolve the substance of the dispute, notwithstanding the respondent's objection pursuant to article 8 MAL.

Indian Act—section 9

Case 14: MAL 8

Canada: Federal Court of Canada, Appeal Division (Marceau, Hugessen and Desjardins, JJ.A.)

2 June, 1989

Iberfreight S.A. et al. v. *Ocean Star Container Line AC and J.W. Lunstedt KG*

Published in English: 104 National Reporter, 164

Commented on by Tetley in [1993] Lloyd's Maritime and Commercial Law Quarterly, 238.

Both applications were dismissed by the motions judge, but were upheld in part by the Federal Court of Appeal. Article 8 of the Model Law, which is enacted by the Commercial Arbitration Act, Revised Statutes of Canada 1985, c.C-34.6, does not require the dismissal of a motion for service *ex juris* nor require the court to decline jurisdiction whenever the contract documents contain an arbitration agreement. Therefore, the application by the defendants concerning service *ex juris* was dismissed.

The court stayed the action against Ocean Star and dismissed the appeal of Lunstedt concerning the arbitration clause. With regard to Ocean Star, the Court stayed the action and referred the matter to arbitration in accordance with the terms of the bill of lading. The application by Lunstedt was dismissed due to a lack of evidence.

Indian Act—sections 9 and 27

Case 15: MAL 8

Canada: Federal Court of Canada, Trial Division (Joyal, J.)

17 January, 1989

Navionics Inc. v. *Flota Maritima Mexicana S.A. et al.*

Published in English: 26 Federal Trial Reporter, 148 Commented on by Tetley in [1993] Lloyd's Maritime and

Commercial Law Quarterly, 238

Article 8 is to be given a fairly strict interpretation and its imperative provision is an exceptional departure from the inherent jurisdiction of the Court to grant stay of proceedings. However, in this case, the court refused to decide if article 8 had been complied with and granted the stay based on its inherent jurisdiction.

A dispute arose between the parties concerning their obligations with respect to a standard-form charter party they had signed. Flota Maritima moved to stay the proceedings brought by Navionics, relying on article 8 of the Model Law as enacted by the Commercial Arbitration Act, Revised Statutes of Canada, 1985, c.C-34.6. The motion was adjourned and before it could be heard, Navionics filed its own motion seeking default judgment against the defendant. The defendant was subsequently granted two extensions in order to allow it to obtain an affidavit. After Flota Maritima was refused any further extension, it filed a statement of defence in order to avoid being held in default.

The court granted the stay of proceedings sought by Flota Maritima. The court relied on section 50(1)(b) of the Federal Court Act, Revised Statutes of Canada, 1985, c F-7, in granting the stay pursuant to its inherent jurisdiction. Article 8 is to be given quite a strict interpretation.

Compare case No. 86, infra

Case 17; MAL 8

Canada: British Columbia Court of Appeal (Carrothers, Southin and Wood, JJ.A.)

26 February, 1990

Stancroft Trust Limited, Berry and Klausner v. *Can-Asia Capital Company, Limited, Mandarin Capital Corporation and Asiamerica Capital Limited*

Published in English: 3 Western Weekly Reports 1990, 665 Commented on by Paterson in Willamette Law Review, Vol. 27, 573.

Under article 8(1) MAL, the fact that one defendant is entitled to an order staying the proceedings does not entitle other defendants to the benefit of the stay.

Mandarin and Asiamerica are British Columbia corporations. Can-Asia is a Hong Kong corporation. Stancroft is a United Kingdom company, Berry resides in London, England, and Klausner resides in Switzerland. The parties had concluded a number of agreements and security instruments. One instrument contained an arbitration clause requiring the resolution of disputes by the London Court of International Arbitration and according to British Columbia law.

The plaintiffs sued the defendants for breach of contract. Can-Asia sought a stay of proceedings, citing the court's inherent jurisdiction and the Model Law as enacted by the International Commercial Arbitration Act, Statutes of British Columbia, 1986, c.14. The other defendants filed statements of defence after their applications to stay the proceedings.

On appeal, the British Columbia Court of Appeal ruled that Can-Asia was entitled to stay under section 8(1) of the Act, but the other defendants were not as they had filed statements of defence. The court upheld section 8(2) of the Act as representing no denial of access to the courts as those who were bound by the section had given up access voluntarily by agreeing to arbitration. As well, laws of a similar nature have existed for almost 300 years. (Leave of appeal was denied by the Supreme Court of Canada.)

The point decided here is important for India also—Indian Act, section 8(1)

Case 18: MAL 5; 8; 16

Canada: Ontario Court of Justice - General Division (Henry J.)

1 March, 1991

Rio Algom Limited v. *Sammi Steel Co.*

Original in English

The interaction of articles 8 and 16 restricts the court's role in arbitrations to determining whether the arbitration clause is *null and void*. Any determination of the*arbitrator's jurisdiction is made by the arbitrator pursuant to article 16.

The parties agreed that Sammi would purchase Rio's steel manufacturing business in Ontario, Quebec and New York State. The agreement provided that the parties each prepare a Closing Date Balance Sheet as soon as possible after closing. Arbitration was provided for if the parties could not resolve any dispute arising out of the Closing Date Balance Sheets. Such a dispute did arise. Sammi followed the required procedure and submitted the matter to an arbitrator. Rio commenced an action in court challenging the jurisdiction of the arbitrator and seeking an order staying the arbitration proceedings. The Chambers judge granted the order finding that the arbitrator's jurisdiction is a threshold issue of contract construction to be decided by the court. Leave to appeal the Chambers judge's order was sought.

The court granted leave to appeal. It found that the Chambers judge's decision had been erroneously based on principles of the domestic arbitration act rather than those found in the Model Law as enacted by the International Commercial Arbitration Act, Statutes of Ontario, 1988, c.30. In particular the court cited article 16 which provides the arbitral tribunal with the power to rule on its own jurisdiction. The court further noted article 8 which restricts court involvement to a determination of whether the arbitration agreement is *null and void*.

Indian Act—sections 8 and 16

Case 19; MAL 8

Canada: British Columbia Supreme Court (Chambers) (Harvey J.)

22 November, 1991

Krutov v. *Vancouver Hockey Club Limited*

Original in English

The mere presence of procedural irregularities in the implementation of the arbitration process, under either the agreement itself or the collective bargaining agreement, will not prevent the dispute from proceeding to arbitration. Krutov, a hockey player residing in Moscow and the Club, a British Columbia corporation, had a contract for playing services of three years' duration. The Club refused to pay Krutov for the second and third seasons and Krulov in turn refused to play. The Club sent the dispute to arbitration pursuant to the agreement. The Club argued that the dispute was automatically subject to arbitration and that article 8 of the Model Law as enacted by the International Commercial Arbitration Act, Statutes of British Columbia, 1986, c.14 contains no discretion for the court to deflect a consensual arbitration. Krutov argued that the contract was *null and void* and thus there was no arbitration agreement. Krutov also argued that procedural irregularities existed making referral to arbitration impossible.

The Court found that the agreement was not *null and void* within the meaning of section 8 of the Act. The procedural irregularities referred to by Krutov concerned time limits and notice requirements. The Court concluded that such irregularities in themselves would not prevent the parties from proceeding to arbitration.

(In making this finding, the court placed particular emphasis on the decision reported as Case 9.)

◆ ◆ ◆ ◆ ◆

Case 20: MAL 1(3)(b)(ii); 3; 8; 10; 11; 16

Hong Kong: High Court of Hong Kong (Kaplan J.)

29 October, 1991

Fung Sang Trading Limited v. *Kai Sun Sea Products and Food Company Limited*

Original in English

Excerpts of judgement in Doyles dispute resolution practice; Asia, Pacific in 1 volume. North Ryde, N.S.W.: CCH International, c1990-Tab 80-036, p.80, 661-80 and in: Yearbook Commercial Arbitration, (Deventer, Netherlands, Kluwer) vol. XVII, 1992, p. 289-303.

Commented on in: Doyles ADR update 5: 4-5, 28 February 1992, and by Pryles, World Arbitration and Mediation Report 2:12:329 (December 1991). Summary published: Yearbook XVIII-1992, International Council for Commercial Arbitration, 11.

Summarized and commercial on by Kaplan, Spruce and Moser in Hong Kong and China Arbitration, Cases and Materials, Butterworths, 1994.

Excerpts published in (1992) 1 Hong Kong Reports (HKLR), 40. (Abstract prepared by the Secretariat)

The plaintiff, a Hong Kong company, asked the court to appoint a second arbitrator, relying on a contracl with anolher Hong Kong company that contained an arbitration clause. The contract was for the sale of soyabean extraction meal FOB Dalian; Dalian, which is in China, was stated to be the place of delivery. The defendant, asserting that there was no valid contract since the person who had signed had no authority to bind it, contended that an arbitrator had no jurisdiction to rule on whether or not a contract had been concluded. Even if an arbitration agreement existed, the arbitration would be domestic and thus have to be conducted by a sole arbitrator.

The court determined the arbitration to be international pursuant to article 1(3)(b)(ii) of the Model Law as enacted by the Hong Kong Arbitration (Amendment) (No. 2) Ordinance, 1989. It regarded delivery (which was to take place outside Hong Kong) as "a substantial part of the obligations of the commercial relationship", without ignoring that payment and nomination of the vessel (which were to take place in Hong Kong) were also important obligations in a contract of sale.

The court refused to deal with the question of whether a valid contract had been concluded since, according to article 16 MAL, it was first for the arbitral tribunal to decide on its jurisdiction. Recognizing the autonomy or separability of the arbitration clause except in the case of *ab initio* illegality of the contract (with reference to English law), the court stated that the decision of the arbitral tribunal was neither final nor exclusive but subject to immediate review under article 16(3) MAL.

In making the appointment under article 11(5) MAL, the court deemed it important that when "appointing on behalf of the defaulting appointing party, it should go out of its way to ensure that no sense of grievance is felt, however unreasonable that attitude might appear to others".

Indian Act: Compare sections 11(8)(b) and 16

Case 28; MAL 1(2); 8

Canada: Saskatchewan Court of Queen's Bench (MacPherson C.J.Q.B.)

19 March, 1993

BWV Investments Ltd. v. *Saskferco Products Inc., UHDE-GmbH, et al.*

Original in English

Unpublished

The parties entered into a series of contractual relationships concerning the construction of a fertilizer plant for Saskferco. The subcontract between UHDE and BVW for the construction contained an arbitration clause requiring that the arbitration take place in Zurich and the interpretation, application and performance of the sub-contract be governed by Swiss law. BWV sued the defendants in court for monies owing on the contract. UHDE applied to have the proceedings stayed in order that the case might be resolved by arbitration. In issue was the application of MAL to this dispute.

The court, stating that despite the provision in article 1(2) that only articles 8, 9, 35 and 36 of MAL apply to arbitration agreements where the place of arbitration is outside the state, found that it could refer to the definitions in MAL by virtue of s. 2(2) of the International Commercial Arbitration Act, Statutes of Saskatchewan 1988-89, c.1-10.2, which enacts MAL. This section provides that all terms used in the Act will have the same meaning as in MAL. The court found that the agreement in question was an international commercial arbitration agreement within the meaning of the Act. The court found that the agreement was void as it conflicted with the Builders' Lien Act, Statutes of Saskatchewan 1984-85-86, c. B-7.1. The agreement would have rendered inapplicable the rights of several lien holders who would not be involved in an arbitration. The court declared the arbitration agreement void and did not grant a stay of proceedings.

Indian Act—sections 8 and 16. But section 8 (in India) does not empower the court to determine validity of the agreement

Case 31: MAL 8

Canada; British Columbia Court of Appeal (Hinkson, Southin and Camming JJ.A.)

10 March, 1992

Gulf Canada Resources Ltd. v. *Arochem International Ltd.*

Published in English: 66 British Columbia Law Reports (2d), 113

Commented on by Tetley in [1993] Lloyd's Maritime and Commercial Law Quarterly, 238

While the court must grant a stay of court proceedings pursuant to article 8 MAL where its terms are satisfied, the court retains some residual jurisdiction to exercise on an application for a stay.

A contract existed between the parties for the delivery of 3,75,000 barrels of crude oil. The contract contained an arbitration clause. The defendant refused delivery and the plaintiff sued for damages. The trial court granted the defendant's request for a stay of court proceedings pending arbitration pursuant to s. 8 of the International Commercial Arbitration Act, Statutes of British Columbia 1986, c. 14, which enacts MAL. The plaintiff appealed.

The court determined that, while s. 8 requires that the court grant a stay unless the arbitration agreement is null and void, inoperative or incapable of being performed, the court still has some residual jurisdiction to exercise. The court may exercise this jurisdiction and refuse to grant a stay should it conclude that one of the parties named in the proceeding is not a parly to the arbitration agreement, the alleged dispute does not come within the terms of the arbitration agreement or if the applicaiion is out of time. The court upheld the trial court's decision to grant the stay of proceedings.

Indian Act—section 8. However, Indian Act does not empower the court to determine that the agreement is void, etc.

Case 32: MAL 7; 8

Canada: Ontario Court, General Division (Zelinski J.)

30 April, 1992

Mind Star Toys Inc. v. *Samsung Co. Ltd.*

Published in English: 9 Ontario Reports (3d), 374

Agreements containing both an arbitration clause and a right to sue will still be subject to article 8 MAL, depending on the particular agreement. Mind Star was a licensee of a product which it sub-licensed to Samsung. The sub-licensing agreement contained an arbitration clause and also a clause providing Mind Star with the right to sue should Samsung fail to perform any of its obligations. Mind Star claimed that Samsung had fundamentally breached the agreement and that Mind Star was entitled to claim damages. The parties agreed that the arbitration clause in the agreement qualified as an arbitration agreement pursuant to article 7 MAL as enacted by the International Commercial Arbitration Act, Revised Statutes of Ontario, 1990, c.1.9.

The court concluded that the right to sue did not qualify the duty to arbitrate. Even disputes concerning the clause creating the right to sue were subject to arbitration. The court found this "consistent with the requirement that the arbitrator will, in the first instance, determine its own jurisdiction, and the scope of its authority." The arbitration clause was operative and as such article 8 MAL required that the parties be referred to arbitration.

This is an important elucidation of article 8, useful for Indian Act also (section 8)

Case 33: MAL 8

Canada: Federal Court of Appeal (Marceau, Desjardins and Décar'y JJ.A.)

29 May, 1992

Ruhrkohle Handel Inter GMBH and National Steel Corp. et al. v. *Fednav Ltd. and Federal Pacific (Liberia) Ltd. and Federal Calumet (The)*

Published in English and French: 3 Federal Court Reports 1992, 98

Commented on by Tetley in [1993] Lloyd's Maritime and Commercial Law Quarterly, 238

In order for the court to grant a stay of proceedings pursuant to article 8 MAL, the party requesting the stay must satisfy the court that the request was made in a timely fashion and that the request was made to the court, not just to the other party.

The parties entered into a charter-party which contained an arbitration clause. The charter-party was subsequently breached. The appellants asked the respondents for an extension of time to "commence suit and/or arbitration". The respondents granted an extension of time to commence arbitration only. The appellants filed a statement of claim for damages which made no mention of arbitration. The respondents filed a statement of defence and counter-claim, and requested a stay of proceedings. Both the Senior Prothonotary and the Trial Division refused the appellants' request that the action be stayed. The appellants appealed.

The court found that while article 8 MAL, which is enacted by the Commercial Arbitration Act, Revised Statutes of Canada 1985, c.C-34.6, requires the court to grant a stay of proceedings and refer the matter to arbitration, such an order is not made as of right. Certain conditions must first be met. The party seeking such an order must demonstrate that a request for arbitration was made in a timely fashion (not later than when submitting their first statement on the substance of the dispute). The court noted that the request for arbitration required in article 8 MAL is a request to the court, not just to the other party. No such request was made to the court here and, therefore, no stay was granted.

Indian Act—section 8

Case 34: MAL 8

Canada: Federal Court of Canada, Trial Division (Joyal J.)

30 September 1992 and 9 October 1992 (identical decisions)

Miramichi Pulp and Paper Inc. v. *Canadian Pacific Bulk Ship Services Ltd.*

Original in English and French

Unpublished

While the Federal Court possesses some permissive jurisdiction over the granting of stays of proceedings, strong reasons are required to overcome the assumption that contracts must be respected and, therefore, article 8 MAL must operate.

The parties entered into a charter-party agreement whereby any dispute would be referred to arbitration in London. A dispute arose and court proceedings were commenced. A stay of these proceedings was granted by the Senior Prothonotary. This decision was appealed.

The court noted the mandatory nature of article 8 MAL (enacted by the Commercial Arbitration Act, Revised Statutes of Canada 1985, c.C-34.6) which requires the court to grant a stay of proceedings and refer matters to arbitration where certain conditions are met. The court also noted the permissive jurisdiction in s. 50 of the Federal Court Act, Revised Statutes of Canada 1985, c.F-7 which allows the Federal Court to grant stays of proceedings in the interest of justice. The court found that the interest of justice generally dictated that contractual agreements be upheld. In order to overcome this assumption, strong reasons are required. The court found that no such strong reasons existed in this case and upheld the decision of the Senior Prothonotary granting the stay.

Indian Act—section 8

Case 35; MAL 8

Canada; Ontario Court, General Division (Day J.)

1 October, 1992

Canada Packers Inc. et al. v. *Terra Nova Tankers Inc. et al.*

Published in English: 11 Ontario Reports (3d), 382

The fact that a claim on which a party seeks arbitration is grounded in tort does not preclude the application of MAL.

The parties entered into a charter-party agreement which contained an arbitration clause. The respondent sued the applicant in both contract and tort. At issue was whether the court should grant a stay of proceedings pursuant to article 8 MAL. The respondent claimed that MAL did not apply to tortious actions and that the absence of the word "commercial" characterizing the term arbitration in the International Commercial Arbitration Act, Revised Statutes of Ontario, 1990, c. 1.9. indicated that MAL would not apply to the situation.

The court found that the fact that a claim is grounded in tort does not preclude arbitration. The court also determined that even though the word "commercial" does not appear in the implementing legislation, it does appear in the schedule to the legislation and as such MAL will apply to commercial arbitrations in Ontario. The court granted the stay of proceedings.

Indian Act—sections 7(1) and 8. Indian section 7(1) recognises an arbitration agreement so long as there is a "defined legal relationship". It can be assumed that "tort" also creates a "defined legal relationship"

Case 36; MAL 8

Canada; Federal Court of Canada, Trial Division (Walsh J.)

19 January, 1993

Nanisivik Mines Ltd. and Zinc Corporation of America v. *F.C.R.S. Shipping Ltd., Canarctic Shipping Co. Ltd. et. al.*

Original in English and French

Unpublished

The mandatory nature of article 8 MAL does not remove the permissive jurisdiction of the Federal Court to grant stays of proceedings pursuant to s. 50 of the Federal Court Act.

Nanisivik and Canarctic entered into a charter-party which required that all disputes of law and fact arising under it be referred to arbitration. The ship sank. The plaintiffs sued in contract and tort. Canarctic argued that the court was required to grant a stay of proceedings and refer the matter to arbitration pursuant to article 8 MAL which is enacted by the Commercial Arbitration Act, Revised Statutes of Canada 1985, c. C-34.6. Nanisivik argued that a stay should not be granted against those parties to the litigation who were not parties to the charter-party.

The court relied on its discretion pursuant to s. 50(1) of the Federal Court Act, Revised Statutes of Canada 1985, c.F-7 rather than on article 8 MAL and granted a stay of proceedings only against Canarctic. In so doing, the court relied on previous Federal Court decisions which determined that article 8 MAL as invoked by an agreement to arbitrate does not affect or impinge on the permissive jurisdiction of the Federal Court (see A/CN.9/SER.C/ABSTRACTS/1, cases 8 and 15).

◆ ◆ ◆ ◆ ◆

Case 38: MAL 8

Hong Kong: High Court (Kaplan J.)

2 March 1991

China State Construction Engineering Corporation, Guangdong Branch v. *Madiford Limited*

Published in English: 1992, Hong Kong Law Digest, C4

Summarized and commented on by Kaplan, Spruce and Moser in Hong Kong and China Arbitration, Cases and Materials, Butterworths, 1994.

Commented on by Kaplan in Asia Law January/February 1995, 23.

(Abstract prepared by Kaplan J.)

The plaintiff agreed to supply lo the defendant the services of a number of Chinese construction workers to carry out certain works in Libya. The defendant admitted that the amount claimed by the plaintiff was correct but ontended that it was not obliged to pay it in full on the basis of a settlement agreement it had reached wilh the plaintiff. The plaintiff had obtained a judgement by default and, in accordance with s. 6. A of the Arbitration Ordinance (with his summons the plaintiff invoked article 8 MAL, the defendant applied for a stay of the proceedings, on the ground that the agreement between the plaintiff and the defendant contained an arbitration clause. The arbitration clause provided that "In case of any incompleteness of the contract, both parties shall reach settlement. If settlement cannot be reached ... the matter may be submitted for arbitration ..," (emphasis added).

The court set aside the judgement by default obtained by the plaintiff as it was satisfied that the defendant had "a reasonable prospect of success".

The court found that MAL was not applicable as the arbitration agreement was entered into before 6 April, 1990, namely the commencement date of the Arbitration (Amendment) (No. 2) Ordinance 1989, by which MAL was made part of the Hong Kong law of arbitration.

The court, applying article 6A of the Arbitration Ordinance, granted the stay of proceedings as it found that there was a valid arbitration agreement. The word "incompleteness" in the arbitration clause was held to be wide enough to cover a failure to perform the contract. The words "may be submitted" in effect meant "shall", as once one party had elected to proceed to arbitration for the resolution of a dispute the other party was obliged to honour the agreement to arbitrate.

The point is relevant for Indian section 7(1) defining an "arbitration agreement"

Case 41: MAL 8(1)

Hong Kong: High Court of Hong Kong (Barnett J.)

24 September, 1992

Guangdong Agriculture Company Limited v. *Conagra International (Far East) Limited*

Published in English: (1993) 1, Hong Kong Law Reports and 1992, Hong Kong Law Digest, H11. Excerpts of judgement published in The Arbitration and Dispute Resolution Law Journal, Part 2, June 1993, 100

Commented on by Kaplan in Asia Law January/February 1995, 23.

Reported on in English: [1992] The Arbitration and Dispute Resolution Law Journal (ADRLJ) 235, (1992) ADRLJ 240, [1993] ADRLJ 240, [1993] ADRLJ 100 and [1994] ADRLJ 49, 295, 307, 291, 290, 298 respectively

(Abstract prepared by Kaplan J.)

The plaintiff sought a summary judgement for damages for short delivery of a shipment of urea. The defendant applied for a stay of the action pending arbitration on the grounds that the agreement with the plaintiff contained an arbitration clause providing that "... In case no settlement can be reached, the case under dispute can then be submitted to the chartered loss adjuster for arbitration ... The arbitration shall take place in Hong Kong and shall take place in accordance with the rules of Hong Kong ...".

The court found that there was a binding arbitration agreement, since all that article 8 MAL required was that the parties plainly agreed to settle any dispute by arbitration.

Compare case No. 63, infra

The court also found that this case involved a real dispute that could be referred to arbitration as required by s. 6A(1) of the Arbitration Ordinance, but not by article 8 MAL. The words * ... or that there is not in fact any dispute between the parties with regard to the matter agreed to be referred :..", omitted from article 8(1) MAL but contained in section 6A(1) of the Arbitration Ordinance, made it clear that under the Arbitration Ordinance only where it was readily and immediately demonstrable that a claim has not been admitted by the party against whom it is made, the matter should be referred to arbitration. The court granted a stay of proceedings.

The point is of practical importance for section 8, Indian Act, as such contentions are often raised in India also

Case 44: MAL 7(2); 8

Hong Kong: High Court of Hong Kong (Kaplan J.)

17 February, 1993

William Company v. *Chu Kong Agency Co. Ltd. and Guangzhou Ocean Shipping Company*

Published in English: 1993, Hong Kong Law Digest, B7

Summarized and commented on by Kaplan, Spruce and Moset in Hong Kong and China Arbitration, Cases and Materials, Butterworths, 1994.

Commented on by Kaplan in Asia Law lanuary/February 1995, 23. (Abstract prepared by the UNCITRAL Secretariat) The plaintiff filed a suit against the defendants requesting damages for loss and damage to its cargo carried under a bill of lading issued by the first defendant in Hong Kong. The bill of lading, which was subject to the Hague- Visby Rules, contained an arbitration clause providing for arbitration in China under Chinese law and an exclusive jurisdiction clause in favour of Chinese courts.

The defendants sought a stay of proceedings in favour of arbitration in China, alternatively a stay on the grounds of the Chinese exclusive jurisdiction clause and/or on the grounds of forum non-conveniens.

The court found that the arbitration clause constituted a valid written agreement to arbitrate. Declining to follow a previous High Court decision to the contrary, namely *Hissan Trading Co Ltd.* v. *Orkin Shipping Corporation* [see A/CN.9/SER.C/ABSTRACTS/2, case 43], the court held that, although the bill of lading was not signed by both parties and the arbitration clause contained therein could not be said to be a written agreement to arbitrate in the sense of article 7(2) MAL, material addressed by one party to the other after the conclusion of the agreement to arbitrate could provide a record of the agreement to arbitrate. In this case it was shown conclusively through the presentation of such material that the parties had agreed on arbitration in China.

As the bill of lading contained both an arbitration and an exclusive jurisdiction clause, the court addressed the question whether the arbitration clause was void. It was held that the claimant had a choice, either to seek arbitration or litigation in China. As the plaintiff opted for a method of dispute resolution not foreseen in the bill of lading, namely litigation in Hong Kong, it was open to the defendants to exercise that choice. By applying for a stay of proceedings pursuant to article 8 MAL, the defendants opted for arbitration in China. The court granted the stay of proceedings.

Indian Act—section 8

Case 57: MAL 8

Hong Kong; High Court of Hong Kong (Kaplan J.)

5 May, 1993

Lucky-Goldstar International (H.K.) Limited v. *Ng Moo Kee Engineering Limited*

Excerpts published in [1993] 1 Hong Kong Law Reports (HKLR), 73

Summarized and commented on by Kapla, Spruce and Moser in Hong Kong and China Arbitration, Cases and Materials, Butterworths, 1994.

(Abstract prepared by the UNCITRAL Secretariat)

The plaintiff, a Hong Kong company and subsidiary of a Korean company, sold sets of elevators to the defendant, a Hong Kong company. The contract contained an arbitration clause which provided for arbitration in a "3rd country, under the rule of the 3rd country and in accordance with the rules of procedure of the International Commercial Arbitration Association".

The plaintiff sued for damages in the Hong Kong courts and the defendant sought a stay of the proceedings pursuant to article 8 MAL.

The plaintiff argued that the arbitration agreement should be considered null since it referred by mistake to an unspecified third country, or inoperative since it referred to a non-existent organization and non-existent rules.

The court found that the arbitration clause sufficiently indicated the parties' intention to arbitrate. It held that the reference to an unspecified third country, to a non-exislent organization and non-exislent rules did not render the arbitration agreement inoperative or incapable of being performed since arbitration could be held in any country other than the countries where the parties had their places of business and under the law of the place of arbitration, which could be chosen by the plaintiff. The court granted the stay of proceedings sought by the defendant and ordered the plaintiff to pay the costs of the proceedings.

Indian Act—section 7. The decision is important, as recognising an elastic clause

Case 61: MAL 8

Hong Kong: High Court of Hong Kong (Kaplan J.)

21 January, 1994

Zhan Jiang E & T Dev Area Service Head Co. v. *An Hau Company Limited*

Original in English

Unpublished

Reported on in English: [1991 The Arbitration and Dispute Resolution Law Journal (ADRLJ) 235, [1992] ADRLJ 240, [1993] ADRLJ 240, [1993] ADRLJ 100 and [1994] ADRLJ 49, 295, 307, 291, 290, 298 respectively.

(Abstract prepared by the UNCITRAL Secretariat)

The plaintiff sued for damages on the ground that the defendant failed to deliver a shipment of wire rods. The defendant requested a stay of the proceedings pursuant to article 8 MAL.

The plaintiff argued that there was no dispute to be referred to arbitration since the defendant in a letter addressed to the plaintiff had admitted liability and offered to compensate the plaintiff. The defendant denied that this letter could be construed as a sufficient admission of liability to justify refusing the stay and argued that it was unable to deliver the wire rods because it could not accept a condition set unilaterally by the plaintiff after the conclusion of the contract that the defendant submit a performance bond.

The court found that the letter referred to by the plaintiff did not constitute an unequivocal admission of liability but was merely a commercial offer to settle. Even if the letters were accepted as an admission of liability, it could clearly not be construed as an admission of the quantum of the claim. The court held that there was a dispute in the sense of article 8 MAL and granted the stay of the proceedings sought by the defendant.

Indian Act—section 8. Compare Case No, 63 infra

Case 63: MAL 8

Hong Kong: High Court of Hong Kong (Kaplan J.)

31 March, 1994

Joong and Shipping Co. Limited v. *Choi Chong-sick (alias Choi Chong-sik) and Chu Ghin Ho trading as Chang Ho Company*

Original in English

Reported on in English: (1992) The Arbitration and Dispute Resolution Law Journal (ADRLJ) 235, [1992] ADRLJ 240, [1993] ADRLJ 240, [1993] ADRLJ 100 and [1994] ADRLJ 49, 295, 307, 291, 290, 298 respectively.

(Abstract prepared by the Secretariat)

The plaintiff sought summary judgement against the defendant for a claim for freight and demurrage, which the defendant had admitted in correspondence with the plaintiff. The defendant requested a stay of proceedings and requested that the matter be submitted to arbitration pursuant to article 8 MAL.

The court, citing its decisions in Guangdong Agriculture Co. Ltd etc. (case 41) and on Zhan Jiang & T. Dev Area Service Head Co. etc. (case 61), found that article 8 MAL was predicated upon the existence of a dispute and that in the present case there was no dispute that could be referred to arbitration since the defendant had admitted the plaintiff's claim unequivocally both as to liability and quantum. The court dismissed the application for a stay and granted the plaintiff a summary judgement for the sum claimed.

Indian Act—section 8. Compare Case No. 61 supra

Case 65: MAL 8(1)

Canada: British Columbia Supreme Court (Mackoff J.)

28 November, 1988

ODC Exhibit Systems Ltd. v. *Lee, Expand International et al.*

Published in English: 41 Business Law Reports, 286

The plaintiff, a British Columbia company, claimed damages from the defendants, including a former general manager of the plaintiff and Expand International, a Swedish company which was the exclusive agent of the plaintiff in Canada, on the ground that they had conspired, deceived and defrauded the plaintiff with a view to terminating the exclusive agency agreement between the plaintiff and Expand International and giving it to the former general manager of the plaintiff. The defendant argued that the court did not have jurisdiction since a breach of contract committed in Sweden was involved and, alternatively, requested a stay of proceedings under s. 8 of the International Commercial Arbitration Act (ICAA, art. 8 MAL) on the basis of an agreement, reached with the plaintiff after the dispute arose, containing an arbitration clause, which provided that "... any dispute arising out of this agreement shall be settled by arbitration ...."

The court found that the plaintiff's action was founded on tort committed in Canada and thus established its jurisdiction. It was found that conspiracy, deceit and fraud were not matters arising out of "this agreement". It was also found that these torts could not have been agreed or even contemplated by the parties as matters that could be settled by arbitration since they were committed before the conclusion of the arbitration agreement. It was thus held that the basic condition precedent for the granting of a stay of proceedings under s. 8, namely that the court action must relate to a matter agreed to be arbitrated, was not met. The court dismissed the defendant's application for a stay of the proceedings.

Indian Act—sections 7 and 8. The ruling is important, as construing the phrase "arising out of

Case 66: MAL 8

Canada: Superior Court of Quebec (Moisan J.)

14 March, 1989

Jean Charbonneau v. *Les Industries A.C. Davie Inc. et. al.*

Published in French: Recueil de jurisprudence du Quebec 1989, 1255

The plaintiff sued for damages caused by the delay in the delivery of a fishing boat, which one of the defendants was to construct and the other, the Minister of Agriculture, to partly finance. The defendants sought a stay of proceedings pursuant to s. 8 of the International Arbitration Arbitration Act (art. 8 MAL) on the ground that the construction contract contained an arbitration clause.

The court found that under the arbitration agreement the Minister of Agriculture was to arbitrate any dispute arising between the parties. It was held that the arbitration clause was inoperative on the ground that the Minister of Agriculture could not act as an impartial arbitrator being a party to the contract. The court dismissed the defendant's application for a stay of the proceedings.

Indian Act—sections 11(2) and 12(4). The Canadian ruling is of great interest for India as the point is raised frequently. But the court has not considered article 12(2) MAL

Case 69: MAL 8(1)

Canada: Ontario Court of Justice, General Division (Blair J.)

24 January, 1994

Onex Corp. v. *Ball Corp.*

Original in English

Unpublished

A dispute arose between the plaintiff and the defendant as to whether the plaintiff had the right under their joint venture agreement to acquire the defendant's share in the joint venture. The parties agreed that the matter should be submitted to arbitration pursuant to an arbitration clause contained in their agreement. However, the plaintiff sought from the court to rectify a provision of the agreement or, alternatively, to declare that provision void on the ground that it contained a drafting mistake and did not actually reflect the parties' agreement, The defendant sought a stay of proceedings and submission of the whole dispute to arbitration.

The court found that the issue whether the arbitral tribunal had the power to rectify the parties' written agreement was a matter of interpretation of the arbitration agreement. It was held that, while the expression arising "under" or "in relation to the construction" of the agreement contained in the arbitration clause was not as broad as the expression "all disputes arising in connection with", which was held by courts to be sufficient to cover the equitable *remedy of rectification,* it was broad enough to cover rectification of the agreement. The court, citing its decision on Gulf Canada etc. (case 31) noted that in doubt the arbitration clause should be interpreted in a manner that would be conducive to arbitration. The court granted a stay of the proceedings and referred the matter to arbitration.

Indian Act—sections 7 and 8. The ruling can be explained on the ground that one who is not a party to the contract is not confined by article 8 MAL

Case 111: MAL 1(1); 8(1)

Canada: Alberta Court of Queen's Bench (Murray J.)

11 August, 1994

Borowski v. *Heinrich Fiedler Perforiertechnik GmbH*

Published in English: (1994) 158 Alberta Reports, 213; and (19941 10 Western Weekly Reports, 623

The plaintiff, an employee of the defendant, sued for damages in lieu of notice of termination of the employment contract and for loss of wages and benefits. The defendant sought a stay of proceedings and submission of the dispute to arbitration, since the employment contract contained an arbitration clause.

The court found that, with regard to the claim for past wages and benefits, there was no dispute to be referred to arbitration, since the defendant had admitted that it owed the plaintiff for past wages and benefits. With regard to damages in lieu of notice of termination, the court found that that was a dispute covered by the arbitration clause, stayed the court proceedings and referred the matter to arbitration.

On the question whether the International Commercial Arbitration Act (I.C.A.A.), which enacted MAL, could apply to a dispute arising from an employment contract, the court held that such a contract created a master and servant relationship and not a commercial relationship of the type falling under the I.C.A.A. (section 4(2) I.C.A.A., which is equivalent to article 1(1) MAL).

Indian Act—sections 7 and 8. This ruling deals with an extremely interesting point, namely, rectification of agreement (by the arbitrator)

Case 70: MAL 8

Canada; Federal Court of Appeal (Mahoney, MacGuigan and Linden, JJ.A.)

10 February, 1994

Nanisivik Mines Ltd. and Zinc Corporation of America v. *Canarctic Shipping Co. Ltd.*

Original in English and French

Published in English: the Arbitration and Dispute Resolution Law Journal, 1996, 6, 117.

The case involved an appeal against the decision of the court of first instance (case 36). There were three issues involved: first, whether the first instance court had discretion as to referring the claim against Canarctic to arbitration and whether it erred in exercising that discretion; second, if the court had no discretion to refer the matter to arbitration, whether it had discretion as to staying the proceedings and whether it erred in the exercise of its discretion; and third, whether, in any event, the court erred in referring the claim of Zinc Corp. to arbitration and, if so, in staying the proceedings in the action by it.

First point

As to the first issue, which was before the Court of Appeal for the first time, the Court of Appeal upheld the decision of the court of first instance that if the conditions of article 8 MAL are met, namely if an arbitration agreement is in writing, is not *null and void* or inoperative or incapable of performance, the court, if asked by a party, has no discretion but is obliged to refer the matter to arbitration ("shall" in article 8 MAL clearly means "must", not "may").

Second point

As to the second issue, the Court of Appeal noted that there were two approaches followed by courts with regard to a stay of proceedings after a mandatory reference has been made. In some cases, courts held that the reference to arbitration is mandatory pursuant to article 8 MAL, but with regard to the stay of the proceedings the courts have a residual "permissive" jurisdiction under section 50 of the Federal Court Act to grant a discretionary stay unless there are "strong reasons" not to (case 15). In other cases, it was held that reference of a matter to arbitration pursuant to article 8 MAL left the courts no discretion but to stay the proceedings (case 9). The Court of Appeal found that the same policy considerations existing in favour of a mandatory legislative requirement that a dispute subject to an arbitration agreement be referred to arbitration seem to be conclusively in favour of the staying of litigation of the same issues until the issuance of an arbitral award. Thus the Court of Appeal, overturning the decision of the court of first instance, held that once a reference to arbitration had been made, there was no residual discretion in the court to refuse to stay the proceedings between the parties to arbitration even though there may be particular issues between them that are not subject to arbitration.

Third point

As to the third issue, the Court of Appeal found that Zinc Corp. was a party to the bill of lading but not to the charterparty out of which the present dispute arose. It was held that the arbitration clause of the charterparty, incorporated in the bill of lading by general reference to the terms and conditions of the charterparty, did not bind the parties to the bill of lading. It was noted that that result could only be achieved by an arbitration clause in a charterparty which expressly provided that it applied to disputes arising in connection with bills of lading that incorporated generally the terms of the charterparty without specific reference to the arbitration clause, or by way of a provision in the bill of lading incorporating the terms and conditions of the charterparty including, by specific reference, its arbitration clause. The Court of Appeal overturned the decision of the court of first instance with regard to the reference of the claim of Zinc Corp, to arbitration on the ground that Zinc Corp. was not bound by the arbitration clause contained in the charterparty, but upheld that decision with regard to the stay of proceedings holding that under section 50(1)(b) of the Federal Court Act the court had discretion to stay the litigation of the claim of Zinc Corp. against Canarctic pending arbitration of Nanisivik's claim.

Indian Act—section 8. The third point in the ruling summarised above is of great legal importance for India, also as it recurs in arguments

Case 72: MAL 8(1)

Canada: Federal Court of Canada, Trial Division (Strayer J.)

22 March, 1994

Continental Resources Inc. v. *East Asiatic Co, (Canada)- et. al.*

Original in English and French

Unpublished

A dispute arose out of a charterparty for loss of cargo, and the plaintiff sued the defendants in court. The defendants requested that the matter be referred to arbitration since the charterparty contained an arbitration clause and sought a stay of the proceedings pursuant to article 8 (1} MAL. The plaintiff argued that the arbitration clause did not preclude the continuance of litigation since the plaintiff had a claim, based on a bill of lading, against the ship and the shipowners, who were not bound by the arbitration clause contained in the charterparty since they were not parties to to the charterparty. The defendant argued that the bill of lading incorporated the terms and conditions of the charterparty, including the arbitration clause, by general reference.

The court held that it was bound to submit the matter to arbitration since the dispute was within the scope of the arbitration agreement and the defendant had not filed its first statement of defence on the substance of the dispute (article 8(1) MAL). The court exercising its discretion under section 50 of the Federal Court Act granted a stay of the proceedings. It was noted that the criteria followed by the court in exercising its discretion included the likelihood of injustice to the defendant if the action proceeded and the unlikelihood of injustice to the plaintiff if it did not. It was also noted that, even if the plaintiff had a claim in tort not covered by the arbitration agreement, the court could still exercise its discretion and grant a stay of proceedings pending arbitration, and the plaintiff could seek the stay to be lifted if after arbitration it still had a claim.

Indian Act—section 8, This ruling is also of great practical importance, as it emphasises the mandatory character of article 8 (section 8, Indian Act)

Case 73: MAL 8(1)

Canada: Ontario Court of Appeal (Morden, Blair and Austin JJ-A.)

25 April, 1994

Automatic Systems Inc. v. *Bracknell Corp. (Canal Contractors) and Chrysler Canada Ltd.*

Original in English

Unpublished

Automatic, a Missouri company, entered into a contract with Chrysler to supply and install a conveyor system at the Chrysler plant in Ontario. Automatic subcontracted part of the work to Bracknell, an Ontario company. The subcontract contained an arbitration clause providing for arbitration in Missouri under Missouri law. Bracknell, which had a lien claim under the Ontario Construction Lien Act against Automatic, sought and obtained a lien certificate and had it registered against the title to Chrysler's land in Ontario. Automatic sued Bracknell for damages and sought a stay of the proceedings and submission of the matter to arbitration. Bracknell declined to arbitrate and Automatic applied to the court for an order referring the matter to arbitration and staying the proceedings.

The court of first instance found that an agreement for international arbitration for an Ontario lien claim was unenforceable since the Ontario Construction Lien Act made provision only for domestic arbitration and dismissed the application of Automatic.

The appellate court found that, having regard to international comity and the strong commitment of the Ontario legislator in support of international arbitration demonstrated through the adoption of MAL, only very clear language in a statute could preclude international arbitration. The appellate court overturned the decision of the court of the first instance on the ground that the Ontario Construction Lien Act by providing only for domestic arbitration did not clearly and expressly preclude international arbitration. The court, without commenting in detail, drew a distinction between the present case and BWV Investments Ltd etc. (case 28; appeal pending) in several respects, including that in the present case the lien had been lifted since Automatic had deposited with the court a letter of credit in the amount of the lien claim and that there were no other lien claimants.

For a sister case, see Case No, 74

Indian Act—section 8. This ruling is concerned with an interesting point, namely, that the existence of a statute with narrow arbitration provisions does not preclude the operation of arbitration clause on other matters

Case 74: MAL 8(1)

Canada: Ontario Court of Appeal (Morden, Blair and Austin JJ.A.)

25 April, 1994

Automatic Systems Inc. v. *E.S. Fox Ltd. and Chrysler Canada Ltd.*

Original in English

Unpublished

Fox was another subcontractor of Automatic (case 73). Unlike the previous case, in the present case the parties disagreed as to whether there was an agreement to arbitrate and the court of first instance did not find it necessary to decide that matter, in view of its decision that at any rate an agreement for international arbitration of an Ontario lien would be unenforceable in Ontario.

The appellate court overturned the decision of the court of first instance and remitted the matter to that court with the question whether there was an agreement to arbitrate between Automatic and Fox and the question of the appropriate relief.

Indian Act—section 8. See comment on case 73, supra

Case 89: MAL 8

Hong Kong; High Court of Hong Kong (Kaptan J.)

16 December, 1994

York Airconditioning & Refrigeration Inc. v. *Lam Kwai Hung Trading as North Sea AC Elect. Eng. Co.*

Original in English

Unpublished (Abstract prepared by the UNCITRAL Secretariat)

The plaintiff, a Hong Kong company, sold to the defendant, a Hong Kong agent of a Chinese company, water cooling machines that were to be installed in Beijing. The contract contained an arbitration clause for arbitration in Beijing under the CIETAC Rules. The defendant paid 30% of the price in Hong Kong, and for the balance a bill of exchange was drawn in Hong Kong on a Hong Kong party and accepted by the defendant. A dispute arose as to the quality of the goods and the defendant failed to honour the bill of exchange upon presentation. The seller sued in Hong Kong. A stay of court proceedings requested by the defendant was not granted by the Master of the court and the defendant appealed.

The court held that under the Chinese law applicable to the sales contract (the law of the place of arbitration), the bill of exchange was to be treated as a separate contract, which was not covered by the arbitration clause contained in the sales contract. In addition, it was held under the Hong Kong law applicable to the bill of exchange that the bill of exchange was a separate contract and a claim on the bill was not covered by the arbitration clause contained in the sales contract. The application for a stay of the court proceedings was dismissed and the claim of the defendant was referred to the appropriate court.

Indian Act—sections 7 and 8. In effect, this ruling lays down that a bill of exchange for payment under the main contract cannot be referred to arbitration

Case 108: MAL 1(3)(b)(iii); 8(1)

Hong Kong; High Court of Hong Kong (Leonard J.)

4 May, 1995

D. Heung & Associates, Architects & Engineers v. *Pacific Enterprises (Holdings) Company Limited*

Original in English

Unpublished

(Abstract prepared by N. Kaplan, Q.C.)

The plaintiff, a Hong Kong company, appointed by the defendant, also a Hong Kong company, as the architect for the entire design of a project in Dongshan Island, China, sued claiming agreed professional fees due by the efendant. The defendant sought a stay of the court proceedings under article 8 MAL and submission of the dispute to arbitration, since their agreement contained an arbitration clause.

The issue was whether, despite the fact that both parties were Hong Kong companies and that the contract was to be partly performed in Hong Kong, an "international arbitration agreement" in the meaning of article 1(3)(b)(ii) was involved. The court found that the subject matter of the dispute was most closely connected to the project in Dongshan, China, and that a substantial part of the defendant's duties related to the entire design and supervision of that project.

The court, noting that article 8(1) MAL was mandatory in its nature, stayed the proceedings, since no party had suggested that the arbitration agreement was null and void or inoperative or incapable of being performed, and in view of the fact that the plaintiff's claim was disputed by the defendant.

Indian Act—section 8

Case 111: MAL 1(1); 8(1)

Canada: Alberta Court of Queen's Bench (Murray J.)

12 August, 1994

Borowski v. *Heinrich Fiedler Perforiertechnik GmbH*

Published in English: (1994) 158 Alberta Reports, 213; and [1994] 10 Western Weekly Reports, 623

The plaintiff, an employee of the defendant, sued for damages in lieu of notice of termination of the employment contract and for loss of wages and benefits. The defendant sought a stay of proceedings and submission of the dispute to arbitration, since the employment contract contained an arbitration clause.

The court found that, with regard to the claim for past wages and benefits, there was no dispute to be referred to arbitration, since the defendant had admitted that it owed the plaintiff for past wages and benefits. With regard to damages in lieu of notice of termination, the court found that that was a dispute covered by the arbitration clause, stayed the court proceedings and referred the matter to arbitration.

On the question whether the International Commercial Arbitration Act (I.C.A.A.), which enacted MAL, could apply to a dispute arising from an employment contract, the court held that such a contract created a master and servant relationship and not a commercial relationship of the type falling under the I.C.A.A. (section 4(2) I.C.A.A., which is equivalent to article 1(1) MAL).

Contrast case 115, infra

Indian Act—section 2(1)(f), which defines "international commercial arbitration" and also contains the words"considered as commercial under any law" etc. The above ruling may be indirectly relevant for that section

Case 112: MAL 8(1)

Canada: Alberta Court of Queen's Bench and Alberta Court of Appeal

13 July, 1994 and 4 October, 1994

Kvaerner Enviropower Inc. v. *Tanar Industries Ltd.*

Published in English: 157 Alberta Reports, 363; and [1994] 9 Western Weekly Reports, 228

Kvaerner, a contractor, applied for a stay of the court proceedings initiated by Tanar, a subcontractor, and for submission of the dispute between them and a third party, which had to pay performance bonds issued in favour of Tanar, to arbitration.

The court stayed the proceedings and referred the dispute between Kvaerner and Tanar to arbitration. While the court considered that the performance bonds in favour of Tanar did not constitute an agreement between the third party and Kvarner to arbitrate their differences, it stayed the court proceedings as between Kvaerner and the third party pending arbitration of the dispute between Kvaerner and Tanar. The Court of Appeal confirmed the decision of the court of first instance.

Indian Act—section 8. The situation above may not literally fall within section 8. But section 151 of the Code of Civil Procedure, 1908 can be utilised

Case 113: MAL 8(1)

Canada: Ontario Court of Justice - General Division (Borins, J.)

10 November, 1994

T1T2 Limited Partnership v. *Canada*

Original in English

Unpublished

The defendant sought a stay of the court proceedings initiated by the plaintiffs and submission of the dispute to arbitration, based on an arbitration clause contained in their contract. The arbitration clause provided that differences between ihe parties should be resolved through arbitration, with the exception of differences "involving a question of law".

The court found that resolving the plaintiff's claims would involve addressing "questions of law", including the application of legal principles to a set of facts, and rejected the application for a stay of proceedings.

Indian Act—sections 7 and 8. The case is of interest, as involving a novel type of arbitration clause which excluded questions of law

Case 114: MAL 8(1) and 16(1)

Canada: British Columbia Supreme Court (Lysyk J.)

18 November, 1994

Globe Union Industrial Corp. v. *G.A.P. Marketing Corp.*

Published in English: [1995] 2 Western Weekly Reports, 696

Globe was a Taiwanese manufacturer who entered into a distribution agreement with G.A.P. granting it a licence to distribute Globe's products in Canada and Mexico. G.A.P. initiated arbitration proceedings under an arbitration clause in the agreement and Globe then commenced the present court proceedings, which G.A.P. sought to stay under s. 8 of the International Commercial Arbitration Act, Statutes of British Columbia, 1986, chapter 14, which enacts MAL.

The court found that, even if the distribution agreement had been terminated between the parties and was assumed to be null and void, it did not mean that the arbitration clause it contained was unenforceable (articles 8(1) and 16(1) MAL). The court also found that the court proceedings were in respect of a matter agreed by the parties to be submitted to arbitration and the fact that G.A.P. responded to Globe's application to enjoin G.A.P. from proceeding with the arbitration did not constitute the taking of a step in the court proceedings so as to justify refusal of a stay.

Indian Act—section 8

Case 115: MAL 8(1)

Canada; Alberta Court of Queen's Bench (Master Funduk)

23 November, 1994

Crystal Rose Home Ltd. v. *Alberta New Home Warranty Program*

Original in English

Unpublished

Crystal, a construction company, was a member of the Warranty Programme, a company designed to provide warranty protection to buyers of new homes. The Warranty Programme terminated Crystal's membership. Crystal initialed court proceedings claiming that it was not in default on its obligation to any home buyers and had not received notice of any such default that would entitle the Warranty Programme to exercise its rights. The contract between the patties provided for arbitration of any dispute "with respect to any matter in relation to this agreement".

The court found that the arbitration clause was not limited in scope to matters expressly addressed in the contract or to matters that were addressed by specific terms of the contract. The court distinguished Borowski v. Heinrich Fieciler (Case 111) as a case where specific words qualified the scope of the arbitration clause. A stay was ordered under the Arbitration Act, Statutes of Alberta, 1991, chapter A-43.1. The court concluded that the arbitration clause was not limited to claims for breach of contract but would extend, for example, to a claim in tort for which the existence of the contract was a relevant fact.

The court thought that whether the statute implementing MAL or an arbitration law dealing only with domestic disputes applied was not relevant to the interpretation of the scope of the arbitration clause. Unless the clause was invalid under either law, it was for the parties between them to decide what was arbitrable.

Indian Act—sections 7 and 8. Contrast case 111. supra

Case 116: MAL 8(1)

Canada: Saskatchewan Court of Appeal

25 November, 1994

BWV Investments Ltd. v. *Saskferco Products Inc. et.al. and UHDE GmbH*

Published in English [1995] 2 Western Weekly Reports, 1

This case involved an appeal against the decision on Case 28, in which the court of first instance had refused to grant a stay of court proceedings declaring the arbitration agreement between BWV, Saskferco, UHDE and others void under both article 8(1) MAL and s. 99(1) of the Builder's Lien Act (B.L.A.), BWV, a subcontractor in a Saskatchevan construction project with head offices in Canada, had filed a builder's lien against the project and sued Saskferco, UHDE, contractors with head offices in Germany, and others under B.L.A.

The issue before the Court of Appeal was whether the arbitration agreement, which was contained in the subcontract between BWV, Saskferco and UHDE, conflicted with B.L.A. and was thus void. The Court of Appeal found that a builders' lien action was not the only method available to determine the amount of money owed in relation to contracts where liens have arisen and that there was no inconsistency between an arbitration agreement and the builders' lien legislation. The Court of Appeal reversed the decision of the court of first instance, stayed the court proceedings and referred the matter to arbitration.

The Court of Appeal considered the question whether to stay the proceed' gs with regard to sub-subcontractors of BWV who had also filed builder's liens against tl project. It was found that, as there was no evidence that the sub-subcontracts incorporated the arbitration agreement, the sub-subcontractors were "third parties" with regard to the dispute between BWV, Saskferco and UHDE. Referring to the United States practice in domestic construction matters to stay third-party actions pending arbitration, the Court of Appeal ordered that the actions by sub-subcontractors be stayed pending the above arbitration, to avoid the problem of multiple concurrent proceedings. A member of the Court of Appeal disagreed with the scope for residual judicial discretion in staying applications set out in *Guif Canada Resources Ltd.* v. *Arochem International Ltd.* (Case 31).

Indian Act—section 8, See comment on case 112, supra

Case 118: MAL 8(1); 23(1)

Canada: Ontario Court of Justice, General Division (Borins J.)

21 December, 1994

Bab Systems, Inc. v. *McLurg*

Original in English

Unpublished

The plaintiff, one of the parties to a franchise agreement, applied to the court seeking judicial relief. Within hours of the court granting certain provisional relief in respect of the application, and adjourning for further particulars, the plaintiff advised the defendant of its intention to submit the dispute to arbitration pursuant to an arbitration clause in their agreement. This oral advice was followed by written confirmation a day later indicating that the plaintiff sought to amend its notice of application, that had been served on the defendant, by discontinuing all relief sought except for certain provisional relief, which was specifically excluded from the scope of the arbitration clause. The plaintiff then sought a court order referring the dispute to arbitration and a stay of the court proceedings, except the claim for provisional relief.

Having concluded that, except for the provisional relief, the relief sought in the application was within the arbitration clause, the court considered, whether the plaintiff had waived arbitration by having brought its dispute before the court, Even assuming a right of unilateral waiver, which was unlikely as the arbitration clause bound all parties to the contract, the court concluded that the waiver had been effectively retracted by reasonable notice of the intention to arbitrate.

The defendant argued that the court should not stay the judicial proceedings under the Ontario equivalent of article 8(1) MAL because the application for stay had been made after the plaintiff had submitted its "first statement on the substance of the dispute" by filing an application with the court. The court held that the word "statement" in article 8(1) MAL meant the first statement in the arbitral process, as distinct from the litigation process. Expressly disagreeing with the interpretation of article 8(1) MAL by the Federal Court of Appeal in Ruhrkohle Handel Inter GmbH v Fednau Ltd. (see Case 33), the court concluded that, since the plaintiff had not submitted its first statement in the arbitral proceedings, within the meaning of articles 23(1) and 8(1) MAL, its request for submission to arbitration was timely. An order was issued referring the parties to arbitration pursuant to their agreement.

Indian Act—section 8

Case 119: MAL 8

Canada: Ontario Court of Justice, General Division (Haley J.)

23 December, 1994

ABN Amro Bank Canada v. *Krupp Mak Maschinenbati GmbH*

Published in Mealey's International Arbitration Report, May 1995, 11.

ABN made a loan to Diesel Inc. (Diesel), a party to a technology licensing agreement with Krupp, which under the terms of the loan was to be assigned to ABN as collateral. Diesel signed a general assignment of its assets to ABN but, although an assignment agreement to which Krupp would be party was prepared, it was never signed. After the loan was made, ABN alleged that the principal owner of Diesel and Krupp had conspired to deceive it and sued Krupp for conspiracy and fraud. In its statement of defence and counterclaim, Krupp, based on an arbitration clause contained in the licensing agreement, sought to stay the proceedings and to have the matter referred to arbitration in Switzerland.

The court held that ABN was not bound to arbitrate because it was not a party to the arbitration clause contained in the licensing agreement between Krupp and Diesel and the assignment of Diesel's assets to ABN did not make it a party to that agreement. It was held that, under article 8 MAL, a party to an arbitration agreement did not include a person claiming through or under a party, as ABN was doing in the present case.

The court further held that Krupp's request for a stay was either no request at all in the meaning of article 8 MAL or an untimely request, since it was filed with Krupp's first statement on the substance of the dispute which implied acceptance of the jurisdiction of the court. The correct procedure pursuant to article 8 MAL was for Krupp to apply for a stay of court proceedings, after receiving the statement of claim but before submitting a statement of defence.

Indian Act—sections 7-8. This ruling is of interest, as it settles the position regarding effect of assignment

Case 128: MAL 8(1)

Hong Kong: Court of Appeal (Nazareth V.P. Bokhary and Liu JJ.A.)

24 November, 1995

Tai Hing Cotton Mill Limited v. *Glencore Grain Rotterdam B.V. and another*

Published in English: [1996] 1 Hong Kong Cases(HKC) 363

(Abstract prepared by Neil Kaplan Q.C.)

Glencore agreed to sell to Tai Hing 1,000 tonnes of raw cotton C&F Hong Kong. The contract provided for arbitration in Liverpool under the Rules of the Liverpool Cotton Association Limited and the contract contained a clause to the effect that the obtaining of an arbitration award should be a condition precedent to the right of either party to start legal proceedings in respect of any arbitrable dispute ("Scott v. Avery-clause").

Disputes arose and the judge granted summary judgement for specific performance of the contract of sale and dismissed Glencore's application for a stay under article 8 (1)MAL

The Court of Appeal considered whether there were grounds for dismissing the application for stay under article 8(1) MAL, despite the existence of the arbitration agreement. Following Guandong Agriculture v. Conagra International (CLOUT Case 41) and Zhan Jian E&T Dev. Area Service Head Co v. An Hau (CLOUT Case 61), the Court of Appeal held that under article 8(1) MAL "the Court is not concerned with investigating whether the Defendant has an arguable basis for disputing the Claim." The Court of Appeal held further that "if a claim is made against him in a matter which is the subject of an arbitration agreement and he does not admit the claim then there is a dispute within the meaning of the Article."

The Court of Appeal set aside the summary judgement and granted a stay under article 8(I) MAL.

Indian Act—section 8(stay) and section 43(3) (arbitration as'a condition precedent)

Case 129: MAL 8(1)

Hong Kong: High Court of Hong Kong (Leonard J.)

19 April, 1996

Nassetti Ettore S.p.a. v. *Lawlon Development Limited*

Original in English

Unpublished

(Abstract prepared by the UNCITRAL Secretariat}

The plaintiff, an Italian company, sold to the defendant, a Hong Kong company, a production line for the manufacture of granite tiles to be delivered to China. The contract provided for arbitration in Stockholm under the auspices of the Stockholm Swedish International Chamber of Commerce.

Disputes arose and the plaintiff applied for summary judgement for payment of the balance due by the defendant under the contract. The defendant applied for an order that all further proceedings in the action should be stayed pursuant to article 8(1) MAL.

Under reference to Tai Hing Cotton Mill Ltd. v. Glencore Grain Rotterdam B.V. and another (CLOUT Case 128), the court held that under article 8(1) MAL "the Court is not concerned with investigating whether the Defendant has an arguable basis for disputing the Claim." The court also held that "the question is whether there is a dispute between the parties in the ordinary sense of that word" and that there is dispute "unless there is an unequivocal admission of liability and quantum".

The court found that it was the obligation of the court to refer the parties to arbitration and ordered that the proceedings be stayed accordingly.

◆ ◆ ◆ ◆ ◆

Case 178: MAL 8(1)

Canada: British Columbia Supreme Court (Huddart J.)

31 January, 1996

Siderurgica Mendes Junior S.A. v. *"Icepearl" (The)*

Original in English

Unpublished

Siderurgica (SMJ) shipped a cargo of steel wire on ihe "Icepearl", which was time-chartered by Norsul International S.A. and owned by Icepearl Shipping Co. The bills of lading were endorsed to Mitsui & Co. (Canada) Ltd., a charterer of part of the vessel. The goods arrived in Vancouver damaged by salt water. SMJ and Mitsui sued Norsul on the bill of lading, claiming damages in contract or iort, or for breach of duty as bailee. Norsul applied for a stay of proceedings and referral to arbitration in New York pursuant to Article 8 of the Commercial Arbitration Act, Revised Statutes of Canada, 1985 (2nd Supplement), Chapter 17, which enacts Article 8(1) MAL An arbitration clause was contained in the charter-party signed by Mitsui and Norsul. The bills of lading included a clause purporting to supersede all previous agreements.

The court applied a line of Canadian and English cases to the effect that an endorsement like that used in the bills of lading did not incorporate the arbitration clause contained in the charter-party. An obligation to arbitrate had to be found in a separate agreement between SMJ or Mitsui and Norsul. As SMJ was not a party to any other agreement with Norsul, no stay could be granted on that ground with respect to that plaintiff.

However, the court then found that, despite the fact that Mitsui sued on the bills of lading, and not the charter-party, the agreement to arbitrate in the charter-party was binding. In addition, the court found that Mitsui and Norsul had agreed that any dispute between them would be referred to arbitration in New York and thus the arbitration clause was enforceable separately from any other provisions of the charter-party. The supersession clause in the bills of lading did not, therefore, prevent Norsul and Mitsui from being bound by the arbitration clause in the charter-party between them.

The court also found that Norsul had not waived its right under the arbitration agreement since it did not submit its application later than the submission of its first statement on the substance of the dispute. The action, by both SMJ and Mitsui, was stayed pending the arbitration between Norsul and Mitsui.

Indian Act—sections 7 and 8

Case 179: MAL 8(1)

Canada: British Columbia Court of Appeal (Macfarlane, Cumming and Prowse, JJ.A.)

4 July, 1995

The City of Prince George v. *A.L. Sims & Sons Ltd.*

Original in English

Published in English: [1995] 9 Western Weekly Reports, 503

The defendant (appellant), Sims, entered into a construction contract containing an arbitration clause with the plaintiff (respondent), the City of Prince George. Plaintiff (respondent) nominated McElhanney Engineering Services Ltd. (McElhanney) as a consultant under the contract. However, there was no arbitration clause in the contract between them. Plaintiff (respondent) commenced an action against defendant (appellant) and McElhanney. Defendant (appellant) applied for an order under Section 15 of the Commercial Arbitration Act, Revised Statutes ,of British Columbia, 1985 (2nd Supplement), Chapter 17, which enacts Article 8 MAL, for a stay of the action. The first instance court found that the arbitration clause was inoperative or incapable of being performed because the action raised broader issues against the co-defendant, McElhanney, which were interrelated with the arbitrable issues between the plaintiff and the defendant. The first instance court also said that it would exercise a residual discretion to refuse the stay where there was a risk of multiple proceedings and inconsistent results. On appeal, the Court of Appeal found that there was a dispute between the parties that involved matters which had been agreed to be submitted to arbitration. The Court of Appeal found that Canadian and English case law was clear that, as a general principle, whenever there are multiple parties and multiple issues, of which some are interrelated and similar, defendants are not barred from invoking an arbitration clause binding them, Amongst the cases referred to by the Court of Appeal was BMW Investments Ltd. v. Saskferco Products Inc. (CLOUT case no. 116 in A/CN.9/SER.C/ABSTRACTS/8).

The Court of Appeal then considered the question of residual discretion to refuse a stay of proceedings in the light of the earlier British Columbia Court of Appeal decision in Gulf Canada Resources Ltd. v. Arochem International Ltd. (CLOUT case no. 31 in A/CN.9/SER.C/ABSTRACTS/2). The Court of Appeal considered that there was, on this issue, no difference in substance between the British Columbia Commercial Arbitration Act and the British Columbia International Commercial Arbitration Act, Statutes of British Columbia, 1986, Chapter 14. The Court of Appeal found that the first instance court had misinterpreted the language of the Court of Appeal in the Gulf Canada decision. The Court of Appeal held that a court had a residual discretion to refuse a stay of proceedings only when a party clearly established that it was not privy to an arbitration agreement. If it is arguable that a party is indeed a party to such an agreement, a stay should be granted and the issue can be resolved in the arbitration.

Indian Act—section 8. Compare case No. 116, Jnfra

Case 180: MAL 8

Canada: British Columbia Supreme Court (Saunders J. in Chambers)

9 May, 1995

Traff et al. v. *Evancic et al.*

Original in English

Unpublished

The plaintiffs commenced an action against the defendants for fraud and breach of trust in relation to an investment scheme. Two Bahamian corporations were also served in the action and sought an order staying the proceedings against them under the International Commercial Arbitration Act, Statutes of British Columbia, 1986, Chapter 14 (which enacts article 8 MAL).

While the proceedings related to allegations of fraud, the plaintiffs also sought an accounting under various agreements relating to the investment scheme. These agreements contained an arbitration clause.

Despite there being different issues, the court granted the stay requested since one of the issues was in respect of a matter agreed to be arbitrated. The court relied on the Gulf

Canada Resources Ltd. v. Arochem International Ltd. decision (CLOUT Case no. 31 in A/ CN.9/SER.C/ABSTRACTS/2),

◆ ◆ ◆ ◆ ◆

Case 181: MAL 8

Canada: British Columbia Supreme Court (Oppal J. in Chambers)

24 March, 1995

Queensland Sugar Corp. v. "Hanjin Jedda" (The)

Original in English

Published in English: [1995] 6 British Columbia Law Reports (3rd) 289

The defendants shipped to the plaintiffs a cargo of raw sugar from Australia to Canada. The latter alleged the cargo was damaged at sea, A charter-party referred all disputes between the parties to arbitration. Two months after the plaintiffs commenced the action, the defendants filed a statement of defence which did not refer to arbitration. After the case was set for trial, the defendants requested the plaintiffs' consent to commence arbitration pursuant to Article 8 of the Commercial Arbitration Act, Revised Statutes of Canada, 1985 (2nd Supplement) Chapter 17, which enacts article 8 MAL.

The court held that the defendants impliedly agreed that the court try the dispute by participating in the litigation process from its commencement.

The court relied on the Gulf Canada Resources Ltd. v. Arochem International Ltd. (CLOUT Case no. 31 in A/CN.9/ SER.C/ABSTRACTS/2) decision and its interpretation of Article 8 MAL to the effect that a stay of proceedings should not be granted if it was applied for out of time; and that it would prejudice the plaintiffs to refer the matter to arbitration when the litigation process was well under way.

Indian Act—section 8

Case 183: MAL 8(1)

Canada: Ontario Court of Appeal (Morden A.C.J.O., Blair and Austin JJ. A.)

25 April, 1994

Automatic Systems Inc. v. *Bracknell Corp.*

Original in English

Published in English: [1994] 18 Ontario Reports (3rd) 257

Automatic Systems, Inc., a Missouri corporation, contracted with Bracknell Corp., an Ontario corporation, for the supply and installation of a conveyor system at a Chrysler plant in Ontario. The contract contained an agreement to arbitrate all disputes arising under it in Missouri in accordance with the law of that State. When Bracknell claimed a statutory construction lien against Automatic, the latter applied tor an order staying the action and referring the parties to arbitration. The application for an order staying the action was denied and Automatic appealed.

The Court of Appeal held that the construction lien legislation should not have been narrowly construed by the court seized of the stay application, rather the court should have enquired whether that legislation prohibited arbitration, The lien statute did not prohibit arbitration but actually contemplated it. The International Commercial Arbitration Act, Revised Statutes of Ontario, 1990, Chapter 1.9, which enacts article 8(1) MAL, was applied since the case fell within its scope and nothing in the lien statute precluded a claim from being arbitrated under the Act. The Court of Appeal made extensive reference to the commitment of the province of Ontario to the policy of international commercial arbitration through enactment of MAL and granted a stay of the proceedings. The Court of Appeal referred in critical terms to the trial judgement in *BWV Investments Ltd.* v. *Saskferco Products Inc. et.al. and UHDE GmbH* (CLOUT case no. 116 in A/CN.9/SER.C/ABSTRACTS/8], which was reversed on appeal in a manner consistent with the result in the present case.

Indian Act—section 8

Case 184: MAL 8(1)

Canada: Federal Court of Canada (Trial Division) (Strayer J.)

22 March, 1994

Continental Resources Inc. v. *The East Asiatic Company (Canada) Inc.*

Original in English

Unpublished

The court was satisfied that there was an arbitration agreement within the meaning of Article 8 of the Commercial Arbitration Act, Revised Statutes of Canada, 1985, 2nd Supplement, Chapter 17, which enacts Article 8(1) MAL, and that, therefore, the matter before it must be referred to arbitration in New York as provided in the charter-party between the litigants. As no statement of defence had been filed by the defendants, they had not submitted any statement on the substance of the dispute to the court so as to justify the refusal of a stay of proceedings.

The court held that there was insufficient evidence that a new agreement had been reached between the parties for arbitration in Vancouver. The court also held that if there was any claim against the defendant vessel, which claim was not precluded by the agreement to arbitrate, it could be stayed pending the conclusion of the arbitration in New York. The court found insufficient evidence to warrant granting such a stay. However, as Article 8 MAL does not address the issue of the terms on which the action before the court should be disposed of, the court used its discretion to grant the stay on condition that the defendants did not rely on prescription or on delay as a defence in the arbitration.

Indian Act—section 8. This decision is important, as authorising conditional stay

Case 186: MAL 8

Canada: Superior Court of Quebec (Ryan J.)

18 May, 1990

A. Bianchi S.R.L. v. *Bilumen Lighting Ltd.*

Original in French

Published in French: Recueil de jurisprudence du Quebec (1990) 1681

In a series of contracts concluded during 1986, Bianchi granted Bilumen the exclusive right to assemble, sell and distribute its products in Canada and the United States. Shortly thereafter, and despite the arbitration clause contained in the contract, Bianchi began judicial proceedings before the Superior Court, claiming damages for breach of contract. The proceedings followed their course, including joint motions for particulars, a demand for a guarantee in respect of the costs of the proceedings and discovery. In March 1990, Bilumen filed a motion for dismissal of the action, pointing to the arbitration clause. Bianchi contested this motion, arguing that Bilumen had tacitly renounced arbitration in view of the various steps undertaken in relation to the judicial proceedings. Given the general policy favouring arbitration, and particularly article 8 MAL, the Superior Court concluded that the delay in invoking the arbitration clause and the steps undertaken in the judicial proceedings did not amount to renunciation of the arbitral procedure. The Superior Court further stated that the mandatory nature of the provision and the absence of judicial discretion required that the parties be referred to arbitration.

Indian Act—section 8. This ruling stresses the mandatory nature of section 8. MAL

Article 9. Arbitration agreement and interim measures by court

It is not incompatible with an arbitration agreement *for* a party to request, *before* or *during arbitral proceedings, from a court an interim measure of protection and for a court to grant such measure.*

Indian Act—section 9 is much more specific, as setting out the various protective measures

Case 11: MAL 8; 9

Canada: Federal Court of Canada, Trial Division (Pinard, J.)

19 February, 1988

Relais Nordik v. *Secunda Marine Services Limited*

Published in English and French: 24 Federal Trial Reporter, 256

A mandatory interim injunction requiring compliance with the terms of a charter party is not an interim measure within the scope of article 9 MAL.

Relais Nordik applied, pursuant to article 9 of the Model Law which is enacted by the Commercial Arbitration Act, Revised Statutes of Canada, 1985, c.C-34.6 for a mandatory interim injunction to force Secunda Marine to comply with the terms of a charter-party signed by both parties.

The Court dismissed the application for an injunction on the grounds that the applicant had not made out a strong prima facie case for an injunction. As well, damages would compensate any loss suffered by the applicant. Moreover, the court held that the remedy sought was not an interim measure within article 9 MAL. The applicant was seen as attempting to have the court rather than the arbitrators resolve the substance of the dispute, notwithstanding the respondent's objection pursuant to article 8 MAL.

◆ ◆ ◆ ◆ ◆

Case 435 — MAL art. 8(1)

Germany: Bundesgerichtshof; III ZR 262/00

10 May, 2001

Original in German

Published in German: VersR 2001, p. 1444; NJW 2001, p. 2176; Betriebs-Berater 2001, p. 1327; DIS-Online Database on Arbitration Law - http://www.dis-arb.de

Abstract prepared by Stefan Kröll and Katja Richter

The decision concerns the question of when a defendant in court proceedings must invoke the existence of an arbitration agreement before being barred from doing so.

The claimant, a German limited company, had brought an action against the defendant, one of its managing directors and shareholders, for a declaration that a decision of the shareholders' meeting to reduce the defendant's power of representation to joint agency was valid. The shareholders' agreement provided that all disputes arising out of it should be referred to arbitration, except for actions to set aside or to declare nullity of a shareholder's decision. The defendant did not challenge the jurisdiction of the tribunal within the time limit set by the court for the defence, but invoked the existence of the arbitration clause before the hearing and before taking any steps on the merits. Nevertheless the two lower courts considered the defendant to be barred from relying on the arbitration agreement by virtue of a provision in the German Code of Civil Procedure (ZPO), which allows defences not raised within a time limit set by the courts to be rejected as untimely.

The Supreme Court reversed this decision and found that the defence was timely. It considered that the relevant provision to address the question of when the existence of an arbitration agreement must be raised is section 1032(1) ZPO (modified article 8 MAL), which as *lex specialis* prevails over the other provisions relied upon by the lower courts. According to section 1032(1) the courts must refer the parties to arbitration if one party invokes the existence of an arbitration agreement before the oral hearing on the substance. Therefore, the expiry of the time limit set for the submission of the defence is, in this respect, irrelevant.

The Supreme Court referred the case back to the lower court to deal with the relevant question of whether the arbitration agreement actually covers the action in question. The action brought by the claimant, though it was not one of the special actions explicitly excluded in the arbitration agreement, is so closely connected to excluded actions that the parties might well have intended it to fall under the exception as well.

Indian Act—section 9. This ruling is very important on the point of mandatory injunction

Case 39: MAL 1(3) (b) (ii), 9

Hong Kong: High Court of Hong Kong (Kaplan J.)

Katran Shipping Co. Ltd. v. *Kenven Transportation Ltd.*

Published in English: 1992, Hong Kong Law Digest, G9

Summarized and commented on by Kaplan, Spruce and Moser in Hong Kong and China Arbitration, Cases and Materials, Butterworths, 1994.

Commented on by Kaplan in Asia Law January/February 1995, 23.

Reported on in English: [1992) The Arbitration and dispute Resolution Law Journal (ADRLJ) 235, [1992] ADRLJ 240, [1993] ADRLJ 240, [1993] ADRLJ 100 and [1994] ADRLJ 49, 295, 307, 291, 290, 298 respectively.

(Abstract prepared by Kaplan)

The defendant, a Hong Kong company, sought to have set aside a Mareva injunction that the court had granted the plaintiff, also a Hong Kong company. The issue before the court was whether it had jurisdiction to grant such an interim measure of protection, in view of the fact that a charter-party agreement entered by the plaintiff and the defendant contained an arbitration clause which provided that "any dispute will be settled before Hong Kong Arbitrators and under British Maritime law ....".

The court, relying on article 1(3)(b)(ii) MAL and its decision on *Fung Sang Trading* v. *Kai Sun Sea Products and Food Co. Ltd.* [see A/CN.9/SER.C/ABSTRACTS/1, case 20], found that MAL covered this dispute, since a substantial part of the obligations provided in the charter-party was to be performed outside Hong Kong.

The court held that the interim measure of protection referred to in article 9 MAL was wide enough to cover a Mareva injunction. "The protection afforded by a Mareva injunction" was held to be "the reduction in the risk of the amount of the claim, or part of it, being dissipated or otherwise put out of the plaintiff's reach before the resolution of the dispute".

The court concluded that it had jurisdiction to grant a Mareva injunction in support of a domestic arbitration carried out in Hong Kong, both under article 9 MAL and s. 14(6) of the Arbitration Ordinance which were identical in regard to domestic arbitration.

Indian Act— section 9. The ruling is important, as dealing with the Mareva injunction

Case 42: MAL 9

Hong Kong: High Court of Hong Kong (Barnett, J.)

2 March, 1992

Interbulk (Hong Kong) Ltd. v. *Safe Rich Industries Ltd.*

Published in English: (1992) 2 Hong Kong Law Reports, 185 and 1992 Hong Kong Law Digest, C7

(Abstract prepared by the Secretariat)

The plaintiff, shipowner, obtained an injunction against the defendant, charterer. The charter-party contained a clause providing for arbitration in England under English law. The defendant sought to have the injunction set aside.

The court held that, pursuant to s. 14(6) of the Arbitration Ordinance, Hong Kong courts had no jurisdiction to grant interim relief, in cases where there was a valid arbitration agreement providing for arbitration elsewhere than in Hong Kong.

The council noted that under article 9 MAL the courts of Hong Kong were empowered to grant an "interim measure of protection" to a party to an arbitration to which MAL applied. The court recognized that it was "... at least open to argument" that a court of a state that had adopted MAL might be more ready to assist a party to an international arbitration agreement, notwithstanding the fact that the arbitration had its seat elsewhere.

Indian Act— section 9. This ruling clarifies that article 9 MAL does not apply where the arbitration is outside the Country

Case 68: MAL 9; 27

Canada: Federal Court of Canada, Trial Division (Denault J.)

3 December 1993

Delphi Petroleum Inc. v. *Derin Shipping and Training Ltd.*

Original in English and French

Unpublished

The plaintiff, a charterer, had a dispute with the defendant, a shipowner, involving freight and demurrage costs. Pursuant to an arbitration clause contained in the charterparty the matter was submitted to a single arbitrator in New York who issued a final award.

The plaintiff, who was not satisfied with the award as far as the claim for demurrage costs was concerned, applied to the court for an interim order in order to secure the evidence of a witness with regard to that claim and a number of additional claims for unjust enrichment, quantum meruit and misrepresentation.

Point 1

The court referred to the travaux préparatoires of MAL (A/CN. 9/264, article 9, paras. 1 and 4) pursuant to sections 4(2)(b), 5 and 6 of the International Commercial Arbitration Act and found that it had jurisdiction to grant an interim order pursuant to article 9 MAL. The court noted that it had a mandate to render assistance in matters of evidence in arbitration but it should avoid taking measures conducive to dilatory tactics of the parties (A/CN. 9/264, article 27, paras. 5-6).

Point 2

The court dismissed the plaintiff's application on the ground that it did not meet the test of rule 466.3(3)(a) of the Federal Rules of Procedure that the witness whose testimony is sought "may have information on an issue in the action" since the issue of demurrage had been decided upon by the arbitrator and the court was not satisfied that the evidence before it demonstrated that the witness had any information on the other issues raised in the application.

Indian Act—section 9. This ruling is important, as laying down the proposition that article 9 MAL can be resorted to, even after the award is pronounced, if the applicant has challenged the award in an appropriate forum

Case 71: MAL 9

Canada: British Columbia Supreme Court (Bouck J)

25 February, 1994

Trade Fortune Inc. v. *Amagalmated Mill Supplies Ltd.*

Original in English

Published in English: The Arbitration and Dispute Resolution Law Journal, 1996, 6, 132.

The plaintiff, a Greek shipowner, claimed payment of demurrage costs on the ground that the defendant, a Canadian charterer, was responsible for a delay in unloading a cargo in Korea. The plaintiff sought and obtained an interim court order designed to secure funds for payment of the claim upon issue of a final decision. The defendant paid into court the full amount of the claim, but sought that the matter be referred to arbitration in London pursuant to an arbitration clause contained in the charterparty, litigation be stayed and the interim order be set aside. The plaintiff agreed to the reference to arbitration and stay of proceedings but objected to the setting aside of the interim court order.

There were two main issues; first, whether interim measures of protection that could be taken by courts (article 9 MAL) included the interim order granted in the present case or whether such an order could be granted only by the arbitral tribunal dealing with the substance of the dispute (article 17 MAL); and second, whether staying the procedures had the effect of setting aside the interim order. On the first issue, the court, referring to the travaux preparatoires of MAL, held that interim court orders designed to protect the applicant from the risk of being unable to enforce a final arbitral award were not incompatible with arbitration (article 9 MAL). The application of the defendant to set aside the interim court order was thus dismissed. On the second issue, the court found that staying the proceedings would not set aside the interim order since the original claim of the plaintiff would not merge into the arbitration award and the plaintiff was thus not prevented from pursuing its claim until it was paid in full. The court ordered a stay of proceedings and dismissed the application of the defendant to set aside the interim court order.

See also cases No. 39 and 58 under article 1, supra

CHAPTER III

COMPOSITION OF ARBITRAL TRIBUNAL

Article 10. Number of arbitrators

(1) *The parties are free to determine the number of arbitrators.*

(2) *Failing such determination, the number of arbitrators shall be three.*

Indian Act—sub-section (1) of section 10 of the 1996 Act deals with the number of arbitrators in an arbitral tribunal and provides that the number of arbitrators shall not be of even number. The Model Law does not contain any such limitation. Where the parties fail to determine the number of arbitrators the Model Law provides that the number of arbitrators shall be three. Sub-section (2) of section 10 of the 1996 Act provides that in such an eventuality, the arbitral tribunal shall consist of a sole arbitrator

Case 20: MAL 1(3)(b)(ii); 3; 8; 10; 11; 16

Hong Kong: High Court of Hong Kong (Kaplan J.)

29 October, 1991

Fung Sang Trading Limited v. *Kai Sun Sea Products and Food Company Limited*

Original in English

Excerpts of judgement in Doyles dispute resolution practice: Asia, Pacific in 1 volume. North Ryde, N.S.W.; CCH International, c1990-Tab 80-036, p.80, 661-80 and in: Yearbook Commercial Arbitration, (Deventer, Netherlands, Kluwer) vol. XVII, 1992, p. 289-303.

Commented on in: Doyles ADR update 5: 4-5, 28 February 1992, and by Pryles, World Arbitration and Mediation Report 2:12:329 (December 1991).

Summary published: Yearbook XVIII-1992, International Council for Commercial Arbitralion, 11.

Summarized and commented on by Kaplan, Spruce and Moser in Hong Kong and China Arbitration, Cases and

Materials, Bulterworths, 1994.

Exerpts published in [1992] 1 Hong Kong Reporls (HKLR), 40.

(Abstract prepared by the UNCITRAL Secretariat)

The plainliff, a Hong Kong company, asked the court to appoint a second arbitrator, relying on a contract with another Hong Kong company that contained an arbitration clause. The contract was for the sale of soybean extraction meal FOB Dalian; Dalian, which is in China, was stated to be the place of delivery. The defendant, asserting that there was no valid contract since the person who had signed had no authority to bind it, contended that an arbitrator had no jurisdiction to rule on whether or not a contract had been concluded. Even if an arbitration agreement existed, the arbitration would be domestic and thus have to be conducted by a sole arbitrator.

The court determined the arbitration to be international pursuant to article 1(3)(b)(ii) of the Model Law as enacted by the Hong Kong Arbitration (Amendment) (No. 2) Ordinance, 1989. It regarded delivery (which was to take place outside Hong Kong) as "a substantial part of the obligations of the commercial relationship", without ignoring that payment and nomination of the vessel (which were to take place in Hong Kong) were also important obligations in a contract of sale.

The court refused to deal with the question of whether a valid contract had been concluded since, according to article 16 MAL, it was first for the arbitral tribunal to decide on its jurisdiction. Recognizing the autonomy or separability of the arbitration clause except in the case of *ab initio* illegality of the contract (with references to English law), the court stated that the decision of the arbitral tribunal was neither final nor exclusive but subject to immediate review under article 16(3) MAL.

In making the appointment under article 11(5) MAL, the court deemed it important that when "appointing on behalf of the defaulting appointing party, it should go out of ts way to ensure that no sense of grievance is felt, however unreasonable that attitude might appear to others".

Indian Act—section 16. The ruling emphasises that under MAL article 16, initially the arbitrator decides whether there is a valid contract. This provision does not exist in India

Case 177: MAL 7 , 10

India: Supreme Court of India

18 November, 1996

MMTC v. *Sterlite Industries (India) Ltd.*

Published in English: Judgments Today [1996] 10 S.C. 390

(Abstract prepared by the UNCITRAL Secretariat)

The case concerned an arbitration clause contained in a contract entered into by the parties.

The clause provided for the appointment of one arbitrator by each party and an umpire to be jointly appointed by those arbitrators.

The appellant sought to rely on the arbitration clause after a dispute arose between the parties. After the respondent claimed that the arbitration clause could not be resorted to, and, therefore, refused to name an arbitrator, the appellant brought an action in the High Court. The High Court rejected the respondent's contention that the arbitration clause was invalid in light of section 10 of the new 1996 Arbitration and Conciliation Act (adapted from article 10 MAL). The aforementioned provision in the Act states that parties are free to determine the number of arbitrators, provided that such number shall not be an even number Special leave was given to appeal to the Supreme Court.

The Supreme Court held that the relevant provision to determine the validity of an arbitration agreement is section 7 of the 1996 Act (adapted from article 7 MAL), which contains the writing requirement. As there is no reference to the number of arbitrators within ihis provision, the Supreme Court concluded that the validity of an arbitration clause does not depend on the number of arbitrators specified therein. The arbitration clause was therefore held to be valid.

Indian Act—section 10, The ruling is important as highlighting the fact that it is this article (MAL) which gives the criterion.

Article 11. Appointment of arbitrators

(1) No person shall be precluded by reason of his nationality from acting as an arbitrator, unless otherwise agreed by the parties.

(2) The parties are free to agree on a procedure of appointing the arbitrator or arbitrators, subject to the provisions of paragraphs (4) and (5) of this article.

(3) Failing such agreement,

   (a) in an arbitration with three arbitrators, each party shall appoint one arbitrator, and the two arbitrators thus appointed shall appoint the third arbitrator; if a party fails to appoint the arbitrator within thirty days of receipt of a request to do so from the other party, or if the two arbitrators fail to agree on the third arbitrator within thirty days of their appointment, the appointment shall be made, upon request of a party, by the court or other authority specified in article 6;

   (b) in an arbitration with a sole arbitrator, if the parties are unable to agree on the arbitrator, he shall be appointed, upon request of a party, by the court or other authority specified in article 6.

(4) Where, under an appointment procedure agreed upon by the parties,

(a) a party fails to act as required under such procedure, or

(b) the parties, or two arbitrators, are unable to reach an agreement expected of them under such procedure, or

(c) a third party, including an institution, fails to perform any function entrusted to it under such procedure, any party may request the court or other authority specified in article 6 to take the necessary measure, unless the agreement on the appointment procedure provides other means for securing the appointment.

(5) A decision on a matter entrusted by paragraph (3) or (4) of this article to the court or other authority specified in article 6 shall be subject to no appeal. The court or other authority, in appointing an arbitrator, shall have due regard to any qualifications required of the arbitrator by the agreement of the parties and to such considerations as are likely to secure the appointment of an independent and impartial arbitrator and, in the *case* of a sole or third arbitrator, shall take into account as well the advisability of appointing an arbitrator of a nationality other than those of the parties.

Indian Act—section 11 differs materially in respect of the situations falling under article 11(4), 11(5) MAL (supra). Indian Act gives power to the Chief Justice. Also, article 11(5) MAL first sentence, is not adopted in India. Section 11 of the 1996 Act empowers the Chief Justice of the High Court concerned or any person or institution designated by him to appoint the arbitrator. Further in the case of International Commercial arbitration, it is the Chief Justice of India, or any person or institution designated by him, who is empowered to appoint the arbitrator. Sub-section (10) of Section 11 empowers the Chief Justice of India or the Chief Justice of the High Court, as the case may be, to make such scheme as he may deem appropriate for dealing with such appointments

Case 13: MAL Articles 1(2); 5; 16

Canada: Ontario District Court, York Judicial District (Mandel, J.)

27 October, 1989

Deco Automotive Inc. v. *G.P.A. Geselkchaft für Pressenautomation mbH*

Original in English

Where an arbitration occurs outside of Canada, pursuant to article 1(2), articles 5 and 16 will not apply.

CPA (a German corporation) entered into a contract with Mareda (a U.S.A. company) to design, manufacture, deliver and put into operation a transfer system. This contract contained references to general conditions (ECE 188), which contained a clause referring disputes to arbitration. The arbitration terms provided for reference of any dispute to the International Chamber of Commerce for resolution through the application of the arbitration conditions of the Economic Commission for Europe (ECE). Mareda assigned the contract to Deco, a Canadian company. Deco refused to pay following disputes with GPA and sued in court for damages. CPA moved to have the action stayed. The court dismissed the motion finding that the reference to arbitration in the ECE rules did not cover the areas in dispute between the parties. Furthermore, the court ruled that where the arbitration is in Canada, then the matter may proceed as set out in Article 16, but where it is not (as in the present case) then article 16 does not apply by virtue of article 1(2). Also based on article 1(2), article 5 of the Model Law restricting judicial intervention does not apply because the place of arbitration is not in Canada.

Indian Act—section 57

Case 20: MAL 1(3)(b)(ii); 3; 8; 10; 11; 16

Hong Kong: High Court of Hong Kong (Kaplan J.)

29 October, 1991

Fung Sang Trading Limited v. *Kai Sun Sea Products and Food Company Limited*

Original in English

Excerpts of judgement in Doyles dispute resolution practice: Asia, Pacific in 1 volume. North Ryde, N.S.W.: CCH International, c1990-Tab 80-036, p. 80, 661-80 and in: Yearbook Commercial Arbitration, (Deventer, Netherlands, Kluwer) vol. XVII, 1992, p. 289-303.

Commented on in: Doyles ADR update 5: 4-5, 28 February 1992, and by Pryles, World Arbitration and Mediation Report 2:12:329 (December 1991).

Summary published: Yearbook XVIII-1992, International Council for Commercial Arbitration, 11.

Summarized and commented on by Kaplan, Spruce and Moser in Hong Kong and China Arbilration, Cases and

Materials, Butterworths, 1994.

Excerpts published in [1992] Hong Kong Reports (HKLR), 40.

(Abstract prepared by the UNCITRAL Secretariat)

The plaintiff, a Hong Kong company, asked the court to appoint a second arbitrator, relying on a contract with another Hong Kong company that contained an arbitration clause. The contract was for the sale of soyabean extraction meal FOB Dalian; Dalian, which is in China, was stated to be the place of delivery. The defendant, asserting that there was no valid contract since the person who had signed had no authority to bind it, contended that an arbitrator had no jurisdiction to rule on whether or not a contract had been concluded. Even if an arbitration agreement existed, the arbitration would be domestic and thus have to be conducted by a sole arbitrator.

The court determined the arbitration to be international pursuant to article 1(3)(b)(ii) of ihe Model Law as enacted by the Hong Kong Arbitration (Amendment) (No.2) Ordinance, 1989. It regarded delivery (which was to take place outside Hong Kong) as "a substantial part of the obligations of the commercial relationship", without ignoring that payment and nomination of the vessel (which were to take place in Hong Kong) were also important obligations in a contract of sale.

The court refused to deal with the question of whether a valid contract had been concluded since, according to article 16 MAL, it was first for the arbitral tribunal to decide on its jurisdiction. Recognizing the autonomy or separability of the arbitration clause except in the case of *ab initio* illegality of the contract (with references to English law], the court stated that the decision of the arbitral tribunal was neither final nor exclusive but subject to immediate review under article 16(3) MAL.

In making the appointment under article 11(5} MAL, the court deemed it important that when "appointing on behalf of the defaulting appointing party, it should go out of its way to ensure that no sense of grievance is felt, however unreasonable that attitude might appear to others".

Indian Act—section 11(8)(b)

Case 40: MAL 7; 11(4)

Hong Kong: High Court of Hong Kong (Kaplan J.)

30 July, 1992

Pacific International Lines (PTE) Ltd. & Another v. *Tsinlien Metals and Minerals Co. Ltd.*

Published in English: 1992, Hong Kong Law Digest, G5; excerpts of judgement in The Arbitration and Dispute Resolution Law Journal, Part 4, December 1992, 240

Summarized and commented on by Kaplan, Spruce and Moser in Hong Kong and China Arbitration, Cases and Materials, Butterworths, 1994. (Abstract prepared by Kaplan J.)

The plaintiff, owner and manager of a vessel which was chartered to the defendant, sought payment of damages for breach of the charter-party with the defendant. When the defendant failed to pay, the plaintiff appointed an arbitrator pursuant to an arbitration clause contained in the charter-party. The defendant failed to appoint a second arbitrator and the plaintiff applied in accordance with article 11(4) MAL for the court to appoint a second arbitrator.

Although the charter-party was not signed by both parties, the court found that there was a charter-party between the plaintiff and the defendant, since there was no doubt from the facts and the pre-voyage communications that the defendant had chartered the vessel of the plaintiff and had paid also certain sums to the plaintiff in accordance with that charter-party. The court concluded that article 7 MAL requiring a written agreement to arbitrate had been complied with and gave the defendant seven days to appoint a second arbitrator, otherwise the court was to appoint him.

◆ ◆ ◆ ◆ ◆

Case 439 — MAL art. 11(4)

Germany: Brandenburgisches Oberlandesgericht; 8 SchH 1/00

26 June, 2000

Original in German

DIS-Online Database on Arbitration Law - *http://www.dis-arb.de*

Abstract prepared by Stefan Kröll and Katja Richter

The decision is about the appointment of an arbitrator by the state courts after the agreed appointment mechanism had failed.

The German and the Italian parties to a construction contract had concluded an arbitration agreement using the standard form of the German Association for Construction Law according to which the arbitration proceedings should be governed by the Arbitration Rules of the German Association for Construction. The rules provided that both parties should appoint one arbitrator who should then agree on the chairman. In case of a failure of agreement the chairman was to be appointed by the President of the "Landgericht" at the employer's place of business. The German party started arbitration proceedings and since the party-appointed arbitrators could not agree on a chairman, they applied to the Brandenburgische Oberlandesgericht (Higher Regional Court) for the appointment of the chairman.

The Court appointed the arbitrator holding that it had jurisdiction and was competent to do so since the parties had implicitly agreed on arbitration in Germany and the initial appointment procedure had failed. Though the parties had not explicitly agreed upon the place of arbitration, the court derived the parties' intent to arbitrate in Germany from the circumstances: (1) the parties had subjected the material issues of their contractual relationship to German law; (2) performance of the contract was due in Germany; (3) the language of the contract was German; (4) the terms of the contract were specified by the "German Standard Terms for Construction" (VoB) and the German Civil Code; and (5) the price was expressed in German currency. The Court found these facts indicative that the parties did not want a foreign arbitral tribunal, composed of foreign arbitrators unfamiliar with German law, to decide their disputes, particularly because they had submitted the arbitral proceedings to German arbitration rules and they had determined that a German Regional Court was competent for all decisions related to the arbitral proceedings.

The Court concluded that the failure of the appointment process originally agreed upon was due to the non-existence of a "Landgericht" (First Instance Court) at the Italian employer's place of business in Bari, and it was competent to appoint the chairman pursuant to Section 1035 (4) ZPO [adopted from article 11(4) MAL]. Contrary to the defendant's submissions, the president of the Court in Bari could not make the appointment. Although the parties were free to agree on a foreign person to decide about the constitution of the tribunal, there were no indications that they had done so. The standard arbitration contract was made for the use within German relationships. It referred to German procedural rules. It assumed that both parties to the arbitration agreement would have their place of business in Germany, and that state courts engaged with acts relating to the arbitration would also apply German law. Therefore, the standard contract could only mean a German person, when it referred to the "competent president of the *Landgericht*".

◆ ◆ ◆ ◆ ◆

Case 59: MAL 11(4)(a)

Hong Kong; High Court of Hong Kong (Leonard J.)

28 September, 1993

China Ocean Shipping Company v. *Mitrans Maritime Panama S.A.*

Original in English

Unpublished

(Abstract prepared by the UNCITRAL Secretariat)

The defendant failed to appoint an arbitrator and the plaintiff sought the appointment of an arbitrator by the court on behalf of the defendant pursuant to article 11(4)(a) MAL. One day before the hearing the defendant indicated its willingness to consent to the appointment of an arbitrator by the court, provided that each party would bear its share of the costs of the proceedings. The plaintiff, who had some difficulty in getting the matter before the court because of problems concerning service of documents, rejected the defendant's offer and asked the court to appoint an arbitrator and order that the defendant pay the costs of the proceedings.

The court found that the defendant had failed to honour its obligation under the arbitration agreement and appoint an arbitrator and that the defendant's conduct was such that it was proper that the plaintiff should be placed in a position in which it would have been if the defendant had honoured its obligation. The court ordered the defendant to pay the costs of the plaintiff occasioned by the application for the appointment of an arbitrator by the court on behalf of the defendant,

Indian Act—section 11. This ruling has great practical importance as it empowers the court to award costs

Case 62: MAL 7(2); 11

Hong Kong: High Court of Hong Kong (Kaplan J.)

2 February, 1994

Oonc Lines Limited v. *Sino-American Trade Advancement Co. Ltd.*

Original in English Unpublished

(Abstract prepared by the UNCITRAL Secretariat)

The plaintiff requested the court to appoint an arbitrator on behalf of the defendant pursuant to article 11 MAL. The defendant objected on the ground that article 7(2) MAL was not complied with since the defendant never signed the charterparty which contained in a rider the arbitration agreement invoked by the plaintiff. The court found that, although the charterparty was not signed by either party, a number of communications exchanged between the parties provided a sufficient record in writing of their agreement to arbitrate. The court appointed an arbitrator on behalf of the defendant.

Indian Act—section 7(2)

Case 101: MAL 1(3); 11(3)(a)

Hong Kong: High Court of Hong Kong (Leonard J.)

27 January, 1995

Private Company "Triple V" Inc. Ltd. v. *Star (Universal) Co. Ltd. and Sky Jade Enterprises Group Ltd.*

Original in English

Published in French: Revue de droit des affaires internationales, 1995, 8, 1008,

(Abstract prepared by the UNCITRAL Secretariat)

The plaintiff, a Russian company, bought from the defendants, two Hong Kong companies, a number of television sets and microwaves. Pursuant to the contract, delivery was to be made in Russia. The contract provided for arbitration in Hong Kong. The plaintiff alleged that the television sets were not delivered at all and the microwaves delivered were defective. The parties failed to agree on a procedure for appointing the arbitrator and the plaintiff requested the court to make the appointment pursuant to article 11(3)(a) MAL. The second defendant argued that it was not part to the contract.

The court found that an international arbitration, as defined in article 1(3] MAL, was involved and that there was *prima facie* evidence of a dispute between the parties, and appointed a sole arbitrator. As to the second defendant, who in fact had not signed the contract, the court found that it was represented by the first defendant and ruled that, in any event, it was at the discretion of the second defendant to challenge the jurisdiction of the arbitrator in accordance with article 16(1) and (3).

◆ ◆ ◆ ◆ ◆

Case 438 — MAL art. 11(3)

Germany: Bayerisches Oberstes Landesgericht; 4Z SchH 1/99

4 June 1999

Original in German

Published in German: Betriebs-Berater 1999, pp.1785 - (headnote and reasons); BayObLGR 1999, p. 72 (headnote) DIS-Online Database on Arbitration Law - *http://www.dis-arb.de*

Abstract prepared by Stefan Kröll

The decision concerns the application for the appointment of an arbitrator by the court.

The claimant had initiated arbitration proceedings against the defendant before the Bavarian Commodities Trading Association (Bayerische Warenbörse) in Munich. The amount claimed was based on four different contracts, only one of which contained a clause providing for "arbitration in Munich". Since the parties were in dispute about the meaning of this arbitration clause and the existence of arbitration clauses for the other contracts they could not agree on an arbitrator. As a result the claimant applied to the court for the appointment of a sole arbitrator.

The Court refused to make the appointment since, in its view, no valid arbitration agreement existed. While the claimant wanted arbitration before a sole arbitrator to be carried out at the seat of the Bavarian Commodities Trading Association, the respondent always intended that the arbitration be conducted under the rules of the Bavarian Commodities Trading Association, which, *inter alia,* provided for a special appeal procedure.

The Court found that the lack of agreement on such an essential issue as the rules to be followed made all arbitration agreements concluded invalid.

◆ ◆ ◆ ◆ ◆

Indian Act—sections 8-16. The case is noteworthy for its extended interpretation of article 8, MAL and reliance on article 16

Case 109: MAL 11(3)(a); 11(5)

Hong Kong: Court of Appeal (Litton, V.P., Liu, J.A and Keith, J.)

7 July, 1995

Private Company "Triple V" Inc. v. *Star (Universal) Co. Ltd. and Sky Jade Enterprises Group Ltd.*

Original in English

Unpublished

(Abstract prepared by the Secretariat)

This case involves an appeal against the decision on Case 101, in which the court had appointed a sole arbitrator pursuant to article 11(3)(a) MAL.

Private Company argued that the Court of Appeal did not have jurisdiction to hear the appeal since the decision of the first instance court dealt with a matter falling within the scope of article 11(3) and, accordingly, was not subject to an appeal (11(5) MAL). The Court of Appeal dismissed that argument holding that article 11(3) applied to cases where the failure to agree on the appointment of an arbitrator was due to the parties failing to agree on a procedure for the appointment of an arbitrator and not on whether there should be an arbitration at all or on whether the arbitration should involve a particular party, as in the present case.

Star argued that the court of first instance had erred since there was no contract between Private Company and Star to arbitrate, in view of the fact that their first contract had been rescinded and their second contract was invalid. The Court of Appeal held that the court of first instance could not examine these arguments in detail without interfering with the jurisdiction of the arbitrator and was correct in forming a prima facie view as to whether there was an agreement to arbitrate, namely that there was no "overwhelming" evidence "that an agreement to arbitrate has been abrogated".

Sky argued that there was no evidence whatsoever that il was a party to the contract between Private Company and Star. The Court of Appeal noted that the first instance court had found that Star had signed the contract both for itself and as agent of Sky; and that there was some evidence that Sky was to be the party to "render performance" under the contract, although the evidence as to agency was found to be extremely weak. On this issue too, the Court of Appeal confirmed the decision of the first instance court holding that it was not for the court to examine the substance of the dispute but for the arbitrator.

Indian Act—section 8. This ruling shows the liberal interpretation placed on Article 8, MAL, by the courts elsewhere

Case 110: MAL 11(3)(b)

Singapore: Chairman, Singapore International Arbitration Centre (SIAC) (Tan Boon Teik, SC)

4 October, 1995

SIAC arb. no. 21 of 1995

Original in English

Unpublished

Disputes arose between the parties to a contract to build and operate a chain of hotels in Indonesia, which contained an arbitration clause. The claimant's notice of arbitration named as respondents a party which had signed the contract and four other parties which had not signed it but had participated in negotiations with the claimant regarding the terms of the contract. The claimant applied to SIAC for appointment of an arbitrator under article 11(3)(b) MAL. The claimant argued that all five respondents named in the notice of arbitration were parties to the contract in that they were all companies within the same group and were inextricably involved in the venture as "affiliates", negotiations regarding the terms of the contract having been undertaken involving all of them. The claimant further argued that all the respondents had to do at that stage was to present an arguable case.

The court held that the issue of joinder of parties was well within the jurisdiction and competence of the arbitrator under article 16 MAL; and that, while all that the claimant had to do was to present an arguable case that all five companies were parties to the contract, the claimant failed to do so. An appointment was made only for an arbitration between the claimant and the respondent who had signed the contract.

Indian Act—section 2(1)(f). The above ruling is of interest, as interpreting the word "commercial".

Article 12. Grounds for challenge

(1) When a person is approached in connection with his possible appointment as an arbitrator, he shall disclose any circumstances likely to give rise to justifiable doubts as to his impartiality or independence. An arbitrator, from the time of his appointment and throughout the arbitral proceedings, shall without delay disclose any such circumstances to the parties unless they have already been informed of them by him.

(2) An arbitrator may be challenged only if circumstances exist that give rise to justifiable doubts as to his impartiality or independence, or if he does not possess qualifications agreed to by the parties, A party may challenge an arbitrator appointed by him, or in whose appointment he has participated, only for reasons of which he becomes aware after the appointment has been made.

Indian Act—section 12(1). In India the disclosure under sub-section (1) must be in writing

Article 13. Challenge procedure

(1) The parties are free to agree on a procedure for challenging an arbitrator, subject to the provisions of paragraph (3) of this article.

(2) Failing such agreement, a party who intends to challenge an arbitrator shall, within fifteen days after becoming aware of the constitution of the arbitral tribunal or after

becoming aware of any circumstance referred to in article 12(2), send a written statement of the reasons for the challenge to the arbitral tribunal. Unless the challenged arbitrator withdraws from his office or the other party agrees to the challenge, the arbitral tribunal shall decide on the challenge.

(3) If a challenge under any procedure agreed upon by the parties or under the procedure of paragraph (2) of this article is not successful, the challenging party may request, within thirty days after having received notice of the decision rejecting the challenge, the court or other authority specified in article 6 to decide on the challenge, which decision shall be subject to no appeal; while such a request is pending, the arbitral tribunal, including the challenged arbitrator, may continue the arbitral proceedings and make an award.

◆ ◆ ◆ ◆ ◆

Case 442 — MAL arts. 13(1); 13(3)

Germany: Oberlandesgericht Köln; 9 Sch 30/00

14 September, 2000

Original in German

DIS-Online Database on Arbitration Law - *http://www.dis-arb.de*

Abstract prepared by Stefan Kröll and Roman Mallmann

The issue in this case concerned time limitations to challenges of arbitrators.

The arbitration proceedings were started in April 1998 and were submitted to the arbitration rules for construction and erection of plants. Oral hearings were held on 7 July 1999 and 18 November 1999. The chairman of the arbitral tribunal informed the claimant on 31 March 2000 that she had taken over a case from a partner leaving her law firm, which involved the filing of a claim against the claimant by another client. One other arbitrator was counsel in another case against the claimant which was pending at the Higher Regional Court even before the arbitration started. After its request of 8 May 2000 to replace both arbitrators had been rejected by the defendant, on 20 June 2000, the claimant initiated challenge proceedings with the Regional Court (Landgericht). The Regional Court held itself not competent to decide and transferred the case to the Higher Regional Court.

The Higher Regional Court, which is competent to resolve challenges to arbitrators pursuant to Section 1062 (1) 1 of the German Civil Procedure Code, held that the claimant's application was filed with undue delay, and consequently in violation of the arbitration rules. The applicable arbitration rules require that the request for challenging an arbitrator must be filed with the court within fourteen days after the opponent refuses to agree to the challenge. The Court did not need to decide on that point as the claimant failed to comply with a second provision of the arbitration rules, which requires that the claimant file its request for challenge "without undue delay" after he became aware of the event giving rise to his complaint. Therefore, the Court dismissed the complaint on procedural grounds without reaching the merits of the case regarding whether justifiable doubts against the impartiality of the arbitrators were given or not.

◆ ◆ ◆ ◆ ◆

Indian Act—section 13 is materially different, as it does not permit the aggrieved party to appeal to the court at that stage. He must wait till the award

Article 14. Failure or impossibility to act

(1) If an arbitrator becomes *de jure* or *de facto* unable to perform his functions or for other reasons fails to act without undue delay, his mandate terminates if he

withdraws from his office or if the parties agree on the termination. Otherwise, if a controversy remains concerning any of these grounds, any party may request the court or other authority specified in article 6 to decide on the termination of the mandate, which decision shall be subject to no appeal.

(2) If, under this article or article 13(2), an arbitrator withdraws from his office or a party agrees to the termination of the mandate of an arbitrator, this does not imply acceptance of the validity of any ground referred to in this article or article 12(21.

Indian Act—section 14

Article 15. Appointment of substitute arbitrator

Where the mandate of an arbitrator terminates under articles 13 or 14 or because of his withdrawal from office for any other reason or because of the revocation of his mandate by agreement of the parties or in any other case of termination of his mandate, a substitute arbitrator shall be appointed according to the rules that were applicable to the appointment of the arbitrator being replaced.

Indian Act—section 15

CHAPTER IV

JURISDICTION OF ARBITRAL TRIBUNAL

Article 16. Competence of arbitral tribunal to rule on its jurisdiction

(1) The arbitral tribunal may rule on its own jurisdiction, including any objections with respect to the existence or validity of the arbitration agreement. For that purpose, an arbitration clause which forms part of a contract shall be treated as an agreement independent of the other terms of the contract. A decision by the arbitral tribunal that the contract is *null and void* shall not entail *ipso jure* the invalidity of the arbitration clause.

(2) A plea that the arbitral tribunal does not have jurisdiction shall be raised not later than the submission of the statement of defence. A party is not precluded from raising such a plea by the fact that he has appointed, or participated in the appointment of an arbitrator. A plea that the arbitral tribunal is exceeding the scope of its authority shall be raised as soon as the matter alleged to be beyond the scope of its authority is raised during the arbitral proceedings. The arbitral tribunal may, in either case, admit a later plea if it considers the delay justified.

(3) The arbitral tribunal may rule on a plea referred to in paragraph (2) of this article either as a preliminary question or in an award on the merits. If the arbitral tribunal rules as a preliminary question that it has jurisdiction, any party may request, within thirty days after having received notice of that ruling, the court specified in article 6 to decide the matter, which decision shall be subject to no appeal; while such a request is pending, the arbitral tribunal may continue the arbitral proceedings and make an award.

Indian Act—section 16 does not permit immediate appeal to the court, unlike article 16(3) MAL. The party must wait till the award

Case 13: MAL Articles 1(2); 5; 16

Canada; Ontario District Court, York Judicial District (Mandel, J.)

27 October, 1989

Deco Automotive Inc. v. *G.P.A. Gesellschaft für Pressenautomation mbH*

Original in English

Where an arbitration occurs outside of Canada, pursuant to article 1(2), articles 5 and 16 will not apply. GPA (a German corporation) entered into a contract with Mareda a U.S.A. company) to design, manufacture, deliver and put into operation a transfer system. This contract contained references to general conditions (ECE 188), which contained a clause referring disputes to arbitration. The arbitration terms provided for reference of any dispute to the International Chamber of Commerce for resolution through the application of the arbitration conditions of the Economic Commission for Europe (ECE). Mareda assigned the contract to Deco, a Canadian company. Deco refused to pay following disputes with GPA and sued in court for damages. GPA moved to have the action stayed. The court dismissed the motion finding that the reference to arbitration in the ECE rules did not cover the areas in dispute between the parties. Furthermore, the court ruled that where the arbitration is in Canada, then the matter may proceed as set out in Article 16, but where it is not (as in the present case) then article 16 does not apply by virtue of article 1(2). Also based on article 1(2), article 5 of the Model Law restricting judicial intervention does not apply because the place of arbitration is not in Canada.

Indian Act—sections 16 and 2(2)

Case 18: MAL 5; 8; 16

Canada; Ontario Court of Justice - General Division (Henry J.)

1 March, 1991

Rio Algom Limited v. *Sammi Steel Co.*

Original in English

The interaction of articles 8 and 16 restricts the court's role in arbitrations to determining whether the arbitration clause is null and void. Any determination of the arbitrator's jurisdiction is made by the arbitrator pursuant to article 16.

The parties agreed that Sammi would purchase Rio's steel manufacturing business in Ontario, Quebec and New York State. The agreement provided that the parties each prepare a Closing Date Balance Sheet as soon as possible after closing. Arbitration was provided for if the parties could not resolve any dispute arising out of the Closing Date Balance Sheets. Such a dispute did arise. Sammi followed the required procedure and submitted the matter to an arbitrator. Rio commenced an action in court challenging the jurisdiction of the arbitrator and seeking an order staying the arbitration proceedings. The Chambers judge granted the order finding that the arbitrator's jurisdiction is a threshold issue of contract construction lo be decided by the court. Leave to appeal the Chambers judge's order was sought.

The court granted leave to appeal. It found that the Chambers judge's decision had been erroneously based on principles of the domestic arbitration act rather than those found in the Model Law as enacted by the International Commercial Arbitration Act, Statutes of Ontario, 1988, c.30. In particular the court cited article 16 which provides the arbitral tribunal with the power to rule on its own jurisdiction. The court further noted article 8 which restricts court involvement to a determination of whether the arbitration agreement is *null and void*.

Indian Act—sections 8 and 16

Case 20: MAL 1(3)(b)(ii); 3; 8; 10; 11; 16

Hong Kong; High Court of Hong Kong (Kaplan J.)

29 October, 1991

Fung Sang Trading Limited v. *Kai Sun Sea Products and Food Company Limited*

Original in English

Excerpts of judgement in Doyles dispute resolution practice: Asia, Pacific in 1 volume. North Ryde, N.S.W.: CCH International, c1990-Tab 80-036, p.BO, 661-80 and in: Yearbook Commercial Arbitration, (Deventer, Netherlands, Kluwer) vol. XVII, 1992, p. 289-303.

Commented on in: Doyles ADR update 5: 4-5, 28 February 1992, and by Pryles, World Arbitration and Mediation Report 2:12:329 (December 1991).

Summary published: Yearbook XVIII-1992, International Council for Commercial Arbitration, 11.

Summarized and commented on by Kaplan, Spruce and Moser in Hong Kong and China Arbitration, Cases and Material, Butterworths, 1994.

Excerpts published in [1992] 1 Hong Kong reports (HKLR), 40.

(Abstract prepared by the Secretariat)

The plaintiff, a Hong Kong company, asked the court to appoint a second arbitrator, relying on a contract with another Hong Kong company that contained an arbitration clause. The contract was for the sale of soybean extraction meal FOB Dalian; Dalian, which is in China, was stated to be the place of delivery. The defendant, asserting that there was no valid contract since the person who had signed had no authority to bind it, contended that an arbitrator had no jurisdiction to rule on whether or not a contract had been concluded. Even if an arbitration agreement existed, the arbitration would be domestic and thus have to be conducted by a sole arbitrator.

The court determined the arbitration to be international pursuant to article 1(3)(b)(ii) of the Model Law as enacted by the Hong Kong Arbitration (Amendment) (No. 2) Ordinance, 1989. It regarded delivery (which was to take place outside Hong Kong) as "a substantial part of the obligations of the commercial relationship", without ignoring that payment and nomination of the vessel (which were to lake place in Hong Kong) were also important obligations in a contract of sale.

The court refused to deal with the question of whether a valid contract had been concluded since, according to article 16 MAL, it was first for the arbitral tribunal to decide on its jurisdiction. Recognizing the autonomy or separability of the arbitration clause except in the case of *ab initio* illegality of the contract (with references to English law), the court stated that the decision of the arbitral tribunal was neither final nor exclusive but subject to immediate review under article 16(3) MAL.

In making the appointment under article 11(5) MAL, the court deemed it important that when "appointing on behalf of the defaulting appointing party, it should go out of its way to ensure that no sense of grievance is felt, however unreasonable that attitude might appear to others".

Indian Act—section 11(8)(b)

Case 27: MAL 16(1)

Argentina: Cámara Nacional de Apelaciones en lo Commercial - Sala

26 September, 1988; judgement hot final

"Enrique C. Wellbers S.A.I.C, A.G. v. Extraktionstechnik Gesellschaft fiir Anlagenbau M.B.M.: S/ Ordinario"

Excerpts published in Spanish: La Ley, 1989-E-302, BuenosAires

In accordance with an arbitration clause contained in a contract of sale FOB port of Hamburg, one of the parties to the contract brought an action before the courts of Argentina for the constitution of the arbitral tribunal. The respondent raised a plea that the arbitral tribunal did not have jurisdiction. It was argued that the courts in Hamburg, the place of performance of the contract, had international jurisdiction over the subject-matter of the contract, and, since the arbitration clause was accessory to the contract of which it forms part, the arbitration clause should follow the fate of the contract.

The court of first instance rejected the plea of lack of jurisdiction. The court of appeals affirmed that the arbitration clause was autonomous, and therefore its validity did not depend on the validity of the contract, on the applicable law or on the court with international jurisdiction to resolve any dispute. The principle of the autonomy of such a clause is internationally accepted and, as such, incorporated in MAL (Article16(I). Although MAL has not been adopted in Argentina, it reflects generally accepted principles in the matter and can be taken into account to make up for the absence of a specific national norm.

◆ ◆ ◆ ◆ ◆

Case 114: MAL 8(1) and 16(1)

Canada: British Columbia Supreme Court (Lysyk J.)

18 November, 1994

Globe Union Industrial Corp. v. *G.A.P. Marketing Corp.*

Published in English: [1995] 2 Western Weekly Reports, 696

Globe was a Taiwanese manufacturer who entered into a distribution agreement with GAP. granting it a licence to distribute Globe's products in Canada and Mexico. G.A.P. initiated arbitration proceedings under an arbitration clause in the agreement and Globe then commenced the present court proceedings, which G.A.P. sought to stay under s. 8 of the International Commercial Arbitration Act, Statutes of British Columbia, 1986, Chapter 14, which enacts MAL.

The court found that, even if the distribution agreement had been terminated between the parties and was assumed to be *null and void*, it did not mean that the arbitration clause it contained was unenforceable (articles 8(1) and 16(1) MAL). The court also found that the court proceedings were in respect of a matter agreed by the parties to be submitted to arbitration and the fact that G.A.P. responded to Globe's application to enjoin G.A.P. from proceeding with the arbitration did not constitute the taking of a step in the court proceedings so as to justify refusal of a stay.

Indian Act—sections 7, 8 and 16, The ruling is of importance as laying down the law as to subsistence of the clause relating to arbitration

Case 127: MAL 16

The Supreme Court of Bermuda (Meerabux J.)

Skandia International Insurance Company and Mercantile & General Reinsurance Company and various others

21 January 1994

Original in English

Unpublished

(Abstract prepared by Jeffrey Elkinson)

This case concerns proceedings initiated in the Supreme Court of Bermuda by Skandia International Insurance Company and other insurance companies ("Skandia and others") for an injunction to restrain Al Amana Insurance and Reinsurance Company Limited ("Al Amana") from continuing legal proceedings against Skandia and others in Kuwait. Skandia and others were reinsurers of Al Amana, a company incorporated under the laws of Bermuda, in respect of real and personal property located in Kuwait and belonging to Alghanim Industries ("Alghanim") and its associated companies. Alghanim sustained extensive property damage in Kuwait during and consequential to the invasion of Kuwait by Iraq in August 1990. Disputes arose as to whether the losses sustained by Alghanim were excluded by virtue of a War Risks Exclusion Clause contained in the reinsurance agreements between Al Amana and Skandia and others.

Al Amana was sued by Alghanim in Kuwait and joined Skandia and others as third parties. Skandia and others argued that the Kuwaiti court had no jurisdiction over them as there were arbitration provisions in the reinsurance agreements with Al Amana. In the meantime, Skandia and others served notices of arbitration on Al Amana and initiated the proceedings in the Supreme Court of Bermuda for an injunction to restrain Al Amana from continuing legal proceedings against them in Kuwait on the ground that there existed an agreement to have their disputes determined by arbitration "at the seat of the defendant party" (*i.e.*, Bermuda).

Al Amana challenged, *inter alia*, the existence of an arbitration clause in one of the reinsurance agreements. Al Amana argued that article *7(2)* MAL requires that, for incorporating an arbitration clause by reference into another document, the reference has to be "such as to make that clause part of the contract," Al Amana submitted that a reference to insurance coverage "as per wording attached" simply incorporated the description of the risks in respect of which reinsurance was effected, but could not incorporate the entirety of the policy and was inadequate to incorporate the arbitration clause contained in another document.

The Supreme Court held that there was *prima facie* evidence that the arbitration agreement existed and satisfied the requirements of article 7(1) MAL and Article 11(2) of the Convention on the Recognition and Enforcement of Foreign Arbitral Awards (New York, 1958). The Supreme Court held, under reference to the travaux préparatoires of the MAL, that the contractual documents do not need to make an explicit reference to the arbitration clause and that general words of incorporation suffice under article 7 MAL. The Supreme Court pointed out, however, that, in any event, a challenge to the existence, validity and scope of the arbitration agreement was a matter to be first determined by the arbitral tribunal under article 16(3) MAL. Accordingly, the Supreme Court granted the injunction restraining Al Amana from continuing with the proceedings brought by it against Skandia and others in Kuwait.

◆ ◆ ◆ ◆ ◆

Case 147; MAL 7(2), 16(1)(3)

Russian Federation: Moscow City Court

13 December, 1994

Original in Russian

Unpublished

The plaintiff appealed to the court on the grounds that the arbitral tribunal had found that as no arbitration agreement existed between the parties, the tribunal had no competence to examine the dispute that had arisen between them.

The court confirmed the right of the arbitral tribunal under article 16(1) MAL to rule on its own jurisdiction. The court found that the question of whether or not a written agreement existed between the parties regarding the procedure for examining disputes had been thoroughly investigated by the arbitral tribunal. The arbitral tribunal had found that at the time of conclusion of the contract, which gave rise to the dispute and which contained an arbitration clause, the person signing the contract on behalf of the defendant did not possess the necessary powers to do so. On these grounds, the court upheld the ruling of the arbitral tribunal, namely that no arbitration agreement existed in writing between the plaintiff and the defendant.

Indian Act—sections 7 and 16

Case 148; MAL 16(2)(3), 34(2)

Russian Federation: Moscow City Court

Decision on the application to set aside the award made by the Court of International Commercial Arbitration at the Russian Federation Chamber of Commerce and Industry in case

No. 214/1993

10 February, 1995

Original in Russian

Unpublished

The plaintiff filed an application to set aside an arbitral award made against it, citing as grounds for doing so the fact that as no arbitration agreement existed between the plaintiff and the defendant, the arbitral tribunal had no jurisdiction to examine the dispute in question. The plaintiff argued that the party signing the contract with the defendant had gone into liquidation as a commercial entity and that the plaintiff was not its legal successor and, hence, not a party to the contract concluded with the defendant which contained the respective arbitration clause. In addition, the plaintiff argued that the contract included an arbitration clause providing for the examination of disputes by the Tribunal of Arbitration at the USSR Chamber of Commerce and Industry, whereas the claim had been brought before the Tribunal of International Commercial Arbitration at the Russian Federation Chamber of Commerce and Industry (TICA), which was not competent to examine the dispute in question.

The court noted that article 16(2) and (3) of the Act of the Russian Federation on "international commercial arbitration" (art. 16 MAL) provided that a plea on the grounds that an arbitral tribunal did not have jurisdiction should be raised not later than the submission of the statement of defence. The court held that the plaintiff (respondent in the arbitral proceedings) had presented to the arbitral tribunal its defence against the claim in which it had stated that it was not the legal successor to the party to the contract which had given rise to the claim and could not be a defendant in the action in question. However, the plaintiff made no reference to the lack of jurisdiction of the arbitral tribunal either in its statement of defence or in the subsequent correspondence with the arbitral tribunal, and had not raised any plea regarding the jurisdiction of the arbitral tribunal during the hearing of the case. The court did not concur with the plaintiff's position that its submission in its statement of defence before the arbitral tribunal that it was not the legal successor and did not recognize itself as a party to the contract should be considered an objection to the jurisdiction of the arbitral tribunal. The court found that those references related exclusively to legal succession in respect of disputed legal relationships and to the validity of claims brought by the plaintiff.

The court did not concur with the plaintiff regarding the lack of jurisdiction of the TICA to examine the dispute in question. In that regard, the court noted that under paragraph 4 of the Statutes on the TICA, which was an annex to the Act of the Russian Federation on "international commercial arbitration", the TICA was the successor to the Tribunal of Arbitration at the USSR Chamber of Commerce and Industry and, in particular, was entitled to settle disputes on the basis of agreement by the parties to refer their disputes to the Tribunal of Arbitration at the USSR Chamber of Commerce and Industry.

The court dismissed the plaintiff's application to set aside the arbitral award.

◆ ◆ ◆ ◆ ◆

Case 441 — MAL arts. 16(3); 31

Germany: Oberlandesgericht Köln; 9 Sch 6/00

20 July, 2000

Original in German

DIS-Online Database on Arbitration Law - *http://www.dis-arb.de*

Abstract prepared by Stefan Kröll

The decision concerned a motion for the setting aside of a preliminary decision by the arbitral tribunal on its jurisdiction, dealing with the question of when a decision by the arbitral tribunal qualifies as an interim decision according to § 1040 (3) of the German Code of Civil Procedure (ZPO) [adopted from article 16(3) MAL].

In the arbitration proceedings between the parties, the claimant requested the tribunal to declare that it did not have jurisdiction in the matter because of the lack of a valid arbitration agreement. On 21 December, 1999, the arbitral tribunal delivered an order without reasons, declaring that the "application of Applicant was rejected." In a further order, delivered on 1 February 2000, the arbitral tribunal corrected the first order and stated that it "rejected the application of Applicant to decide the issue of jurisdiction by way of an intermediate decision according to § 1040 para. 3 ZPO" and that "The arbitral tribunal will decide on its jurisdiction in the final award." Claimant moved to have this order set aside.

The Court dismissed the motion and held that the decisions of the arbitral tribunal could not be made subject to separate judicial review. The first order could not be an award according to § 1054 ZPO [adopted from article 31 MAL] because it did not comply with the formal requirements (reasons) for an award. Nor was it an interim decision according to § 1040(3) 3 ZPO because the arbitral tribunal had not intended to make a decision regarding its jurisdiction, but merely rejected the procedural application to decide on its jurisdiction by way of an interim decision. This interpretation is confirmed by the second order. A decision on the jurisdiction will only be made in the final award, and may only be reviewed by a court in a motion for setting aside or a motion for recognition and enforcement of the award.

The decision of the Court did not require an oral hearing in terms of § 1063(2) ZPO. The decision did not concern the formal setting-aside procedure according to § 1059 ZPO [article 34 MAL], but referred to an award of the arbitral tribunal that did not become binding on the parties.

Indian Act—Sections 16 and 34(2)

Case 182: MAL 5; 16; 34

Canada: Superior Court of Quebec (Tellier J.)

9 September, 1994

International Civil Aviation Organization (ICAO) v. *Tripal Systems Pvt. Ltd.*

Original in French

Published in French: Recueil de jurisprudence du Québec [1994] 2560

In February 1990, ICAO entered into a contract with Tripal for the conception, construction and installation of an airport in Hanoi, Vietnam. The contract included an arbitration clause as well as a clause that preserved any immunity that might accrue to ICAO. Following the commencement of arbitral proceedings to resolve a dispute between the parties, ICAO raised its immunity to contest the arbitral tribunal's competence.

Considering that the issue was one of mixed fact and law, the arbitral tribunal, in order to rule on the objection, decided to hear all evidence. ICAO then asked the Superior Court of Quebec to declare that it enjoyed an absolute immunity from judicial process of any kind. Tripal responded with its own motion for dismissal on the grounds that only the arbitral tribunal was competent at that stage of the proceedings.

The Superior Court granted the motion for dismissal of the declaratory motion, having decided that the arbitral tribunal alone was competent to decide the immunity issue. To this end, the Superior Court examined the conditions regulating judiciary intervention in the arbitral process (articles 16 and 34 MAL) and concluded that these were not met. The Superior Court refused to intervene on the basis of article 5 MAL. However, it noted that once the arbitral tribunal had declared itself competent, the Superior Court would be competent to review this decision in accordance with article 16(3) MAL, should a party so request.

Indian Act—sections 5, 8 and 16. As to immunity, see section 86, Code of Civil Procedure, 1908

Article 17. Power of arbitral tribunal to order interim measures

Unless otherwise agreed by the parties, the arbitral tribunal may, at the request of a party, order any party to take such interim measure of protection as the arbitral tribunal may consider necessary in respect of the subject-matter of the dispute. The arbitral tribunal may require any party to provide appropriate security in connection with such measure.

Indian Act—section 17

CHAPTER V

CONDUCT OF ARBITRAL PROCEEDINGS

Article 18. Equal treatment of parties

The parties shall be treated with equality and each party shall be given a full opportunity of presenting his case.

Indian Act—section 18

MAL 146: 18, 34(2)

Russian Federation: Moscow City Court

10 November, 1994

Original in Russian

Unpublished

The plaintiff, whose claim in arbitration proceedings had been dismissed, filed an application to have the award set aside on the grounds that in the course of the arbitration proceedings article 18 of the Russian Federation Act on "international commercial arbitration" (corresponding to art. 18 MAL) had been violated in that the parties had not been treated with equality and the award was in conflict with public policy.

The plaintiff argued that the decision to dismiss ihe claim had been made despite the fact that the defendant partially acknowledged the claim brought against it. In that regard, the court held that such acknowledgement did not constitute grounds for setting aside the award since, in making the award, the arbitrators were not bound by an acknowledgement of the claim.

Since the plaintiff failed to establish that the award was in conflict with public policy, its claim in that respect was found to be unjustified. At the same time, the court noted that a procedural infringement in the arbitral proceedings had no relevance to the notion of "public policy". On the basis of the facts presented, the court dismissed Ihe plaintiff's application to set aside the arbitral award.

Article 19. Determination of rules of procedure

(1) Subject to the provisions of this Law, the parties are free to agree on the procedure to be followed by the arbitral tribunal in conducting the proceedings.

(2) Failing such agreement, the arbitral tribunal may, subject to the provisions of this Law, conduct the arbitration in such manner as it considers appropriate. The power conferred upon the arbitral tribunal includes the power to determine the admissibility, relevance, materiality and weight of any evidence.

Indian Act—section 19. The Indian Act adds a provision that the arbitrator is not bound by the Evidence Act or the Code of Civil Procedure

Article 20. Place of arbitration

(1) The parties are free to agree on the place of arbitration. Failing such agreement, the place of arbitration shall be determined by the arbitral tribunal having regard to the circumstances of the case, including the convenience of the parties.

(2) Notwithstanding the provisions of paragraph (1) of this article, the arbitral tribunal may, unless otherwise agreed by the parties, meet at any place it considers appropriate for consultation among its members, for hearing witnesses, experts or the parties, or for inspection of goods, other property or documents.

Indian Act—section 20

Article 21. Commencement of arbitral proceedings

Unless otherwise agreed by the parties, the arbitral proceedings in respect of a particular dispute commence on the date on which a request for that dispute to be referred to arbitration is received by the respondent.

Article 22. Language

(1) The parties are free to agree on the language or languages to be used in the arbitral proceedings. Failing such agreement, the arbitral tribunal shall determine the language or languages to be used in the proceedings. This agreement or determination, unless otherwise specified therein, shall apply to any written statement by a party, any hearing and any award, decision or other communication by the arbitral tribunal.

(2) The arbitral tribunal may order that any documentary evidence shall be accompanied by a translation into the language or languages agreed upon by the parties or determined by the arbitral tribunal.

Indian Act—section 22

Article 23. Statements of claim and defence

(1) Within the period of time agreed by the parties or determined by the arbitral tribunal, the claimant shall state the facts supporting his claim, the points at issue and the relief or remedy sought, and the respondent shall state his defence in respect of these particulars, unless the parties have otherwise agreed as to the required elements of such statements. The parties may submit with their statements all documents they consider to be relevant or may add *a* reference to the documents or other evidence they will submit.

(2) Unless otherwise agreed by the parties, either party may amend or supplement his claim or defence during the course of the arbitral proceedings, unless the arbitral

tribunal considers it inappropriate to allow such amendment having regard to the delay in making it.

Indian Act—section 23

Case 16: MAL 1; 5; 23(1); 34, especially 34(2)(a)(iii)

Canada: British Columbia Court of Appeal (Hutcheon, Proudfoot and Giggs, JJ.A.)

24 October, 1990

Quintette Coal Limited v. *Nippon Steel Corp. et al.*

Published in English and French: Canada Supreme Court Reports 1990 volume 2

"Published in English: 1 Western Weekly Reports, 1991, 219".

Commented on by Telley in [1993] Lloyd's Maritime and Commercial Law Qarlerly, 238.

Commented on by Paterson in Williamette Law Review, Vol. 27,573.

The appropriate standard of review of arbitral awards is one which preserves the autonomy of the forum chosen by the parties and minimizes judicial intervention. Quintette, a Canadian company, agreed to supply coal to the respondent, a Japanese company. Their agreement provided that any contract disputes would be submitted to binding arbitration under British Columbia Law. Accordingly, a dispute concerning the interpretation of a contract clause outlining a pricing mechanism was referred to arbitration and an award rendered. Quintette, relying on sections 5 and 34 of the Model Law as enacted by the International Commercial Arbitration Act, Statutes of British Columbia, 1986, c. 14 sought to set aside the award on the grounds that the arbitrators had exceeded their jurisdiction by dealing with a matter not contemplated by or falling within the scope of the submission to arbitration. The Court of Appeal upheld the lower court's affirmation of the award. The Court noted the world-wide trend toward restricting the scope of judicial intervention into commercial arbitration. The award could be justified under the terms of the contract so the Court was prevented from intervening under article 34(2)(a)(iv) of the British Columbia Act (which is the same as article 34(2)(a)(iii) of the Model Law).

(The Supreme Court of Canada denied leave to appeal from the British Columbia Court of Appeal judgment on 13 December, 1990.)

Indian Act—section 34. The above case is of importance as illustrating the liberal approach towards awards

Case 118: MAL 8(1); 23(1)

Canada: Ontario Court of Justice, General Division (Borins J,)

21 December, 1994

Bab Systems, Inc. v. *McLurg*

Original in English

Unpublished

The plaintiff, one of the parties to a franchise agreement, applied to the court seeking judicial relief. Within hours of the court granting certain provisional relief in respect of the application, and adjourning for further particulars, the plaintiff advised the defendant of its intention to submit the dispute to arbitration pursuant to an arbitration clause in their agreement. This oral advice was followed by written confirmation a day later indicating that the plaintiff sought to amend its notice of application, that had been served on the defendant, by discontinuing all relief sought except for certain provisional relief, which was specifically excluded from the scope of the arbitration clause. The plaintiff then sought a court order referring the dispute to arbitration and a stay of the court proceedings, except the claim for provisional relief.

Having concluded that, except for the provisional relief, the relief sought in the application was within the arbitration clause, the court considered, whether the plaintiff had waived arbitration by having brought its dispute before the court. Even assuming a right of unilateral waiver, which was unlikely as the arbitration clause bound all parties to the contract, the court concluded that the waiver had been effectively retracted by reasonable notice of the intention to arbitrate.

The defendant argued that the court should not stay the judicial proceedings under the Ontario equivalent of article 8(1) MAL because the application for stay had been made after the plaintiff had submitted its "first statement on the substance of the dispute" by filing an application with the court. The court held that the word "statement" in article 8(1) MAL meant the first statement in the arbitral process, as distinct from the litigation process. Expressly disagreeing with the interpretation of article 8(1) MAL by the Federal Court of Appeal in Ruhrkohle Handel Inter GmbH v Fednau Ltd. (see Case 33), the court concluded that, since the plaintiff had not submitted its first statement in the arbitral proceedings, within the meaning of articles 23(1) and 8(1) MAL, its request for submission to arbitration was timely. An order was issued referring the parties to arbitration pursuant to their agreement.

Indian Act—section 8

Article 24. Hearings and written proceedings

(1) Subject to any contrary agreement by the parties, the arbitral tribunal shall decide whether to hold oral hearings for the presentation of evidence or for oral argument, or whether the proceedings shall be conducted on the basis of documents and other materials. However, unless the parties have agreed that no hearings shall be held, the arbitral tribunal shall hold such hearings at an appropriate stage of the proceedings, if so requested by a party,

(2) The parties shall be given sufficient advance notice of any hearing and of any meeting of the arbitral tribunal for the purposes of inspection of goods, other property or documents.

(3) All statements, documents or other information supplied to the arbitral tribunal by one party shall be communicated to the other party. Also any expert report or evidentiary document on which the arbitral tribunal may rely in making its decision shall be communicated to the parties.

Indian Act—section 24

Article 25. Default of a party

Unless otherwise agreed by the parties, if, without showing sufficient cause,

(a) the claimant fails to communicate his statement of claim in accordance with article 23(1), the arbitral tribunal shall terminate the proceedings;

(b) the respondent fails to communicate his statement of defence in accordance with article 23(1), the arbitral tribunal shall continue the proceedings without treating such failure in itself as an admission of the claimant's allegations;

(c) any party fails to appear at a hearing or to produce documentary evidence, the arbitral tribunal may continue the proceedings and make the award on the evidence before it.

Indian Act—section 25

Article 26. Expert appointed by arbitral tribunal

(1) Unless otherwise agreed by the parties, the arbitral tribunal

(a) may appoint one or more experts to report to it on specific issues to be determined by the atbitral tribunal;

(b) may require a party to give the expert any relevant information or to produce, or to provide access to, any relevant documents, goods or other property for his inspection.

(2) Unless otherwise agreed by the parties, if a party so requests or if the arbitral tribunal considers it necessary, the expert shall, after delivery of his written or oral report, participate in a hearing where the parties have the opportunity to put questions to him and to present expert witnesses in order to testify on the points at issue.

Indian Act—section 26

Article 27. Court assistance in taking evidence

The arbitral tribunal or a party with the approval of the arbitral tribunal may request from a competent court of this State assistance in taking evidence. The court may execute the request within its competence and according to its rules on taking evidence.

Indian Act—section 27

CHAPTER VI

MAKING OF AWARD AND TERMINATION OF PROCEEDINGS

Article 28, Rules applicable to substance of dispute

(1) The arbitral tribunal shall decide the dispute in accordance with such rules of law as are chosen by the parties as applicable to the substance of the dispute. Any designation of the law or legal system of a given Stale shall be construed, unless otherwise expressed, as directly referring to the substantive law of that State and not to its conflict of laws rules.

(2) Failing any designation by the parties, the arbitral tribunal shall apply the law determined by the conflict of laws rules which it considers applicable.

(3) The arbitral tribunal shall decide *ex aequo et bono* or as amiable compositeur only if the parties have expressly authorized it to do so.

(4) In all cases, the arbitral tribunal shall decide in accordance with the terms of the contract and shall take into account the usages of the trade applicable to the transaction.

Indian Act—section 28

Article 29. Decision making by panel of arbitrators

In arbitral proceedings with more than one arbitrator, any decision of the arbitral tribunal shall be made, unless otherwise agreed by the parties, by a majority of all its members. However, questions of procedure may be decided by a presiding arbitrator, if so authorized by the parties or all members of the arbitral tribunal.

Indian Act— section 29

Article 30. Settlement

(1) If, during arbitral proceedings, the parties settle the dispute, the arbitral tribunal shall terminate the proceedings and, if requested by the parties and not objected to

by the arbitral tribunal, record the settlement in the form of an arbitral award on agreed terms.

(2) An award on agreed terms shall be made in accordance with the provisions of article 31 and shall state that it is an award. Such an award has the same status and effect as any other award on the merits of the case.

Indian Act—section 30

Article 31. Form and contents of award

(1) The award shall be made in writing and shall be signed by the arbitrator or arbitrators. In arbitral proceedings with more than one arbitrator, the signatures of the majority of all members of the arbitral tribunal shall suffice, provided that the reason for any omitted signature is stated.

(2) The award shall state the reasons upon which it is based, unless the parties have agreed that no reasons ate to be given or the award is an award on agreed terms under article 30.

(3) The award shall state its date and the place of arbitration as determined in accordance with article 20(1). The award shall be deemed to have been made at that place.

(4) After the award is made, a copy signed by the arbitrators in accordance with paragraph (1) of this article shall be delivered to each party.

Indian Act—section 31

Case 10: MAL 31(2); 34

Canada: Superior Court of Quebec (Gonthier J.)

16 April, 1987

Navigation Sonamar Inc. v. *Algoma Steamships Limited and others*

Published in French: "Requeils de Jurisprudence du Quebee 1987, 1346". Commented on by Tetley in (1993) Lloyd's Maritime and Commercial Law Quarterly, 238.

The court ruled that arbitrators cannot be criticized for expressing themselves as commercial men and not as lawyers. Where the agreement between the parties does not specify the form of the award, that form is governed by article 31(2).

In accordance with the arbitration clause contained in a charter-party agreement concluded on 9 January, 1981, the parties submitted to arbitration a dispute concerning their respective liabilily with regard to certain damages that resulted from the grounding, on 26 April, 1984, of the vessel that was the subject of the charter-party. The applicant (Navigation Sonomar), based on alleged lack of coherent and comprehensible reasons, submitted an application to set aside the award rendered on 29 October, 1986.

The Superior Court dismissed the application. The court ruled that the reasons were adequate, taking into account not only what was expressly stated but also what was implicit in the award. Arbitrators cannot be criticized for expressing themselves as commercial men and not as lawyers.

Indian Act—section 31(3) also requires reasons.
The above ruling can be utilised, for its interpretation

Case 12: MAL 31; 34

Canada: Federal Court of Canada, Trial Division (Denault J.)

7 April, 1988

D. Frampton & Co. Ltd. v. *Sylvio Thibeault and Navigation Harvey & Fréres Inc.*

Original in English and French

With respect to an application to set aside an arbitral award, the powers of the court are limited to examining the award on the basis of the restrictive provisions of article 34 of the Model Law, as those provisions are reproduced in the Commercial Arbitration Code, S.R.C. 1985, c.C-34.6. The court cannot draw authority from article 34(4) MAL to refer the matter back to the arbitral tribunal and request that it consider the question of the applicable rate of interest where that question was not originally considered by the arbitrators.

Thibeault and Navigation Harvey requested the court to set aside an arbitral award where only two out of the three arbitrators had submitted their opinion. Where a defendant signed the charter-party which contained the arbitration clause, that defendant is personally involved in the charter-party since he signed it in his personal capacity. However, the court allowed the application of another defendant who had signed the charter-party while acting as president of his company. According to the court, the defendant is bound by the charter-party in his official capacity but not in his personal capacity. The decision of the arbitrator to involve that defendant personally was beyond the scope of the submission to arbitration in that it affected a third party who was not a party to the arbitration.

The application of Navigation Harvey to set aside the arbitral award was dismissed even though only two arbitrators rendered the award. Article 31 MAl provides that "the signatures of the majority of all members of the arbitral tribunal shall suffice, provided that the reason for any omitted signature is stated". That reason was formally given to the court by the president of the tribunal. The application for homologation of the arbitral award was allowed.

◆ ◆ ◆ ◆ ◆

Case 441—MAL arts. 16(3); 31

Germany: Oberlandesgericht Köln; 9 Sch 6/00

20 July, 2000

Original in German

DIS-Online Database on Arbitration Law - *http://www.dis-arb.de*

Abstract prepared by Stefan Kröll

The decision concerned a motion for the setting aside of a preliminary decision by the arbitral tribunal on its jurisdiction, dealing with the question of when a decision by the arbitral tribunal qualifies as an interim decision according to § 1040 (3) of the German Code of Civil Procedure (ZPO) [adopted from article 16(3) MAL].

In the arbitration proceedings between the parties, the claimant requested the tribunal to declare that it did not have jurisdiction in the matter because of the lack of a valid arbitration agreement. On 21 December, 1999, the arbitral tribunal delivered an order without reasons, declaring that the "application of Applicant was rejected." In a further order, delivered on 1 February, 2000, the arbitral tribunal corrected the first order and stated that it "rejected the application of Applicant to decide the issue of jurisdiction by way of an intermediate decision according to § 1040 para. 3 ZPO" and that "The arbitral tribunal will decide on its jurisdiction in the final award." Claimant moved to have this order set aside.

The Court dismissed the motion and held that the decisions of the arbitral tribunal could not be made subject to separate judicial review. The first order could not be an award according to § 1054 ZPO [adopted from article 31 MAL] because it did not comply with the formal requirements (reasons) for an award. Nor was it an interim decision according to § 1040(3) 3 ZPO because the arbitral tribunal had not intended to make a decision regarding its jurisdiction, but merely rejected the procedural application to decide on its jurisdiction by way of an interim decision. This interpretation is confirmed by the second order. A decision on the jurisdiction will only be made in the final award, and may only be reviewed by a court in a motion for setting aside or a motion for recognition and enforcement of the award.

The decision of the Court did not require an oral hearing in terms of § 1063(2) ZPO. The decision did not concern the formal setting-aside procedure according to § 1059 ZPO [article 34 MAL], but referred to an award of the arbitral tribunal that did not become binding on the parties.

Indian Act—section 34(4).

Article 32. Termination of proceedings

(1) The arbitral proceedings are terminated by the final award or by an order of the arbitral tribunal in accordance with paragraph (2) of this article.

(2) The arbitral tribunal shall issue an order for the termination of the arbitral proceedings when:

   (a) the claimant withdraws his claim, unless the respondent objects thereto and the arbitral tribunal recognizes a legitimate interest on his part in obtaining a final settlement of the dispute;

   (b) the parties agree on the termination of the proceedings;

   (c) the arbitral tribunal finds that the continuation of the proceedings has for any other reason become unnecessary or impossible.

(3) The mandate of the arbitral tribunal terminates with the termination of the arbitral proceedings, subject to the provisions of articles 33 and 34(4).

Indian Act—section 32

Article 33. Correction and interpretation of award; additional award

(1) Within thirty days of receipt of the award, unless another period of time has been agreed upon by the parties:

   (a) a party, with notice to the other party, may request the arbitral tribunal to correct in the award any errors in computation, any clerical or typographical errors or any errors of similar nature;

   (b) if so agreed by the parties, a party, with notice to the other party, may request the arbitral tribunal to give an interpretation of a specific point or part of the award.

   If the arbitral tribunal considers the request to be justified, it shall make the correction or give the interpretation within thirty days of receipt of the request. The interpretation shall form part of the award.

(2) The arbitral tribunal may correct any error of the type referred to in paragraph (1)(a) of this article on its own initiative within thirty days of the date of the award.

(3) Unless otherwise agreed by the parties, a party, with notice to the other party, may request, within thirty days of receipt of the award, the arbitral tribunal to make an additional award as to claims presented in the arbitral proceedings but omitted from the award. If the arbitral tribunal considers the request to be justified, it shall make the additional award within sixty days.

(4) The arbitral tribunal may extend, if necessary, the period of time within which it shall make a correction, interpretation or an additional award under paragraph (1) or (3) of this article.

(5) The provisions of article 31 shall apply to a correction or interpretation of the award or to an additional award.

Indian Act—section 33

Case 208: MAL 33(1)

Singapore: Singapore International Arbitration Centre (SIAC) (Lawrence Boo, Presiding Arbitrator)

6 February, 199B; SIAC Arb. no. 6 of 1996

Original in English

Unpublished

The respondents succeeded in an arbitration and were awarded costs to be assessed by the Presiding Arbitrator. In the subsequent assessment of costs, the respondents were awarded $177,500 for costs and $4,163 for disbursements.

The respondents later realized that they had omitted to include in their certificate of costs, disbursements in the sum of $25,690.00 representing the costs of survey reports prepared by the respondents' witnesses and their. Fees for attendances at the arbitration hearing. They applied for a correction of the award for costs to include this amount. The claimant argued that the words are to correct in the award any errors in computation, any clerical or typographical errors or any errors of a similar nature in SIAC Rule 28.1 (similar to Article 33(1) MAL) are narrower than the term accidental slip or omission used in the Arbitration Act Chapter 10 (1980 edition), which English courts had interpreted to include even errors in a bill of costs due to a mistake by solicitors representing a party [See *Chessum Chessum & Sons* v. *Gordon*, (1901) 1 King's Bench (English Law Reports) 644].

The Presiding Arbitrator held however that the words in SIAC Rule 28.1 (Article 33(1) MAL) were in substance not narrower than the term "accidental slip or omission" in that an error in computation would include miscalculations, use of wrong data in calculations, omission of data in calculations and a clerical or typographical error would include mistakes made in the course of typing or drafting the award. The term "errors of a similar nature" if read as meaning errors of the "same kind" would also include errors or mistakes of commission as well as of omission which had been inadvertently made or had never been intended by the tribunal. Accordingly, the Presiding Arbitrator considering that Article 33 MAL was best understood as used in contradistinction to errors of judgement, whether of law or of fact, for which a tribunal is not empowered to correct, held that it had jurisdiction to correct the certificate of costs.

Indian Act—section 33(1)(b). The above ruling is of interest as interpreting the meaning of the expression "error"

CHAPTER VII

RECOURSE AGAINST AWARD

Article 34. Application for setting aside as exclusive recourse against arbitral award

(1) Recourse to a court against an arbitral award may be made only by an application for setting aside in accordance with paragraphs (2) and (3) of this article.

(2) An arbitral award may be set aside by the court specified in article 6 only if:

(a) the party making the application furnishes proof that:

(i) a party to the arbitration agreement referred to in article 7 was under some incapacity; or the said agreement is not valid under the law to which the parties have subjected it or, failing any indication thereon, under the law of this State; or

(ii) the party making the application was not given proper notice of the appointment of an arbitrator or of the arbitral proceedings or was otherwise unable to present his case; or

(iii) the award deals with a dispute not contemplated by or not falling within the terms of the submission to arbitration, or contains decisions on matters beyond the scope of the submission to arbitration, provided that, if the decisions on matters submitted to arbitration can be separated from those not so submitted, only that part of the award which contains decisions on matters not submitted to arbitration may be set aside; or

(iv) the composition of the arbitral tribunal or the arbitral procedure was not in accordance with the agreement of the parties, unless such agreement was in conflict with a provision of this Law from which the parties cannot derogate, or, failing such agreement, was not in accordance with this Law; or

(b) the court finds that:

(i) the subject-matter of the dispute is not capable of settlement by arbitration under the law of this State; or

(ii) the award is in conflict with the public policy of this State.

(3) An application for setting aside may not be made after three months have elapsed from the date on which the party making that application had received the award or, if a request had been made under article 33, from the date on which that request had been disposed of by the arbitral tribunal.

(4) The court, when asked to set aside an award, may, where appropriate and so requested by a party, suspend the setting aside proceedings for a period of time determined by it in order to give the arbitral tribunal an opportunity to resume the arbitral proceedings or to take such other action as in the arbitral tribunal's opinion will eliminate the grounds for setting aside.

Indian Act—section 34

Case 10: MAL 31(2); 34

Canada: Superior Court of Quebec (Gonthier J.)

16 April, 1987

Navigation Sonamar Inc. v. *Algoma Steamships Limited and others*

Published in French: "Requeils de Jurisprudence du Quebec 1987, 1346". Commented on by Tetley in [1993] Lloyd's Maritime and Commercial Law Quarterly, 238.

The court ruled that arbitrators cannot be criticized for expressing themselves as commercial men and not as lawyers. Where the agreement between the parties does nol specify the form of the award, that form is governed by article 31(2).

In accordance with the arbitration clause contained in a charter-party agreement concluded on 9 January, 1981, the parties submitted to arbitration a dispute concerning their respective liability with regard to certain damages that resulted from the grounding, on 26 April, 1984, of the vessel that was the subject of the charter-party. The applicant (Navigation Sonomar), based on alleged lack of coherent and comprehensible reasons, submitted an application to set aside the award rendered on 29 October, 1986.

The Superior Court dismissed the application. The court ruled that the reasons were adequate, taking into account not only what was expressly stated but also what was implicit in the award. Arbitrators cannot be criticized for expressing themselves as commercial men and not as lawyers.

Indian Act—section 31(3). Compare Case No. 11 above, under MAL article 31

Case 12: MAL 31; 34

Canada: Federal Court of Canada, Trial Division (Denault J,)

7 April, 1988

D. Frampton & Co. Ltd. v. *Sylvio Thibeault and Navigation Harvey & Fréres Inc.*

Original in English and French

With respect to an application to set aside an arbitral award, the powers of the court are limited to examining the award on the basis of the restrictive provisions of article 34 of the Model Law, as those provisions are reproduced in the Commercial Arbitration Code, S.R.C. 1985, c.C-34.6, The court cannot draw authority from article 34(4) MAL to refer the matter back (o the arbitral tribunal and request that it consider the question of the applicable rate of interest where that question was not originally considered by the arbitrators.

Thibeault and Navigation Harvey requested the court to set aside an arbitral award where only two out of the three arbitrators had submitted their opinion. Where a defendant signed the charter-party which contained the arbitration clause, that defendant is personally involved in the charter-party since he signed it in his personal capacity. However, the court allowed the application of another defendant who had signed the charter-party while acting as president of his company. According to the court, the defendant is bound by the charter-party in his official capacity but not in his personal capacity. The decision of the arbitrator to involve that defendant personally was beyond the scope of the submission to arbitration in that it affected a third party who was not a party to the arbitration.

The application of Navigation Harvey to set aside the arbitral award was dismissed even though only two arbitrators rendered ihe award. Article 31 MAL provides that "the signatures of the majority of all members of the arbitral tribunal shall suffice, provided that the reason for any omitted signature is stated". That reason was formally given to the court by the president of the tribunal. The application for homologation of the arbitral award was allowed.

Indian Act—section 34(2)

Case 16: MAL 1; 5; 23(1); 34, especially 34(2)(a)(iii)

Canada: British Columbia Court of Appeal (Hutcheon, Proudfoot and Giggs, JJ.A.)

24 October, 1990

Quintette Coal Limited v. *Nippon Steel Corp. et al.*

Published in English and French: Canada Supreme Court Reports 1990 volume 2

"Published in English: 1 Western Weekly Reports, 1991, 219."

Commented on by Tetley in [1993] Lloyd's Maritime and Commercial Law Quarterly, 238.

Commented on by Paterson in Williamette Law Review, Vol. 27, 573.

The appropriate standard of review of arbitral awards is one which preserves the autonomy of the forum chosen by the parties and minimizes judicial intervention.

Quintette, a Canadian company, agreed to supply coal to the respondent, a Japanese company. Their agreement provided that any contract disputes would be submitted to binding arbitration under British Columbia Law. Accordingly, a dispute concerning the interpretation of a contract clause outlining a pricing mechanism was referred to arbitration and an award rendered. Quintette, relying on sections 5 and 34 of the Model Law as enacted by the International Commercial Arbitration Act, Statutes of British Columbia, 1986, c. 14 sought to set aside the award on the grounds that the arbitrators had exceeded their jurisdiction by dealing with a matter not contemplated by or falling within the scope of the submission to arbitration.

The Court of Appeal upheld the lower court's affirmation of the award. The Court noted the world-wide trend toward restricting the scope of judicial intervention into commercial arbitration. The award could be justified under the terms of the contract so the Court was prevented from intervening under article 34(2)(a)(iv) of the British Columbia Act [which is the same as article 34(2)(a)(iii) of the Model Law].

[The Supreme Court of Canada denied leave to appeal from the British Columbia Court of Appeal judgment on 13 December 1990.)

__Indian Act—section 34(2)__

MAL 146: 18, 34(2)

Russian Federation: Moscow City Court

10 November 1994

Original in Russian

Unpublished

The plaintiff, whose claim in arbitration proceedings had been dismissed, filed an application to have the award set aside on the grounds that in the course of the arbitration proceedings article 18 of the Russian Federation Act on international commercial arbitration (corresponding to art. 18 MAL) had been violated in that the parties had not been treated with equality and the award was in conflict with public policy.

The plaintiff argued that the decision to dismiss the claim had been made despite the fact that the defendant partially acknowledged the claim brought against it. In that regard, the court held that such acknowledgement did not constitute grounds for setting aside the award since, in making the award, the arbitrators were not bound by an acknowledgement of the claim.

Since the plaintiff failed to establish that the award was in conflict with public policy, its claim in that respect was found to be unjustified. At the same time, the court noted that a procedural infringement in the arbitral proceedings had no relevance to the notion of public policy.

On the basis of the facts presented, the court dismissed the plaintiff's application to set aside the arbitral award.

◆ ◆ ◆ ◆ ◆

Case 148: MAL 16(2)(3), 34(2)

Russian Federation: Moscow City Court

Decision on the application to set aside the award made by the Court of International Commercial Arbitration at the Russian Federation Chamber of Commerce and Industry in case No. 214/1993

10 February, 1995

Original in Russian

Unpublished

The plaintiff filed an application to set aside an arbitral award made against it, citing as grounds for doing so the fact that as no arbitration agreement existed between the plaintiff and the defendant, the arbitral tribunal had no jurisdiction to examine the dispute in question. The plaintiff argued that the party signing the contract with the defendant had gone into liquidation as a commercial entity and that the plaintiff was not its legal successor and, hence, not a party to the contract concluded with the defendant which contained the respective arbitration clause. In addition, the plaintiff argued that the contract included an arbitration clause providing for the examination of disputes by the Tribunal of Arbitration at the USSR Chamber of Commerce and Industry, whereas the claim had been brought before the Tribunal of International Commercial Arbitration at the Russian Federation Chamber of Commerce and Industry (TICA), which was not competent to examine the dispute in question.

The court noted that article 16(2) and (3) of the Act of the Russian Federation on "international commercial arbitration" (art. 16 MAL) provided that a plea on the grounds that an arbitral tribunal did not have jurisdiction, should be raised not later than the submission of the statement of defence. The court held that the plaintiff (respondent in the arbitral proceedings) had presented to the arbitral tribunal its defence against the claim in which it had stated that it was not the legal successor to the party to the contract which had given rise to the claim and could not be a defendant in the action in question. However, the plaintiff made no reference to the lack of jurisdiction of the arbitral tribunal either in its statement of defence or in the subsequent correspondence with the arbitral tribunal, and had not raised any plea regarding the jurisdiction of the arbitral tribunal during the hearing of the case. The court did not concur with the plaintiff's position that its submission in its statement of defence before the arbitral tribunal that it was not the legal successor and did not recognize itself as a party to the contract should be considered an objection to the jurisdiction of the arbitral tribunal. The court found that those references related exclusively to legal succession in respect of disputed legal relationships and to the validity of claims brought by the plaintiff.

The court did not concur with the plaintiff regarding the lack of jurisdiction of the TICA to examine the dispute in question. In that regard, the court noted that under paragraph 4 of the Statutes on the TICA, which was an annex to the Act of the Russian Federation on international commercial arbitration, the TICA was the successor to the Tribunal of Arbitration at the USSR Chamber of Commerce and Industry and, in particular, was entitled to settle disputes on the basis of agreement by the parties to refer their disputes to the Tribunal of Arbitration at the USSR Chamber of Commerce and industry.

The court dismissed the plaintiff's application to set aside the arbitral award.

◆ ◆ ◆ ◆ ◆

Case 149: MAL 34(2)

Russian Federation: Moscow City Court

18 September, 1995

Original in Russian

Unpublished

The plaintiff, against whom an arbitral award had been made, applied to have the award set aside, arguing that the award was in conflict with the public policy of the Russian Federation, since it obliged the plaintiff (respondent in the arbitral proceedings) to pay the defendant (claimant in the arbitral proceedings) a sum of money in foreign currency whereas the plaintiff did not have a foreign currency account.

The court did not agree that the award made by the arbitral tribunal ordering the Russian plaintiff (respondant) to make the payment in foreign currency was in conflict with the public policy of the Russian Federation, even if the plaintiff did not have foreign currency at its disposal. In that connection, the court noted that, in the enforcement of the award, the competent court had the option of modifying the arrangements and procedures for enforcement.

◆ ◆ ◆ ◆ ◆

Case 436 — MAL art. 34(2)(a)(iv)
Germany: Bayerisches Oberstes Landesgericht; 4Z Sch 17/98
24 February, 1999
Original in German
DIS-Online Database on Arbitration Law - *http://www.dis-arb.de*
Abstract prepared by Stefan Kröll

The decision is about a motion for setting aside an award because of procedural errors made in the composition of the arbitral tribunal.

The claimant, a potato farmer, had initiated arbitral proceedings before the arbitral tribunal of the potato industry at the Bavarian Commodities Trading Association against the defendant, a potato trader. After an award was rendered in favour of the defendant, the claimant appealed the award to the Highest Arbitral Tribunal of the Bavarian Commodities Trading Association. The claimant appointed a farmer as his arbitrator. The defendant successfully challenged this arbitrator, as well as the substitute nominated by claimant. Arbitrator C, a trader, was finally appointed for the claimant and claimant's challenge of arbitrator C was dismissed by the Highest Arbitral Tribunal composed of three traders. The claimant applied to the courts to have this award set aside for procedural irregularities in the appointment process.

The court granted the application and set aside the award on the basis of § 1059 (2) (1 b, d) Code of Civil Procedure [ZPO; equivalent to article 34(2)(a)(iv) MAL]. It held that the procedure employed by the Highest Arbitral Tribunal with regard to the appointment and challenge of arbitrator C violated § 1032 ZPO of the then-applicable German Arbitration Law. According to § 1032 ZPO (old version) in conjunction with § 1045 ZPO (old version), which could not be derogated from, the motion of the claimant to challenge arbitrator C had to be decided by a court, not by the Highest Arbitral Tribunal. Because the court might have decided differently on the challenge, and the Highest Arbitral Tribunal might have decided—in a different composition - differently on the outcome of the appeal, the court affirmed that the procedural mistake had potentially caused an unfavourable outcome for the claimant.

Also, the court held that the refusal of the Highest Arbitral Tribunal to appoint the substitute arbitrator nominated by the claimant for the successfully challenged first arbitrator had been a procedural error. According to the applicable arbitration rules it was not mandatory that the party appointed arbitrator come from the list of arbitrators. The *list was only to be used as a recommendation.*

◆ ◆ ◆

Case 437 — MAL art. 34(2)(b)(ii)
Germany: Bayerisches Oberstes Landesgericht; 4Z Sch 14/98
24 February, 1999
Original in German

Published in German: BayObLGZ 1999, 55-57 (headnote and reasons); BayObLGZ 1999; Nr 14, JMBl BY 1999, 73 (headnote); NJW-RR 2000, 807-808 (headnote and reasons); Betriebs-Berater, Beilage 12 zu Heft 50/2000 (RPS), p.24 DIS-Online Database on Arbitration Law - http://www.dis-arb.de

Abstract prepared by Stefan Kröll

The procedural prerequisites for the recognition and declaration of enforceability of a foreign award in Germany were at issue in this case.

The claimant had applied to the court to have an award rendered by a tribunal under the auspices of the Court of Arbitration of the Chamber of Commerce and Industry of the Russian Federation in its favour recognized and declared enforceable in Germany. During the written preliminary proceedings, the defendant asked the German court in a brief to deny the motion, alleging *inter alia* that he had not been given proper notice of the arbitration proceedings and did not know the person who had signed the arbitration agreement on his behalf. The German court ordered an oral hearing at which the claimant did not appear while the defendant's representative orally repeated his request to deny the motion referring to the reasons stated in his brief.

The Bavarian Higher Regional Court refused to recognize the award and declare it enforceable since the claimant failed to make a procedurally valid request at the oral hearing before the Court. Since the defendant raised potential grounds to refuse recognition [§ 1059 (2) (1b), (1c), (1d) ZPO (the equivalent of article 34(2)(a)(ii), (iii), (iv) MAL)] the Court was required to hold an oral hearing (§ 1063 (2) ZPO). According to §§ 128 (1), 297 ZPO it is required that, in the case of a mandatory oral hearing, any motion by a party has to be made at the oral hearing by way of an oral application or an oral reference to the written application. Where an application does not fulfil the requirements of the German Code of Civil Procedure, the Court may not decide on the merits of the motion (§ 308 ZPO: Principle of Party Disposition). Because the defendant failed to appear at the scheduled hearing, and therefore did not make his motion in the way required by the German Code of Civil Procedure, the Court had to deny the declaration of recognition and enforceability of the award paying no regard to the merits of the case.

◆ ◆ ◆ ◆ ◆

Case 440 — MAL art. 34(2)(a)(iv)

Germany: Oberlandesgericht Köln; 9 Sch 15/99

22 December, 1999

Original in German

DIS-Online Database on Arbitration Law - *http://www.dis-arb.de*

Abstract prepared by Stefan Kröll

The decision concerns an application for the recognition and enforcement of an award rendered by a tribunal in Germany.

In 1989, the parties had entered into a lease agreement containing an arbitration clause. After the termination of the lease, the claimant sent a request for arbitration to the defendant and nominated its arbitrator. Since the defendant did not appoint its arbitrator within the time provided for in the arbitration agreement, the claimant, in accordance with the agreement, appointed the arbitrator for the defendant. The two arbitrators rendered an award in favour of claimant who moved to have it recognized and declared enforceable.

The Court granted the motion rejecting the objection by the defendant that the tribunal was not properly formed (ZPO §1059 (2) (1d)), [adopted from article 34(2)(a)(iv)) MAL]. It held that the procedure adopted was in line with the agreement of parties, in that it provided for a tribunal, which can be appointed by one party only if the other party did not participate in the appointment process. The Court considered such an agreement to be valid on the basis of the old arbitration law, applicable to the issue since the agreement was entered into before 1 January 1998. (Art. 4 § 1 SchiedsVfG). It held that since the party agreed on such a procedure, the principle of party autonomy requires such agreements to be held valid, as long as it does not violate other principles such as the requirement of neutrality of the tribunal. That principle, however, is sufficiently protected by the right of each party to challenge the arbitrators, but the defendant did not take advantage of this right. Finally, it did not find a causal relationship between the appointment procedure and the decision of the arbitral tribunal.

◆ ◆ ◆ ◆ ◆

Case 444 — MAL art. 34(2)(b)(ii)

Germany: Oberlandesgericht Dresden; 11 Sch 08/01

8 May, 2001

Original in German

Published in German: Betriebs-Berater, Beilage 7 zu Heft 43/2000 (RPS), p. 22

DIS-Online Database on Arbitration Law - *http://www.dis-arb.de*

Abstract prepared by Stefan Kröll

The decision concerned a motion for recognition and enforcement of two awards.

The claimant obtained an award ordering the respondent to give the consent necessary for a transfer of property as well as an award ordering the respondent to pay the cost including the advance payment made by claimant for the arbitrators' fees. Claimant moved to have both awards recognized and enforced.

The Court granted the motion. It found that in relation to the award on the merits that the declaration of enforceability had only declaratory meaning, since the award replaced the declaration of respondent's consent *ipso iure*. According to § 1055 ZPO (civil procedure statute), an arbitral award has the same effect as a final judgement, and is not subject to appeal before a court. Where such judgement ordered a party to make a declaration of intention, the judgement itself replaced the declaration without further manifestation of will by the party (§ 894 ZPO).

With regard to the award on the costs, the Court stated that the action for recognition and enforcement was not an appeal against the award, so that most objections raised by the respondent were inadmissible. A wrong method of calculation of the amount in controversy and a false decision on costs do not by themselves violate the *ordre public* (article 34(2)(b)(ii) MAL). The Court also dismissed the objection that the award violated public policy because the arbitrators had been fixing their own compensation.. The Court found that the tribunal only determined that respondent had to reimburse claimant for the advance payments made, which was allowed according to the established practice of the Federal Supreme Court (BGH), and did not render a judgment on its own fees.

Indian Act—section 34(2)(ii). This is a very important case on the point of award in foreign currency

Case 182: MM 5; 16; 34

Canada: Superior Court of Quebec (Tellier J.)

9 September, 1994

International Civil Aviation Organization (ICAO) v. *Tripal Systems Pty. Ltd.*

Original in French

Published in French: Recueil de Jurisprudence du Québec [1994] 2560

In February 1990, ICAO entered into a contract with Tripal for the conception, construction and installation of an airport in Hanoi, Vietnam. The contract included an arbitration clause as well as a clause that preserved any immunity that might accrue to ICAO. Following the commencement of arbitral proceedings to resolve a dispute between the parties, ICAO raised its immunity to contest the arbitral tribunal's competence. Considering that the issue was one of mixed fact and law, the arbitral tribunal, in order to rule on the objection, decided to hear all evidence. ICAO then asked the Superior Court of Quebec to declare that it enjoyed an absolute immunity from judicial process of any kind. Tripal responded with its own motion for dismissal on the grounds that only the arbitral tribunal was competent at that stage of the proceedings.

The Superior Court granted the motion for dismissal of the declaratory motion, having decided that the arbitral tribunal alone was competent to decide the immunity issue. To this end, the Superior Court examined the conditions regulating judiciary intervention in the arbitral process (articles 16 and 34 MAL) and concluded that these were not met. The Superior Court refused to intervene on the basis of article 5 MAL. However, it noted that once the arbitral tribunal had declared itself competent, the Superior Court would be competent to review this decision in accordance with article 16(3) MAL, should a party so request.

Indian Act—sections 16 and 34(2)

Case 185: MAL 34(4); 36(b)(ii)

Canada: Quebec Court of Appeal (Vallerand, Brossard and Dussault, JJ.A.)

15 June, 1990

Transport de cargaison (Cargo Carriers) v. *Industrial Bulk Carriers*

Original in French

Published in French: Revue de droit judiciaire [1990] 418

Cargo Carriers, whose cargo ship travels between Niger and Spain, contracts with Industrial Bulk for port services. A dispute arose concerning sums incurred and paid by Industrial for services rendered while Cargo's ship was moored in Bilbao. Cargo opposed the enforcement of the arbitral award rendered in Industrial's favour for two reasons.

First, the award was said to order payment by Cargo of a sum greater than that expended by Industrial. The court rejected this argument on the grounds that it was equivalent to an application for the setting aside of the award and that this was within the exclusive jurisdiction of the arbitral tribunal under article 34 MAL.

Second, Cargo argued that the award provided for reimbursement of a bribe paid by Industrial to the port authority in Bilbao and that it would be contrary to Canadian public policy for Quebec courts to enforce such an award. The court rejected this argument, accepting the arbitrator's interpretation of the nature of the payment in question. The court further stated that the payment was in the nature of a ransom as opposed to a bribe because Industrial had no other choice but to pay the escalating demurrage charges to enable the ship to leave the port. The court distinguished between a bribe, which it defined as intrinsically immoral for both the offerer and the receiver, and a ransom, which involves immorality only on the part of the blackmailer. An arbitral award imposing the reimbursement of a sum paid as ransom does not violate Canadian public policy and therefore Cargo could not resist recognition and execution of the award on the basis of article 36(b)(ii) MAL.

A motion for leave to appeal to the Supreme Court of Canada was denied.

Indian Act—section 34(2)(b)(ii)

CHAPTER VIII
RECOGNITION AND ENFORCEMENT

Article 35. Recognition and enforcement

(1) An arbitral award, irrespective of the country in which it was made, shall be recognized as binding and, upon application in writing to the competent court, shall be enforced subject to the provisions of this article and of article 36.

(2) The party relying on an award or applying for its enforcement shall supply the duly authenticated original award or a duly certified copy thereof, and the original arbitration agreement referred to in article 7 or a duly certified copy thereof. If the award or agreement is not made in an official language of this State, the party shall supply a duly certified translation thereof into such language.

Indian Act—sections 44-60

Case 29: MAL 2;35;36

Canada: Ontario Court, General Division (While J.)

30 January, 1992

Kanto Yakin Kogyo Kabushiki-Kaisha v. *Can-Eng Manufacturing Ltd.*

Published in English: 7 Ontario Reports (3d), 779

Commented on by Tetley in (1993) Lloyd's Maritime and Commercial Law Quarterly, 238

Concluding an agreement prior to the existence of legislation implementing MAL will not mean that MAL will not apply to arbitrations taking place pursuant to the agreement.

The parties concluded an agreement which contained an arbitration clause and provided that arbitration would take place in Tokyo. Arbitration of an issue arising out of the agreement was held and an award was made. Kanto Yakin sought to enforce the award in Ontario, The court found that, despite the fact that the agreement was concluded prior to the coming into force of the International Commercial Arbitration Act, Revised Statutes of Ontario, 1990, c. 1.9, which enacts MAL, the agreement was still an arbitration agreement governed by the Act and was enforceable as such.

◆ ◆ ◆ ◆ ◆

Case 30: MAL 35;36

Canada: Ontario Court, General Division (Feldman J.)

13 February 1992; appeal pending in the Ontario Court of Appeal

Robert E. Schreter v. *Casmac Inc.*

Published in English: 7 Ontario Reports (3d), 608

Commented on by Tetley in [1993] Lloyd's Maritime and Commercial Law Quarterly, 238

For the purposes of MAL, an arbitral award does not merge in a judgment which confirms it. The court should not re-open the merits of an arbitral award where there has been no misconduct, simply on the grounds of ensuring conformity with public policy.

The agreement between the parties provided that the law of the state of Georgia, United States of America, would govern and that disputes arising out of the agreement would be determined by binding arbitration to take place in Atlanta. An arbitral award in favour of Schreter was subsequently confirmed by the Georgia court. Gasrnac challenged the enforcement of the award in Ontario on a number of procedural grounds, all of which were rejected by the court. Gasmac claimed that the award had merged in the Georgia court judgment and could therefore only be enforced in Ontario as a foreign judgement. Gasmac also claimed that the acceleration of royalty payments for breach of contract was contrary to the public policy of Ontario.

The court found that article 35 MAL as enacted by the International Commercial Arbitration Act, Revised Statutes of Ontario, 1990, c. 1.9 made recognition and enforcement of arbitral awards mandatory. The court found no indication in articles 35 or 36 that awards should be considered to merge in judgments which confirm them. The court indicated that to make such a finding would "create a gaping hole in the scope of the Act." The court determined that the facts did not warrant re-opening the arbitral award on public policy grounds pursuant to article 36(1)(b)(ii) MAL. The court enforced the arbitral award.

Indian Act—sections 48(1) and 57(1). The ruling is important, on the question of merger

Case 117: MAL 35

Canada: Ontario Court of justice, General Division (Somers J.)

19 December 1994

Murmansk Trawl Fleet v. *Bimman Realty Inc.*

Original in English

Unpublished

The plaintiff sought to enforce in Ontario a final arbitral award issued in New York with regard to a dispute arising from its contract with the defendant. The application was made after the right to appeal the award in New York State had expired but the defendant argued that the award should not be enforced in Ontario, since no steps had been taken to have it confirmed (made binding) under New York law.

The court held that it was not necessary that the foreign award be confirmed in order to be enforceable in Ontario. The court, referring to the decision on Case 30, based this conclusion on a public policy favouring the avoidance of delays that were ensuing from court proceedings and providing for a more efficient dispute resolution where the parties have chosen arbitration.

◆ ◆ ◆ ◆ ◆

Case 233; MAL 35(1); 36(1)(b)(ii)

Zimbabwe: Harare High Court (fudge Chatikobo); Judgment No. HH-133-97

10 July and 20 August 1997

Durco (Pvt) Ltd. v. *Dajen (Pvt) Ltd.*

Original in English

Published in English in 1997(2) Zimbabwe Law Reports 199 (Harare)

Two parties, a grain producer and a miller, had submitted their dispute to a single arbitrator which resulted in an award in favour of the miller. As a third party was involved who had not been a party to the arbitration, it was feared that further proceedings might ensue. Accordingly, it was felt to be in the interests of all concerned to submit to a second arbitration which would be binding on all three parties.

The second arbitration, before a panel of three arbitrators, however, resulted in an award against the miller. The miller refused to comply with the second award and the grain producer applied to the High Court for its recognition and enforcement under article 35 MAL. The miller opposed the award on the grounds that it would be contrary to public policy to enforce the award in terms of article 36(1)(b)(ii) MAL, contending that since there was already an award it would offend the principle of finality in arbitration to enforce the second award.

The court held that, by agreeing to submit to a second arbitration, the miller had waived its rights to finality of the first award. Accordingly, the miller was now bound by the second award and the court ordered that it should be recognised and enforced. The miller appealed (see CLOUT case no. 234) to the Supreme Court.

◆ ◆ ◆ ◆ ◆

Case 234; MAL 35(1); 36(1)(b)(ii)

Zimbabwe: Supreme Court of Zimbabwe (Judges of Appeal: Muchechetere, Ebrahim and Sandura); Judgment No. SC 141/98

22 June and 7 September, 1998

Dajen (Pvt.) Ltd. v. *Durco (Pvt.) Ltd.*

Original in English

Unpublished

The miller, the unsuccessful party in CLOUT case no. 233, appealed to the Supreme Court. In dismissing the appeal, the Supreme Court held that the principle of finality did not destroy or supplant a party's power to waive any right derived from an award and that this is what the miller had done by submitting to the second arbitration.

Indian Act—section 34 has no provision as to waiver

Article 36. Grounds for refusing recognition or enforcement

(1) Recognition or enforcement of an arbitral award, irrespective of the country in which it was made, may be refused only:

(a) at the request of the party against whom it is invoked, if that party furnishes to the competent court where recognition or enforcement is sought proof that:

(i) a party to the arbitration agreement referred to in article 7 was under some incapacity; or the said agreement is not valid under the law to which the parties have subjected it or, failing any indication thereon, under the law of the country where the award was made; or

(ii) the party against whom the award is invoked was not given proper notice of the appointment of an arbitrator ot of the arbitral proceedings or was otherwise unable to present his case; or

(iii) the award deals with a dispute not contemplated by or not falling within the terms of the submission to arbitration, or it contains decisions on matters beyond the scope of the submission to arbitration, provided that, if the decisions on matters submitted to arbitration can be separated from those not so submitted, that part of the award which contains decisions on matters submitted to arbitration may be recognized and enforced; or

(iv) the composition of the arbitral tribunal or the arbitral procedure was not in accordance with the agreement of the parties or, failing such agreement, was not in accordance with the law of the country where the arbitration took place; or

(v) the award has not yet become binding on the parties or has been set aside or suspended by a court of the country in which, or under the law of which, that award was made; or

(b) if the court finds that:

(i) the subject-matter of the dispute is not capable of settlement by arbitration under the law of this State; or

(ii) the recognition or enforcement of the award would be contrary to the public policy of this State.

(2) If an application for setting aside or suspension of an award has been made to a court referred to in paragraph (1)(a)(v) of this article, the court where recognition or enforcement is sought may, if it considers it proper, adjourn its decision and may also, on the application of the party claiming recognition or enforcement of the award, order the other party to provide appropriate security.

Indian Act—sections 44-60

Case 29: MAL 2;35;36

Canada: Ontario Court, General Division (While J.)

30 January, 1992

Kanto Yakin Kogyo Kabushiki-Kaisha v. *Can-Eng Manufacturing Ltd.*

Published in English: 7 Ontario Reports (3d), 779

Commented on by Tetley in [1993] Lloyd's Maritime and Commercial Law Quarterly, 238

Concluding an agreement prior to the existence of legislation implementing MAL will not mean that MAL will not apply to arbitrations taking place pursuant to the agreement.

The parties concluded an agreement which contained an arbitration clause and provided that arbitration would take place in Tokyo. Arbitration of an issue arising out of the agreement was held and an award was made. Kanto Yakin sought to enforce the award in Ontario. The court found that, despite the fact that the agreement was concluded prior to the coming into force of the International Commercial Arbitration Act, Revised Statutes of Ontario, 1990, c. 1.9, which enact; MAL, the agreement was still an arbitration agreement governed by the Act and was enforceable as such.

◆ ◆ ◆ ◆ ◆

Case 30; MAL 35;36

Canada: Ontario Court, General Division (Feldman J.)

13 February, 1992; appeal pending in the Ontario Court of Appeal

Robert E. Schreter v. *Gasmac Inc.*

Published in English: 7 Ontario Reports (3d), 608

Commented on by Tetley in [I993] Lloyd's Maritime and Commercial Law Quarterly, 238

For the purposes of MAL, an arbitral award does not merge in a judgment which confirms it. The court should not re-open the merits of an arbitral award where there has been no misconduct, simply on the grounds of ensuring conformity with public policy.

The agreement between the parties provided that the law of the state of Georgia, United States of America, would govern and that disputes arising out of the agreement would be determined by binding arbitration to take place in Atlanta, An arbitral award in favour of Schreter was subsequently confirmed by the Georgia court. Gasmac challenged the enforcement of the award in Ontario on a number of procedural grounds, all of which were rejected by the court. Gasmac claimed that the award had merged in the Georgia court judgment and could therefore only be enforced in Ontario as a foreign judgement. Gasmac also claimed that the acceleration of royalty payments for breach of contract was contrary to the public policy of Ontario.

The court found that article 35 MAL as enacted by the International Commercial Arbitration Act, Revised Statutes of Ontario, 1990, c. 1.9 made recognition and enforcement of arbitral awards mandatory. The court found no indication in article 35 or 36 that awards should be considered to merge in judgments which confirm them. The court indicated that to make such a finding would "create a gaping hole in the scope of the Act." The court determined that the facts did not warrant re-opening the arbitral award on public policy grounds pursuant to article 36(1)(b)(ii) MAL. The court enforced the arbitral award.

◆ ◆ ◆ ◆ ◆

Case 36: MAL 8

Canada: Federal Court of Canada, Trial Division (Walsh J.)

19 January, 1993

Nanisivik Mines Ltd. and Zinc Corporation of America v. *F.C.R.S. Shipping Ltd., Canarctic Shipping Co. Ltd. et al.*

Original in English and French

Unpublished

The mandatory nature of article 8 MAL does not remove the permissive jurisdiction of the Federal Court to grant stays of proceedings pursuant to s. 50 of the Federal Court Act.

Nanisivik and Canarctic entered into a charter-party which required that all disputes of law and fact arising under it be referred to arbitration. The ship sank. The plaintiffs sued in contract and tort. Canarctic argued that the court was required to grant a stay of proceedings and refer the matter to arbitration pursuant to article 8 MAL which is enacted by the Commercial Arbitration Act, Revised Statutes of Canada 1985, c. C-34.6. Nanisivik argued that a stay should not be granted against those parties to the litigation who were not parties to the charter-party.

The court relied on its discretion pursuant to s. 50(1) of the Federal Court Act, Revised Statutes of Canada 1985, c.F-7 rather than on article 8 MAL and granted a stay of proceedings only against Canarctic. In so doing, the court relied on previous Federal Court decisions which determined that article 8 MAL as invoked by an agreement to arbitrate does not affect or impinge on the permissive jurisdiction of the Federal Court (see A/CN.9/SER.C/ABSTRACTS/ 1, cases 8 and 15).

◆ ◆ ◆ ◆ ◆

Case 443— MAL arts. 36(1)(a)(i); 36(1)(b)(ii)

Germany: Oberlandesgericht Dresden; 11 Sch 06/98

13 January, 1999

Original in German

DIS-Online Database on Arbitration Law - *http://www.dis-arb.de*

Abstract prepared by Stefan Kröll and Roman Mallmann

The case concerned the recognition and enforcement of a foreign award, in particular the defences of "lack of a valid arbitration agreement" and "violation of public policy".

The original dispute arose out of a contract for the sale of industrial plants by the claimant to the defendant who refused payment alleging defects in the delivered plants. The claimant initiated arbitration proceedings on the basis of an arbitration clause contained in its standard terms based on the widely used United Nations Economic Commission for Europe (ECE) General Conditions of Sale and Standard Form Contracts. It asserted that a copy of its standard terms was given to the defendant's representative during the negotiations. After taking evidence on that point, the arbitrator rendered an arbitral award in favour of the claimant, awarding it approximately 850,000 German Marks (DM) plus interest between 10% and 16%. Furthermore, the award granted the claimant reimbursement of 162,000 DM for legal expenses.

Upon an application by the claimant the Court declared the award enforceable in Germany rejecting the objections by the defendant that no valid arbitration agreement had been was concluded and that the interest rate violated public policy.

The Court found that, on the basis of the old German arbitration law (applicable to all agreements concluded before 1998), that the parties had entered into a valid arbitration agreement. According to the relevant former Section 1027(2) ZPO (civil procedure statute) the arbitration agreement did not have to meet any form requirements. Therefore, the arbitration agreement could be validly agreed upon on the basis of the law applicable to the sales contract. Under German law, standard conditions of contract may become part of the contract, if the party using the standard conditions refers to them in any manner in the contract or in the pre-contractual correspondence with the other party. Such a reference to an arbitration agreement would not violate German public policy since also under German law standard conditions can become part of a contract in the same way.

The Court further concluded that also the liquidated interest rate of 14% would not make the enforcement of the award contrary to public policy. The Court found, that the arbitral award did not violate German *ordre public* in granting the claimant reimbursement of his legal expenses, which were in the present case less than 5% of the value of the whole case. Finally, the arbitral award was declared enforceable, although the actual interest rate was not stated in the award itself.

◆ ◆ ◆ ◆ ◆

Case 37; MAL 36(1)(b)(ii)

Canada: Ontario Court, General Division (Eberle J.)

12 March, 1993

Arcata Graphics Buffalo Ltd. v. *Movie (Magazine) Corp.*

Original in English

Unpublished

In order to refuse to enforce an award as contrary to public policy (article 36(1)(b)(ii) MAL) the award must be contrary to the morality of the community of the enforcing State.

The arbitral award in question included interest at the rate of 1.5% per month with no annual interest rate. This violated s. 4 of Canada's Interest Act which imposes limits on interest rates not expressed annually. The respondent argued that to give force to this provision would be contrary to public policy and thus contrary to article 36(1)(b)(ii) MAL enacted by the International Commercial Arbitration Act, Revised Statutes of Ontario, 1990, c.1.9.

The court adopted the principle that to refuse to enforce an award pursuant to article 36(1)(b)(ii) MAL the award must be contrary to the essential morality of the state in question. The court upheld the award.

◆ ◆ ◆ ◆ ◆

Case 67: MM 36(1)(a)(ii)

Canada; Saskatchewan Court of Appeal (Vancise, Wakeling and Gerwing JJ.A.)

17 September, 1991

AAMCO Transmissions Inc. v. *Kunz*

Published in English: 97 Saskatchewan Reports, 5

The appellant terminated a franchise agreement with the respondent citing as reasons, inter alia, the respondent's failure to file business reports and to pay fees with the result that its indebtedness to the appellant had continued to increase at a rapid rate. The matter was submitted to arbitration in the U.S. pursuant to an arbitration clause, which however, contained a proviso excluding from arbitration matters arising from "... termination by AAMCO which is based in whole or in part upon the fraudulent acts of Franchisees or Franchisee's failure to deal honestly and fairly with any customer or Franchisees's failure to accurately report his gross receipts to AAMCO ...". The arbitral tribunal found in favour of the appellant, who subsequently sought to have the award recognized and declared enforceable by the courts in Canada.

The court of first instance refused to recognize the arbitral award. On appeal, at issue was whether the award dealt with a matter "not contemplated by or not falling within the terms of the submission to arbitration", or whether it contained "decisions on matters beyond the scope of the submission to arbitration" (article 36(1)(a)(ii) MAL. The appellant argued that the proviso mentioned above should be interpreted narrowly so as to cover only fraudulent or quasi-fraudulent actions and not termination for failure of the franchisee to file reports. The respondent argued that the dispute dealt with a matter which clearly was not contemplated by the parties or did not fall within the arbitration agreement.

The appellate court found that the failure of the respondent to file business reports was explicitly mentioned in the arbitration clause as a non-arbitrable matter and dismissed the appeal upholding the decision of the court of first instance.

◆ ◆ ◆ ◆ ◆

Case 76: MAL 36(1)(a)(iv)

Hong Kong: High Court of Hong Kong (Kaplan J.)

13 July, 1994

China Nanhai Oil Joint Service Corporation, Shenzhen Branch v. *Gee Tai Holdings Co. Ltd.*

Original in English

Reported on in English: [1992] The Arbitration and Dispute Resolution Law Journal ADRLJ 235, [1992] ADRLJ 240, [1993] ADRLJ 240. [1993] ADRLJ 100 and [1994] ADRLJ 49, 295, 307, 291, 290, 298 respectively

(Abstract prepared by the UNCITRAL Secretariat)

The plaintiff sought from the court leave to enforce an arbitration award rendered by the Shenzhen Subcommission of the China International Economic and Trade Arbitration Commission (CIETAC). The defendant opposed the enforcement of the award on the grounds that the composition of the arbitral tribunal was not in accordance with the agreement of the parties, which provided for arbitration by CIETAC, Beijing and not CIETAC, Shenzhen [sec. 44(2)(e) of the Hong Kong Arbitration Ordinance, same as article 36(l)(a)(iv) MAL].

The court held that CIETAC, Shenzhen did not have jurisdiction to decide this dispute, because a Chines court would not allow a Shenzhen arbitrator, who, at the time the dispute was arbitrated, could not arbitrate in Beijing, to decide a case referred to CIETAC, Beijing. However, the court found that the defendant had waived its right to raise the jurisdictional objection since it participated in the Shenzhen arbitration without clearly reserving its right to later object to the award on the grounds that the tribunal lacked jurisdiction. The court declared the award enforceable and held that, even if the defendant had not waived its rights to object on the grounds of lack of jurisdiction, the court would still declare the award enforceable since it was satisfied that the defendant basically obtained what it had agreed to, that is arbitration conducted by three CIETAC arbitrators under CIETAC rules

◆ ◆ ◆ ◆ ◆

Case 88: MAL 36(1)(a)(ii)

Hong Kong: High Court of Hong Kong (Kaplan J.)

16 December, 1994

Nanjing Cereals, Oils and Foodstuffs Import & Export Corporation v. *Luckmate Commodities Trading Ltd.*

Original in English

Unpublished

(Abstract prepared by the UNCITRAL Secretariat)

The plaintiff obtained an arbitration award from the China International Economic and Trade Arbitration Commission (CIETAC) ordering the defendant to pay the purchase price of Peruvian fishmeal, which the defendant had bought from the plaintiff. The defendant failed to pay and the plaintiff applied to the court for leave to enforce the arbitral award. The court granted leave for enforcement and the defendant requested the court to set aside the leave because it was not given a sufficient opportunity to present its case as to the quantum of the claim (sec. 44 of the Hong Kong Arbitration Ordinance, which is identical to article 36(1)(a)(ii) MAL). The defendant based its argument on the fact that the arbitral tribunal formed its opinion as to the amount of the claim "through independent investigation".

The court found that the defendant had ample opportunity to present its own evidence as to the amount of the claim but failed to do so. It was held that even if there were grounds for the court to set aside the award, it was at the discretion of the court to do so, since MAL provided that enforcement "maybe refused" (emphasis added). The court dismissed the application to set aside the leave for enforcement of the arbitral award.

◆ ◆ ◆ ◆ ◆

Case 185: MAL 34(4); 36(b)(ii)

Canada: Quebec Court of Appeal (Valierand, Brossard and Dussault, JJ. A.)

15 June, 1990

Transport de cargaison (Cargo Carriers) v. *Industrial Bulk Carriers*

Original in French

Published in French: Revue de droit judiciaire [1990] 418

Cargo Carriers, whose cargo ship travels between Niger and Spain, contracts with Industrial Bulk for port services. A dispute arose concerning sums incurred and paid by Industrial while Cargo's ship was moored in Bilbao. Cargo opposed the enforcement of the arbitral award rendered in Industrial's favour for two reasons. First, the award was said to order payment by Cargo of a sum greater than that expended by Industrial, The court rejected this argument on the grounds that it was equivalent to an application for the setting aside of the award and that this was within the exclusive jurisdiction of the arbitral tribunal under article 34 MAL.

Second, Cargo argued that the award provided for reimbursement of a bribe paid by Industrial to the port authority in Bilbao and that it would be contrary to Canadian public policy for Quebec courts to enforce such an award. The court rejected this argument, accepting the arbitrator's interpretation of the nature of the payment in question. The court further stated that the payment was in the nature of a ransom as opposed to a bribe because Industrial had no other choice but to pay the escalating demurrage charges to enable the ship to leave the port. The court distinguished between a bribe, which it defined as intrinsically immoral for both the offerer and the receiver, and a ransom, which involves immorality only on the part of the blackmailer. An arbitral award imposing the reimbursement of a sum paid as ransom does not violate Canadian public policy and therefore Cargo could not resist recognition and execution of the award on the basis of article 36(b)(ii) MAL.

A motion for leave to appeal to the Supreme Court of Canada was denied,

◆ ◆ ◆ ◆ ◆

Case 233: MAL 35(1); 36(1)(b)(ii)

Zimbabwe: Harare High Court (Judge Chatikobo); Judgment No. HH-133-97

10 July and 20 August, 1997

Durco (Pvt.) Ltd. v. *Dajen (Pvt.) Ltd.*

Original in English

Published in English in 1997(2) Zimbabwe Law Reports 199 (Harare)

Two parties, a grain producer and a miller, had submitted their dispute lo a single arbitrator which resulted in an award in favour of the miller. As a third party was involved who had not been a party to the arbitration, it was feared that further proceedings might ensue. Accordingly, it was felt to be in the interests of all concerned to submit to a second arbitration which would be binding on all three parties. The second arbitration, before a panel of three arbitrators, however, resulted in an award against the miller. The miller refused to comply with the second award and the grain producer applied to the High Court for its recognition and enforcement under article 35 MAL. The miller opposed the award on the grounds that it would be contrary lo public policy to enforce the award in terms of article 36(l)(b)(ii) MAL, contending that since there was already an award it would offend the principle of finality in arbitration to enforce the second award. The court held that, by agreeing to submit to a second arbitration, the miller had waived its rights to finality of the first award. Accordingly, the miller was now bound by the second award and the court ordered that it should be recognised and enforced. The miller appealed (see CLOUT case no. 234) to the Supreme Court.

◆ ◆ ◆ ◆ ◆

Case 234: MAL 35(1); 36(1)(b)(ii)

Zimbabwe: Supreme Court of Zimbabwe (Judges of Appeal: Muchechetere, Ebrahim and Sandura); Judgment No. SC 141/98

22 June and 7 September, 1998

Dajen (Pvt.) Ltd. v. *Durco (Pvt.) Ltd.*

Original in English

Unpublished

The miller, the unsuccessful party in CLOUT case no. 233, appealed to the Supreme Court. In dismissing the appeal, the Supreme Court held that the principle of finality did not destroy or supplant a party's power to waive any right derived from an award and that this is what the miller had done by submitting to the second arbitration.

Compare same case—case No. 234 under article 35

Case 443— MAL arts. 36(1)(a)(i); 36(1)(b)(ii)

Germany: Oberlandesgericht Dresden; 11 Sch 06/98

13 January, 1999

Original in German

DIS-Online Database on Arbitration Law - *http://www.dis-arb.de*

Abstract prepared by Stefan Kröll and Roman Mallmann

The case concerned the recognition and enforcement of a foreign award, in particular the defences of "lack of a valid arbitration agreement" and "violation of public policy".

The original dispute arose out of a contract for the sale of industrial plants by the claimant to the defendant who refused payment alleging defects in the delivered plants. The claimant initiated arbitration proceedings on the basis of an arbitration clause contained in its standard terms based on the widely used United Nations Economic Commission for Europe (ECE) General Conditions of Sale and Standard Form Contracts. It asserted that a copy of its standard terms was given to the defendant's representative during the negotiations. After taking evidence on that point, the arbitrator rendered an arbitral award in favour of the claimant, awarding it approximately 850,000 German Marks (DM) plus interest between 10% and 16%. Furthermore, the award granted the claimant reimbursement of 162,000 DM for legal expenses.

Upon an application by the claimant the Court declared the award enforceable in Germany rejecting the objections by the defendant that no valid arbitration agreement had been was concluded and that the interest rate violated public policy.

The Court found that, on the basis of the old German arbitration law (applicable to all agreements concluded before 1998), that the parties had entered into a valid arbitration agreement. According to the relevant former Section 1027(2) ZPO (civil procedure statute) the arbitration agreement did not have to meet any form requirements. Therefore, the arbitration agreement could be validly agreed upon on the basis of the law applicable to the sales contract. Under German law, standard conditions of contract may become part of the contract, if the party using the standard conditions refers to them in any manner in the contract or in the pre-contractual correspondence with the other party. Such a reference to an arbitration agreement would not violate German public policy since also under German law standard conditions can become part of a contract in the same way.

The Court further concluded that also the liquidated interest rate of 14% would not make the enforcement of the award contrary to public policy. The Court found, that the arbitral award did not violate German *ordre public* in granting the claimant reimbursement of his legal expenses, which were in the present case less than 5% of the value of the whole case. Finally, the arbitral award was declared enforceable, although the actual interest rate was not stated in the award itself.

EXPLANATORY NOTE BY THE UNCITRAL SECRETARIAT ON THE MODEL LAW ON INTERNATIONAL COMMERCIAL ARBITRATION*

1. The UNCITRAL Model Law on International Commercial Arbitration was adopted by the United Nations Commission on International Trade Law (UNCITRAL) on 21 June 1985, at the close of the Commission's 18th annual session. The General Assembly, in its resolution 40/72 of 11 December 1985, recommended "that all States give due consideration to the Model Law on International Commercial Arbitration, in view of the desirability of uniformity of the law of arbitral procedures and the specific needs of international commercial arbitration practice".
2. The Model Law constitutes a sound and promising basis for the desired harmonization and improvement of national laws. It covers all stages of the arbitral process from the arbitration agreement to the recognition and enforcement of the arbitral award and reflects a worldwide consensus on the principles and important issues of international arbitration practice. It is acceptable to States of all regions and the different legal or economic systems of the world.
3. The form of a model law was chosen as the vehicle for harmonization and improvement in view of the flexibility it gives to States in preparing new arbitration laws. It is advisable to follow the model as closely as possible since that would be the best contribution to the desired harmonization and in the best interest of the users of international arbitration, who are primarily foreign parties and their lawyers.

A. BACKGROUND TO THE MODEL LAW

4. The Model Law is designed to meet concerns relating to the current state of national laws on arbitration. The need for improvement and harmonization is based on findings that domestic laws are often inappropriate for international cases and that considerable disparity exists between them.

1. Inadequacy of domestic laws

5. A global survey of national laws on arbitration revealed considerable disparities not only as regards individual provisions and solutions but also in terms of development and refinement. Some laws may be regarded as outdated, sometimes going back to the nineteenth century and often equating the arbitral process with court litigation. Other laws may be said to be fragmentary in that they do not address all relevant issues. Even most of those laws which appear to be up-to-date and comprehensive were drafted with domestic arbitration primarily, if not exclusively, in mind. While this approach is understandable in view of the fact that even today the bulk of cases governed by a general arbitration law would be of a purely domestic nature, the unfortunate consequence is that traditional local concepts are imposed on international cases and the needs of modern practice are.often not met.
6. The expectations of the parties as expressed in a chosen set of arbitration rules or a "one-off" arbitration agreement may be frustrated, especially by a mandatory provision of the applicable law. Unexpected and undesired restrictions found in national laws relate, for example, to the parties' ability effectively to submit future

* *This note has been prepared by the secretariat of the United Nations Commission on International Trade Law (UNCITRAL) for informational purposes only; it is not an official commentary on the Model Law: A commentary prepared by the Secretariat on an earlier draft of the Model Law appears in document A/CN.9/264(reproduced in UNCITRAL Yearbook, Vol. XVI-1985) (United Nations Publication, Sales No. E. 87.V.4)*

disputes to arbitration, to their power to select the arbitrator freely, or to their interest in having the arbitral proceedings conducted according to the agreed rules of procedure and with no more court involvement than is appropriate. Frustrations may also ensue from non-mandatory provisions which may impose undesired requirements on unwary parties who did not provide otherwise. Even the absence of non-mandatory provisions may cause difficulties by not providing answers to the many procedural issues relevant in an arbitration and not always settled in the arbitration agreement.

2. Disparity between national laws

7. Problems and undesired consequences, whether emanating from mandatory or non-mandatory provisions or from a lack of pertinent provisions, are aggravated by the fact that national laws on arbitral procedure differ widely. The differences are a frequent source of concern in international arbitration, where at least one of the parties is, and often both parties are, confronted with foreign and unfamiliar provisions and procedures. For such a party it may be expensive, impractical or impossible to obtain a full and precise account of the law applicable to the arbitration.

8. Uncertainty about the local law with the inherent risk of frustration may adversely affect not only the functioning of the arbitral process but already the selection of the place of arbitration. A party may well for those reasons hesitate or refuse to agree to a place which otherwise, for practical reasons, would be appropriate in the case at hand. The choice of places of arbitration would thus be widened and the smooth functioning of the arbitral proceedings would be enhanced if States were to adopt the Model Law which is easily recognizable, meets the specific needs of international commercial arbitration and provides an international standard with solutions acceptable to parties from different States and legal systems.

B. SALIENT FEATURES OF THE MODEL LAW

1. Special procedural regime for international commercial arbitration

9. The principles and individual solutions adopted in the Model Law aim at reducing or eliminating the above concerns and difficulties. As a response to the inadequacies and disparities of national laws, the Model Law presents a special legal regime geared to international commercial arbitration, without affecting any relevant treaty in force in the State adopting the Model Law. While the need for uniformity exists only in respect of international cases, the desire of updating and improving the arbitration law may be felt by a State also in respect of non-international cases and could be met by enacting modern legislation based on the Model Law for both categories of cases.

a. Substantive and territorial scope of application

10. The Model Law defines an arbitration as international if "the parties to an arbitration agreement have, at the time of the conclusion of that agreement, their places of business in different States" [article 1(3)]. The vast majority of situations commonly regarded as international will fall under this crilerion. In addition, an arbitration is international if the place of arbitration, the place of contract performance, or the place of the subject-matter of the dispute is situated in a State other than where the parties have their place of business, or if the parties have expressly agreed that the subject-matter of the arbitration agreement relates to more than one country.

11. As regards the term "commercial", no hard and fast definition could be provided, Article 1 contains a note calling for "a wide interpretation so as to cover matters arising from all relationships of a commercial nature, whether contractual or not".

The footnote to article 1 then provides an illustrative list of relationships that are to be considered commercial, thus emphasizing the width of the suggested interpretation and indicating that the determinative test is not based on what the national law may regard as "commercial".

12. Another aspect of applicability is what one may call the territorial scope of application. According to article 1(2), the Model Law as enacted in a given State would apply only if the place of arbitration is in the territory of that State. However, there is an important and reasonable exception. Articles 8(1) and 9 which deal with recognition of arbitration agreements, including their compatibility with interim measures of protection, and articles 35 and 36 on recognition and enforcement of arbitral awards are given a global scope, *i.e.* they apply irrespective of whether the place of arbitration is in that State or in another State and, as regards articles 8 and 9, even if the place of arbitration is not yet determined.

13. The strict territorial criterion, governing the bulk of the provisions of the Model Law, was adopted for the sake of certainty and in view of the following facts. The place of arbitration is used as the exclusive criterion by the great majority of national laws and, where national laws allow parties to choose the procedural law of a State other than that where the arbitration takes place, experience shows that parties in practice rarely make use of that facility. The Model Law, by its liberal contents, further reduces the need for such choice of a "foreign" law in lieu of the (Model) Law of the place of arbitration, not the least because it grants parties wide freedom in shaping the rules of the arbitral proceedings. This includes the possibility of incorporating into the arbitration agreement procedural provisions of a "foreign" law, provided there is no conflict with the few mandatory provisions of the Model Law. Furthermore, the strict territorial criterion is of considerable practical benefit in respect of articles 11, 13, 14, 16, 27 and 34, which entrust the courts of the respective State with functions of arbitration assistance and supervision.

b. Delimitation of court assistance and supervision

14. As evidenced by recent amendments to arbitration laws, there exists a trend in favour of limiting court involvement in international commercial arbitration. This seems justified in view of the fact that the parties to an arbitration agreement make a conscious decision to exclude court jurisdiction and, in particular in commercial cases, prefer expediency and finality to protracted battles in court.

15. In this spirit, the Model Law envisages court involvement in the following instances. A first group comprises appointment, challenge and termination of the mandate of an arbitrator (articles 11, 13 and 14), jurisdiction of the arbitral tribunal (article 16) and setting aside of the arbitral award (article 34). These instances are listed in article 6 as functions which should be entrusted, for the sake of centralization, specialization and acceleration, to a specially designated court or, as regards articles 11, 13 and 14, possibly to another authority (*e.g.* arbitral institution, chamber of commerce). A second group comprises court assistance in taking evidence (article 27), recognition of (he arbitration agreement, including its compatibility with court-ordered interim measures of protection (articles 8 and 9), and recognition and enforcement of arbitral awards (articles 35 and 36).

16. Beyond the instances in these two groups, "no court shall intervene, in matters governed by this Law". This is stated in the innovative article 5, which by itself does not take a stand on what is the appropriate role of the courts but guarantees the reader and user that he will find all instances of possible court intervention in this Law, except for matters not regulated by it (*e.g.*, consolidation of arbitral proceedings,

contractual relationship between arbitrators and parties or arbitral institutions, or fixing of costs and fees, including deposits). Especially foreign readers and users, who constitute the majority of potential users and may be viewed as the primary addressees of any special law on international commercial arbitration, will appreciate that they do not have to search outside this Law.

2. Arbitration agreement

17. Chapter II of the Model Law deals with the arbitration agreement, including its recognition by courts. The provisions follow closely article II of the Convention on the Recognition and Enforcement of Foreign Arbitral Awards (New York, 1958) (hereafter referred to as "1958 New York Convention"), with a number of useful clarifications added.

a. Definition and form of arbitration agreement

18. Article 7(1] recognizes the validity and effect of a commitment by the parties to submit to arbitration an existing dispute ("compromis") or a future dispute ("clause compromissoire"). The latter type of agreement is presently not given full effect under certain national laws.

19. While oral arbitration agreements are found in practice and are recognized by some national laws, article 7(2) follows the 1958 New York Convention in requiring written form. It widens and clarifies the definition of written form of article 11(2) of that Convention by adding "telex or other means of telecommunication which provide a record of the agreement", by covering the submission-type situation of "an exchange of statements of claim and defence in which the existence of an agreement is alleged by one party and not denied by another", and by providing that "the reference in a contract to a document" (*e.g.* general conditions) "containing an arbitration clause constitutes an arbitration agreement provided that the contract is in writing and the reference is such as to make that clause part of the contract".

b. Arbitration agreement and the courts

20. Articles 8 and 9 deal with Iwo important aspects of the complex issue of the relationship between the arbitration agreement and resort to courts. Modelled on article 11(3) of the 1958 New York Convention, article 8(11) of the Model Law obliges any court to refer the parties to arbitration if seized with a claim on the same subject-matter unless it finds that the arbitration agreement is *null and void,* inoperaiive or incapable of being performed. The referral is dependent on a request which a party may make not later than when submitting his first statement on the substance of the dispute. While this provision, where adopted by a State when it adopts the Model Law, by its nature binds merely the courts of that State, it is not restricted to agreements providing for arbitration in that State and, thus, helps to give universal recognition and effect to international commercial arbitration agreements.

21. Article 9 expresses the principle that any interim measures of protection that may be obtained from courts under their procedural law (e.g. pre-award attachments) are compatible with an arbitration agreement. Like article 8, this provision is addressed to the courts of a given State, insofar as it determines their granting of interim measures as being compatible with an arbitration agreement, irrespective of the place of arbitration. Insofar as it declares it to be compatible with an arbitration agreement for a party to request such measure from a court, the provision would apply irrespective of whether the request is made to a court of the given State or of any other country. Wherever such request may be made, it may not be relied upon, under the Model Law, as an objection against the existence or effect of an arbitration agreement.

3. Composition of arbitral tribunal

22. Chapter III contains a number of detailed provisions on appointment, challenge, termination of mandate and replacement of an arbitrator. The chapter illustrates the approach of the Model Law in eliminating difficulties arising from inappropriate or fragmentary laws or rules. The approach consists, first, of recognizing the freedom of the parties to determine, by reference to an existing set of arbitration rules or by an ad hoc agreement, the procedure to be followed, subject to fundamental requirements of fairness and justice. Secondly, where the parties have not used their freedom to lay down the rules of procedure or a particular issue has not been covered, the Model Law ensures, by providing a set of suppletive rules, that the arbitration may commence and proceed effectively to the resolution of the dispute.

23. Where under any procedure, agreed upon by the parties or based upon the suppletive rules of the Model Law, difficulties arise in the process of appointment, challenge or termination of the mandate of an arbitrator, Articles 11, 13 and 14 provide for assistance by courts or other authorities. In view of the urgency of the matter and in order to reduce the risk and effect of any dilatory tactics, instant resort may be had by a party within a short period of time and the decision is not appealable.

4. Jurisdiction of arbitral tribunal

a. Competence to rule on own jurisdiction

24. Article 16(1) adopts the two important (not yet generally recognized) principles of "Kompetenz-Kompetenz" and of separability or autonomy of the arbitration clause. The arbitral tribunal may rule on its own jurisdiction, including any objections with respect to the existence or validity of the arbitration agreement. For that purpose, an arbitration clause shall be treated as an agreemenl independent of the other terms of the contract, and a decision by the arbitral tribunal that the contract is *null and void* shall not entail *ipso jure* the invalidity of the arbitration clause. Detailed provisions in paragraph (2) require that any objections relating to the arbitrators' jurisdiction be made at the earliest possible time.

25. The arbitral tribunal's competence to rule on its own jurisdiction, *i.e.* on the very foundation of its mandate and power, is, of course, subject to court control. Where the arbitral tribunal rules as a preliminary question that it has jurisdiction, article 16(3] provides for instant court control in order to avoid unnecessary waste of money and time. However, three procedural safeguards are added to reduce the risk and effect of dilatory tactics: short time-period for resort to court (30 days), court decision is not appealable, and discretion of the arbitral tribunal to continue the proceedings and make an award while the matter is pending with the court. In those less common cases where the arbitral tribunal combines its decision on jurisdiction with an award on the merits, judicial review on the question of jurisdiction is available in setting aside proceedings under article 34 or in enforcement proceedings under article 36.

b. Power to order interim measures

26. Unlike some national laws, the Model Law empowers the arbitral tribunal, unless otherwise agreed by the parties, to order any party to take an interim measure of protection in respect of the subject-mailer of the dispute, if so requested by a party (article 17). It may be noted that the article does not deal with enforcement of such measures; any State adopting the Model Law would be free to provide court assistance in this regard.

5. Conduct of arbitral proceedings

27. Chapter V provides the legal framework for a fair and effective conduct of the arbitral proceedings. It opens with two provisions expressing basic principles that

permeate the arbitral procedure governed by the Model Law. Article 18 lays down fundamental requirements of procedural justice and article 19 the rights and powers to determine the rules of procedure.

a. Fundamental procedural rights of a party

28. Article 18 embodies the basic principle that the parties shall be treated with equality and each party shall be given a full opportunity of presenting his case. Other provisions implement and specify the basic principle in respect of certain fundamental rights of a party. Article 24(1) provides that, unless the parties have validly agreed that no oral hearings for the presentation of evidence or for oral argument be held, the arbitral tribunal shall hold such hearings at an appropriate stage of the proceedings, if so requested by a parly. It should be noted that article 24(1) deals only with the general right of a party to oral hearings (as an alternative to conducting the proceedings on the basis of documents and other materials) and not with the procedural aspects such as the length, number or timing of hearings.

29. Another fundamental right of a party of being heard and being able to present his case relates to evidence by an expert appointed by the arbitral tribunal. Article 26(2) obliges the expert, after having delivered his written or oral report, to participate in a hearing where the parties may put questions to him and present expert witnesses in order to testify on the points at issue, if such a hearing is requested by a party or deemed necessary by the arbitral tribunal. As another provision aimed at ensuring fairness, objectivity and impartiality, article 24(3) provides that all statements, documents and other information supplied to the arbitral tribunal by one party shall be communicated to the other party, and that any expert report or evidentiary document on which the arbitral tribunal may rely in making its decision shall be communicated to the parties. In order to enable the parties to be present at any hearing and at any meeting of the arbitral tribunal for inspection purposes, they shall be given sufficient notice in advance (article 24(2)).

b. Determination of rules of procedure

30. Article 19 guarantees the parties' freedom to agree on the procedure to be followed by the arbitral tribunal in conducting the proceedings, subject to a few mandatory provisions on procedure, and empowers the arbitral tribunal, failing agreement by the parties, to conduct the arbitration in such a manner as it considers appropriate. The power conferred upon the arbitral tribunal includes the power to determine the admissibility, relevance, materiality and weight of any evidence.

31. Autonomy of the parties to determine the rules of procedure is of special importance in international cases since it allows the parties to select or tailor the rules according to their specific wishes and needs, unimpeded by traditional domestic concepts and without the earlier mentioned risk of frustration. The supplementary discretion of the arbitral tribunal is equally important in that it allows the tribunal to tailor the conduct of the proceedings to the specific features of the case without restraints of the traditional local law, including any domestic rules on evidence. Moreover, it provides a means for solving any procedural questions not regulated in the arbitration agreement or the Model Law.

32. In addition to the general provisions of article 19, there are some special provisions using the same approach of granting the parties autonomy and, failing agreement, empowering the arbitral tribunal to decide the matter. Examples of particular practical importance in international cases are article 20 on the place of arbitration and article 22 on the language of the proceedings.

c. Default of a party

33. Only if due notice was given, may the arbitral proceedings be continued in the absence of a party. This applies, in particular, to the failure of a party to appear at a hearing or to produce documentary evidence without showing sufficient cause for the failure [article 25(c).] The arbitral tribunal may also continue the proceedings where the respondent fails to communicate his statement of defence, while there is no need for continuing the proceedings if the claimant fails to submit his statement of claim [article 25(a), (b)].

34. Provisions which empower the arbitral tribunal to carry out its task even if one of the parties does not participate are of considerable practical importance since, as experience shows, it is not uncommon that one of the parties has little interest in co-operating and in expediting matters. They would, thus, give international commercial arbitration its necessary effectiveness, within the limits of fundamental requirements of procedural justice.

6. Making of award and termination of proceedings

a. Rules applicable to substance of dispute

35. Article 28 deals with the substantive law aspects of arbitration. Under paragraph (1), the arbitral tribunal decides the dispute in accordance with such rules of law as may be agreed by the parties. This provision is significant in two respects. It grants the parties the freedom to choose the applicable substantive law, which is important in view of the fact that a number of national laws do not clearly or fully recognize that right. In addition, by referring to the choice of "rules of law" instead of "law", the Model Law gives the parties a wider range of options as regards the designation of the law applicable to the substance of the dispute in that they may, for example, agree on rules of law that have been elaborated by an international forum but have not yet been incorporated into any national legal system. The power of the arbitral tribunal, on the other hand, follows more traditional lines. When the parties have not designated the applicable law, the arbitral tribunal shall apply the law, i.e. the national law, determined by the conflict of laws rules which it considers applicable.

36. According to article 28(3), the parties may authorize the arbitral tribunal to decide the dispute *ex aequo et bono* or as amiables compositeurs. This type of arbitration is currently not known or used in all legal systems and there exists no uniform understanding as regards the precise scope of the power of the arbitral tribunal. When parties anticipate an uncertainty in this respect, they may wish to provide a clarification in the arbitration agreement by a more specific authorization to the arbitral tribunal. Paragraph (4) makes clear that in all cases, *i.e.* including an arbitration ex aequo et bono, the arbitral tribunal must decide in accordance with the terms of the contract and shall take into account the usages of the trade applicable to the transaction.

b. Making of award and other decisions

37. In its rules on the making of the award (articles 29-31), the Model Law pays special attention to the rather common case that the arbitral tribunal consists of a plurality of arbitrators (in particular, three). It provides that, in such case, any award and other decision shall be made by a majority of the arbitrators, except on questions of procedure, which may be left to a presiding arbitrator. The majority principle applies also to the signing of the award, provided that the reason for any omitted signature is stated.

38. Article 31(3) provides that the award shall state the place of arbitration and that it shall be deemed to have been made at that place. As to this presumption, it may be noted that the final making of the award constitutes a legal act, which in practice is

not necessarily one factual act but may be done in deliberations at various places, by telephone conversation or correspondence; above all, the award need not be signed by the arbitrators at the same place.

39. The arbitral award must be in writing and state its date. It must also state the reasons on which it is based, unless the parties have agreed otherwise or the award is an award on agreed terms, *i.e.* an award which records the terms of an amicable settlement by the parties. It may be added that the Model Law neither requires nor prohibits "dissenting opinions".

7. Recourse against award

40. National laws on arbitration, often equating awards with court decisions, provide a variety of means of recourse against arbitral awards, with varying and often long time-periods and with extensive lists of grounds that differ widely in the various legal systems. The Model Law attempts to ameliorate this situation, which is of considerable concern to those involved in international commercial arbitration.

a. Application for setting aside as exclusive recourse

41. The first measure of improvement is to allow only one type of recourse, to the exclusion of any other means of recourse regulated in another procedural law of the State in question. An application for setting aside under article 34 must be made within three months of receipt of the award. It should be noted that "recourse" means actively "attacking" the award; a party is, of course, not precluded from seeking court control by way of defence in enforcement proceedings (article 36). Furthermore, "recourse" means resort to a court, *i.e.* an organ of the judicial system of a State; a party is not precluded from resorting to an arbitral tribunal of second instance if such a possibility has been agreed upon by the parties (as is common in certain commodity trades).

b. Grounds for setting aside

42. As a further measure of improvement, the Model Law contains an exclusive list of limited grounds on which an award may be set aside. This list is essentially the same as the one in article 36(1), taken from article V of the 1958 New York Convention: lack of capacity of parties to conclude arbitration agreement or lack of valid arbitration agreement; lack of notice of appointment of an arbitrator or of the arbitral proceedings or inability of a party to present his case; award deals with matters not covered by submission to arbitration; composition of arbitral tribunal or conduct of arbitral proceedings contrary to effective agreement of parties or, failing agreement, to the Model Law; non-arbitrability of subject-matter of dispute and violation of public policy, which would include serious departures from fundamental notions of procedural justice.

43. Such a parallelism of the grounds for setting aside with those provided in article V of the 1958 New York Convention for refusal of recognition and enforcement was already adopted in the European Convention on International Commercial Arbitration (Geneva, 1961). Under its article IX, the decision of a foreign court setting aside an award for a reason other than the ones listed in article V of the 1958 New York Convention does not constitute a ground for refusing enforcement. The Model Law takes this philosophy one step further by directly limiting the reasons for setting aside.

44. Although the grounds for setting aside are almost identical to those for refusing recognition or enforcement, two practical differences should be noted. Firstly, the grounds relating to public policy, including non-arbitrability, may be different in substance, depending on the State in question (*i.e.* State of setting aside or State of enforcement). Secondly, and more importantly, the grounds for refusal of recognition

or enforcement are valid and effective only in the State (or States) where the winning parly seeks recognition and enforcement, while the grounds for setting aside have a different impact: The setting aside of an award at the place ot origin prevents enforcement of that award in all other countries by virtue of article V(1)(e) of the 1958 New York Convention and article 36(1)(a)(v) of the Model Law.

8. Recognition and enforcement of awards

45. The eighth and last chapter of the Model Law deals with recognition and enforcement of awards. Its provisions reflect the significant policy decision lhat the same rules should apply to arbitral awards whether made in the country of enforcement or abroad, and that those rules should follow closely the 1958 New York Convention.

a. Towards uniform treatment of all awards irrespective of country of origin

46. By treating awards rendered in international commercial arbitralion in a uniform manner irrespective of where they were made, the Model Law draws a new demarcation line between "international" and "non-international" awards instead of the traditional line belween "foreign" and "domestic" awards. This new line is based on substantive grounds rather than territorial borders, which are inappropriate in view of the limited importance of the place of arbitration in international cases. The place of arbitration is often chosen for reasons of convenience of the parties and the dispute may have little or no connection with the State where the arbitration takes place. Consequently, the recognition and enforcement of "international" awards, whether "foreign" or "domestic", should be governed by the same provisions.

47. By modelling the recognition and enforcement rules on the relevant provisions of the 1958 New York Convention, the Model Law supplements, wilhout conflicting with, the regime of recognition and enforcement created by that successful Convention,

b. Procedural conditions of recognition and enforcement

48. Under article 35(1) any arbitral award, irrespective of the country in which it was made, shall be recognized as binding and enforceable, subject to the provisions of article 35(2) and of article 36 (which sets forth the grounds on which recognition or enforcement may be refused). Based on the above consideration of the limited importance of the place of arbitration in international cases and the desire of overcoming territorial restrictions, reciprocity is not included as a condition for recognition and enforcement.

49. The Model Law does not lay down procedural details of recognition and enforcement since there is no practical need for unifying them, and since they form an intrinsic part of the national procedural law and practice. The Model Law merely sets certain conditions for obtaining enforcement: application in writing, accompanied by the award and the arbitration agreement (article 35(2)).

c. Grounds for refusing recognition or enforcement

50. As noted earlier, the grounds on which recognition or enforcement may be refused under the Model Law are identical to those listed in article V of the New York Convention. Only, under the Model Law, they are relevant not merely to foreign awards but to all awards rendered in international commercial arbitration. While some provisions of that Convention, in particular as regards their drafting, may have called for improvement, only the first ground on the list (*i.e.* "the parties to the arbitration agreement were, under the law applicable to them, under some incapacity") was modified since it was viewed as containing an incomplete and potentially misleading conflicts rule. Generally, it was deemed desirable to adopt, for the sake of harmony, the same approach and wording as this important Convention.

•••